AGAINST PERFECTIONISM:
DEFENDING LIBERAL NEUTRALITY

D1616244

In a democracy, political authority should be determined independently of the religious, philosophical, and ethical ideals that often divide us. This notion, called liberal neutrality, challenges one of the oldest insights of the Western philosophical tradition in politics. At least since Plato the defenders of perfectionism have insisted that statecraft is akin to 'soulcraft,' and political questions about the justification of state power have followed from ethical questions about what is valuable in life and about how we should live if we are to live well.

Against Perfectionism defends liberal neutrality as the political morality most appropriate for democratic societies. Steven Lecce investigates the theoretical foundations of liberalism, bringing together classic and contemporary arguments about the implications of pluralism for liberal equality. He surveys three classic debates over the grounds and limits of tolerance, and investigates the limitations of perfectionism as a guide to law and public policy in pluralist societies. Lecce ultimately proposes a version of neutrality that answers the critiques recently levelled against it as a political ideal. Presenting sophisticated and groundbreaking arguments, *Against Perfectionism* is a call to rethink current concepts of law and public policy in democratic societies.

STEVEN LECCE is an assistant professor in the Department of Political Studies at the University of Manitoba.

STEVEN LECCE

Against Perfectionism

Defending Liberal Neutrality

UNIVERSITY OF TORONTO PRESS
Toronto Buffalo London

© University of Toronto Press Incorporated 2008
Toronto Buffalo London

www.utppublishing.com

Printed in Canada

ISBN 978-0-8020-9212-0 (cloth)
ISBN 978-0-8020-9447-6 (paper)

Printed on acid-free paper

Library and Archives Canada Cataloguing in Publication

Lecce, Steven, 1970–
    Against perfectionism : defending liberal neutrality / Steven Lecce.

    Includes bibliographical references and index.
    ISBN 978-0-8020-9212-0 (bound). – ISBN 978-0-8020-9447-6 (pbk.)

    1. Liberalism – Philosophy.   2. Political Science – Philosophy.
    3. Liberalism – Moral and ethical aspects.   I. Title.

    JC575.L43 2008   320.51′3   C2007-904952-4

This book has been published with the help of a grant from the Canadian
Federation for the Humanities and Social Sciences, through the Aid to
Scholarly Publications Program, using funds provided by the Social Sciences
and Humanities Research Council of Canada.

University of Toronto Press acknowledges the financial assistance to its
publishing program of the Canada Council for the Arts and the Ontario
Arts Council.

University of Toronto Press acknowledges the financial support for its
publishing activities of the Government of Canada through the Book
Publishing Industry Development Program (BPIDP).

For my family
Antonio, Denise, and Michelle

Contents

x   Contents

Acknowledgments

This book has been several years in the making, and I have incurred numerous debts along the way. My first one is to Richard Vernon, who supervised my doctoral work at the University of Western Ontario. The argument of this book builds on that work, and both were substantially improved by the patient, meticulous, and insightful feedback he so generously offered over the years. I am grateful for both his teaching and his friendship; he will always be my exemplar of what it means to be a scholar.

The following individuals were kind enough to comment on various draft chapters and, in some cases, the entire manuscript: Charles Jones, Michael Milde, Douglas Long, Daniel Weinstock, and Timothy Cobban.

Chapter 3 was published earlier in *Contemporary Political Theory* as 'The Clapham Omnibus Revisited: Liberalism against Democracy' (March 2003), and chapter 6 in *Political Studies* as 'Contractualism and Liberal Neutrality: A Defence' (October 2003). I thank anonymous readers from both journals for their helpful suggestions, and for editorial permission to reprint this material here.

Stephen Kotowych, my editor at the University of Toronto Press, was incredibly helpful and supportive all along the way; I thank him, and the Press, for their unwavering professionalism. Two anonymous readers from the Press offered thoughtful, detailed, and incisive comments and criticisms, which have made for a better book. I would also like to thank Ian MacKenzie for copy editing the text.

This book emphasizes the centrality of institutions to liberal justice, and so it is appropriate that I should thank a number of institutions without which the work presented here would have been impossible: the Social Science and Humanities Research Council of Canada; the Ontario

Graduate Scholarship Program; the Faculty of Graduate Studies and Department of Political Science at the University of Western Ontario; my new friends at/through the Centre de recherche en ethique de l'Université de Montréal, especially Samantha Brennan, Matthew Clayton, Colin MacLeod, Shauna Van Praagh, and Daniel Weinstock; and, finally, the most important and enduring source of institutional support in my life, my family, Tony, Denise, and Michelle Lecce. Without their love and support, this book would not exist (nor would I, for that matter) so I dedicate it to them.

This book has also been improved indirectly by a number of people whose friendship has enabled its author to be happier and saner than he would be otherwise: Margaret Hancock, Ian Anderson, Rebecca Hancock, Tim and Janelle Cobban, Robert Racco, Steven Bray, Ryan Whyte, Tara Mimnagh, Andrew Bacsa, Chris Morrison, Kari Townsend, Matthew Armstrong, and Carmen Lynch.

My greatest debt is to Rachael Hancock, whom I had the sense to marry shortly after the first draft of this manuscript was completed. Our marriage (and friendship) is, by far, my greatest accomplishment in life, and I will always be grateful for her love and inspiration.

AGAINST PERFECTIONISM:
DEFENDING LIBERAL NEUTRALITY

Introduction

This book is about the justification of liberalism, not its history. But history is not irrelevant to the justificatory project either.[1] In the face of intractable conflict, over time, the view arose that states should accept religious pluralism and abandon attempts to impose religious conformity. That view adopted *freedom* as a value, in attributing to individuals a right to choose, and it adopted *equality* as a value, in detaching states from claims to religious privilege. The conjunction of these two values, in the form of a scheme of equal rights, is at the heart of what would later be called 'liberalism,' whether we think of it as a view that sustains the political arrangements of current Western states or, instead, as a critical theory that presses all states, including Western ones, to a fuller recognition of equality.

Even this brief characterization of liberalism leads directly to a paradox, which is the starting point for the argument of this book. On the one hand, it stresses the fact of pluralism – not just religious pluralism but, as time went on, a whole range of different and mutually exclusive beliefs about what is valuable in life – beliefs arising from all the social, cultural, demographic, and economic changes that have accompanied the emergence of liberal democracy as a political form. On the other hand, in stressing equality, liberalism presents the demand that political arrangements be justifiable to all those who are subject to them. Given the very diversity of belief on which it seems to depend, this demand is, obviously, a challenge, for in the face of diversity, will everyone be persuaded by the same reasons?

For early social contract thinkers in the liberal tradition, political legitimacy was based upon the consent of every reasonable person.[2] This ideal of legitimacy, together with the existence of profound disagreement about the nature of religious salvation or human flourishing, implied that arguments for religious freedom (and against intolerance), to be mutually acceptable, would have to be based upon distinctively political considerations – a 'political morality' – that abstracted from the religious and ethical controversies that made toleration necessary in the first place. On this contractualist and *anti-perfectionist* view, the liberal theory of political legitimacy imposed principled limits on the kinds of goods that states could justifiably pursue.

The second, *perfectionist*, approach found its classic expression in nineteenth-century Victorian England; it rejected both of the above-mentioned claims in asserting that (1) ethical pluralism raises no distinctively political problems, so reasonable consent must be rejected as the foundation of legitimate political authority; and (2) political morality *must* be based upon a comprehensive account of human well-being or flourishing. On the perfectionist view, whether or not people should be free to think or to act in certain unconventional or unorthodox ways in the absence of governmental interference depends crucially upon whether or not such thoughts or actions are likely to contribute to their living decent, or ethically valuable, lives. Governments must necessarily discriminate, then, between the diverse and contested beliefs and values of their citizens – if and where they can, they should promote and encourage those that are true, and discourage or prevent those that are false. There is no distinctively political morality, then: politics *is* morality.

This book defends contractualism as the best justification for liberal political demands, and argues that state neutrality between contested ethical ideals (anti-perfectionism) is a fundamental requirement of liberalism so justified. By now, this general position has become quite familiar, as many of the world's leading contemporary political philosophers endorse differing versions of it.[3] But while the general position is well known, many of the arguments commonly deployed to support (and challenge) it rest upon unsatisfactory and mistaken interpretations of its core concepts. This makes a critical analysis of its normative underpinnings more important than ever – a task that the book undertakes in three steps.

Part One introduces the contractual argument by examining the ways in which liberalism has been defended against its strongest critics. It does so by exploring three historic debates about the legitimacy of enforcing contested ethical ideals, in the context of religious, cultural, and sexual pluralism: the seventeenth-century controversy between John Locke and Jonas Proast over the grounds and limits of religious toleration; the nineteenth-century dispute between J.S. Mill and James Fitz-james Stephen on the role of the state in enforcing character ideals; and, finally, the twentieth-century debate between H.L.A. Hart and Lord Devlin on the ethical bases of the criminal law. The controversies that occupy the first three chapters represent the clearest, most well thought out, historical expressions of the liberal and anti-liberal positions on toleration, and the conceptual clarity that emerges from these dialogical clashes is indispensable in helping us to understand and, in the end, assess what is at issue between contemporary liberals and their critics. Ultimately, these academic controversies continue to pursue questions that first emerged in public debate about the legitimacy of state action in various areas of law and public policy.

Part Two advances the contractual argument for state neutrality between competing ethical ideals through a critique of its primary rival conception of political morality – *liberal perfectionism*. Liberal perfectionists share with many critics of liberalism the assumption that states *are* responsible for the moral and ethical well-being of their citizens. Accordingly, they reject altogether the suggestion that states can pursue perfectionist goals only within the boundaries that are fixed by contractually generated principles of justice. But they also maintain that people should enjoy a wide range of civil and political liberties, because the personal autonomy to which such liberties contribute is, in the end, a central aspect of any good or flourishing human life. Part Two demonstrates that perfectionism is fundamentally inadequate as a basis for liberal political morality for two primary reasons: first, it either underestimates or completely ignores the conceptual and political problems created by ethical pluralism; and, second, it is incapable of justifying, and is sometimes actually inconsistent with, many of the civil and political freedoms that liberals have reason to champion. It argues for this conclusion by evaluating the claims of two of the world's leading contemporary legal and political philosophers – Joseph Raz and Ronald Dworkin. Perfectionism is thus critically and interpretively deficient from a liberal point of view, and this conclusion prepares the way for the alternative account of liberalism defended in Part Three.

Part Three explains and defends a version of liberalism that emerges from its founding controversies and the failure of perfectionism. An egalitarian ideal of human relations, combined with certain basic facts of political life, leads us to embrace a form of procedural democracy. This ideal and those facts, in turn, make contractualism the most appropriate test of political legitimacy, because collective self-determination is compatible with equal freedom only when democratic decision-making is, itself, tempered by principles that are reasonably acceptable to everyone. A form of state neutrality between comprehensive and contested ethical ideals emerges as a central feature of liberal political morality, because pluralism ensures that the social contract that yields these regulative principles cannot proceed without it.

Part One, then, concerns selected historical controversies. Parts Two and Three concern contemporary theories and my critical response to them. So why is Part One integral to this book's argument? Like any other political theory, liberalism can be understood in historical terms. As a tradition of political thought that has developed over roughly the last three hundred years, it may be identified by a series of political causes espoused by liberals (say, religious toleration), by claims about the functioning of society and the economy (for example, the protection of markets and the links between economic incentives, material prosperity, and personal freedom), and, finally, by claims about the fundamental principles of political morality (say, that victimless immoralities should be legally permitted).

The causes, social ideals, and principles that make up the liberal tradition can be studied from a variety of perspectives, with history differently related to each of them.[4] If we are interested in learning about liberalism, then, we might ask at least four different questions: (1) the genetic question – *How* did liberal views and political practices come about? (2) the functional question – What *purpose* has liberalism served in shaping the social, legal, political, and economic practices that it has? (3) the semantic question – What universe of *meaning* has both constructed and reflected those practices? and, finally, (4) the normative question – How *defensible* or attractive are the principles of political morality that have emerged in the liberal tradition?

While the first three questions are undoubtedly fascinating, I leave them to historians of ideas, sociologists, and students of ideology, respectively. In this book, my goal instead is to defend a particular *kind* of liberal political morality against its numerous critics, both historical and contemporary, and this goal motivates the choice to include some political philosophers and to exclude others. For example, some might wonder how a book-length treatment of liberalism could dispense with utilitarianism since, historically, utilitarians such as Jeremy Bentham and James Mill were political progressives who exerted a powerful influence on the evolution of liberal attitudes to legislation and public policy in a variety of areas. However, while many early utilitarians were also liberals, the idea that there is some property called 'utility' to be maximized by state action is utterly inconsistent with the version of liberalism to be defended here. A neutral state has no overarching goals beyond securing people justice in the distribution of basic resources and opportunities, leaving them to decide for themselves which projects, commitments, and relationships are ultimately worth pursuing. Similarly, some might wonder why a defence of liberal neutrality should begin with Locke, to the extent that his arguments for toleration appear to depend on both controversial religious and metaphysical premises,[5] together with an associated doctrine of natural rights long since discredited in many quarters. But the premise of my argument for neutrality in this book is the idea of a political community as a fair procedure that depends on the reasonable endorsement of its equal members and, as I argue below, this is Locke's real legacy for contemporary liberal theory.[6]

In any event, there is reason to doubt whether the project of writing *the* history of liberalism is a plausible one.[7] While the liberal tradition does display a considerable degree of unity and continuity, surely no political cause, vision of society, or principle of political morality has been endorsed by all liberals of any particular generation, let alone through the centuries and across national boundaries.[8] This is no embarrassment, however, because rather than trying to extract a single ideal type from this multiplicity of different but related liberal views, I hope to defend a normative political morality that can help shape law and public policy under contemporary conditions of diversity better than its rivals can. From the viewpoint of normative political theory, 'history is a laboratory for arguments,'[9] and the historical controversies occupying the first three chapters of the book are argumentative building-blocks for the theory of liberal neutrality defended later on. The choice of particular historical cases is therefore selective, but not arbitrarily so.

Chapter 1, as noted above, introduces and investigates the seventeenth-century polemic between John Locke, neutralist liberalism's founding father, and Jonas Proast, his most vigorous critic, over the grounds and limits of religious toleration. This controversy is both historically and conceptually important, as Locke's three arguments for tolerating dissenters continue to influence contemporary liberal theories of justice and, as we shall see, recent perfectionist critics have inherited the several argumentative strands of Proast's critique. At bottom, this debate is about what, if anything, religious or ethical pluralism implies about the foundations of political morality, and the failure of Proast's objections reveals certain pervasive problems with state perfectionism.

Locke argues that the persecution of religious dissenters is illegitimate for three interrelated sets of reasons: (1) the *contractual* one – because consent is the basis of legitimate political authority, and no rational person would grant states the authority to compel religious observances or beliefs; (2) the *epistemic* one – because coercion works on the will of its victims, and people cannot choose what to believe, religious persecution is irrational to the extent that it cannot achieve its stated objective, namely, forcing people to believe what is true; (3) the *pluralist* one – because people ultimately disagree about the path to salvation, and religious observation is such a vital interest of theirs, they will not consent to political authority that ignores this fact by enforcing whichever religious views happen to be dominant at the time.

Proast's critique is the historical source of what are probably the three most important and enduring objections to liberalism, all of which are found in contemporary perfectionist writings. For Proast, when we are judging the legitimacy of persecuting minorities, what matters is not what they *believe* but rather whether or not their beliefs are actually *true*. Although what people have reason to consent to might change in relation to what they happen to believe, what people believe has no effect whatsoever upon what happens to be objectively true. And if the whole truth is, as Proast maintains, the only possible foundation for political morality, then Locke's social contract device is entirely redundant, and liberalism is unjustified.

This leads to Proast's second main objection, which is that rational people who took their fundamental interests seriously – in this case, eternal salvation – might agree to curtail the magistrate's authority to compel religious beliefs and practices, but *only if and when such beliefs and practices were false*. For Proast, Locke's case for liberal toleration depends essentially upon either a controversial epistemic thesis about the limits of human knowledge or, even worse, upon a sceptical one about the falsity of all religious beliefs.

Proast's objection raises two interrelated questions that dominate the contemporary liberal/anti-liberal debate, and this explains his importance to the argument of the book as a whole: what place, if any, does epistemology occupy in the contractual defence of liberalism; and if that defence does presuppose a particular epistemological view, then how is liberalism 'neutral' in any meaningful sense? Parts Two and Three of the book answer these questions. The contemporary debate about the status of liberal neutrality has derailed on both sides, as it were, by focusing on the wrong thing (epistemology) instead of the right one (simple pluralism), and the Locke-Proast controversy illustrates the difference with unparalleled clarity, and also what hinges on it.

Chapter 2 introduces the main components of perfectionist (autonomy-based) liberalism through a critical examination of the writings of its most important classical exponent – John Stuart Mill. It outlines Mill's famous liberty principle, explains the utilitarian and perfectionist considerations that underlie his ideal of personal autonomy, and assesses the extent to which liberalism defended on this basis is, in fact, vulnerable to the challenges of its most comprehensive nineteenth-century critic – James Fitzjames Stephen. Within the context of the book's overall argument, the Mill-Stephen debate serves an analogous function to the controversy surveyed in the first chapter but, this time, in connection with the role that philosophical ethics play, or should play, in the defence of liberalism.

While many of Stephen's objections rely on deeply flawed (but unfortunately common) readings of *On Liberty*, others point to certain persistent vulnerabilities of perfectionist, or autonomy-based, forms of liberalism. Whereas Locke's contractualist liberalism purports to avoid judgements about the nature of good, or ethically valuable, lives, on the grounds that liberal tolerance is precisely a response to ethical disagreement of this very kind, Mill sets out to demonstrate the specific character ideal upon which, he claims, liberalism *must* be based. For Mill, political liberty is an essential precondition of the individuality, authenticity, eccentricity, and contrariety that are constitutive aspects of human well-being. Liberty is not simply a regulative or procedural value, then, designed to express some independently justified notion of fairness or impartiality between rival ethical perspectives; it is *itself* one such perspective in competition with many others, and the one that states are, Mill claims, duty-bound to promote. Chapter 2 suggests that because pluralistic societies are characterized by ethical disagreement that also extends to the value of personal autonomy, this makes the latter a poor candidate as the justificatory basis for mutually acceptable principles of political restraint. While Mill's perfectionist liberalism is clearly not a sceptical one, it does not take pluralism, or pluralism of the right kind, nearly seriously enough, and it also provides an insecure basis for the civil and political freedoms that liberals have reason to value. While a controversial view of human flourishing cannot plausibly serve as the basis of justified state power in a democratic, that is to say, plural, society, Mill's enormous influence on the development of contemporary liberal theory – particularly Raz's and the later Dworkin's – has largely concealed this. By exposing what's wrong with Mill, we also expose what's wrong with Raz and Dworkin, and thereby provide the motivational appeal and structural outlines of a better, anti-perfectionist strategy. These themes are further developed in chapters 4 through 6 in connection with contemporary liberal-perfectionist writings.

Chapter 3 revisits a classic debate between Professor H.L.A. Hart and Lord Devlin occasioned in response to the publication of what became known as the Wolfenden Report in Britain during the late 1950s. The Committee on Homosexual Offences and Prostitution was asked to re-evaluate the state of British criminal law in connection with homosexuality and prostitution, and it recommended, by a twelve to one majority, that (1) homosexual practices in private between consenting adults should no longer be punishable as criminal offences and (2) while public solicitation should be driven off the streets as an offensive nuisance to third parties, prostitution per se should be decriminalized. Before criminal sanctions may be justifiably deployed in order to extirpate immoral activities, that is, such activities must clearly involve some *other-regarding* feature such as indecency, corruption, or exploitation.

Chapter 3 also outlines the reasoning behind Devlin's rejection of the Wolfenden Report, explains Hart's broadly Millian defence of it, and argues that commentators, including Hart himself, are wrong to conclude that the implausibility of Devlin's 'Disintegration Thesis' decisively settles the matter. Devlin claims that violations of a community's public morality are treasonous, even when perpetrated in private and by consenting adults, because they weaken the social solidarity that alone makes peaceful coexistence possible. Although Hart's refutation of this suggestion is quite convincing, it ignores Devlin's most important argument for intolerance, one that threatens to expose certain contradictions in the egalitarian foundations of liberal democracy. For Devlin, the only convincing justification for democratic government – a form of political rule that accords each citizen equal rights – is equality. Majoritarian decisions, that is, take everyone's interests equally into account. However, by constraining the ability of democratic majorities to enforce and, thus, sustain their public morality, minority rights appear to aggregate interests unevenly to the extent that they give undue weight to relatively unpopular points of view. Devlin maintains that taking equality seriously necessitates effectively unrestricted democratic sovereignty, and that this implies that liberal toleration is actually undemocratic. Without having figures to support it, my suspicion is that Devlin's democratic argument for intolerance, while incoherent, is actually the most

widely held belief about the relationship between democratic governance and unconventional cultural, religious, or sexual practices – that
is, the belief that majorities should be allowed to repress unpopular practices not because the beliefs that underpin that repression are true, but
simply because they are *held* by a majority of democratic citizens, all of
whom are equally entitled to share in the political power that licenses it.
In this sense, liberalism is undemocratic precisely because it urges
restraint. Today, we hear this all of the time in connection with issues
such as same-sex marriage and pornography, and also in demands to
limit the judiciary's ability to strike down democratically enacted legislation as unconstitutional. Because democratic equality is the argumentative premise of the liberal theory defended in Part Three of the book, it
is important to demonstrate why the democratic argument *for* intolerance is mistaken, and this explains the significance of the Hart–Devlin
debate.[10] Showing why Devlin is wrong contributes to a better understanding of the relationship between liberalism and democracy in contemporary political theory and practice and, as we shall see, refuting his
argument also helps us to locate the place and role of deliberation in the
form of procedural democracy that emerges later in the book.

Chapter 4 criticizes the most sophisticated and comprehensive perfectionist defence of liberal toleration in the contemporary literature, that
of Joseph Raz. Raz's liberal theory embodies a type of full continuity
between values, reasons, and principles of political morality, one that
makes political freedom a requirement of general moral principles that
are not, themselves, essentially political. For Raz, governments must
enable individuals to pursue valid conceptions of the good, and discourage them from pursuing evil or empty ones. Because personal autonomy
is an essential aspect of human well-being, however, state action in pursuit of perfectionist values will not, Raz thinks, unduly compromise individual liberty.

Chapter 4 outlines Raz's reinterpretation of Mill's liberty principle,
explains the moral theory upon which that reinterpretation is based, and
argues that the theory of toleration constructed out of these elements is
(1) incoherent, because it is not consistently derivable from the moral
theory that allegedly grounds it, and (2) intolerant, because it is incompatible with a due regard for individual liberty. These failings are symptomatic of perfectionist political moralities generally, and showing why
this is so lends additional justificatory support to the alternative contractualist approach subsequently explicated in Part Three of the book. In
essence, Raz's theory is the problem to which the argument found in the

remainder of the book is the solution, hence the centrality of diagnosing that problem accurately, and constructing the subsequent argument in light of this diagnosis.

Chapter 5 outlines and examines Ronald Dworkin's latest argument for liberal neutrality. Since 1978, Dworkin has argued that governments must remain neutral between rival theories of what is valuable in life in order for them to treat those under their authority with equal concern and respect. Until recently, that is, he interpreted neutrality as a distinctively political virtue, one constitutive of the overall character of a just, or egalitarian, society; as a by-product of a principle of political organization required by justice (equality), neutrality neither implied nor depended upon any particular ethical view of the good life for individuals. Dworkin now thinks that liberalism requires ethical, as opposed to distinctively political, foundations, in order to respond to a number of powerful anti-liberal objections, so he has abandoned the methodological discontinuity characteristic of social contract theories in favour of a liberal political morality that is continuous with an abstract or philosophical account of human flourishing, which he calls the 'challenge model' of ethics.

Chapter 5 also examines the challenge model of ethics, and concludes that it is simultaneously too abstract to exclude political perfectionism, and too comprehensive to embody the kind of state neutrality that Dworkin seeks to justify. The burden of his case thus falls squarely upon the original distributive argument developed in his 'What Is Equality?' series of papers. Unfortunately, the simplifying counterfactual assumptions required by the hypothetical auction/insurance scheme generate whatever ethical neutrality they do by means of a type of implied or closet contractualism. Unlike Dworkin's challenge model, then, the auction *does* yield neutrality, but only because it has been antecedently constrained in a variety of ways that call into question his claim that it embodies an instance of continuity after all. This finding is significant, because it reveals that abstract or subtle forms of perfectionism like Dworkin's fare no better than comprehensive ones like Raz's at justifying liberalism and, accordingly, any sound justificatory strategy must make ethics and politics at least partially discontinuous. I develop precisely such a strategy in Part Three of the book.

Chapter 6 exposes the deficiencies of an important criticism of liberal neutrality found in the recent literature that threatens contractualist liberalism from the inside, as it were – the *reflexivity thesis*. Contemporary contractualists such as Barry, Nagel, and Rawls rely upon a broadly Lockean view of legitimacy to argue that state perfectionism is illegitimate because free and equal citizens would not reasonably consent to it. Simon Caney, Simon Clarke, and Joseph Chan all reject this claim. They maintain that even if the contractualist premise is defensible, the neutralist conclusion is not, because the epistemic notions that contractualists deploy to establish that reasonable people would reject perfectionist principles of justice also contaminate neutralist ones, making *them* reasonably rejectable as well. The contractual argument for liberal neutrality is thus, they claim, undermined by its very own epistemic presuppositions.

Chapter 6 also explains the contractual ideal of political legitimacy and the type of neutrality it yields, before outlining the reflexivity thesis as presented by its three advocates. It then distinguishes between moral and epistemic conceptions of reasonableness to illustrate that the reflexivity thesis gains whatever limited appeal it has from conflating the two. Finally, it builds upon this foundational (but neglected) distinction, to construct a novel argument for neutrality that is elaborated and defended throughout the remainder of the book, one whose steps avoid the type of self-defeating epistemic premises that adherents of the reflexivity thesis (and even some contractualists) mistakenly think indispensable to contractualist liberalism. So state enforcement of contested ethical ideals is illegitimate *once* we are committed to contractualism, but this conclusion assumes rather than defends the ideal of moral equality that is commonly thought to make reasonable agreement the appropriate test of political legitimacy in the first place.

Chapter 7 addresses this issue by arguing that *democratic* equality, not moral equality, is the reason for adopting contractualism, and it explicates that premise in a way that evades another difficult objection to liberalism – the *circularity thesis*. Social contract theorists maintain that reasonable agreement is the proper standard of political legitimacy. In order for this method of justification to yield determinate results, however, certain motivational and/or informational constraints on the contracting parties must be introduced because, otherwise, there is no way of knowing precisely which principles it actually legitimates or excludes, and that is, of course, its whole point. An obvious way of discriminating between the myriad such potential constraints is to derive them from the underlying conception of equality that they model – the conception that recommends contractualism. But if the constraints that are ultimately introduced are selected on the basis of their according with some given conception of what political morality antecedently requires (equality), then the idea of hypothetical agreement at the core of the contractualist justificatory strategy seems entirely redundant – contractualist principles of justice are supposed to be derived from reasonable agreement, but such agreement, so the objection runs, is instead actually and tautologically derived from justice. The very notion of reasonableness that is supposed to test the relative legitimacy of candidate neutralist versus perfectionist principles of justice actually depends upon those principles for its content – hence the *circularity thesis*.

Chapter 7 distinguishes distributive from relational conceptions of egalitarianism, and defends *democratic equality*, an interpretation of the latter, as the normative premise of contractualist liberalism. Because democratic citizens are entitled to press claims upon one another simply by virtue of their status *as* equal citizens, their fundamental rights and obligations are specifiable without reference to things such as their differing talents at choosing comprehensive goals, or their varying capacities for behaving justly. If we take certain Lockean insights about ethical disagreement and the coercive nature of politics seriously, we are logically committed to a form of procedural democracy very broadly understood, and contractualism is the political morality of democratic citizenship. There is no independently describable condition of society that democratic institutions must produce and subsequently conform to, so the contractually generated principles of justice that regulate these institutions cannot plausibly be said to be undemocratic, and this means that both the conceptual and political dimensions of the circularity thesis unravel. The chapter ends by considering the place and role of deliberation in this account of liberalism.

Chapter 8 criticizes the epistemic turn in Rawls's latest formulation of justice-as-fairness, and defends simple as opposed to 'reasonable' pluralism as essential to the contractualist argument for liberalism. In *Political Liberalism*, Rawls introduces a whole family of new ideas – public reason, overlapping consensus, and the notion of a free-standing political conception – to rectify what he considers to be serious deficiencies in the argument of *A Theory of Justice*. Most of these defects stem, he thinks, from his failure to fully appreciate the distinction between simple and *reasonable* pluralism, and the problems created by the latter for the stability of a democratic society. Certain burdens of judgement are allegedly of central significance for the democratic understanding of toleration, because they limit what can be contractually justified through the public use of reason. Rawls's conception of the reasonable is quite obscure, and it contains both moral and epistemic argumentative strands that are fused in complicated and often subtle ways. Chapter 8 assesses the influence and importance of each of these respective strands on Rawls's overall position, because if reasonable pluralism has the significance for contractualism that Rawls thinks it does, my earlier refutation of the reflexivity thesis is undermined – it clearly and essentially depends upon the very distinction between morality and epistemology that Rawls's new argument collapses. It is worth considering, then, whether, or to what extent, contractualism actually requires an epistemology of the kind that Rawls now offers us, and if one is needed, whether this effectively reopens the door to the reflexivity thesis. The two strands of the reasonable must therefore be disentangled.

Chapter 8 reviews Rawls's contractual argument in *Theory* for the equal basic liberty and difference principles, explains how the primary modifications of that argument in *Political Liberalism* are connected to the fact of reasonable pluralism, and, finally, examines these modifications in connection with the overlapping consensus account of stability. The chapter concludes that (1) Rawls's reasoning underlying that account is circular and (2) the epistemic ideas that generate this circularity are actually dispensable to the contractual argument for liberalism, which can be more persuasively defended without them. Once the original position is specified to model the ideal of democratic equality, only the fact of simple pluralism is relevant to the reasoning of hypothetical contractors selecting principles of justice. Aside from reinforcing an account of political stability that is viciously circular, then, there is simply no work left for an epistemic theory of pluralism to do. This suggests that the epistemic turn at work in Rawls's recent writings, as well as the secondary literature it has influenced, is a mistake. Chapter 8 explains what these findings imply about the type of methodological abstraction that a contractual theory of political morality must rely upon, and suggests that there are persuasive reasons for favouring Thomas Scanlon's formulation of contractualism over Rawls's.

Chapter 9 summarizes the four-part argument first sketched in chapter 6, and subsequently developed in chapters 7 and 8. An egalitarian ideal of human relations combined with certain basic facts of political life leads us to embrace a form of procedural democracy. This ideal and those facts, in turn, make contractualism the most appropriate test of political legitimacy, because collective self-determination is compatible with equal freedom only when democratic decision-making is, itself, tempered by principles that are reasonably acceptable to everyone. A form of state neutrality between comprehensive and contested ethical ideals emerges as a central feature of liberal political morality, because (simple) pluralism ensures that the social contract that yields these regulative principles cannot proceed without it. Chapter 9 explains and defends the particular form of ethical neutrality required by the contractual argument for liberalism, and considers the place that neutrality so understood occupies within liberal political morality as a whole.

Recently, a number of critics have challenged the idea of a distinctive political morality of the kind defended in this book, on the grounds that 'the personal is political.' Chapter 10 responds to this challenge by distinguishing between several ways that the personal is political and also between various ways of applying political principles to personal conduct. While the personal is indeed sometimes relevantly political, then, equality as a norm of personal conduct is not, strictly speaking, required by egalitarian justice. The enemy of equality is not partiality per se, but sub-forms of partiality that lead to hierarchy, subordination, and oppression. The real question is not, Is the personal political? Of course it is. The real question is, *how* political is the personal? And the answer to *that* question does little to undermine the case for neutralist liberalism. Or so I argue in chapter 10.

PART ONE

Three Classic Controversies

1 Putting Up with Heresy

1.1 Introduction

Locke's *Letter concerning Toleration* is widely regarded as one of liberal-ism's canonical founding texts, as well as one of the most important con-tributions in the history of that idea. After the Letter's publication in 1689, Locke engaged anonymously in a polemic with one of its earliest critics, Jonas Proast, a chaplain at All Souls College, Oxford. In 1690, Proast published *The Argument of the Letter concerning Toleration Briefly Con-sider'd and Answer'd*. Later that year, *Locke countered with A Second Letter con-cerning Toleration*. Proast followed in 1691 with *A Third Letter concerning Toleration*. In 1692, Locke published his *Third Letter for Toleration*. Twelve years passed before Proast replied with *A Second Letter to the Author of the Three Letters for Toleration*. Locke began *A Fourth Letter for Toleration* but had yet to complete it at the time of his death in 1704.

In his classic study of Locke's political philosophy, John Dunn main-tains that 'every philosophical argument is a moment in social history but it is also *ex hypothesi* a philosophical argument.'[1] In this chapter, I focus on Locke's three central arguments for restraint as found in the original *Letter concerning Toleration*, together with Proast's strongest objec-tions to them. While Locke develops a number of related arguments elsewhere, I take these three to be of greater philosophical importance, and introduce the others only to the extent that they contribute to understanding them.

The discussion will be primarily analytical. By ignoring the extensive controversies surrounding the contextualization of Locke's ideas, I am not suggesting that, in Dunn's idiom, social history is irrelevant to philo-sophical argument.[2] Within the context of this chapter, however, the focus on conceptual analysis seems justified for two reasons: first, much of Locke's political philosophy is itself concerned with identifying criteria for political morality that are outside the contingencies of particular historical communities. The Lockean state of nature is intentionally ahistorical and abstract precisely because it is meant to provide a normative foundation for assessing the legitimacy of existing political institutions; and Locke's contractual case for toleration places restrictions on the extent to which *any* society's conventional moral understanding is a legitimate basis for coercing its members. As he says in *A Letter concerning Toleration*, 'The civil power is the same in every place; nor can that power, in the hands of a Christian prince, confer any greater authority upon the Church, than in the hands of a heathen; which is to say, just none at all.'[3] His theory of natural rights is deduced from the premises of natural freedom and equality and the argument proceeds logically to conclusions meant to be as certain as conclusions of a mathematical proof.[4] Locke's arguments for toleration, then, are both embedded within an analytical view of political justification, and developed according to a model of demonstrative normative theory that he outlines in the *Essay concerning Human Understanding*.[5] Conceptual analysis is appropriate since it takes both Locke's substantive aims and methodology seriously.

Second, Locke's attempts at deriving principled limits on the power of the state illustrate some of the paradigmatic challenges of liberal theory. Students of contemporary liberalism – those of Rawls, Raz, and Dworkin, for instance – should pay particular attention to Locke since his arguments for toleration illustrate some of the internal tensions that are endemic to liberal theory. In Locke, we find a serious confrontation with the problems facing liberal theory then *and* now, problems that perpetually face liberal theorists because they arise from the starting premise of liberal thought – equal freedom.[6] If liberal political theory embodies certain internal tensions that have their historical roots in the conflicts of the seventeenth century, then many of Locke's problems are shared by contemporary liberals. A study of modern theories of toleration has much to gain from an appreciation of these tensions. Conceptual analysis is sensitive to the historical continuities in the idea of toleration and allows for an examination of its complexities.[7]

In section 2 of the chapter, I outline Locke's contractual, epistemic, and pluralist arguments for tolerating religious dissenters. In section 3, I set out the substance of Proast's critique. In section 4, I refute that critique and explain how and why Locke's arguments are building-blocks for the neutralist version of liberalism defended later in the book, particularly in connection with contractualism and public reason.

1.2 The Contractual Argument

In the original *Letter concerning Toleration,* Locke maintains that 'the business of laws is not to provide for the truth of opinions, but for the safety and security of the commonwealth, and of every particular man's goods and person.'[8] Political association aims solely at the advancement of 'civil interests' such as 'life, liberty, health, and indolency of body; and the possession of outward things, such as money, lands, houses, furniture, and the like.'[9] Perfectionist considerations,[10] then, are illegitimate as grounds for state action since political authority cannot rightfully extend beyond these 'civil concernments.' This is the conclusion and not, as some critics[11] maintain, the premise of Locke's case for toleration, and the *Letter* contains three separate arguments to support it. The first 'contractual' one grounds a principle of restraint in the terms of political association that free and equal individuals would hypothetically agree to; the second one shifts from the issue of 'commission' or legitimacy to epistemic considerations regarding the 'impertinence' of coercion at altering beliefs; the final 'pluralist' argument builds on the first by explaining how the sociological fact of ethical disagreement influences the context and, therefore, the terms of political association that the contractual device yield.

Locke's first argument for the claim that 'the care of souls is not committed to the civil magistrate, any more than to other men'[12] is grounded in a contractual view of political justification[13] familiar to readers of the *Second Treatise of Government.* The magistrate has no 'commission' to enforce religious beliefs for two independent reasons: first, because 'it appears not that God has ever given any such authority to one man over another as to compel anyone to his religion.'[14] The absence of any plausible evidence for the existence of divinely sanctioned religious authority renders any putative claim to it spurious. Locke makes a similar claim in the *First Treatise of Government* by noticing that even if Adam's heir is the sole legitimate ruler of mankind, as Filmer maintains, one cannot possibly know *who* that person is. In the absence of divine designation, which one does not have, Filmer's principle is useless as it leads to no determinate result. Second, no such 'commission' can be vested in the magistrate by the consent of the people since 'no man can so far abandon the care of his own salvation as blindly to leave it to the choice of any other, whether prince or subject, to prescribe to him what faith or worship he shall embrace.'[15] While consent is the basis of all legitimate Lockean political authority, there are certain things to which 'no man' will rationally assent. But why is this so?

Locke begins *The Second Treatise of Government* by considering 'what state all men are naturally in.'[16] He characterizes it in terms of 'perfect freedom' and 'equality.'[17] The freedom in question consists of man's liberty to order his actions and dispose of his possessions and person as he thinks fit, 'within the bounds of the law of nature, without asking leave, or depending upon the will of any other man.'[18] The equality in question is juridical, and not substantive. Thus, while 'age,' 'virtue,' 'excellency,' and 'birth,' for instance, may establish a 'just precedency' for some, all such qualitative distinctions consist with the equality of jurisdiction or 'dominion.' The conjunction of these two premises – natural freedom and equality – amounts to the claim that there is no natural right to political rule: 'all the power and jurisdiction is reciprocal, no one having more than another.'[19] The law of nature commands the self-preservation of all, and within its bounds, men are free from the will of others.

The 'state of nature'[20] is simply Locke's designation, then, for *any* relationship between *any* individuals that has not been modified by either particular acts of aggression, which initiate a state of war, or by the establishment of a mutually recognized authority to arbitrate disputes between them, which institutes a commonwealth: 'Wherever any two men are who have no standing rule and common judge to appeal to on earth for the determination of controversies of right betwixt them, there they are still in the state of nature, and under all the inconveniences of it.'[21] These 'inconveniences' are central to Locke's contractual argument for toleration because they are directly linked to the very limits he places on the normative force of consent.

Locke faces a motivational objection in explaining the origins of political society, which he recognizes. Why would anyone consent to the establishment of political authority when 'he be absolute lord of his own person and possessions, equal to the greatest, and subject to nobody'?[22] The answer lies in the distinction between the *existence* of a right, and its *value*. In the Lockean state of nature, all possess a natural right[23] to freedom, but 'the enjoyment of it is very uncertain, and constantly exposed to the invasion of others'[24] for three reasons. First, the lack of mutually acceptable standing rules to decide controversies makes the law of nature inoperable among men. Being inherently 'biased by their interest,' individuals 'are not apt to allow of it as a law binding to them in the application of it to their particular cases.'[25] In the absence of a regulatory principle established by common consent, there is no impartial basis for resolving controversies. Second, the lack of an indifferent judge renders everyone simultaneously an interpreter, judge, and executioner of the law in his or her own case. Finally, the state of nature often 'wants power to back and support the sentence when right, and to give it due execution.'[26] Inadequate enforcement mechanisms make the violation of natural rights relatively easy.

Partiality threatens freedom and equality by perverting both the interpretation and the application of natural law. Appropriately, Locke begins the *Second Treatise* by defining the political problem as the need for an impartial judge to settle disputes. Free and equal individuals consent to the establishment of a commonwealth solely to remedy the inconveniences of the state of nature and thereby secure their natural rights. By excluding the private judgement of every particular member as to the proper resolution of controversies, the community 'comes to be umpire, by settled standing rules, indifferent and the same to all parties.'[27] In this way, consent both creates and restricts the scope of political authority by identifying internal limits on the concept of the state:

> But though men when they enter into society give up the equality, liberty and executive power they had in the state of nature into the hands of society, to be so far disposed of by the legislative as the good of the society shall require; yet it being only with an intention in everyone the better to preserve himself his liberty and property (for no rational creature can be supposed to change his condition with an intention to be worse), the power of society, or legislative constituted by them, can never be supposed to extend further than the common good; but is obliged to secure everyone's property by providing against those defects above-mentioned that made the state of nature so unsafe and uneasy.[28]

Without political society, natural rights to freedom and equality are insecure. *Hence*, individuals consent to the establishment of political society to secure those rights. The central implication of this inference is that any exercise of political power over the beliefs or actions of individuals that do not threaten those rights is illegitimate. Since 'no rational creature' would consent to worsening his condition, and since absolute and arbitrary power not only continues but worsens[29] the 'inconveniences' of state of nature, legitimate authority (that to which rational creatures consent) must invariably be limited.

We are now better positioned to understand Locke's claim that the magistrate lacks 'commission' to enforce religious beliefs. In the first *Letter concerning Toleration*, Locke tells us that 'no man can, if he would, conform his faith to the dictates of another. All the life and power of true religion consists in the inward and full persuasion of the mind; and faith is not faith without believing.'[30] If true (soul-saving) religion consists of inward persuasion, and if one cannot simply *choose* what to believe, then in no rational contract would one consent to empowering the magistrate to enforce religious views against one's own convictions. Since no benefits accrue from hypocritically professing a faith that one rejects, religious compulsion or intolerance is not plausibly among the terms of political association that free and equal individuals would reasonably consent to: 'For force from a stronger hand, to bring a man to a religion which another thinks the true, being an injury which in the state of nature every one would avoid; protection from such injury is one of the ends of a commonwealth, *and so every man has a right to toleration.*'[31] Securing salvation, then, cannot 'in reason' be reckoned among the aims of political association, and religious persecution is illegitimate, even if it successfully alters beliefs.

In the *Essay concerning Toleration*, Locke points out that the magistrate 'can right me against my neighbour but cannot defend me against my God.'[32] This thought is reintroduced some twenty years later in the *Letter* and related to the contractual argument for restraint. Locke sees nothing inherently irrational in 'turning merchant' upon the prince's command, since a magistrate is able to compensate for one's unfortunate financial ruin: 'In case I have ill-success in trade, he is abundantly able to make up my loss in some other way.'[33] But with respect to religious faith, 'What security can be given for the Kingdom of Heaven?'[34] Locke's point is about the relative costs and, therefore, the rationality of consent to various political measures. When errors may be adequately compensated for, consent may not be unreasonable; if they produce disastrous or irreparable consequences (such as eternity in hell), the limits of political trust have been reached, and consent to such authority is absurd.

In joining the Lockean commonwealth, individuals incur an obligation to submit their controversies to the resolution of public judgement. Natural law principles are thus rendered operative by the establishment of an authority to interpret and pronounce on its requirements. In order to remedy 'men being biased by their interest,' such authority must rule by 'standing laws.' In practice, standing laws are required because, without them, subjection to a ruler implies subjection to his arbitrary, personal rule.[35] So there is a necessity for impartiality in the *application* of standing rules. But meeting this requirement assumes a prior impartiality in their *interpretation*. Before a standing rule can be applied impartially to adjudicate between competing interests or convictions, it must be interpreted in a sufficiently abstract way so as not to reinstate partiality at a different (interpretive) level. Unless a standing rule's interpretation is itself somehow related to shared or, at bare minimum, potentially shareable, interests or convictions, it cannot serve the function that Locke attributes to it. Indeed, this insight is at the foundation of contemporary liberalism – while Locke nowhere uses the term *public reason*, some variant of that idea is essential to every contractual theory of justification, as we shall see shortly.

In the *Third Letter for Toleration*, Locke suggests that if a standing rule or principle can be defended only by relying on self-evidence, private intuition, or revelation, members of the public will obviously fail to interpret it in convergent ways. The perfectionist principle 'Enforce not your religion, but only true religion,' for instance, is meant by its advocates to restrict legitimate compulsion to the enforcement of orthodox or *true* convictions; political authority regulated by it will allegedly eradicate falsehood and uphold truth. But *anyone* with any religious beliefs comes within the principle's ambit to the extent that one cannot believe in something without also thinking it to be true. As Locke says, 'Everyone is orthodox to himself.'[36] Insofar as the principle empowers everyone, the distinction between 'your religion' and 'true religion' is entirely without force.[37] Both those with true *and* false beliefs are not only authorized but, in fact, *compelled* by conscience to coerce others. Since the principle fails to embody any type of standing rule at all, the state of nature is thereby restored: all interpret *true* religion as their own. Principles such as 'Enforce the true religion' are therefore insufficiently public to make consent to political authority that acts upon them rational. In this way, the contractual argument yields the further claim that religious persecution is illegitimate because it is inconsistent with the public use of reason.

Appeals to non-generalizable values in politics, when successful, transform the state into a vehicle for the protection of the interests of some, but not of others. To the extent that this is the case, natural rights to freedom and equality are destroyed. The insecure and unsafe partiality characteristic of the state of nature is not only restored, but is now also backed by collective force. Locke's contractual argument for toleration, then, makes some form of public reason a necessary condition of political legitimacy. Ultimately, public reason makes the interpretive impartiality of standing rules possible by identifying the *types* of interests that both can and cannot legitimately be submitted for public deliberation.

1.2.1   The Epistemic Argument

Locke's first argument for toleration in the *Letter* – the contractual one – concerns internal limits on the concept of the state. Since hypothetical norms of practical reasoning define what a state is,[38] limits to political authority are found in the very terms of political association. Locke's second argument, however, shifts the argumentative ground from internal questions of legitimacy to external ones related to the *means* of political enforcement:

> In the second place, the care of souls cannot belong to the civil magistrate, because his power consists only in outward force; but true and saving religion consists in the inward persuasion of the mind, without which nothing can be acceptable to God. And such is the nature of the understanding that it cannot be compelled to the belief of anything by outward force. Confiscation of estate, imprisonment, torments, nothing of that nature can have any such efficacy as to make men change the inward judgment that they have framed of things.[39]

Locke thinks that this argument 'absolutely determines' the controversy, and if its constitutive claims are in fact true,[40] it appears to do so. Political authority consists exclusively in 'outward force'; it 'gives laws' and 'compels with the sword.'[41] But religion of the 'true and saving' variety involves 'the inward persuasion of the mind.'[42] One can grow rich, then, by practices that one dislikes; one can be cured by remedies in which one disbelieves; but '[one] cannot be saved by a religion that [one] distrusts.'[43] If only an inward persuasion of the mind procures acceptance with God, then coercion is 'absolutely impertinent' towards the salvation of souls since it cannot influence belief. Only 'light and evidence' can change opinions, and such light 'can in no manner proceed from corporeal sufferings.'[44] Individuals cannot be compelled to be saved, and must be left to their own consciences.

One important implication of this argument is the doubt that it casts on the actual motives of religious persecutors. For if coercion cannot alter belief, and if belief is an indispensable element of true faith, then persecutors cannot, if they are at all rational, be interested in what they claim to be – the saving of souls. Indeed, all three of Locke's arguments in the original *Letter,* but particularly the second one, demonstrate the extent to which intolerance is mere partisanship. This point is clear from the perspectives of both the victims and perpetrators of intolerance. If one focuses on the victims, incentives and threats do not encourage, but pervert, their deliberative processes. Coercion and manipulation, Locke thinks, are as sure ways to make them consider religious matters properly 'as it would be for a prince to bribe and threaten a judge to make him judge uprightly.' If they do anything at all, such pressures normally reinforce, rather than alter, existing beliefs.[45] And persecutors, themselves, seem interested in defending truth and opposing 'schism' only when 'they have the civil magistrate on their side'; when they lack the power to carry on persecuting others, 'then they can bear most patiently, and unmovedly, the contagion of idolatry, superstition, and heresy in their neighbourhood.'[46] The irrationality of religious coercion together with the selectivity of its application make clear that persecutors are motivated by 'interest'[47] and 'temporal dominion,'[48] not truth.

Locke's second argument initially seems to suggest that a particular conception of epistemology is foundational to his case for toleration. In the *Essay concerning Human Understanding*, he famously compares the original state of the human mind to 'white paper void of all characters, without any *ideas*.' At the core of Locke's epistemic empiricism is the notion that sensation and reflection are, together, exhaustive of the sources of all the ideas that human beings are capable of having.[49] This 'white paper' is transformed and coloured by both perceptions of external objects, and by the internal operation of the mind reflecting upon itself. The raw materials of reason and knowledge originate 'from *experience*; in that all our knowledge is founded, and from that it ultimately derives itself.'[50] In the *Essay*, Locke suggests that only the individual who is 'not content to live lazily on scraps of begged opinions' has 'raised himself above the alms-basket.'[51] The proper employment of the faculties with which God has entrusted individuals consists in their thinking for themselves: 'It is not worth while to be concerned what he says or thinks who says or thinks only as he is directed by another.'[52] Most people, Locke maintains, take things upon trust and 'misemploy their power of assent, by lazily enslaving their minds to the dictates and dominion of others.'[53] Truth is accessible only if people are willing to properly exercise their minds.

Locke's rejection of innate ideas places experience at the centre of what human beings can know.[54] This epistemic claim, however, has two possible implications for toleration – one liberal, the other not. If the pursuit of truth requires experience, then a principle of non-interference is suggested by that very consideration. Truth requires experience, and people cannot experience things if they are constrained from doing so. The Lockean theory of knowledge, then, seems to entail a commitment to limited government. But there is another, less decidedly liberal, interpretation available here. If experience is somehow related to the discovery of truth – either religious or secular – then perhaps this provides the state with even more of a decisive reason for *controlling* what people experience and reflect upon. Even if states cannot directly manipulate peoples' beliefs, they can clearly shape the environments within which such beliefs are formed. Remember, Locke's second argument is about the nature of belief, not the limits of political legitimacy. And within this narrower discussion, more sophisticated and indirect measures such as banning heretical books are likely to be radically less 'impertinent' at influencing religious convictions.

We should be wary, then, of relying too heavily on the epistemic case for toleration as suggested in the *Essay*. While Locke does defend a particular view about the initial acquisition of ideas in the *Essay*, the *Letter* focuses primarily, if not exclusively, on how beliefs are *changed*: 'It is only light and evidence that *can work a change* in men's opinions.'[55] The notion that persecution is unlikely to alter religious beliefs is compatible with a variety of differing explanations as to their genesis. As one commentator notes, 'The argument of the letter is neutral as to whether we can get at the truth in religious questions; all Locke seeks to show is that we are not more likely to reach it by submitting to persecution.'[56]

The epistemology of the *Essay* is relevant to Locke's second argument in the *Letter*, but only indirectly. Locke's discussion of the limits of human understanding is meant to explain the origins of ethical disagreement. As a result of varying natural capacities, efforts, and interests, for example, truth affects people's minds differentially. Accordingly, there is no consensus about it. In this way, epistemology connects with toleration by explaining what it is that makes a principle of restraint necessary – namely, ethical disagreement. Locke's particular views about the grounds and limits of knowledge, however, are not essentially tied to toleration. They simply explain why it is required.[57]

1.2.2 The Pluralist Argument

Locke's third argument – what I shall call the argument from pluralism – is not really a separate argument, but rather an empirical observation that influences the context and, therefore, the outcome of the contractual procedure (argument 1):

In the third place, the care of the salvation of men's souls cannot belong to the magistrate, because, though the rigour of laws and the force of penalties were capable to convince and change men's minds, yet would not that help at all to the salvation of their souls. For there being but one truth, one way to heaven, what hopes is there that more men would be led into it, if they had no other rule to follow but the religion of the court, and were put under a necessity to quit the light of their own reason; to oppose the dictates of their own consciences; and blindly to resign themselves to the will of their governors, and to the religion which either ignorance, ambition, or superstition had chanced to establish in the countries where they were born?[58]

David Wootton misleadingly calls this argument a 'sceptical one,'[59] but it is the brute fact of pluralism – simple ethical disagreement – that grounds Locke's claim that the salvation of souls cannot 'belong to the magistrate.' Even if one supposes, with Locke, that 'the Scripture ... has for at least these sixteen hundred years contained the only true religion in the world,'[60] and one further accepts that religious beliefs *can* be compelled, one would still not authorize magistrates to compel such beliefs since, the odds are, they would impose the wrong ones. If, for example, there are ninety-nine false religions for one that *I know* to be true, the odds are ninety-nine to one that I will be coerced into believing what is false. Since the magistrates of the world are as divided by religious opinions as they are by conflicting interests, individuals compelled to follow them in their faith would 'owe their eternal happiness or misery to the places of their nativity'[61] – obviously an absurd conclusion. It is pluralism, then, that makes submitting religious beliefs[62] to the authoritative demands of the state irrational.

Pervasive ethical disagreement also refutes the suggestion, made by Proast and others, that political and clerical authority is somehow epistemically privileged in religious matters. For if princes were endowed with superior insight into the nature of religious truth, then one would expect to find religious consensus among the 'lords of the earth.'[63] But since this is clearly not the case, such knowledge 'cannot be looked upon as the peculiar possession of any sort of men.'[64] The princes of the world are as infected with the depraved nature of mankind as the rest of their brethren. To the extent that this is true, it makes no sense to surrender one's judgement to them.

In the *Third Letter for Toleration*, Locke continues this argument by rejecting the suggestion that magistrates are commissioned by God and the law of nature to propagate the true religion. Insofar as this alleged commission cannot be executed without magistrates themselves being judges of what is true,[65] religious compulsion is not plausibly mandated by the law of nature, since pluralism renders its execution self-defeating for the reasons outlined above.

1.3. Proast on Locke

At first glance, one of the most remarkable things to be found in Proast's replies is the repeated suggestion that Locke ultimately has only one argument for restraint.[66] Notwithstanding the fact that Locke restates each of his three key arguments not once but three times in the original *Letter*, Proast persists in maintaining that the contractual and pluralist ones are both reducible to the argument from belief. Of the former, Proast asserts that 'if all the Reason which the Author denies that Magistrates have any Commission or Authority to punish for Matters of Religion, ends in the unfitness of Force to convince Men's understanding (as, upon examination, it will appear it does) the onely strength of that Letter may lie in that.'[67] Of the latter, he maintains similarly that 'this Argument, from the Magistrate's being as liable to error as the rest of mankind, concerns none but those, who assert that every Magistrate has a Right to use Force to promote his own Religion, whatever it be: Which I think no man that has any religion will assert: And for this reason, I could not be obliged to consider it as a distinct Argument.'[68] This makes it initially tempting to perceive Proast as either disingenuous or careless. However, Proast's conflation of Locke's three separate (but admittedly related) arguments ultimately reflects his commitment to a conception of political authority in which the distinction between legitimacy and efficacy is itself collapsed.

Because Proast assumes that the only plausible limitations on 'commission' are rooted in either the impertinence of penalties or the falsity of one's beliefs, he finds in Locke only what he is already predisposed to see: an argument about the inefficacy of coercion, which he (quite reasonably) takes to be false, and a secret scepticism about religious truth, which is obviously indefensible from both of their points of view. So, for Proast, the only distinct argument that Locke offers is the one from belief. Precisely what view of political authority generates this myopically selective reading of the *Letter*?

In response to Locke's contention that the impertinence of penalties 'absolutely determines' the controversy, Proast writes,

For this is indeed the Point upon which this Controversy turnes: If all Force and Compulsion be utterly useless and unserviceable to the promoting these Ends; then to use it for that purpose, will be only to abuse it; which no man can have a Right to do: But if, on the contrary, such a degree of outward Force as has been mentioned, be really of great and even necessary Use for the advancing these ends ... then it must be acknowledged, that there is a Right somewhere to use it for the advancing those Ends; unless we will say (what without Impiety cannot be said) that the Wise and Benign Disposer and Governour of all things has not furnish'd Mankind with competent Means for the promoting his own Honour in the World, and the Good of Souls.[69]

Proast claims several important things here. First, the existence of a 'Right' is conditional upon the instrumentality of 'Force and Compulsion' in 'advancing' the particular end in question – in this case, salvation. The legitimacy of coercing others depends upon the extent to which such compulsion actually secures its putative ends, as well as upon the objective validity of the ends themselves. This perfectionist view of authority can be represented thus: if means (M) are either instrumentally useful or necessary to bringing about effect (E), and E is objectively valuable (or true, good), then there is a right to M. Authority is therefore both conditional upon empirical observations about the effects and limits of coercion, and a direct and unmediated consequence of normative truth.

The second important point about this passage is Proast's inference from 'someone' necessarily having a right to M to the further claim that such a right is held by the magistrate. The perfectionist view of authority outlined above suggests that the right to compel religious orthodoxy resides with the magistrate because of the scope and efficacy of the means at his disposal: 'What better course can men take to provide for this [to make them care for their salvation against their passions], than by vesting the Power I have described, in him who bears the Sword?'[70]

Finally, if Proast's view of authority is coherent, it implicitly undermines Locke's entire conceptualization of the political problem, as well as the contractual device he develops in response to it. Individuals who disagree about truth cannot rationally consent to the enforcement of ethical or religious orthodoxy. Within Locke's contractual framework, then, pluralism is clearly relevant to toleration: limits on authority are found in the basic terms of political association, and such terms are, in turn, influenced by the fact that contractors disagree about what is true.

But Proast's conception of authority renders ethical disagreement largely irrelevant to issues of legitimacy. Although ethical disagreement ultimately creates the need for tolerance, it has no bearing upon a view of authority that asserts that if means (M) are either instrumentally useful or necessary to effect (E), and E is objectively valuable (or 'true,' or 'good'), then there is a right to M. For Proast, whether the magistrate has the authority to compel obedience to the Church of England depends upon Anglicanism's *truth*. Since what individuals actually *think* about the matter cannot possibly affect *that* question, pluralism raises no distinctively political concerns for toleration.

Alongside the implicit claim that contractualism is the wrong way to think about principles of restraint, Proast levels a much more difficult objection. He thinks that even if one accepts Locke's characterization of the political problem as the need for mutually acceptable adjudicative principles, hypothetical consent will still fail to yield anti-perfectionism.

Locke denies that the enforcement of religious orthodoxy against dissenters can 'in reason' be reckoned among the aims of political association, since such authority represents 'an injury which in the state of nature everyone would avoid; protection from such injury is one of the ends of a commonwealth.' The contractual argument attempts to specify the type of state that is in the moral interests of its citizens. Proast seizes upon this to discredit the idea that consent to religious compulsion is inherently irrational and, therefore, illegitimate. If salvation is better provided for when the magistrate is entrusted and obliged to see that no person neglect his soul, then 'it is every man's true Interest, that the care of his Soul should not be left to himself alone, but that the Magistrate should be so far entrusted with it as I contend that he is.'[71]

By relying on the perfectionist view of authority outlined above, this claim clearly expresses Proast's conflation of two of Locke's distinct arguments. If coercion assists in the genesis of orthodox religious belief, and such belief is itself a prerequisite for salvation, then the magistrate may rightfully use such force, since all have an interest in eternal life. The limits of Proastian political legitimacy are identical with those of instrumental efficacy.

Later in the book, we shall see that there are convincing reasons for rejecting perfectionist justifications of political authority, particularly from a liberal point of view. Proast's focus on 'true Interest,' however, raises an acute problem for Locke within the very assumptions of the contractual argument itself. Salvation is obviously a paramount concern for religious believers. But the faithful themselves are often the first to acknowledge the extent to which 'Prejudice and Passion' can distort or replace the 'Reasons and Motives' that ought to determine their religious beliefs.[72] Locke clearly shares Proast's view of human weakness and temptation. The contractual argument assumes this by seeing political association as a remedy for the partisanship of the state of nature. Natural law, which is God's law, is often misinterpreted by self-interested and passion-driven individuals. The core of the pluralist argument, in turn, assumes an egalitarianism of human depravity. Because princes are as infected with the depraved nature of mankind as the rest of their brethren, they are neither ethically nor epistemically privileged. If this is so, however, then it is unclear why self-admittedly weak and vulnerable individuals would rationally withhold their consent to an authority that compels them to fulfil their religious obligations.

Coercion of this type clearly frustrates first-order desires by preventing people from indulging in behaviour that they, de facto, wish to engage in. But if the satisfaction of such desires (for drunkenness, adulterous sex, idolatry) actually harms their moral interests by leading, say, to eternal damnation, then people arguably have compelling self-interested reasons to be frustrated in this way. This view fits naturally with a perfectionist view of well-being since the latter identifies the content of our highest-order interests.

Individuals often have (second-order) desires to want things other than they do. Some substance abusers, for instance, voluntarily subject themselves to extremely difficult and painful rehabilitative programs in an effort to change what they strongly want. By consciously attempting to transform the nature of their wants, individuals attempt to change *who* they are. Indeed, hierarchically structured intentions such as these seem to manifest central aspects of both personhood and rationality.[73]

In a magisterial work[74] on the making of the modern identity, Charles Taylor develops a related idea by way of a distinction between two types of deliberation. He suggests that the peculiarly human capacity to formulate second-order desires takes place within the context of 'strong,' as opposed to 'weak,' evaluation. 'Weak evaluation' is essentially concerned with outcomes, and the criteria it uses are external to the self. When a weak evaluator eschews a desired option, she does so because of its contingent incompatibility with a preferred alternative. A strong evaluator, by contrast, engages herself in a self-reflexive inquiry related to the qualitative worth of her various desires. A desired consummation is shunned by the strong evaluator, not because of its incommensurability with another object of her will, but since the kind of person she aspires to be would be compromised by satisfying it.[75]

The idea of normative second-order desires is naturally aligned with a perfectionist view of well-being. A theory of human flourishing identifies the noble, worthy, and integrated activities that are, or ought to be, the objects of one's de facto desires. Proast's internal critique of Locke's contractual argument appeals to the value of a type of moral paternalism implied by this link. Proast thinks that consent to religious persecution is rational because it ultimately secures people's higher-order interest in salvation. The idea of normative (second-order) desires makes contractually self-imposed coercion rational. One consents to being forced to do what is in one's best interests.

Analogies between physical paternalism (compelling people to wear seatbelts) and moral paternalism (compelling people to live ethically) are highly problematic. As H.L.A. Hart points out, it is 'quite unclear why forcing a person under the threat of legal penalties to conform to moral requirements ... should be regarded as securing for him welfare or a good of any kind.'[76] Indeed, unless some criterion of 'harm' is identified that is independent of the alleged impiety or immorality of certain conduct or beliefs, moral welfare and moral harm simply become synonyms for conformity to, and deviation from, conventionally held beliefs.

But Locke *shares* Proast's belief that their society's conventional religious understandings – those of the Anglican Church – are in fact true.[77] He cannot dismiss Proast's argument about second-order or 'true Interests' as easily as he does the perfectionist view of authority, because it arises within the contractual framework of justification that he, himself, has constructed. From behind a 'veil of ignorance,'[78] hypothetical contractors would likely select anti-perfectionist principles of political morality. In the absence of any detailed knowledge about the nature of true faith, consent to religious coercion is senseless. Individuals cannot rationally authorize the state to coerce them into securing their higher-order interests since no one knows, or can know, where such interests lie. Lockean contractors, however, are not similarly ignorant. If the Anglican Church really is a vehicle for the attainment of eternal life, and if individuals have an interest in securing salvation, what makes consent to religious intolerance in its name irrational? Locke's argument from pluralism is clearly offered as an answer to this question. From a contractual point of view, one's certainty in Christ, for example, does not make consent to Christian intolerance rational, since one can never be similarly certain that those wielding power will share this conviction.[79] But Proast's view of authority rejects the idea that ethical disagreement has any bearing upon principles of restraint. As a result, he thinks that it is contractually rational to limit coercion only when the beliefs that are enforced are false. Ultimately, the argument says, Locke must be a sceptic.[80]

Locke's anti-perfectionism is reducible to scepticism, however, only if, following Proast, he begs the question by assuming that ethical truth can be directly identified with his personal views. With this Proastian assumption in place, intolerant authority is justified not because it enforces one's own ethical beliefs – no political privilege can legitimately be derived simply from the bare assurance one has in the truth of one's convictions; phenomenologically, everyone is equally positioned[81] – but rather because truth is fortunately enshrined in the actual historical community to which one belongs. For Proast, the privilege of belonging to the Church of England *is* differentially distributed between various individuals depending upon *where* they live, and the church to which they belong. Outsiders such as French Catholics and internal dissenters such as English atheists are therefore not only legitimate targets of intolerance, they are themselves precluded from legitimately persecuting others. As Proast says, 'The power I ascribe to the Magistrate, is given to him, to bring men, not to his *own*, but to the *true* Religion.'[82] Since truth is a necessary condition for the justification of religious intolerance, and Catholicism is manifestly false, Proast thinks that Locke's concern with Protestant minorities in France betrays a sceptical premise – the principle empowers only the orthodox.

If Proast's claim makes (any) sense, then Locke's contractual argument generates agent-relative and context-dependent principles of restraint. That is to say, it leads to perfectionism if the contracting members of a commonwealth hold true beliefs, and to anti-perfectionism when these beliefs are false. As an implication, the content of political morality identified through consent is dependent, among other things, upon the ethnicity and religion of the hypothetical contractors in question. The appropriateness of restraint or intolerance will vary with their ethical beliefs: are we dealing with Protestants or Catholics!?

Clearly, the distinction at the core of Proast's principle is circular and nonsensical because it assumes what we need, but do not have: an independent criterion of truth. Locke realizes, but Proast cannot see, that it is *French Catholic political authorities*, not Oxbridge Protestant pamphleteers, whose religion will be the basis of coercive enforcement in France. Indeed, if such a criterion were available, it would be difficult to explain the existence of the ethical disagreement that prompted the need for a principle of restraint in the first place. Locke and Proast agree on Catholicism's perversity, but the authorities to whom the principle must apply in

France do not. While unanimity would render Proast's equivocation[83] mildly coherent within a particular normative consensus (a mutually acceptable criterion of truth would, in principle, not only adjudicate, but eliminate controversy), the very ethical disagreement that generates the need for tolerance renders it absurd. Such disagreement may result either from disputes between different political jurisdictions where conflicting cultural and religious groups make mutually exclusive ethical claims (the English vs the French), or from overlapping communal attachments, which create conflicts *within particular jurisdictions* (English dissenters).

Principles of restraint must somehow accommodate, not ignore, the fact that toleration is needed in a context of interpretive disagreement – a clash of incompatible perspectives is what sets the political and conceptual problem. But the principle advanced by Proast neglects this by appealing to a *sub specie aeternitatis* notion of truth. The political adjudication of interpretive conflict becomes a background, or secondary, problem. This explains Proast's focus on the relative merits of various *means* of enforcement. Since religious truth is self-evidently enshrined in the Church of England, religious persecution is a purely technical matter constrained only by empirical limitations on the use of force.

1.4 Contractualism and Abstraction in Liberal Political Morality

Locke's focus on minorities in the *Letters on Toleration* signals a recognition of the conceptual as well as the political problems of this view. His attempt to identify a set of specifically political, and therefore ethically neutral, entitlements and obligations is meant to accommodate them. Whereas Proast sees nothing distinctive about the political problem raised by ethical disagreement for perfectionist principles of restraint, Locke's entire methodological approach – abstraction – is framed to deal with it.

Locke's contractualist case for anti-perfectionism and, by implication, any similar argument, crucially depends upon sustaining both what we may call *ethical* and *political abstraction*. Locke's argument escapes Proast's charge of scepticism, that is, only to the extent that these two interrelated ideas are defensible. In the absence of a moral requirement (fairness? impartiality?) to articulate principles of political morality that are relatively autonomous from contested conceptions of ethical value, what, other than scepticism, could possibly motivate anti-perfectionism? On the other hand, if there are compelling moral reasons to adopt this strategy, then Proast's critique fails.

In Locke's writings, *ethical abstraction* is primarily a heuristic device that represents a substantive thesis about moral equality. Since the justification of civil and political liberties is disassociated from, among other things, the particular ethical norms that individuals endorse, an equality of (political) moral standing obtains between them. The constitutional aspects of Locke's political vision are rooted in this idea. As specified in the state of nature, moral equality identifies fixed limits to all forms of legitimate political authority.

Political abstraction, by contrast, relates not to the limits on the constituent power that creates a commonwealth, but to the discursive principles that regulate and ultimately make possible the ongoing political life of a self-governing community of equals. Political abstraction takes two forms in Locke: constraints on political deliberation, which are based upon the premise of moral equality. These are closely related to the discursive limits of 'civil communication' and embody a theory of *public reasoning*; and a counterfactual test for principles of governmental restraint related to the issue of political minorities.

The Lockean state of nature, that state that 'all Men are naturally in,' represents an attempt to devise normative criteria for social criticism that are external to the cultural practices and political arrangements to which they apply. The intuitive idea is the need for critical distance: unless social criticism is undertaken in light of norms that are somehow defensible independently of the contexts that produce them, it amounts to little more than a rationalization of the ethical status quo. In order to rectify the defects of history and the contamination of moral concepts by tradition, self-interest, and partiality, Locke articulates an ahistorical criterion for morality: 'The project was to devise a criterion which was outside history, in terms of which to judge the moral status of the present political culture.'[84] Analytically, the state of nature's ahistoricity enables it to operate as an Archimedean critical vantage point outside the contingencies of time and place.

Recall that the natural freedom and equality that characterizes this state obtains by virtue of individuals' identical positioning within the normative order of God's creation. The law of nature, which is the law of God, is identifiable through reason. The contractual argument for the institution of a commonwealth both assumes and relies upon this (God-given) faculty to identify limits to *all* forms of legitimate political authority. Thus, while 'age,' 'virtue,' 'excellency of parts,' 'merit,' and 'birth' often establish 'a just precedency' for some over others, these inequalities all consist with the equality in respect of 'jurisdiction or dominion'[85] whereby all are entitled to their natural freedom from the will or authority of any other individuals. This moral equality sets fixed limits to the constituent power of a commonwealth since the terms of political association can never legitimately transgress it.

Let us call this strategy *ethical abstraction*. The Lockean state of nature *abstracts* from certain palpable differences between human beings to establish an underlying moral equality between them. This juridical structure does not assume that individuals share equally in either natural endowments or personal achievements. In principle, Locke accepts the idea that superiority of intellect is a title to authority, but since the faculty of reason is a common possession, everyone is adequately equipped for self-direction: 'Creatures of the same species and rank promiscuously born to all the same advantages of nature, and the use of the same faculties, should also be equal one amongst another without subordination or subjection.'[86] By 'the same advantages,' Locke either intends a minimal threshold capacity for self-direction beyond which differences are irrelevant, or a stipulative conceptual claim about the intimate link between the human 'species' and its 'faculties.' In the latter case, this capacity is equally distributed *in principle* – to speak of human beings is *pro tanto* to imply self-direction. Contra Filmer's argument for the rightful ascendancy of Adam's heirs, the absence of a 'manifest declaration' by the 'lord and master of them all' allows everyone the freedom that is required to fulfil God's intentions.

Certain observable differences between human beings are therefore bracketed or set aside as irrelevant from the moral point of view. Differential natural distributions in talent, intelligence, and strength, for example, are not implausibly *denied*; they are *ignored* in favour of a deeper egalitarianism. In Locke's argument, ethical abstraction is both methodological and substantive: methodologically, the state of nature abstracts from historical contingency to afford a critical perspective in the assessment of a society's conventional moral understandings; substantively, a particular conception of moral equality emerges from this process. Ethical abstraction, then, both identifies, and is identical to, Locke's thesis about moral equality. This thesis establishes hypothetical consent as the appropriate constitutional expression of equal freedom.

Ethical and political abstraction are tied together in Locke's thought by his particular understanding of the relationship between government and civil society. Individuals consent to the establishment of a commonwealth to remedy the inconveniences of their natural condition. Legitimate political authority results from a trust given by its members. This trust can only occur, then, if there already exists a people to constitute it.[87] Although the rights that set fixed limits to all possible forms of political association are natural, the constituent power that itself creates a particular form of government is conventional. The capacity for rational self-direction that grounds Locke's thesis of moral equality also implies that individual agents are responsible for the political arrangements that they institute. Political authority is, therefore, a rational construction bounded by the central purpose of *its* creators – the protection of equal freedom.[88]

One implication of the artificiality of political institutions is that these may be constructed in a host of different ways, provided, of course, that moral equality is respected. This proviso, however, is not a sufficient condition for the persistence of a self-governing community of equals. One cannot deduce a moral culture or an entire legal system from this all-important but minimal constraint. Since the post-constitutional life of a commonwealth will involve the contextual interpretation of what moral equality requires, certain discursive principles are also needed to regulate the disagreements that will inevitably arise from this. Within the range of political alternatives satisfying moral equality, only those also incorporating certain discursive norms of *publicity* make the ongoing mutual acceptability of 'standing rules' possible.

The conceptual and temporal priority of a people over the government it institutes reveals that ethical abstraction is a feature of humanity as a whole. Political abstraction, on the other hand, is a feature of Lockean *civil* society. This takes two forms: constraints on political argument that link moral equality to the limits of communicability through a requirement of *public reasoning*; and a counterfactual test for principles of governmental restraint grounded in the problem of political minorities as raised in the Locke-Proast polemic.

There is a clear analogy between Locke's thoughts on the limits of 'civil communication' in the *Essay concerning Human Understanding* and the first component of political abstraction. In book 3, chapter 3 of the *Essay*, Locke suggests that a certain kind of abstraction is an indispensable precondition for the mutual intelligibility of language. The greater part of all human languages consists of 'general terms,' not as a result of neglect or accident, 'but of reason and necessity.'[89] This rational necessity is traceable to the purposive aspect of language, as well as to certain limits on communicability. As with virtually everything else in Locke's thought, language is quintessentially purposive: 'Men learn names and use them in talk with others only that they may be understood.'[90] A speaker achieves this, however, only when the particular word that she uses to express an idea *converges* or *coincides* with the idea such a sound elicits in the mind of her interlocutor. Since this cannot be done by names applied to particular things with which the speaker alone is acquainted, reason suggests the necessity of 'general words.'[91]

These 'general words' make the mutual intelligibility of language possible 'by separating [it] from the circumstances of time and place and any other *ideas* that may determine this or that particular existence. By this way of abstraction [general words] are made capable of representing more individuals than one.'[92] A trivial example would be the difference between my saying '355 Piccadilly St' or 'PTAPAN,' which presumably mean nothing to anyone unacquainted with my neighbourhood or intellectual interests, and 'home' or 'philosophical society,' which do convey certain basic ideas because of conventional parameters on the use of such words.

In chapter 9 of the same book, Locke links the 'imperfection of words' to a distinction between two uses of language. For 'the recording of our own thoughts,' whereby we talk to ourselves, as it were, any words suffice. Words represent ideas, and the ideas that they express originate in the same 'understanding' as the words themselves. Since Locke conceives of language as the medium through which ideas are both developed and expressed – 'talking to ourselves' is identical to *thinking* – it is conceptually impossible to misunderstand one's own words. Paradoxically, then, the 'right use and perfection of language'[93] is internal monologue.

The second use is 'the communicating of our thoughts to others.' This is divided into two further categories with each entailing different limitations – 'civil' and 'philosophical' discourse. The 'civil use' of words has at its central aim the 'upholding [of] common conversation and commerce about the ordinary affairs and conveniences of civil life in the societies of men one amongst another.'[94] This embodies a convenient arrangement for managing or accommodating conflicting interests or perspectives in the absence of shared regulative norms. It is an essentially dialogical and largely anarchic process.[95] Other than convention or 'propriety,' there is no linguistic 'standing rule' to determine or settle disputed meanings.

By contrast, the 'philosophical use' of words serves to 'convey the precise notions of things, and to express in general propositions certain and undoubted truths which the mind may rest upon and be satisfied with in its search after true knowledge.'[96] Unlike states, voluntary (truth-seeking) associations such as churches or scientific societies *can* self-impose stipulative definitions because of their prior commitments to shared norms. While propriety may regulate civil or 'common conversation' fairly well, it is unhelpful in philosophical discourse since convention cannot plausibly establish the precise signification of philosophical ideas and the words that express them. Complex (moral) ideas such as justice and virtue, for instance, are irreducible to 'propriety' for two reasons. First, there is scarce 'any name of any very complex *idea*... which, in common use, has not a great latitude and which, keeping within the bounds of propriety, may not be made the sign of far different *ideas*';[97] and second, disagreements about such complex ideas are likely to extend themselves to controversies over the criteria of propriety. Philosophical discourse is therefore similar to the monological conception of language in which, individually or through a voluntary association of our fellows, we 'talk' to ourselves.

One way of understanding the central issue at stake in the Locke-Proast controversy over toleration is in terms of the distinction Locke draws between civil and philosophical discourse. In the third and fourth letters on toleration, Locke repeatedly complains that Proast cannot appreciate the difference between the minimal requirements of persuasively talking to oneself, or to those of a similar mind, and talking to others who often disagree with us. The former case raises an epistemic problem in which one's particular vantage point or perspective is mostly irrelevant to the question of truth – for example, how could it matter whether it is you or I who asks, 'What is virtue'? Politics, however, raises the issue of perspective in the most acute way *because* it is defined by the disjunction of our respective answers to this question.

In the third and fourth letters, Locke repeatedly points out the incoherence of an argumentative strategy that essentially depends for its success upon the *imposition* of one's personal interpretation of a philosophical principle on one's interlocutor. Consider a dispute between individuals A (Proast) and B (Locke) about principle P ('enforce the *true* religion'). B may, and often does, interpret complex philosophical principles such as P differently from A. To the extent that the success of A's strategy's presupposes A and B's unanimity about the content of P, nonconvergence in this regard is fatal to its stated objective (promoting the *true* religion).

Proast claims that his principle forbids French monarchs from repressing Protantism in France because of Catholicism's manifest falsity. Locke responds by saying, 'The mass, in France, is as much supposed the truth, as the liturgy here. And your way of applying force will as much promote popery in France, as protestantism in England. And so you see how serviceable it is to make men receive and embrace the truth that must save them.'[98] Proast's strategy, then, is a paradigmatic example of the confusion inherent within P above. It is not he, but Frenchmen, who will interpret religious 'truth' in France. Proast's argument makes sense only if French authorities adopt his religious perspective. Logically, this is absurd since it is *disagreement* not *consensus* that generates the debate over toleration. Once French authorities adopt Proast's convictions, toleration becomes politically useless and conceptually impossible.

For Locke, political institutions are artificial – they are constructions of reason. Reason, in turn, is understood primarily in terms of a faculty and its exercise, as opposed to any pre-existing set of conclusions. What constraints, then, do the limits of communicability briefly identified above place upon *political reasoning* between individuals conceived of as free and equal?

Locke's contractual argument for principles of political morality must operate in a context of interpretive uncertainty. To remedy the inconveniences of the state of nature, mutually acceptable standing rules must adjudicate between conflicting interests and values. But to be identifiable and operative, standing rules will, themselves, have to survive interpretive differences and lead to convergent results. This requirement identifies the motivation for, as well as the limits of, the constraints of public reasoning. Political discourse must somehow be limited to civilly defined interests that can potentially survive a plurality of interpretations. As general words make the mutual intelligibility of language possible, public reason allows for the possibility of standing rules by abstracting from the very contested conceptions of ethical value that generate their need.

Civil communication differs from philosophical communication insofar as the former is designed as a convenience for upholding 'common conversation and commerce about ... ordinary affairs,' not as a path to normative truth. Churches, for example, are not analogous to states, because, as voluntary associations, the former are, but the latter are not, characterized by prior commitments to shared ethical norms. Indeed, it is precisely the *absence* of such norms that creates the distinctively political problem of accommodating ethical disagreement. Together with Locke's premise of equal freedom, this task generates a publicity requirement in the rational construction and sustenance of political institutions.

Political authority respects agents' moral equality and rationality only if the norms that it imposes are shared or, at bare minimum, potentially shareable, by all. For Locke, the existence of a self-governing and plural-

istic community presupposes certain constraints on political deliberation as identified by the limits of 'civil communication.' Unless collective
action is kept within such limits, the state is nothing more than a vehicle
for the *imposition* of certain peoples' contested norms and self-understandings on others. The constraints of public reason, therefore, allow
for the political expression of a collective 'we' or 'us.' Public reason both
presupposes and sustains Lockean community.

At the first stage of Locke's argument, a hypothetical contract limits
the constituent power of a commonwealth to ensure that the terms of
political association are consistent with natural rights. But as Locke's
debate with Proast makes clear, this is not the only point at which equal
freedom is potentially threatened. Political authority justified by self-evidence, intuition, or divine inspiration, for instance, is equally worrying.
By privileging the interpretive powers of some over others, philosophical
justifications for collective action destroy equal freedom at a second, and
no less important, discursive stage.

For Locke, the principles of political morality that specify rights and
obligations must be the object of reasonable agreement if a self-governing community of equals is to be possible. In the absence of such a contract, mutually acceptable adjudicative principles are non-existent, and
politics is simply the imposition of certain (dominant) normative self-
understandings on others. A commonwealth, therefore, presupposes a
certain degree of interpretive convergence. Locke expresses the political
need for this convergence through standing rules. But if standing rules
are possible only when these are understood, interpreted, and applied in
convergent ways (remember the principle 'enforce the *true* religion'),
then pluralism and mutual acceptability suggest that these be limited to
what Locke calls civil interests. The limits of communicability make
philosophical principles poor candidates for standing rules – their
(self?) evidence is rarely persuasive except to members of the voluntary
associations that constitute the limited normative consensus in question.

With this in mind, the crucial link in Locke's argument between
equality, publicity, and abstraction is clear: the (political) abstraction
characteristic of public reason is nothing other than the discursive manifestation of moral equality. By abstracting from their ethical disputes and
reasoning publicly about their civil interests, members of the Lockean
commonwealth respect each other's equal moral standing and God-given
deliberative powers. In this way, moral equality is preserved beyond the
original conventional act that institutes a civil society and is extended to
the ongoing political life of a self-governing community.

Besides the requirement of discursive publicity, political abstraction also manifests itself via a counterfactual claim about the interchangeability of political actors in the contractual justificatory scheme. We saw earlier that toleration is the expression of a natural rights claim that places liberty of conscience outside the scope of *all* forms of legitimate political authority. Locke's distinction between the 'business' of civil government from that of religion yields 'fixed and immovable'[99] boundaries that separate the two. Since limits to political authority are found in the original grant of power to the magistrate, and commonwealths are instituted only to protect the equal freedom of their members, the 'civil power is the same in every place.'[100]

One implication of this claim is that the distribution of political rights and obligations should be *insensitive* to contextual differences between contractors both within and between particular commonwealths.[101] The state of nature's ahistoricity is the pre-political expression of this Lockean intuition – differential endowments of talent and personal achievement do not affect the egalitarian distribution of natural rights. Proast's view of political authority implicitly violates this by being both agent-relative and context-dependent. One's rights are dependent upon *what* one believes; this, in turn, is contingent upon *where* one lives (are you French or English?)

In the *Second Treatise*, Locke characterizes the political problem as the need for mutually acceptable adjudicative principles or standing rules within a commonwealth. In his subsequent exchanges with Proast, however, the argumentative scope is expanded to include the issue of political minorities. To the extent that the contractual argument yields internal limits on the authority of all states, identical principles of political restraint will be implemented in a variety of radically dissimilar contexts. Such principles will affect Protestants in France and Italy, as well as Catholics in England.[102] Indeed, the shift from writing in English in the *Two Treatises* to Latin in the *Letter concerning Toleration* is symptomatic of the broader audience for whom the *Letter* was intended.[103]

1.5 Conclusion

The conjunction of Locke's claim that the civil power is the same in every place with the empirical observation that different authorities believe in mutually exclusive religions (the argument from pluralism) yields a Lockean veil of ignorance device beyond the need for discursive publicity. In his polemic with Proast, Locke introduces this idea by asking, even if one accepts the legitimacy of religious persecution for truth, what if authorities disagree with one's interpretation of it? Granting that Protestantism is undoubtedly true (as Locke thinks), how would adopting Proast's principle of persecution affect one's interests in France, where Catholicism is the state religion? Locke suggests that the proper, or contractual, way to think about principles of political morality in a pluralistic setting is to ask the following question: Is our favoured distribution of rights and obligations consistently defensible in abstraction from detailed knowledge about our particular interests and ethical convictions? The fact that moral equality is preserved only to the extent that an affirmative answer is reached says something profound and important that is often overlooked even today, namely, that political philosophy is *not* simply individual practical reason, or personal ethics, writ large.

Now this conclusion (and reference to a Lockean veil of ignorance) sounds ominously Rawlsian, so one might worry whether, in trying to refute Proast, I have ultimately read Rawls back into Locke, as it were. As we shall later see, the autonomy of political morality and the epistemic constraints found in the contractual situation *are* key components of what Rawls now calls *political* liberalism. But the worry just noted is misplaced, and we should take Rawls at face value when he gestures[104] towards classical social contract theorists in the opening pages of his magisterial work. What the Locke-Proast controversy teaches us is that equality and pluralism make the social contract device indispensable for thinking about political justice, so it is no accident that Rawls, and other contemporary contractualists such as Barry, Larmore, Nagel, and Scanlon, end up with the justificatory framework that they do. As one commentator rightly notes, 'Readers of *A Theory of Justice* ought to wonder more than they do about the contractarian form in which Rawls presents his theory of justice as fairness.'[105] This chapter has sought to rectify this speculative deficit, by explaining why reasonable agreement should be the test of political legitimacy in plural societies.

2 Freedom for Eccentrics

2.1 Introduction

Locke's contractualism reflects a distinctive conception of political morality designed to accommodate deep and pervasive ethical pluralism. Lockean principles of toleration emanate from a view of political legitimacy in which the basic terms of political association among individuals conceived of as free and equal set internal constraints on the powers of states to coercively influence religious beliefs. As such, a defining feature of Locke's case is the extent to which pluralism requires that principles of *political* morality be specified in abstraction from the contested moral, religious, or philosophical ends favoured by different citizens within the particular political community to which they are meant to apply. If Locke's argument succeeds, then we can identify what governments may and may not legitimately do to people in the absence of a comprehensive statement about what such individuals are, or should ideally become.

A second and very different argumentative strand in this history of the idea of toleration is found in the liberal social and political philosophy of John Stuart Mill.[1] Isaiah Berlin has fittingly called Mill's *On Liberty* 'the clearest, most candid, persuasive, and moving exposition of the point of view of those who desire an open and tolerant society.'[2] This chapter introduces the central elements of perfectionist (autonomy-based) liberalism through a critical examination of Mill's writings. Section 2 introduces the argument of *On Liberty* and highlights its central claims. Section 3 discusses James Fitzjames Stephen's *Liberty, Equality, Fraternity* as the most comprehensive contemporary objection to Mill's arguments for toleration. Section 4 examines the extent to which Mill's liberty principle both is, and is not, vulnerable to Stephen's attack. Section 5 exposes seemingly insurmountable problems with ethical justifications for liberal politics, and this sets the stage for the critique of contemporary perfectionism found later in the book. Ultimately, the strength of Mill's liberalism is paradoxically also the source of a potentially devastating weakness. Insofar as Millean toleration is based upon the value of personal autonomy, liberty is not simply a regulative or procedural value designed to express some independently justified notion of fairness or impartiality between rival comprehensive conceptions of the good; it is *itself* one such conception in competition with many others. Since pluralistic societies are characterized by ethical disagreement that also extends to the value of personal autonomy, the latter is not plausibly the basis for a mutually acceptable principle of governmental restraint. While Mill's liberalism is clearly not a sceptical one, it overlooks many of the problems related to pluralism that Locke thinks recommend neutrality.

2.2 The Liberty Principle

Since its original publication in 1859, Mill's *On Liberty* has spawned innumerable and seemingly endless interpretive disputes over the meaning and range of the 'one very simple principle' for which it is rightly famous.[3] Much of the secondary literature concerns itself with what Mill intended by *harm*, as though the key to unlocking many of *On Liberty*'s riddles could be settled by a stipulative definition of that term. Interestingly, though, the idea of harm plays virtually no role in the essay's second and third chapters, which, arguably, form the justificatory core of Mill's defence of toleration: 'Of the Liberty of Thought and Discussion' (chapter 2) is a utilitarian case for liberty as an indispensable precondition for truth-seeking and social progress. The primary injury caused by the suppression of thought and discussion is to 'the human race,'[4] not to assignable individuals as required by the principle of liberty itself. Individual rights, therefore, play no foundational role within the argument of chapter 2; 'Of Individuality, as One of the Elements of Well-Being' (chapter 3) makes the notion of harm derivative from a perfectionist theory of vital interests. After its first mention in the introduction, the idea of harm is not reintroduced before chapter 4, where it is treated as an implication of arguments presented elsewhere.

While the concept of harm does play a key expository function in the argument of *On Liberty*, an interpretation of Mill's liberalism that begins with this idea is not likely to get very far. Harm is an essentially contested concept having no clear or indisputable meaning. A more promising (and charitable) interpretive tack is to develop an appreciation for the context and purposes for which Mill's arguments are designed. As one commentator notices, the dispute between Mill and his critics is not usefully identified as a controversy over which is the better conception of harm, but rather which variant of that idea 'answers more adequately to the purposes for which the concept is deployed.'[5] What are those purposes, then?

Mill begins *On Liberty* by suggesting that while the struggle between liberty and authority is 'the most conspicuous feature'[6] in the political histories of Greece, Rome, and England, recent democratizing transformations in the location of sovereignty have not altered the need for a principled balance between these two competing tendencies. Among the ancients, this contest manifested itself as a clash between subjects and their government. Since the interests of authorities were supposed to be necessarily antagonistic to those over whom they ruled, the demand for liberty was simply a plea for protection against the tyranny of political rulers. But the historical shift away from monarchical or aristocratic forms of government toward increasingly democratic ones has had the unfortunate effect of alleviating the perceived need for demands of this type: 'As the struggle proceeded for making the ruling power emanate from the periodical choice of the ruled, some persons began to think that too much importance had been attached to the limitation of the power itself.'[7] It is widely thought that since democratic authority is legitimated by, and expresses, the popular will, a democratic people cannot conceivably tyrannize itself.

Mill rejects the intuition underlying this complacency since it rests upon a false analogy between individual and collective self-direction. In the case of one isolated individual, self-government means precisely that: the government of each by herself. Since the subject and object of volition are identical (X wills something for X), it is difficult to make sense of how an autonomous individual could tyrannize herself. But democratic sovereignty raises no similar empirical or conceptual difficulty. For Mill, phrases such as 'self-government' and 'the power of the people over themselves'[8] are highly misleading. Democratic majoritarian decision-rules produce a situation in which the will of the people entails the will of the 'most numerous or the most active *part* of the people.'[9] As such, the absurdity of individual self-tyranny cannot be straightforwardly extended to collectivities because a situation where X wills something for herself is not analogous to one in which everyone (X, Y, and Z) wills something for

X. Collective self-determination is not the government of each by herself, but of each by all of the rest. A democratic people may coherently desire to oppress its minorities and, thus, the limitation on the power of its government 'loses none of its importance when the holders of power are regularly accountable to the community, that is, to the strongest part therein.'[10]

So one important background consideration to Mill's argument is a rejection of any necessary conceptual link between democratic decision-making and individual liberty. This does not imply that Mill is an anti-democrat, but it does mean that the justification of democracy will have to rest upon different, perhaps utilitarian or egalitarian, grounds. Another such consideration is Mill's belief that majoritarian tyrannies do not normally restrict themselves to using political functionaries as their agents: societies often limit deviation from their prevailing opinions and feelings by means other than civil penalties: 'To extend the bounds of what may be called the moral police, until it encroaches on the most unquestionably legitimate liberty of the individual, is one of the most universal of all human propensities.'[11] Thus, a concern for liberty makes constraints on the power of both public opinion *and* political authority indispensable.

Mill's 'very simple principle' is designed to circumscribe an inviolable area within which individuals are to be free from both political *and* social intolerance. As he says, 'There needs protection also against the tyranny of prevailing opinion and feeling; against the tendency of society to impose, by other means than civil penalties, its own ideas and practices as rules of conduct on those who dissent from them.'[12]

Mill's understanding of social intolerance is linked to his appraisal of 'custom' and this, in turn, appears to derive from a distinction Jeremy Bentham draws in *An Introduction to the Principles of Morals and Legislation.*[13] Bentham contrasts what he calls 'the principle of sympathy and antipathy' with that of 'utility.' By the former, he understands a principle that approves or disapproves of certain actions, not on account of their tending to increase or diminish the happiness of the party whose interest is in question, 'but merely because a man finds himself disposed to approve or disapprove them: holding up that approbation or disapprobation as a sufficient reason for itself, and disclaiming the necessity of looking out for any extrinsic ground.' For Bentham, this is 'the negation of all principle' since the ethical standard of right and wrong that it supplies is reducible to the personal preferences of different self-interested individuals. Utility, on the other hand, embodies such an 'extrinsic ground' by providing a test for the appropriateness of one's approbation and disapprobation.

Throughout his writings, Mill clearly endorses a variant of Bentham's distinction between genuine moral disapproval based upon reasoned 'principle' and the reactionary disapprobation that expresses little more than the deification of conventional opinion and habit. For example, in *The Subjection of Women*, Mill writes that 'a stupid person's notions and feelings may be confidently inferred from those which prevail in the circle by which the person is surrounded.'[14] In *On Liberty*, we are similarly told that those who allow custom and not personal choice to determine their 'plan of life' are 'ape-like.'[15]

While the precise location of the appropriate boundary between liberty and authority is a subject 'on which nearly everything remains to be done,'[16] the 'magical influence of custom'[17] prevents the people of any given age and country from even inquiring into whether the line can, or should be, drawn differently from where it already is. *On Liberty* begins with Mill's lamentation of the fact that people believe that 'their feelings on subjects of this nature are better than reasons, and render reasons unnecessary.'[18] An opinion on a point of conduct 'not supported by reasons,' however, amounts to nothing more than 'one person's preference'; and if such reasons, when solicited and given, appeal only to similar or identical preferences held by others, 'it is still only many people's liking instead of one'[19] and, thus, of no greater justificatory force. Mill's distinction between self-evident 'feelings' or 'likings' versus 'reasons' is therefore similar[20] to that reflected in Bentham's contrast between sympathy and antipathy versus utility. Both Bentham and Mill reject custom as a plausible ethical foundation for political morality since it identifies conventional agreement about a particular normative rule as a relevant ground of its prescriptive force, and does so independently of extrinsic reasons.

Communities can be tyrannical, then, not only through the coercive impositions of their political functionaries, but also by their failure to insulate minorities from powerful conformist social pressures unsupported by what are taken to be principled reasons. For Mill, these 'dislikings' or 'preferences' form 'a hostile and dreaded censorship.'[21] Philosophers, no less than the general public, mistakenly inquire into what things society ought to like or dislike rather than 'questioning whether its likings or dislikings should be a law to individuals.'[22] Since there is no recognized principle by which the propriety or impropriety of government interference with individual liberty is customarily tested,

'people decide according to their personal preferences.'[23] The 'Introductory' to *On Liberty* makes it clear that Mill's overriding aim is to rectify
this indeterminacy, and he proposes

> one very simple principle, as entitled to govern absolutely the dealings of
> society with the individual in the way of compulsion and control, whether
> the means used be physical force in the form of legal penalties, or the moral
> coercion of public opinion. That principle is, that the sole end for which
> mankind are warranted, individually or collectively, in interfering with the
> liberty of action of any of their number, is self-protection. That the only pur-
> pose for which power can be rightfully exercised over any member of a civ-
> ilized community, against his will, is to prevent harm to others.[24]

In the paragraph immediately following the principle's enunciation, Mill
qualifies it by rejecting its applicability to: (1) 'children, or ... young persons below the age which the law may fix as that of manhood or woman-
hood,' (2) 'those who are still in a state to require being taken care of by
others,' and finally, (3) 'those backward states of society in which the
race itself may be considered as in its nonage.'[25] Whether in dealing with
children, imbeciles, or barbarians, then, the principle of liberty has 'no
application to any state of things anterior to the time when mankind
have become capable of being improved by free and equal discussion.'[26]
We are told that despotism is a legitimate mode of government in dealing with these classes of individuals, provided that such despotic authority is efficient and has their improvement as its primary goal.

Once spelled out, the 'appropriate region of human liberty' circumscribed by the principle comprises first 'the inward domain of conscious-
ness,' which demands 'liberty of thought and feeling; absolute freedom
of opinion and sentiment on all subjects, practical and speculative, scientific, moral or theological.'[27] The 'liberty of expressing and publishing
opinions'[28] is also protected by most of the same reasons that establish
liberty of conscience in Mill's comprehensive sense. Second, the principle requires 'liberty of tastes and pursuits; of framing the plan of our life
to suit our own character.'[29] Finally, from this liberty of each individual
follows, within the same limits, the 'liberty of combination'[30] among
them. These liberties are thought of by Mill as categorically binding
requirements of free societies: whatever its form of government, no society in which these liberties are not, on the whole, respected is free; and a
society is completely free only if they exist absolute and unqualified.[31]

A critical assessment of Mill's principle will emerge through our examination of the extent to which it both can and cannot withstand the most important historical objections that have been levelled against it. Nonetheless, a few preliminary remarks are in order. First, while the principle relies on the coherence of a distinction between action that is harmless, and action that is harmful, to others, it does not itself supply the normative criteria for identifying the content of these respective categories. This will have to be specified, then, in relation to other more foundational ideas, which are to be developed elsewhere in *On Liberty*. Also, Mill sometimes reformulates 'harm to others' as 'concerns others.' This ambiguity is problematic since these are obviously very different criteria, and much interpretive reconstruction must be done before the limits of Mill's principle can be given any definite shape. Second, since the principle is intended only for individuals satisfying certain developmental and minimum competency thresholds, the absoluteness that Mill attributes to it must somehow refer to its *force* or indefeasibility rather than to its *range* of application. This reading is supported both by Mill's exemption of certain classes of *persons* as set out in the applicability restrictions 1–3 above, as well as certain classes of *actions* or *subjects* as implied by the need for a principle.[32] Finally, the precise distinction between 'compulsion' and 'remonstrance' will have to be made clear since the former is said to violate, while the latter allegedly respects, individual sovereignty.

Notoriously, many commentators have questioned the extent to which a moral right to liberty can consistently be given a utilitarian foundation.[33] They have also suggested that, among other things, Mill's refinements of Benthamite utilitarianism as expressed, say, in the distinction between higher and lower pleasures, entail a more sophisticated appreciation for the complexities of human character *and*, paradoxically, a subversion of the chief motive underlying the utilitarian approach to ethics.[34] But whether this is so or not, there is little doubt as to Mill's motivation in '[forgoing] any advantage which could be derived to [his] argument from the idea of abstract right, as a thing independent of utility.'[35] As Bentham sought to show, the 'Law of Nature,' like all such expressions, is simply a contrivance for 'prevailing upon the reader to accept the author's sentiment or opinion as a reason for itself.' This is why, for Mill, 'utility in the largest sense, grounded on the permanent interests of man as a progressive being' is 'the ultimate appeal on all ethical questions.'[36] Unless the principle of liberty can be given a utilitarian or 'extrinsic' justification, it amounts to little more than a highly sophisticated personal preference for freedom.

A central unifying theme that runs throughout *On Liberty* is the intimate connection between liberty and diversity. Whether Mill is arguing for liberty of discussion (chapter 2), of lifestyles (chapter 3), or actions (chapter 4), diversity is everywhere critical to his case. But these two ideas are differently linked depending upon which of Mill's two general argumentative strands they are located in. In his utilitarian argument for liberty, diversity is presented as a causal precondition of social progress. Within this strand, it may not necessarily matter whether diversity arises as a result of individual choice. In places, Mill gives credence to the provisional value of toleration by writing of diversity as a natural fact that seems to sever any connection it may have with liberty and individual choice. In his perfectionist argument for 'individuality,' however, diversity emerges as both a by-product and precondition for personal choice. To the extent that meaningful choice cannot be exercised without a plurality of available options, this second argumentative strand connects toleration and diversity through the intrinsic value of choice.

The utilitarian/social progress argument is found (mainly) in chapter 2 of *On Liberty*; the perfectionist defence of liberty as a constitutive element of well-being is developed in chapter 3. However, since Mill's social progress argument combines *both* a claim about liberty as instrumentally related to truth *and* an epistemic thesis about the nature of rationally justified belief, the utilitarian and perfectionist strands of his case for toleration are not self-contained and interpenetrate one another. Ultimately, the preconditions for holding justified beliefs (which are conducive to utility) are the very ones most expressive of 'individuality' (perfectionism).

On Liberty is perhaps most famous for its justification of liberty of thought and discussion found in its second chapter. There, Mill tells us that even if 'all mankind minus one, were of one opinion, and only one person were of the contrary opinion, mankind would be no more justified in silencing that one person, than he, if he had the power, would be justified in silencing mankind.'[37] Were an opinion merely a 'personal possession of no value except to the owner' and its suppression simply a 'private injury,'[38] then the propriety of censoring it *would* depend upon whether it was shared by many or few individuals as required by the principle of utility. But Mill evades the intolerant implications of such an argument by viewing censorship primarily in terms of *public* harm: 'The peculiar evil of silencing the expression of an opinion is, that it is robbing the human race; posterity as well as the existing generation.'[39] The collective benefit of what Mill calls 'discussion' (to which the public harm of censorship is a corollary) is the foundation of a complex and distinctively utilitarian argument for toleration that connects liberty to diversity, diversity to truth, and truth to social progress.

Mill argues for the utility of diversity (which liberty sustains) on four distinct grounds. The first two depend upon ethical confrontation,[40] that is, on a roughly dialectical account of ethical progress in which truth emerges from the confrontation of the rival ethical views that liberty and, thus, diversity, make possible. The last two embody a thesis about the preconditions for justified belief. Mill's argument, therefore, divides itself neatly into two halves: a sociological claim about the causal conditions necessary for ethical progress, given Mill's understanding of the fragmented nature of ethical truth; and a thesis about the proper *manner* in which ethical truths should be held by rational beings.

First, the opinion that authorities attempt to suppress may possibly be true: 'Who can compute,' Mill writes, 'what the world loses in the multitude of promising intellects combined with timid characters, who dare not follow out any bold, vigorous, independent train of thought, lest it should land them in something which would admit of being considered irreligious or immoral?'[41] The primary noxious effect of a ban on unorthodox opinion is not to the heretical themselves, but to third parties whose 'whole mental development is cramped'[42] by their non-exposure to different and conflicting ideas.

Second, though the silenced opinion might be wrong, it may, and very often does, contain a portion of the truth. Liberty of thought and discussion is, therefore, a critical precondition for the syntheses that result from the clashes of such rival views.

The final two grounds, by contrast, concern not the content but the *manner* in which 'truth ought to be held by a rational being.'[43] Truth gains more even by the errors of individuals who think for themselves than by those who cling accidentally to it as one superstition among others. How can this be? Even if the orthodox opinion contains the whole truth, unless it is vigorously and earnestly contested, it will be held 'in the manner of a prejudice, with little comprehension or feeling of its rational grounds.'[44] Complete liberty of contradicting and disproving our opinion is, therefore, the very condition that justifies our assuming its truth.

Finally, unless our opinion, however true, is vigorously contested, 'the meaning of the doctrine itself will be in danger of being lost, or enfeebled, and deprived of its vital effect on the character and conduct.'[45] True opinions, thus held, amount to nothing more than 'dogma,' 'a mere formal profession, ineffacious for good, but cumbering the ground, and preventing the growth of any real and heartfelt conviction, for reason or personal experience.'[46]

As stated, the argument defends freedom of 'discussion,' not 'expression,' since only the former is conceptually related to the dialectical relationship between conflicting ethical ideas sharing the truth between them. Expression, after all, is not necessarily dialogical. Additionally, only such discussion as pertains to the subjects enumerated above is protected by Mill's utilitarian argument for diversity. While 'expression' could conceivably include spray-painting graffiti or urinating on the steps of Parliament in protest, for instance, 'discussion' is much narrower: it appears to involve putting forth in a respectful[47] manner substantive ethical positions designed to elicit reasoned discourse about their merits. This reading fits well with Mill's repeated uses of the terms 'doctrine' and 'creed,' together with such expressions as 'the great practical concerns of life' and 'moral and human subjects' in connection with the idea of 'discussion.'[48] And while the precise boundaries of areas such as 'morals, religion, politics, social relations, and the business of life' are somewhat vague and admittedly difficult to draw, it would seem that Mill intended for these to be exhaustive of the discussion that diversity must sustain. This does not imply that beyond them, Mill is committed to censorship; the argument is simply that the collective interests at stake are such that, *within this range*, utility can *never* be promoted by intolerance.

It should now be clear how Mill's argument derives liberty of thought and discussion from the utilitarian value of diversity, as opposed to, say, some thesis about the natural right of individuals to be free. Mill's limitations on the authority of society and government to interfere with individuals' freedom of thought and discussion emerge from the benefits of such restraints to the general interest. Individuals must be left as free as possible from various pressures to conform, not because they have *natural rights* to consideration of this sort, but because the unacceptable collective costs of intolerance mandate that they *should* be given legal rights to this protection. In this view, rights are distributed to individuals on the basis of considerations of aggregate welfare. As such, rights to free thought and discussion are not natural in the Lockean sense, nor are the individual right-bearers their intended beneficiaries. At least within the context of his discussion in chapter 2, then, Mill is completely warranted in saying that he forgoes any advantage that could be derived from basing his argument on a notion of abstract right, independent of utility.

Since liberty of thought and discussion is conditionally dependent upon its contribution to the common good, it explicitly *does not* establish rights to an inviolable sphere of individual discretionary authority that may be legitimately invoked to constrain utility-maximizing policies. For the reasons adumbrated above (the fragmentation of ethical truth, the rarity of certain 'judicial faculties,' etc.), these rights are themselves a central vehicle for maximizing aggregate welfare. As a result, they are logically indefensible to the extent that they conflict with it.

In one obvious sense, then, chapter 2 of *On Liberty* is a purely utilitarian argument rooted in the social benefits to be derived from freedom and diversity in the access to truth. Mill's first and second argumentative strands are best understood in precisely these terms. The theory of justified belief articulated in his third and fourth claims also implies a view about what it means to be a free person. Liberty is not simply the absence of external impediments – whether societal or governmental – but a feature of having a particular internal disposition of character and mind to which such freedom contributes. Mill tells us that rational beings ought to hold truths only after subjecting them to critical examination; the ethical doctrines that emerge from the dialectical syntheses that he describes must be passionately endorsed and reflectively defended to both shape and express character. But if this is so, the argument is no longer a purely utilitarian one: somewhere along the way, Mill has moved from an instrumental defence of diversity towards one in which negative liberty is a constitutive element of a more comprehensive character ideal.

The priority that Mill accords to liberty in his utilitarian account of moral rights is rooted in its conceptual and empirical connections to what he calls 'individuality.' Because of these links, when custom or tradition rather than individual choice is the rule of personal conduct, 'there is wanting one of the principal ingredients of human happiness, and quite the chief ingredient of individual and social progress.'[49] The core of individuality is the importance of the capacity and exercise of self-defining autonomous choice. Such choice is related to a distinction Mill draws between higher and lower pleasures. In effect, Mill claims that individuality is one of the leading essentials of well-being, and also that his theory of higher pleasures supports his principle of liberty.

In *Utilitarianism*, Mill tells us that the 'creed' that accepts utility as the foundation of morals holds that 'actions are right in proportion as they tend to promote happiness, wrong as they tend to produce the reverse of happiness.'[50] In its classical, or Benthamite, formulation, happiness is understood as pleasure and the absence of pain; unhappiness, as pain and the privation of pleasure. The classical utilitarian view identifies the content of each category as resting upon a distinction between different subjective mental states. Pleasure and freedom from pain are the only things desirable as ends; all desirable ends are pursued either for the pleasure inherent in themselves, or as a means to the promotion of pleasure and the prevention of pain.

Almost immediately after explaining the principle of utility in its classical formulation, Mill adds that it is 'quite compatible with the principle of utility to recognize the fact, that some *kinds* of pleasure are more desirable and more valuable than others.'[51] How, then, are we to distinguish between them? What makes one pleasure more valuable than another if not simply because the former is more strongly desired? Mill answers, 'Of two pleasures, if there be one to which all or almost all who have experience of both give a decided preference, irrespective of any feeling of moral obligation to prefer it, that is the more desirable pleasure.'[52] As he famously says, 'It is better to be a human being dissatisfied than a pig satisfied; better to be Socrates dissatisfied than a fool satisfied. And if the fool, or the pig, is of a different opinion, it is because they only know their own side of the question. The other party to the comparison knows both sides.'[53] So whatever else Mill intends by this distinction, its essence is *not* captured by a simple contrast between subjective mental states; it relates to various types of activities or forms of life that are somehow qualitatively distinguishable in kind.

In chapter 3 of *On Liberty*, Mill extends his arguments for freedom of thought and discussion (chapter 2) to include the need for 'different experiments in living' that would allow for 'free scope' to be given to 'varieties of character.'[54] Notwithstanding the undeniable benefits of historically accumulated wisdom, it is the 'privilege and proper condition of a human being'[55] to use and interpret such wisdom in her own way. Tradition and custom are merely presumptive evidence of the veracity of such collective insight, and one's deference to them should be mitigated by at least three considerations: first, the experience of others, and their interpretation of it, may be too narrow or unrelated to one's own; second, such experience may be 'unsuitable': 'customs are made for customary circumstances, and customary characters; and [one's] circumstances or [one's] character may be uncustomary';[56] finally, even though customs are good, and 'suitable' to oneself, to conform to custom *as* custom does not educate or develop in oneself any of the qualities 'which are the distinctive endowment of a human being.'[57]

The central element of this distinctive endowment is the capacity for, and the exercise of, *choice*: 'The human faculties of perception, judgment, discriminating feeling, mental activity, and even moral preference, are exercised only in making a choice. He who does anything because it is the custom makes no choice.'[58] Mill's preoccupation with the despotism of custom should now be readily understandable. Social intolerance is the standing hindrance to human progress because in inhibiting autonomous choice, it is responsible for preserving individuals in a state of permanent moral and intellectual immaturity. The connection between diversity and individuality should also be clear, given the centrality of choice to Mill's account of well-being. Not only do people have radically dissimilar tastes; they also require different conditions for their spiritual development. Because of differences between people on their sources of pleasure and their susceptibilities to pain, unless there is a corresponding diversity in their modes of life, 'they neither obtain their fair share of happiness, nor grow up to the mental, moral, and aesthetic stature of which their nature is capable.'[59] He writes, 'If a person possesses any tolerable amount of common sense and experience, his own mode of laying out his existence is the best, not because it is the best in itself, but because it is his own mode.'[60]

There are (at least) two ways in which choice can be related to Mill's theory of higher pleasures, given what he says about its centrality to individuality. First, the connection between autonomous choice and the higher pleasures could be criterial.[61] If whatever one chooses autonomously is the criterion for what is a higher pleasure, one cannot be mistaken about this so long as such a choice is undertaken with a relevant and adequately wide range of experiences under one's belt. In this view, the content of one's higher pleasures can change when the pattern of one's autonomous choices do. Second, the relationship between autonomous choice and the higher pleasures could be an evidential one. In this case, while informed choice is evidence that what is chosen is a higher pleasure, a further criterion of the latter is still needed.

Mill's metaphors in *On Liberty* are instructive in showing how his argument for individuality is ambivalent about which of these two possibilities he endorses. On the one hand, a person whose desires and impulses are not the product of choice 'has no character, no more than a steam-engine has a character.'[62] To build character, then, one must choose one's plan of life for oneself. Through a successive number of self-defining choices, one *constructs* a character from a wide array of possibilities. So while Bentham conceives of individuality as a psychological datum[63] for utility calculations, for Mill it represents a character ideal that is the *result* of choice. If whatever one chooses is best *because* one has chosen it, choice is a criterion of value. Mill supports this reading himself in *Utilitarianism* when he says that 'the sole evidence it is possible to produce that anything is desirable, is that people do actually desire it.'[64] The appropriate region of human liberty spelled out by Mill's principle in the Introductory is therefore a statement of the freedoms that are indispensable to the exercise of autonomous thought and action. Liberty is important because it allows for people to pursue the objects of their desire. In doing so, they live autonomous or potentially valuable lives.

Elsewhere, however, Mill relies upon the second, or evidential, view by treating individuality as a given that should guide one's choices: 'Human nature is not a machine to be built after a model, and set to do exactly the work prescribed for it, but a tree, which requires to grow and develop itself on all sides, according to the tendency of the inward forces which make it a living thing.'[65] The ideas of 'tendencies' or 'inward forces' suggest a standard to which choice ought to conform. As such, liberty is important not because of any conceptual link it has with choice, but because the diversity it sustains increases the likelihood that radically dissimilar individuals will stumble upon an experiment in living that suits their idiosyncratic natures. If this reading of Mill is sound, then the implications of his principle are potentially less libertarian than one might be inclined to think at first glance: if what matters for individuality is diversity per se, then nothing seems to preclude the use of coercion to produce it. One can imagine *mandating* (on utilitarian grounds) experiments in living on unwilling participants to provide a maximum range of lifestyles for others to choose from. While those compelled to experimentation would potentially have *their* individuality violated, two considerations mitigate our assigning this consideration pre-emptive weight. First, Mill introduces the argument of chapter 3 as an extension of various claims for freedom of thought and discussion presented in chapter 2. There, however, we find a utilitarian argument that distributes rights to individuals for the sake of *collective* benefits. While the choice/individuality connection represented by the criterial link discussed above does preclude coercion-induced diversity, we are now dealing with the second 'inward tendencies' argument. And *within this argument,* nothing seems to preclude extending the collectivist bent of chapter 2 into a perfectionist case for coerced diversity – such inward tendencies are not themselves chosen. Failed individual experiments could yield net collective benefits even when they are the result of coercion or manipulation. For example, similarly natured X, Y, and Z can now safely avoid a particular experiment in living since a state-induced go of it has completely ruined W. Second, while individuals are most often best able to discern what their 'natures' require, this can only be an empirically based and, therefore, defeasible presumption. In cases of a disjunction between what people prefer and what suits their natures, perhaps the latter should take precedence. As one perceptive critic notices, we 'can choose shoes to fit our feet; but we cannot very easily choose our foot size. Despite his commitments to personal liberty and development, Mill sometimes seems so devoted to the pre-given uniqueness of each individual's character that he denies any significant character-shaping role to choice.'[66] If the value of a life comes less from its being self-chosen and more from making the right choices (which Mill's man-tree metaphor implies), wouldn't coercion be justified in dealing with singularly unreflective and, hence, misguided individuals? If suitability is a central determinant of well-being, is a lifestyle any less suitable for being forced?

When one combines the distinction between higher and lower pleasures as found in *Utilitarianism* with the argument of chapter 3 in *On Liberty*, one is left with a rather complex ideal of personal freedom. While the content of higher pleasures will differ substantially across various individuals, only those who have developed their distinctive endowments will be happy in Mill's sense of that term. Mill is not committed, then, to the view that autonomous people are necessarily happy; his position entails the rather different claim that only people with self-chosen lives *can* be. If the constitutive elements of individuality are necessary features of the moral and intellectual make-up of those susceptible to the higher pleasures, then personal autonomy is a necessary but not sufficient condition of well-being. The sufficiency condition is established only when a pleasure with an autonomous pedigree actually conforms to, or expresses, an individual's potentially unique and pre-given nature. Paradoxically, then, Mill's perfectionist ideal of individuality consists in the intentional shaping of one's character through self-chosen projects, relationships, and commitments in conformity to an inner standard that is simultaneously a precondition for, but not itself the result of, choice.

Taken together, Mill's utilitarian and perfectionist arguments for toleration suggest that liberty is both intrinsically and instrumentally valuable. Within the utilitarian argument of chapter 2, liberty emerges as an essential precondition of social progress; in chapter 3, given the centrality of choice to individuality, liberty is a constitutive element of human flourishing. Ultimately, Mill's conception of both social progress and utility cannot be specified independently of his notion of what it means to be a free person.

2.3 Stephen on Mill

In 1874, James Fitzjames Stephen published *Liberty, Equality, Fraternity,* which is still widely recognized as one of the most comprehensive critiques of Mill's arguments for toleration. Stephen's wide-ranging discussion of Mill has three main components: a general methodological objection to the approach to politics that Mill adopts in *On Liberty;* a challenge to the cogency of the liberty principle; and finally, a rejection of Mill's utilitarianism together with the overly optimistic picture of human nature and social progress upon which it rests. Stephen's central claim is that 'there are a vast number of matters in respect of which men ought not to be free; they are fundamentally unequal, and they are not brothers at all, or only under qualifications which make the assertion of their fraternity unimportant.'[67]

In the *Subjection of Women,* Mill argues that the subordination of women is 'an isolated fact in modern social institutions; a solitary breach of what has become their fundamental law.'[68] Except for this anomalous violation of equality as the world's central regulative principle, the law of the strongest has been entirely abandoned. For Stephen, however, Millian progress does not diminish the role of force in society; it simply changes its form. Parliamentary government, he tells us, is but a 'mild and disguised form of compulsion. We agree to try strength by counting heads instead of breaking heads, but the principle is exactly the same.'[69] Mill's attempted reformulation of the bases of legitimate majoritarian decision-making is an idealization of what *really* matters politically. In democratic politics, it is not the wisest or most rational side that wins; all other things being equal, appeals to extrinsic principle have no greater political weight than sheer prejudice. A particular position is determinative 'by enlisting the largest amount of active sympathy in its support.'[70] Therefore, political minorities yield to majorities not because their numerical inferiority convinces them that they are wrong, but simply *because* they are minorities. For Stephen, power is 'the essential thing'[71] in whatever form it takes. Mill's distinction, then, between a civilized and a barbarous society is overdrawn. The difference between them is not that the former relies on persuasion while the latter uses coercion, but that 'force is (or ought to be) guided with greater care'[72] in a civilized community.

This idea of a continuum as opposed to a simple dichotomy between persuasion and coercion is expressed through Stephen's indiscriminate use of the term 'force' to encompass both. That the distinction between them is a quantitative one with no particular normative weight raises a key problem for Mill's 'one very simple principle.' Towards the beginning of his book, Stephen makes a number of concessions to Mill: he accepts that people are often mistaken in their judgements of good and evil, and of truth and falsehood; they have conflicting ideas of happiness; they are not half sceptical enough; and they are far too inclined to meddle and persecute. In short, Stephen endorses what he refers to as 'the commonplaces about liberty and toleration.'[73] Unfortunately, Mill's principle in *On Liberty* translates such commonplaces into an axiomatic restriction on political authority in general. But for Stephen, the expediency of using either promises or threats to encourage or prevent actions and beliefs invariably depends upon 'the circumstances of the case, upon the nature of the act prevented, and the nature of the means by which it can be prevented.'[74] Since the 'method of specific experience is in politics the only one from which much good can be got,' 'every attempt to lay down theoretical limits to the power of governments must necessarily fail.'[75] In seeking to limit, as opposed to guiding, political authority, Mill's principle – and by implication, liberalism – is 'a serious embarrassment to rational legislation'[76] because of its insensitivity to contextual subtleties. Rather than identifying fixed and inviolable individual rights upon which political authority must never encroach, we must 'confine ourselves to such remarks as experience suggests about the advantages and disadvantages of compulsion and liberty respectively in particular cases.'[77]

This observation about the limitations of abstract principle in politics carries over into a similar claim about the absurdity of a general right to liberty. Stephen takes Mill to be the most articulate representative for the 'popular view' that uses 'pathetic language' to glorify 'the religious dogma of liberty.'[78] For Stephen, however, the eulogizers of liberty should ask themselves, 'Who is left at liberty to do what, and what is the restraint from which he is liberated?' before 'going into ecstasies over any particular case of it.'[79] Since neither the value of liberty nor the disvalue of coercion can be established independently of the triadic relationship identified in Stephen's formulation – person A is free from restraint B to do or become C – the absolute protection established by Mill's principle must be abandoned in favour of a prudential guideline that reads somewhat as follows: coercion is inexpedient when (1) the end that justifies it

is bad or worthless, (2) the end is good but the coercion used is not calculated to obtain it, and, finally, (3) when both the end is good and the
means undertaken are effective but the cost is too great.[80]

Liberty, Equality, Fraternity is the first full statement of what has probably
been the most persistent worry about Mill's principle since the publication of *On Liberty.* Human beings in society are so closely connected to
one another that it is notoriously difficult to say how far the influence of
acts of the most personal character may extend: 'The sentiments of the
founder of a great religion, the reflections of a great philosopher, the calculations of a great general may affect the form of the mould in which the
lives, thoughts, and feelings of hundreds of millions of men may be
cast.'[81] Therefore, Mill's attempt to distinguish between self-regarding
and other-regarding actions is 'like an attempt to distinguish between
acts which happen in time and acts which happen in space. Every act happens at some time and in some place, and in like manner every act that
we do either does or may affect both ourselves and others.'[82] Insofar as
Mill's foundational distinction cannot be sustained, the argument of *On
Liberty* is conceptually incoherent and politically useless. Since there is no
interference with personal freedom that Mill's principle constrains on
Stephen's reading of 'affect,' it is singularly useless at achieving its central
purpose – protecting as wide an area of individual liberty as possible.

For our purposes, one of Stephen's most important objections to *On
Liberty* is his outright denial of the possibility of moral neutrality in legislation. Though Stephen uses religion as the paradigmatic example in his
case for non-neutrality, we may extend his comments to secular ethics
more generally.[83] For Stephen, there are only three possible relations in
which legislation can stand towards religion in general, and toward various particular faiths: (1) it may proceed on the assumption that one religion is true and all others false, (2) it may proceed on the assumption
that more than one religion is respectable and it may favour them in the
same or different degrees, (3) finally, it may proceed on the assumption
that all religions or that some religions are false. Since 1–3 are exhaustive, it is 'simply impossible that legislation should be really neutral as to
any religion that is professed by any large number of the persons legis-
lated for. He that is not for such a religion is against it.'[84] Real neutrality
is possible only in connection with forms of religion and, by implication,
experiments in living, that are professed by so few that they can be
regarded as irrelevant.[85]

Stephen draws two inferences from this impossibility of ethical neutrality – one political, the other psychological. If governments *cannot*

avoid acting upon assumptions about the validity of contested ethical views, then they 'should not be afraid, when the occasion arises, to take account of the question whether this religion or that is true, whether this moral doctrine or that is well founded. I protest, in short, against the dogma which appears to be received by so many people in these days, that statesmen, as such, are bound to treat all religions ... as having an equal claim to be regarded as true.'[86] Like Proast, then, Stephen is committed to the view that ethics and politics are purely continuous so that no distinctively political considerations mediate the extent to which governments may act on the basis of perfectionist values.

The second inference concerns the necessary instability of liberal political institutions given the complex, perhaps internally contradictory, nature of a tolerant psychological disposition. Since ethical and religious controversies 'go to the core and root of life' and 'express the deepest convictions of men,'[87] Stephen thinks that support for political neutrality will be forthcoming only to the extent that such disputes are regarded as mere differences of opinion or preference. But once this happens, they have 'really [been] decided in the sceptical sense, though people may not like to acknowledge it formally.'[88] Stephen's position implies that support for liberal political institutions will be forthcoming only from citizens who have abandoned their most powerful and compelling ethical convictions. If accurate, this view renders the stability of tolerant or neutralist institutions crucially dependent upon widespread scepticism or indifference.[89]

Within the utilitarian argument of chapter 2 in *On Liberty*, diversity is a causal precondition for social progress – for Mill, the telos of tolerance is truth. Yet the picture of ethical progress that Mill paints there largely assumes, rather than argues for, the connection between liberty and diversity. Additionally, the perfectionist argument in chapter 3 implies either that *only freedom* is capable of stimulating the capacities necessary to frame, pursue, and rationally revise one's plan of life, or that freedom does so *better* than anything else. Stephen seizes on both of these ideas to reject the connection that Mill wants to draw between liberty and progress, on the one hand, and liberty and individuality, on the other. While progress clearly requires originality, originality consists in thinking for oneself, 'not in thinking differently from other people.'[90] As for the link between liberty and individuality, Stephen thinks that 'if you want zealous belief, set people to fight. Few things give men such a keen perception of the importance of their own opinions and the vileness of the opinions of others as the fact that they have inflicted and suffered persecution for them.'[91] For him, the tacit assumption that pervades almost all of Mill's writings is the idea that 'the removal of restraints usually tends to invigorate character.'[92] Since Mill's argument is an empirical claim about the causal efficacy of liberty at strengthening character, it invites counter-arguments such as Stephen's – namely, that habitual exertion is 'the greatest of all invigorators of character, and restraint and coercion in one form or another is the great stimulus to exertion.'[93]

Stephen's final set of objections involves the extent to which Mill's principle of liberty and his egalitarianism are consistently derivable from his utilitarianism. It is unclear how Stephen's triadic reformulation of the liberty principle violates Mill's utilitarian premise. He suggests that if a particular goal can be successfully pursued through intolerant but efficient means and the accrued benefits clearly outweigh the costs, then governments have the authority to do so. Stephen wonders how Mill can defend individual rights to liberty where intolerance is, on balance, utility-maximizing.[94] The absoluteness of Mill's principle is even more problematic within a utilitarian argument since it implies that, self-protection apart, 'compulsion must always be a greater evil in itself than the absence of any object which can possibly be obtained by it.'[95]

On the opening page of *The Subjection of Women*, Mill maintains that 'the legal subordination of one sex to the other ... is wrong in itself, and now one of the chief hindrances to human improvement.'[96] For Stephen, this statement is tautological since 'human improvement' supplies the criterion of right and wrong. Mill's utilitarianism must claim that the legal subordination of women is wrong *because* it is inexpedient and then provide empirical evidence to support this contention. Similarly, in *Utilitarianism*, Mill writes that society between human beings, except within a master–slave relationship, 'is manifestly impossible on any other footing than that the interests of all are to be consulted.'[97] Stephen translates Mill's claim about the injustice of inequality as follows: it is inexpedient that any law should recognize any inequality between human beings. Mill's case for the disutility of intolerance trades heavily upon the conceptual link between autonomy and the permanent interests of mankind as progressive beings. However, equality is a relational value not similarly connected to individuality in any obvious way. Mill's distinction between higher and lower pleasures also suggests that individuals with differentiated moral and intellectual endowments will develop radically dissimilar capacities for utility-maximization. Stephen wonders how it makes sense to treat qualitatively different pleasures equally within a consequentialist ethical theory devoted to maximizing the higher ones. Given that the

pleasures experienced by various individuals are often both quantita-
tively and qualitatively different, why should an inegalitarian distribution
of rights be necessarily sub-optimal from a utilitarian point of view?[98] If
liberty and equality really are justified by reference to their capacity for
maximizing the total aggregate of pleasure or happiness, then they are
not independent principles capable of constraining inegalitarian distributions of rights. As Stephen perceptively points out, 'although ... the
whole drift ... of the doctrines of the school to which Mr Mill belongs ...
leads to the conclusion that equality is just only if and in so far as it is
expedient, Mr Mill gives to equality a character different from other
ideas connected with justice.'[99]

2.4 Stephen Examined

Stephen's first methodological objection concerns the absurdity of
reducing politics to general axiomatic principles: 'I do not believe that
the state of our knowledge is such as to enable us to enunciate any "very
simple principle as entitled to govern absolutely the dealings of society
with the individual in the way of compulsion and control"'[100] But Mill
restricts the application of his principle both to agents satisfying certain
minimum competency requirements, and to narrowly specified *categories*
of subject matter encompassed by the idea of 'discussion.' If we interpret
'absolutely' in Mill's formulation to mean the range of the principle's
application, then there is a blatant contradiction at work here. On the
other hand, if 'absolutely' refers to the force of the principle's application over the range that Mill carefully sets out, then such an inconsistency disappears. Tentatively, this indicates that Stephen's objection
confuses the issues of force and range by mistakenly assuming that
because Mill's principle is to regulate liberty 'absolutely,' the liberty it
defends must be 'absolute,' or unrestricted. His reading of *On Liberty* is
myopic, since chapter 5, 'Applications,' identifies a number of instances
in which the state may legitimately restrict liberty – public safety, public
decency, and compulsory education, to mention but a few. So while
Mill's initial formulation of his principle is somewhat careless or misleading, his subsequent examples make it amply clear that he does *not* understand its range in the manner suggested by Stephen's objection. While
the principle seeks to rule out paternalism and moralistic interferences
with personal freedom, its scope is actually quite limited: it says *nothing*,
for instance, about questions of distributive justice, common defence,
tax structures and their economic impacts, and so on.

Seen in this light, Mill's argument neither abandons the particularity of experience for the sake of abstract principles designed to apply everywhere, nor suggests that liberty should be absolute or unrestricted. His claim is simply that within the narrowly construed area whose boundaries are coextensive with 'discussion' and 'individuality,' the interests at stake are such that restricting liberty can never promote them. Outside of this area, utilitarian calculations rooted in experience are perfectly legitimate. Thus, while the success of Mill's argument rides on the extent to which he correctly identifies 'permanent interests' and their empirical/conceptual links with liberty, he is not guilty of oversimplifying the complexity of politics.

Stephen's aversion to reducing politics to axioms and his rejection of principled limitations on the scope of political authority is based upon the value of *experience*. Particular experience, alone, allows for the accumulation of collective wisdom and, thus, for the possibility of political sagacity. For Stephen, Mill's 'very simple principle' is pedagogically and politically deficient because it appears to inhibit this. But a principle designed to protect personal autonomy evades this general objection since the maximization of experience is precisely what motivates it. Thus, there is a sense in which Stephen is guilty of the very charge that he levels at Mill: his indictment suggests that all general principles are similarly hostile to the subtlety of experience, notwithstanding the fact that the *content* of Mill's principle is predicated upon its value. At the heart of Stephen's general objection to generality in political analysis lies a devastating logical contradiction. Finally, it is difficult to see how an argument that has the centrality of experience as its premise ends up defending intolerance. Persecution contracts, rather than expands, the range of available experiences.

Stephen's second objection attributes to Mill the highly implausible view that there is a class of actions that is purely self-regarding, or free from social consequences. This claim has two related components: first, Mill's idea of harm is allegedly far too ambiguous to be useful; second, since the self- versus other-regarding distinction is non-existent (whatever harm means), the principle is incoherent.

Throughout *On Liberty*, Mill uses two types of expressions to differentiate between the self- and other-regarding spheres: in some places, one finds 'what only regards himself,' 'conduct which affects only himself,' 'which concerns only himself,' 'things wherein the individual alone is concerned'; in other places, however, one finds 'concern the interests of others,' 'affects the interests of no one but himself,' 'affects the interests

of others,' and 'damage to the interests of others.' Clearly, there is a crucial difference between simply affecting others in a causal sense (emotionally, physically, and psychologically) and affecting the interests of
others. By contextualizing these various locutions within Mill's broader
argument for toleration, his meaning becomes clear.

In chapter 4 of *On Liberty*, Mill continues the discussion of chapter 1 by
returning to the issue of 'harm.' In attempting to specify the area of conduct for which individuals are to be made responsible to society, Mill tells
us that this conduct 'consists in not injuring the interests of one another;
or rather certain interests which, either by express legal provision or by
tacit understanding, ought to be considered as rights.'[101] If we take this
for Mill's most careful statement of intent, then Mill's conception of
harm cannot simply mean 'to adversely affect,' or even 'to adversely affect
others' interests'; to 'harm' is to adversely affect interests important
enough to ground rights. Which interests are these, then?

In the final chapter of *Utilitarianism*, Mill links the ideas of utility, interests, and rights in connection with the notion of justice:

> Justice is a name for certain classes of moral rules, which concern the essen-
> tials of human well-being more nearly, and are therefore of more absolute
> obligation, than any other rules for the guidance of life; and the notion
> which we have found to be of the essence of the idea of justice, that of a
> right residing in an individual, implies and testifies to this more binding
> obligation ... The moral rules which forbid mankind to hurt one another
> (in which we must never forget to include wrongful interference with each
> other's freedom) are more vital to human well-being than any maxims, how-
> ever important, which only point out the best mode of managing some
> department of human affairs.[102]

The idea of 'harm' at the core of Mill's principle, then, refers to assaults
upon 'the essentials of human well-being.' The similarity between this
formulation and 'the permanent interests of man as a progressive being'
in *On Liberty* is striking and should not be overlooked. Given Mill's argument in chapter 3, there is ample reason to assume that it is the interests
in security and personal autonomy, or 'individuality,' that ground the
rights that are the essence of justice.

If harm amounts to a violation of the rules of justice, and such rules
are specified in relation to the necessary but not sufficient conditions of
human well-being, then Mill is *not* committed to the view attributed to
him by Stephen, for a number of reasons. While one could be seriously

affected by the action of another simply because of one's extraordinarily sensitive nature, for instance, an interest must be supported by extrinsic reasons. Whether someone is painfully affected is an empirical matter requiring no appeal to standards of evaluation. But there is a selection process at work in Mill's argument whereby certain interests are singled out and assigned priority. This process *cannot* be undertaken simply through empirical assessments of psychological or subjective mental states; it requires an appeal to criteria of importance, which is exemplified through Mill's use of expressions such as 'permanent interests,' 'essentials of human well-being,' and the like. Stephen's claim that 'every mode of differing from a man which causes him pain infringes his liberty of thought to some extent'[103] is therefore irrelevant, even if true. Since Mill's contrast between self- and other-regarding actions is a normative conclusion rather than the reporting of a natural fact, it is not vulnerable to arguments such as Stephen's, which assert that every action may potentially affect others.

Stephen's third main objection involves a similar confusion. For him, the ideal of moral neutrality is politically impossible, and the notion of a general right to liberty is absurd. However, even a cursory reading of chapter 5 of *On Liberty* demonstrates that Mill neither defends neutrality nor a general right to liberty. Mill tells us that a public officer or anyone else may legitimately prevent a person from crossing an unsafe bridge 'without any real infringement of his liberty'[104] if there is no time to warn him of the immanent danger. Since 'liberty consists in doing what one desires,'[105] and such an individual presumptively does not want to fall into the river under the bridge, such a constraint is justified. In another example, to the extent that taxation is required for the subsidization of public services, the state may legitimately consider which 'commodities the consumers can best spare' and 'select those of which it deems the use, beyond a very moderate quantity to be positively injurious.'[106] As such, the taxation of 'stimulants, up to the point which produces the largest amount of revenue ... is not only admissible, but to be approved of.'[107] Finally, Mill takes it as an 'almost self-evident axiom, that the State should require and compel the education, up to a certain standard, of every human being who is born its citizen.'[108]

Stephen's conflation of the issues of force and range in the absoluteness of Mill's principle leads him to read the conception of liberty at its core as licence. But these three examples identified above suggest that negative liberty is a constitutive element of a perfectionist view of well-being that is not indiscriminate in the way that Stephen thinks. Liberty as

licence is violated by every restraint, including laws preventing danger-
ous bridge-crossing, taxation, and laws mandating compulsory education. Since Mill's fifth chapter is intended to illustrate his principles, we
may charitably assume that these examples are at least consistent with
them. However, Mill's self- versus other-regarding distinction is compatible with these three particular examples only if liberty is understood, not
as licence, but as related to autonomy. In the bridge example, then, we
are justified in preventing someone from crossing because his judgement about the relative risks of doing so is uninformed. Mill's use of the
qualifier 'real' in the sentence 'with no real infringement of his liberty'
indicates that the liberty in question is justifiably restricted either
because it is unimportant or outweighed by a competing consideration
such as autonomy. In the case of taxing alcohol at higher rates than food,
for example, the state is not neutral between competing conceptions of
a worthwhile life, but actively engaged in discriminating between them.
Finally, compulsory education restricts liberty (to drop out or refuse to
send one's children to school) because schooling is essential to the development of the capacities for individuality. Mill is not committed to
defending a right to liberty per se (which would be absurd), but only to
those basic liberties that are conceptually related to the exercise of
autonomous thought and action. Mill's distinction 'between acts that are
self-regarding and those that are other-regarding was not an arbitrary
compromise between the claims of license and other values. It was
intended to define political independence, because it marked the line
between regulation that connoted equal respect and regulation that
denied it.'[109]

So Mill's argument is *not* vulnerable to Stephen's attack on three different fronts. First, Stephen's methodological objection relies upon a
profoundly mistaken reading of *On Liberty*. The principle of liberty tells
us what to do (tolerate) *only* when particularly important interests of *others* are not at stake. When such interests are involved, then utilitarian calculations about the benefits and costs of regulation come into play, but
Mill's principle itself supplies no general formula for carrying them out.
Second, Mill is not refuted by Stephen's suggestion that every action may
potentially affect others. This claim conflates a normative proposition
with empirical statements about subjective dispositions. Finally, the
absurdity of a general right to liberty is not a liability for Mill's position
since it eschews neutrality in favour of a perfectionist conception of well-
being.

2.5 A Utilitarian Defence of Liberalism?

Mill's central difficulty is that he must demonstrate how the institution of a system of moral rights within which the right to (equal) liberty is accorded priority can be defended on utilitarian grounds. This problem manifests itself in three interrelated ways. First, while the principle of utility must itself supply all reasons for and against any action or policy, *On Liberty* introduces a principle that is not only distinct in its content from that of utility, but also seems to require us to ignore the latter within a potentially wide range of circumstances.

Clearly, there is no formal inconsistency involved in assenting to two exceptionless principles such as 'Always act so as to maximize happiness' and 'In the absence of harm to others, never restrict liberty.' But their conjunction implies that Mill must establish not only that one principle (liberty) follows from the other (utility), but also that the two *cannot* conflict. For one thing, strict adherence to the principle of liberty will have the effect of maximizing utility 'only on very questionable assumptions about the predictability and regularity of human affairs.'[110] Much empirical evidence must be offered to support this convergence. For another, their seemingly inevitable divergence creates a lexical problem: if utility and liberty desiderate distinct and sometimes conflicting values, how can a self-professed utilitarian consistently accord priority to the latter?

While the first and second sets of objections concern the extent to which the primacy of liberty can be given a utilitarian justification, the third relates to the particular *type* of constraint at work in the one very simple principle. Although utilitarianism is a consequentialist and aggregative morality that most often has as its chief aim the maximization of the sum of happiness (however defined and measured), the argument of *On Liberty* distributes moral rights to individuals so as to constrain such maximization. Since the principle of liberty is indifferent to the aggregate amount of utility that its implementation might yield, it is best understood as a moral constraint on the pursuit of happiness rather than an efficient strategy for its promotion. But if this is the case, then the argument for toleration is no longer a consequentialist one and, as such, it requires different foundations, and this creates further problems for Mill.

Ultimately, Mill appears to be caught on the horns of a dilemma: on the one hand, if, *per impossibile*, liberty and happiness are *identical*, then the tension between them dissolves, but only because the argument is no longer a consequentialist one – under the guise of utility, Mill is making perfectionist claims about the invariant essentials of human well-being, and, from a structural point of view at least, this brings the foundation of his liberalism perilously close to a natural rights doctrine of the kind he officially repudiates; on the other hand, if liberty is one among many necessary elements of utility in the largest sense, then what reason can Mill have for its lexical priority in relation to all the others?

There is an uneasy balance between the essentialist and consequentialist argumentative strategies found in *On Liberty*, and the potentially intolerant and inegalitarian implications of Mill's liberalism are avoided only if he is willing to abandon consequentalism. Officially at least, Mill disavows an appeal to abstract right in his defence of toleration. However, this claim is also coupled with the idea that there are certain moral rights rooted in vital individual interests that are both independent of social or conventional recognition and adapted to essential and invariant features of human nature. Furthermore, respect for these interests mandates that equality is the only possible basis for a stable political community.

The general form of Mill's argument, then, differs from the particular utilitarian reason ('general utility') that he advances for enforcing individual claims that are to embody moral rights. This general form reproduces some important features inherent in the conception of universal rights as used in the criticism of law and society. For an individual to have a moral right there must be extrinsic reasons of special weight that explain why she should have the liberty or advantage secured by it. Such a right has a peremptory character as the basis for social or legal demands on others and may potentially have weight even relative to law or established convention.

In short, there is a great disjunction between the general form of analysis that stipulates that aggregative considerations are to ground distributive claims and Mill's particular conception of utility.[111] The general form of Mill's argument implies that the reason for conceding certain legal or other positive social rights is utility. The creation and sustenance of these rights is the proper thing for governments to do because of their utility-maximizing consequences. In connection with Mill's argument for freedom of thought and discussion, this does not entail that individuals have moral rights to the advantages secured by such protection. But Mill's specific criteria for moral rights are 'the essentials of human well-being,' things that 'no human being can possibly do without'; 'it is a claim we have on our fellow creatures to join in making safe for us the very groundwork of our existence.' Despite Mill's official repudiation of

abstract right, then, moral rights are justified by reference to 'the separate good in some form of the individuals who are to receive these rights
and on the footing that the good is not merely of value as a contribution
to pooled or aggregate welfare.'[112] Mill's argument for the moral right to
liberty is premised upon a theory of basic needs, which links freedom to
the development of distinctively human capacities. As Isaiah Berlin
notices, although '[Mill's] reasons are drawn from experience and not
from a priori knowledge, the propositions themselves are very much like
those defended on metaphysical grounds by the traditional upholders of
the doctrine of natural rights.'[113]

   If this is so, then Mill faces a potentially insurmountable dilemma. On
the one hand, the bases of moral rights are identified independently of
general utility and the argument is not a consequentialist one; on the
other, the reason for protecting such individual goods by legal enforcement *is* general utility, and their status as moral rights is dependent upon
this being the case. As such, Mill's criterion for the identification of
moral rights has two components: the 'permanent interests of man as a
progressive being' must be at play, *and* their legal and social enforcement must advance general utility. So if Mill's justification of moral
rights is to avoid internal contradiction, it must somehow establish not
only that the two halves of its criterion may coincide, but that they *cannot*
diverge, so that general utility must always require general rules providing legal or social protection of such forms of individual good for everyone. Therefore, Mill is caught on the horns of another dilemma. The
needed utility/equal freedom coincidence can be established stipula-
tively if 'utility' is simply Mill's word for a situation in which the permanent interests of all individuals are fully protected by law or social
convention. But if this is the case, then general utility cannot logically be
a reason for such legal or social protection. Mill's statement that the
legal subordination of women is 'wrong in itself, and now one of the
chief hindrances to human improvement' illustrates this problem well.
To the extent that 'human improvement,' or utility, supplies the content
of right and wrong, Mill is arguing that sexual inequality is wrong
because it is wrong. Utility, liberty, and equality no longer conflict only
because they are analytically equivalent.

   More plausibly, if utility *does* refer to varying levels of aggregate welfare, then the internal consistency of Mill's two-pronged criterion for
moral rights depends upon his establishing that differentiated rights or
unequal liberties can never have the effect of maximizing it. Therefore,
it must always be the case that equal freedom is utility-optimal. Since

Mill's distinction between higher and lower pleasures implies that human beings have qualitatively different capacities for maximizing utility, this egalitarian baseline is surely difficult to sustain. Mill's alterations to the Benthamite notion of utility embody a more sophisticated understanding of human motivation, but they do not avoid, and perhaps even exacerbate, its inegalitarian results.

2.6 Conclusion

There are further problems related to limitations of perfectionist liberalism generally. While autonomy, or individuality, clearly provides toleration with an extrinsic or principled foundation, such a justification may ultimately be an inappropriate response to pluralism for a number of reasons. First, whether any particular conception of autonomy is an essential aspect of individual well-being is inherently controversial. Basing a principle of political restraint on such a contentious ethical claim allows anyone who disputes its validity to reject liberal toleration itself. If we characterize liberalism as a political morality developed in response to pluralism – that is, deep doctrinal conflict – then the idea that any one contested doctrine from amidst that selfsame conflict could provide the justification for a mutually acceptable scheme of basic civil and political liberties seems rather hopeless. To argue for toleration in this way is tantamount to granting rights to others on the condition that they accept what (some) liberals conceive of as ultimately valuable in life – a strange view of toleration indeed.

Second, personal autonomy is not only politically controversial to the extent that there is de facto disagreement regarding its ultimate value, but ethically as well. Are the constitutive elements of Mill's individuality, for instance, either necessary or sufficient conditions of human well-being? Are there really no other worthwhile ways to live – ways much less individualistic and more traditional? Should governments protect or at least not impede only actions or lifestyles that express such values?

Finally, Mill's argument supplies no reason for states to refrain from coercively interfering with beliefs or practices that are not dependent upon the rational revision of one's identity and ends. The intolerant implications of his utilitarianism are evaded only because of the conceptual tie between utility and autonomy. But his argument has nothing to say to sceptics or persecutors uninterested in truth or maximizing utility. Persecution is often undertaken to *silence* truth. Also, since consequentialism is Mill's official position, one can easily imagine cases where interfering with people's choices can help to promote *other values*; or, alternatively, where restricting choices *now* can enable individuals to choose some goods autonomously *in the future*. For a number of reasons, then, it is unclear why personal autonomy is a necessary condition of the individual freedoms of the sort that liberal toleration has traditionally protected. Political intolerance is often devastating, not because it impedes or artificially distorts rational deliberation, but simply because it forces people away from whatever happens to be important and central to their lives.

Part 2 of this book will examine whether the most sophisticated contemporary variants of Millian (perfectionist) liberalism – those of Joseph Raz and Ronald Dworkin – can evade these difficulties, or whether, in fact, there is something problematic about perfectionism per se that makes it a bad foundation for liberal political morality.

3 Is Prostitution Unpatriotic?

3.1 Introduction

In 1954, the Committee on Homosexual Offences and Prostitution (the 'Wolfenden Committee') was appointed to consider the state of British criminal law in relation to homosexuality and prostitution. The committee submitted its findings in September 1957 and recommended by a twelve to one majority that homosexual practices between consenting adults in private should no longer be a crime. As to prostitution, they found unanimously that, while it should not be made illegal, legislation should be introduced to drive it off the streets since public solicitation was an offensive nuisance to third parties. As one commentator has noticed, the normative bases for the committee's recommendations 'are strikingly similar to those expounded by Mill in his essay *On Liberty*.'[1]

The committee members saw the criminal law's primary functions as the preservation of public order and decency, the protection of citizens from what is offensive and injurious, and the provision of adequate safeguards against the exploitation and corruption of others, especially the mentally or physically vulnerable. A central implication of this particular understanding of criminal law is found in section 61 of the report, which tells us that 'there must remain a realm of private morality and immorality which is, in brief and crude terms, not the law's business.'[2] No act of immorality should be made a criminal offence, then, unless it is also accompanied by some *other-regarding* feature such as indecency, corruption, or exploitation.

The publication of the Wolfenden Report precipitated a famous intellectual exchange during the 1960s between Patrick Devlin, then a member of the House of Lords and a distinguished writer on criminal legislation, and H.L.A. Hart, professor of jurisprudence in the University of Oxford. Devlin explicitly denied the idea that there is a private realm of morality into which the law cannot legitimately enter. For him, any Millian attempt to resolve questions about the legitimacy of legally enforcing moral obligations by distinguishing immoralities that implicate public interests from those that are merely private was doomed to failure. He further maintained that the morality that the law must enforce should be popular or conventional morality. Hart attempted to vindicate a modified version of John Stuart Mill's position by rejecting both of these propositions.

At least initially, it is tempting to read this controversy as an earlier round of the 'liberal-communitarian'[3] debate that came to dominate much Anglo-American political philosophy from the early 1980s onwards. Devlin's primary justification for enforcing a community's constitutive public morality against its deviants is to promote and sustain social *solidarity* or *cohesion*. Along with present-day communitarians such as MacIntyre, Sandel, Taylor, and Walzer, he thinks that political solidarity must be based upon a shared way of life that is both protected by, and expressed through, a public morality. Hart, in turn, anticipates contemporary liberals such as Dworkin and Rawls by claiming that public moralities must, themselves, be subjected to critical scrutiny and tested against what are allegedly more universal and, thus, critical values.[4] But a characterization of the Hart–Devlin dispute limited to the relative importance of *community* alone misses Devlin's most powerful case for intolerance.

While Devlin's famous 'disintegration thesis' has generally been dismissed as incoherent, commentators, including Hart himself, surprisingly overlook an interesting but largely unnoticed companion argument that is clearly more promising. Embedded within Devlin's remarkable claim that transgressions of a political community's constitutive morality are treasonous is another one based upon the importance of majoritarian decision-making to communal solidarity, *and* in the egalitarian presuppositions of democracy. This second line of argument for intolerance appeals to equality and choice – values that liberals cannot consistently reject. As such, it seems to render liberal democracy oxymoronic for the following reason. Liberalism justifies the toleration of dissent by appealing to the value of a self-chosen life; it recommends stringent constitutional limits on the power of political authorities in the name of both equality and personal autonomy. Democracy, which also espouses equality and autonomy, presupposes the ability of a community to follow its own lights politically. But how can these two desiderata ever be rendered consistent? Any political morality that prevents democratic majorities from using the law (including the criminal law) to influence the conditions within which autonomous lives are shaped appears at least prima facie self-defeating: 'Latent or explicit, the idea of a profound opposition between majoritarian politics and constitutionally anchored restraints remains a commonplace of contemporary political theory.'[5] Because of the particular construction that he gives it, however, the fact that this tension or 'opposition' is a familiar one only *adds* to the importance and interest of Devlin's critique. Even some fifty years after its initial publication, it should lead theorists of liberalism and democracy alike to address what has recently been called 'one of the great unresolved questions of contemporary political philosophy'[6] – namely, what should the bases of social unity and political stability be in pluralistic communities?[7]

This chapter explores the links between democratic institutions and liberal values through a reassessment of the Hart–Devlin debate. Devlin's democratic argument forms part of a larger and more familiar case that has been termed the 'disintegration thesis.' Accordingly, I begin in section 2 by briefly describing that thesis before turning to the democratic argument itself. In section 3, I explain why Hart's case against the disintegration thesis is very persuasive, but unsatisfactory in connection with Devlin's democratic argument, which he largely ignores. In section 4, I establish the failure of a recent communitarian reading of the disintegration thesis to show that Devlin's original argument is more problematic for liberals than this subsequent reinterpretation. Without having figures to support it, I suspect that Devlin's argument is actually a sophisticated version of the most widely held contemporary belief about the relationship between democratic governance and unconventional cultural, religious, or sexual practices – that is, the notion that majorities should be allowed to repress unpopular practices not because the beliefs that underpin that repression are true, but simply because they are held by a majority of democratic citizens, all of whom are equally entitled to share in the political power that licenses it. In this sense, *liberalism* is undemocratic precisely because it urges restraint. Today, we hear this all of the time in connection with issues such as same-sex marriage and pornography, and in populist criticisms of the judicial review of democratically enacted legislation of all kinds. For this reason, Devlin's argument assumes a new importance. I conclude by sketching some of the possible resources available to liberals in answering this potentially troublesome objection. Whichever conclusions we finally draw, we are better positioned to understand the ways in which liberalism and democracy both are, and are not, mutually supportive by engaging with, rather than ignoring, Devlin's most important claim.

3.2 Devlin's Disintegration Thesis

In The *Enforcement of Morals*, Lord Devlin inquires as to whether, and on what grounds, society has the authority to 'pass judgement ... on matters of morals'[8] and to use the weapon of the criminal law to enforce its verdicts. His affirmative answer to these questions is rooted in a particular a priori conception of what constitutes a society. For Devlin, a society consists of 'a community of ideas'[9] about the way its members should behave and govern their lives. The moral and political structure of every society is held together by 'the invisible bonds of common thought,' which embody a fundamental agreement about 'what is good and what is evil.'[10]

Now, the Wolfenden Report's litmus test for legitimate state interference with alleged immorality is whether the act in question would, in itself, damage the interests of non-consenting parties. In the absence of indecency, corruption, or exploitation, the act is a private one beyond the reach of political authority, whether immoral or otherwise. For Devlin, on the other hand, deviant behaviour is inherently antisocial independently of its impact on particular non-consenting individuals since it threatens the social cohesion that a publicly shared morality expresses and sustains. Thus, beliefs or practices in violation of the 'fundamental agreement' lead 'society [to] disintegrate' and its members to 'drift apart.'[11]

This view of society and its attendant notion of disintegration preclude setting theoretical limits to the power of the state to legislate against immorality. Since society is entitled to protect itself from both internal and external threats, the Wolfenden Report's attempt to define an inviolable area of private morality into which the law may not legitimately interfere breaks down. In a now-famous analogy, Devlin writes,

> The law of treason is directed against aiding the king's enemies and against sedition from within. The justification for this is that established government is necessary for the existence of society and therefore its safety against violent overthrow must be secured. But an established morality is as necessary as good government to the welfare of society. Societies disintegrate from within more frequently than they are broken up by external pressures. There is disintegration when no common morality is observed and history shows that the loosening of moral bonds is often the first stage of disintegra-

tion, so that society is justified in taking the same steps to preserve its moral code as it does to preserve its government and other essential institutions.[12]

If the suppression of vice is as much the law's business as the suppression of subversive activities, then it is as impossible to define a sphere of private morality (and immorality) as it is to define one of private subversive activity.

On one reading, Devlin seems to *equate* a society with its shared morality at any given time so that a change in the latter is tantamount to the destruction of the former. On another, less circular, reading, Devlin is not straightforwardly identifying a society with its public morality, but making a predictive or causal claim. Social cohesion or integration depends upon a shared set of convictions about the proper way for human beings to live. This fundamental agreement is what binds people together in society. By implication, then, anything that threatens or actually weakens this tie endangers the social cohesion that a public morality makes possible. Since both immorality and treason *are capable* in their nature of threatening the existence of society, neither can be safely placed beyond the scope of the criminal law by fixed principles of political legitimacy. To render individuated non-consensual harm a minimum threshold requirement for the legal suppression of immorality (as the Wolfenden Committee does) is to miss the way in which deviant behaviour produces a collective injury by weakening social solidarity.

Since the legal enforcement of a public morality is justified by the value of social cohesion per se, the propriety of tolerating or suppressing particular activities is relative to the dominant existing ethical belief system in any given society. This has two results. First, unless truly immoral practices or beliefs are, for some reason, inherently more divisive than others, Devlinite legislators must enforce whatever moral convictions are dominant, including grossly unjust (because inegalitarian or oppressive) ones. Second, and as a result, the limits of tolerance will vary dramatically from society to society. Not surprisingly, this proposal is diametrically opposed to the methodological abstraction at the core of contractualist justifications of toleration that attempt to identify principles of restraint on more universal grounds.[13] Devlin's discussion of polygamy illustrates both of these implications well: 'Polygamy can be as cohesive as monogamy ... What is important is not the quality of the creed but the strength of the belief in it. The enemy of society is not error but indifference.'[14] Whether polygamy or homosexuality, for instance, should be criminalized or permitted ultimately depends upon the extent to which they offend against whatever particular form of sexual union is dominant within the constitutive public morality of the society in question.

3.2.1 The Democratic Argument

Devlin identifies two different possible objectives to be pursued through the legal enforcement of moral obligations. He calls the first the 'Platonic ideal'[15] in which the state exists to promote virtue among its citizens. In this view of the state's function, whatever power is sovereign 'must have the right and duty to declare what standards of morality are to be observed as virtuous and must ascertain them as it thinks best.'[16] Devlin rejects this idea as unacceptable to Anglo-American thought insofar as it 'invests the State with power of determination between good and evil, destroys freedom of conscience and is the paved road to tyranny.'[17]

The alternative end is that society may legislate to preserve itself. While we have already seen this described via Devlin's disintegration thesis, the argument he deploys in contrasting it with the Platonic ideal introduces a new set of concerns. These centre on the link between intolerance and a particular conception of democracy.

Under the Platonic ideal, legislators must paternalistically determine what is good for their subjects. Even if they undertake this monumental task non-arbitrarily and to the best of their abilities, given the relevant available evidence at their disposal, it is still their judgement, alone, that determines the rights and liberties to be granted. As Devlin writes, 'It is against this concept of the State's power that Mill's words are chiefly directed.'[18] Under the disintegration thesis, however, law-makers are not required to make any judgements about what is good or bad since the morals that they must enforce are those already widely accepted in their community. Their mandate is to preserve the essentials of their society, not to reconstruct them according to their own potentially idiosyncratic ethical ideas.

The disintegration thesis, however, clearly raises an obvious epistemic problem: how are legislators to ascertain the moral principles that are widely accepted, and how 'wide' is wide enough? Devlin's standard is 'the viewpoint of the man in the street – or to use an archaism familiar to all lawyers – the man in the Clapham omnibus. He might also be called the right-minded man.'[19] While this person is an 'ordinary reasonable man,' Devlin also identifies him as 'the man in the jury box'[20] to call attention to three important points. First, since the verdict of a jury must be unanimous, a moral principle can be given the force of law only if 'twelve men and women drawn at random from the community can be expected not only to approve but to take so seriously that they regard a breach of it as fit for punishment.'[21] Second, juries are asked to return verdicts only after argument, instruction, and deliberation. To be enforceable, a moral principle must be similarly deliberated and not merely the product of a 'snap judgment.'[22] Finally, 'the jury box is a place in which the ordinary man's views on morals become directly effective.'[23]

So if the man on the Clapham omnibus believes that a practice is immoral and also believes that no right-minded member of his society could think otherwise, then it *is* immoral for the purpose of the criminal law. Devlin's claim that society may use the criminal law to preserve morality as it does to safeguard anything else that is essential to its continued existence is thus tempered by a restraining principle, which we are now better positioned to elucidate. That principle is that 'there must be toleration of the maximum individual freedom that is consistent with the integrity of society.'[24] The limits of tolerance are therefore co-extensive with the integrity of society, and this integrity, in turn, is established by the morals of the reasonable man. This argumentative structure has two implications: nothing should be punished by law that does not lie beyond the limits of tolerance; and such limits are breached whenever 'intolerance, indignation, and disgust' is 'deeply felt and not manufactured.'[25]

Devlin anticipates the objection that his position reduces morality to a question of fact by pointing to a link between democratic government and equality. A belief in the value of democracy cannot be predicated upon an egalitarian distribution of intellectual endowments among humans since empirical evidence easily refutes this suggestion. On the other hand, it does presuppose 'that [individuals] have at their command – and that in this they are all born in the same degree – the faculty of telling right from wrong.'[26] For Devlin, this epistemic moral egalitarianism 'is the whole meaning of democracy, for if in this endowment men were not equal, it would be pernicious that in the government of any society they should have equal rights.'[27]

At the core of the disintegration thesis, then, there is also an argument for the enforcement of moral obligations rooted in the egalitarian foundations of democracy. If human beings are equally endowed by God or nature with the power of reason and the strength of mind to subdue vicious promptings, then 'there can be no objection to morality being a matter for the popular vote.'[28] There is epistemic strength in numbers. For Devlin, an objection to this moral populism is sustainable only upon the view that the opinion of the 'trained and educated mind'[29] is a source of morals superior to that of the ordinary person. If the end of rational inquiry is the law of God, then this law is inadmissible as a basis for legislation in a secular society because it obviously assumes belief in a divinity as a law-giver; but if reliance is instead placed upon the opinions of rationalist philosophers to determine the content of morality, 'what is obtained except to substitute for the voice of God the voice of the Superior Person?'[30]

Polemically, this argument is highly ingenious because it conceives of principled limitations on the scope of democratic decision-making as inherently anti-egalitarian. If coherent, it renders liberalism internally inconsistent. Liberals often value democracy because its procedural mechanisms express an underlying moral equality between human beings. Majoritarian decisions are thought to take everyone's interests equally into account. However, by constraining the ability of democratic majorities to enforce their public morality, minority rights appear to aggregate interests unevenly to the extent that they give undue weight to relatively unpopular points of view. Devlin's central claim is that taking equality seriously necessitates effectively unrestricted democratic sovereignty. Given that liberals are also democrats, they will be hard-pressed to justify toleration without simultaneously abandoning the egalitarianism that recommends democracy in the first place.

3.3 Hart on Devlin

Hart's critique of the disintegration thesis is powerful and succeeds in disposing of much of it very compellingly. Paradoxically, however, his critique shifts the burden of Devlin's position almost entirely to the democratic argument itself, which Hart ultimately fails to deal with in a satisfactory manner.

In his Harry Camp lectures at Stanford University in 1962, Hart begins his assessment of the disintegration thesis by distinguishing between two levels of moral analysis. Devlin's claim that a society may preserve its public morality as it does anything else that is central to its continued existence is not advanced as, itself, a feature of English popular morality, but as a moral claim that he held to be true. The example of polygamy discussed above shows that his position is complex to the extent that it endorses a certain relativity in the application of a principle of political morality that he believes to be universally valid. Notwithstanding the fact that the principles of public morality that are legitimately enforceable will vary from society from society, Devlin's claim that morals laws are appropriate means of preserving social cohesion does not. As such, the apparent disjunction between the view from the Clapham omnibus and that of the social theorist is highly misleading – while the passengers want their morality enforced because it is *true*, and Devlin wants it enforced simply because it is *shared*, neither is a relativist in any meaningful sense.

The question as to whether the fact that certain conduct is by common standards immoral is sufficient to justify its criminalization, therefore, implies a distinction between the ethical code actually accepted and shared by a given social group, and certain general moral principles used in the criticism of existing social institutions, including that code itself. Hart calls the former 'positive' and the latter 'critical'[31] morality. A utilitarian, for example, who maintains that criminal law should be developed and enacted so as to maximize the greatest happiness for the greatest number is unconcerned with the question of whether the utilitarian morality is or is not already endorsed as the positive morality of the society to which he applies that critical principle. Even if utilitarianism *is* widely accepted, *that* is not the reason why its recommendations should be followed.

Since the enforcement of a public morality requires justificatory support from some general critical principle, then, as Hart argues, the legitimacy of this imposition cannot be established or refuted by pointing, as Devlin does,[32] to the actual practices of any particular society. Hart's analytical point of departure in considering the plausibility of the disintegration thesis is his contention that Devlin's position, like the utilitarian's, is one of critical morality. The issue between liberals and their critics is therefore not reducible to the question of which positive morality should be enforced, as some have recently claimed,[33] but instead whether the enforcement of positive morality is, itself, morally justified.

Once the idea that a society may legitimately take the steps required to preserve its organized existence is seen as a critical principle, its plausibility as such may be considered. Hart does so by distinguishing between two possible interpretations of the disintegration thesis. According to the moderate thesis, a recognized morality is instrumentally valuable to the preservation of society from dissolution or collapse. In this view, the fact that certain immoral acts may not harm, endanger, or corrupt others when done in private does not tell conclusively against intolerance. Such acts cannot be viewed in isolation from their effects on the shared morality since breaches of it are offences against society as a whole by weakening social cohesion. The extreme thesis, on the other hand, sees the enforcement of morality as intrinsically valuable, independently of considerations regarding the extent to which putatively immoral acts weaken social cohesion. Unlike the moderate thesis, this view is not a consequentialist one.

Devlin's analogy between immorality and treason suggests that his claim that the preservation of a society's public morality is necessary for its continued existence is a causal and empirical proposition. If this is so, then the continued existence of society is plainly distinguishable from the preservation of its morality as the former is a desirable consequence of the latter. Interpreted in this way, Devlin's position is a variant of the moderate thesis and his argument is a utilitarian one. Hart's central objection to this is that it entails 'Utilitarianism without the benefit of facts.'[34] While no society could exist without a morality that mirrored and reinforced the law's proscription of conduct injurious to others, there is 'no evidence to support, and much to refute, the theory that those who deviate from conventional sexual morality are in other ways hostile to society.'[35]

This lack of empirical evidence leads Hart to interpret the disintegration thesis as a necessary conceptual truth. On this extreme view, the enforcement of morality is not justified consequentially by reference to its ability in preserving society from decay; the recognized morality is, itself, *identical* to such societal preservation. As stated, the argument therefore shifts from the intelligible claim that some shared set of moral principles is essential to the existence of any society to the notion that a society is identical with its morality as manifested at any given moment in its history. The counterintuitive implications of this should be obvious:

> The former proposition might be even accepted as a necessary rather than an empirical truth depending upon a quite plausible definition of society as a body of men who hold certain moral views in common. But the latter is absurd. Taken strictly, it would prevent us saying that the morality of a given society had changed, and would compel us instead to say that one society had disappeared and another one taken its place. But it is only on this absurd criterion of what it is for the same society to continue to exist that it could be asserted without evidence that any deviation from a society's shared morality threatens its existence.[36]

For Hart, Devlin's conflation between the necessity for *a* moral code with the preservation of its particular substantive character is rooted in his failure to appreciate the inherently multi-tiered aspect of positive moralities.

A positive morality is not simply an amalgam of historically specific norms and customs, but a vehicle for the transmission and expression of what Hart calls 'universal values.'[37] Whatever else they contain, all social moralities provide in some degree for 'such universal values as individual freedom, safety of life, and protection from deliberately inflicted harm.'[38] These values are worth enforcing at virtually any cost to those who violate them since a society in which they are not generally recognized is neither empirically nor logically possible. Even if it were so, 'such a society could be of no practical value for human beings.'[39] Devlin's disintegration thesis must therefore be turned on its head: the preservation of any particular society from dissolution is desirable only to the extent that it secures for human beings some measure of these universal values. As Hart writes, 'Whether or not a society is justified in taking steps to preserve itself must depend both on what sort of society it is and what the steps to be taken are.'[40]

So while a society cannot safely tolerate deviation from these universal values, it can certainly survive and, as Mill sought to demonstrate so forcefully, perhaps even benefit from differences in other components of its prevalent morality. There is also a distinction between what Hart calls '*formal* values,' which embody the 'spirit or attitude of mind which characterises the practice of a social morality' from the '*material* values'[41] of its particular rules or content. The former enable individuals to see questions of conduct from a more impersonal point of view and to apply general rules of conduct impartially. The moral attitude produces and sustains a sense of reciprocity in which the wants, expectations, and interests of others are taken into account. In adapting one's conduct to a system of reciprocal claims, one learns self-discipline and control. These are 'universal virtues and indeed constitute the specifically moral attitude to conduct.'[42] For Hart, while they are learnt in conforming to the morality of some particular society, their value does not derive from that fact: 'No principles of critical morality which paid the least attention to the most elementary facts of human nature and the conditions in which human life has to be led could propose to dispense with them.'[43] Thus, there is an important distinction to be drawn between the preservation of morality in this critical sense, and mere 'moral conservatism,' which attempts to 'freeze into immobility'[44] dominant public moralities. Neither the existence of universal values nor the specifically moral attitude to conduct precludes radical changes in a society's positive morality. Both can and, in fact, do survive such transformations.

3.3.1 The Democratic Argument Considered

One remarkable feature of Hart's response to the disintegration thesis is the relative lack of attention it pays to the democratic argument for the enforcement of a public morality. Only four short pages at the end of *Law, Liberty and Morality* are directly devoted to addressing this issue. The substance of Hart's response is a contrast between democracy and what he calls 'moral populism,' or the view that 'the majority have a moral right to dictate how all should live.'[45] Devlin's argument confuses these two ideas since it moves from the acceptable principle that political power is best entrusted to the majority to the untenable claim that democratic power 'is beyond criticism and must never be resisted.'[46] For Hart, democratic principles do not support the imposition of a popular morality on a deviant minority, even when the majority is 'overwhelming' and expressive of 'intolerance, indignation, and disgust.'[47]

Hart, however, unfortunately says very little by way of elucidating the precise content of these democratic principles. Without a clear statement of them in hand, it is not immediately obvious why Devlin's position amounts to a 'misunderstanding of democracy.'[48] Since the scope of legitimate majoritarian decision-making is obviously related to its underlying justification, this oversight is troublesome. Democracy can be justified in a variety of ways with each having different implications for minority rights. For example, democratic procedures could be justified instrumentally on the basis of their capacity for identifying right answers or optimal outcomes as jury trials, for instance, are thought to be reliable indicators of guilt.[49] This first, or 'right-answer,' conception is problematic to the extent that it seemingly renders the processes that it recommends dispensable. We can know that a procedure is more likely than not to reach the best outcomes only if we already have some independent idea of what such outcomes look like. But once we know this, why not appeal directly to those outcomes? Rousseau's treatment of political minorities in the *Social Contract* is symptomatic of this link between political strength and epistemic efficacy – the outvoted minority must accept not only that they are outvoted, but also that they are wrong.[50] On another view, democracy may be the best way of aggregating preferences to maximize utility.[51] This utilitarian rationale is particularly worrisome within the context of discussions about the enforcement of morality, both since the idea of aggregating and maximizing anything is out of place, and because, for a number of familiar reasons, utilitarianism may sanction unacceptable trade-offs between agents. As critics[52] have pointed out, the maximization of utility is a particularly unstable foundation for minority rights unless one introduces extraneous constraints. Finally, democracy could be an institutional embodiment of procedural fairness between agents conceived of as free and equal.[53] Even though this view is intuitively appealing and appears to be Devlin's, Hart provides no argument to illustrate why unconstrained majoritarianism violates rather than follows from procedural fairness.

One such argument has been advanced by Ronald Dworkin,[54] who perceives an internal inconsistency in Devlin's democratic case for the enforcement of moral obligations. Often, 'morality,' 'moral beliefs,' or 'moral convictions' are anthropological expressions used to identify whatever subjective attitudes a particular group displays about the propriety of human conduct or goals. But these expressions can also be used in a discriminatory sense 'to contrast the positions they describe with prejudices, rationalizations, matters of personal aversion or tastes, arbitrary stands, and the like.'[55] Since Devlin's Clapham omnibus argument relies on the anthropological view of morality, democratic principles do not call for its enforcement because the belief that prejudices, personal aversions, and rationalizations do not justify restricting another's freedom is, itself, a critical and fundamental component of 'our popular morality.'[56]

For Dworkin, then, what 'is shocking and wrong is not [Devlin's] idea that the community's morality counts, but his idea of what counts as the community's morality.'[57] On the one hand, Dworkin's argument is similar to Hart's since it distinguishes between positive (anthropological) and critical (discriminatory) morality; on the other, it illustrates in acute form two central problems of identification. If only moral positions in the discriminatory sense are democratically pursuable, then we need some mutually acceptable method of testing both what 'our' popular morality (really) contains, and also of distinguishing moral reasoning from simple 'rationalization.' Unless this can be done without begging the question, disagreements over the alleged immorality of, say, homosexuality simply transfer themselves to epistemic controversies over what is to count as acceptable moral 'evidence.' For instance, is the Bible sufficient to condemn sodomy as unnatural, or is medical science the proper authority? Is a traditional morality inherently unreasoned or the only reliable source of ethical wisdom? As Locke sought to convince Proast, everyone's morality is 'critical' or 'discriminatory' to himself, so there is reason to suspect that Dworkin's suggestion is politically, though not ethically, useless.

3.4 A Communitarian Reinterpretation of the Disintegration Thesis?

Robert George has recently offered a reinterpretation[58] of Devlin's disintegration thesis that is meant to withstand Hart's criticisms. George identifies himself as an exponent of what he calls 'the central pre-liberal tradition of thought'[59] about morality, politics, and law. Within this tradition, of which Proast and Stephen are notorious members, laws forbidding 'powerfully seductive and corrupting vices'[60] may assist people in establishing and preserving virtuous characters in four general ways: (1) by preventing the self-corruption that ensues from engaging in immoral conduct, (2) by minimizing the chances that others will emulate the bad example set by such behaviour, (3) by preserving the 'moral ecology in which people make their morally self-constituting choices,' (4) and, finally, by educating people about the content of moral right and wrong.[61]

This concern for a society's moral ecology implies that the fundamental distinction relevant to legislators charged with upholding public morality is between acts that are moral and immoral, and not between allegedly public and private ones. On the one hand, then, the tradition's position is similar to Devlin's in denying a realm of private morality; on the other, it is based upon the ethical character of a community's members, not social cohesion per se.

For George, Devlin's disintegration thesis does not claim, as Hart took him to be claiming, that the protection of a society's public morality is necessary to prevent the breakdown of social order. A society characterized by radical moral pluralism may very well continue to be one in which people live in close proximity to one another in a state of peace and security. But since a society means more than simply an aggregation of peaceful individuals living in close proximity, the price of toleration is 'the loss of a distinctive form of interpersonal integration in community understood as something worthwhile for its own sake.'[62] What does this mean?

George clarifies this communitarian understanding of public morality by pointing to Devlin's image of individuals drifting apart in pluralistic societies. He draws an analogy of his own between societal disintegration resulting from the infringement of a dominant morality and the dissolution of a 'marital friendship.'[63] Once spouses cease to integrate their lives around common interests, commitments, or concerns, they 'drift apart'; they may continue to coordinate their activities in a variety of ways for 'extrinsic purposes,' but their relationship is 'instrumentalized' and they no longer 'understand, and thus no longer experience, themselves as *integrally* related in the way they once were.'[64]

Similarly, the central societal locus for this interpersonal integration is a set of shared moral principles that binds people together as members of one political community. Social cohesion is, thus, not only instrumentally valuable as a means of preserving order, but also intrinsically so because the 'identification of one's own interests and well-being with that of others to whom one is *thus integrally related* is essential to community.'[65] Toleration inevitably weakens this integration.

Hart's critique of the disintegration thesis loses its force, then, once it is understood that Devlin does not suppose that social disorder will ensue whenever social cohesion is lost. 'Disintegration' involves a qualitative shift in a community's character; it amounts to a fragmentation of the distinctive self-understanding among a collectivity of individuals integrally related through their public morality. Seen in this light, the defensibility of Devlin's thesis does not require evidence linking pluralism about fundamental principles of sexual morality to social chaos or civil war; nor does it trivially imply that one society replaces another whenever a shift in its dominant morality occurs.

This interpretive claim is complemented by a prescriptive one. For Devlin, the truth or falsity of an alleged moral obligation is irrelevant to the question of whether it is legitimately enforceable by law. For George, by contrast, this must be modified to accommodate 'the traditional and correct view that morals laws are morally justified only when the morality they enforce is true.'[66] Social cohesion is, thus, only conditionally valuable. The erosion of a hitherto dominant public morality sanctions its enforcement against dissidents only to the extent that its injunctions are, in fact, true.

Recall that this position – that the state exists to promote virtue and discourage vice among its citizens – is the very Platonic ideal that Devlin abandons as the paved road to tyranny. George defends against this criticism by contrasting the reasoning of a legislator committed to his principle with one following Devlin's. In democracies, the Platonic ideal protects individuals and unpopular minorities by requiring that political authorities *reason* publicly about the content of human well-being and the true norms of morality. While the law may forbid *any* genuine immorality, authorities cannot legislate against acts that are not truly immoral. The Platonic ideal therefore places a powerful internal limit on the reach of the law to enforce moral obligations. On the other hand, Devlin's unmodified disintegration thesis renders social cohesion unconditionally valuable so that public authorities may suppress anything that a large enough majority strongly *perceives* to be immoral. Ultimately, it is this view that represents 'the real threat of tyranny.'[67]

There are two different possible viewpoints from which to consider the Platonic ideal and, ultimately, from the vantage point of policy-makers, George's position inevitably *collapses into* Devlin's with the implication that both of their respective principles of restraint have roughly the same impact on civil liberties. For better or worse, depending upon one's point of view, they are equally intolerant.

The fundamental epistemic premise of the central tradition is the possibility for human beings to *reason* about the content of well-being and the requirements of morality. Unless individuals can, in principle, distinguish between authentic moral knowledge and mere superstition or prejudice, the claim that political authorities may properly enforce only the former is absurd. For this reason, George connects Devlin's repudiation of the Platonic ideal to an endorsement of a form of moral non-cognitivism that denies the existence of this requisite ability. Devlin, however, cannot consistently hold this view for two reasons: first, his democratic argument for intolerance is *premised upon* an epistemic moral egalitarianism in which individuals are equally endowed with the capacity to discern right and wrong; and second, the proposition that the legal enforcement of morality is justified in preventing social disintegration is, itself, an irreducibly moral claim and is, as such, inconsistent with this type of scepticism. While Devlin does say that the exclusion of the irrational is a 'comparatively unimportant process' and that in choosing between a number of rationally acceptable options 'reasoning will get [us] nowhere' so that we must rely on 'feeling,'[68] this merely establishes the possibility of reasonable pluralism. Devlin's claim that reason has inevitable limits is a far cry from the non-cognitivism attributed to him by George.

Even if Devlin *does* hold this view, however, it is inessential to a rejection of the Platonic ideal for the following reason. Consider three different societies that emerge as implications of George's position:

1 Non-integrated but peaceful societies characterized by 'instrumentalized' interpersonal relations
2 Societies whose members identify their interests and well-being with others to whom they are, thus, *integrally related* around wicked or unjust public moralities
3 Intrinsically valuable societies whose members are *integrally related* around authentically virtuous or just public moralities

There are two very different vantage points from which to consider these societies. First, there is the transcendent position of the social theorist looking down from her academy and assessing the extent to which each one conforms to the principles of right reason. From this perspective, societies 2 and 3 are plainly distinguishable and the tradition's principle – 'enforce only authentically virtuous moralities' – is intelligible. The social theorist can safely accept the Platonic principle of restraint since society 2 is thereby precluded from enforcing its positive morality. The second perspective, however, is that of the legislators themselves who will have to decide which principles of public morality to enforce against deviants. But from this view – the only one with any practical relevance – the distinction between 'enforce whatever morality you happen to sub-scribe to' and 'enforce the true morality' is *no distinction at all* since one cannot believe something without also thinking it to be true.[69] George maintains that as the power to deregulate does not appear to induce peo-ple of a libertarian bent to become anarchists, the power to enforce morality for the sake of virtue is unlikely to induce the tradition's supporters to become 'moral extremists,' 'fanatics,' or 'rigorists.'[70] But 'extreme,' 'fanatical,' and 'rigoristic' are almost always pejorative adjec-tives levelled at one's adversaries and are rarely, if ever, self-applied. To the extent that everyone's morality is critical to herself, George's Platonic ideal is reducible to Devlin's position but plagued by the additional worry that idiosyncratic conceptions of virtue and vice are not filtered out by any requirement of popular support. One way of preventing societies 2 and 3 from both enforcing their respective dominant conceptions of eth-ical truth is to claim that reason or critical morality allows only one set of universally binding moral obligations so that permissible positive moral-ities will be everywhere alike. But this response simply avoids or ignores the political problem that a principle of restraint should be designed to accommodate – namely, reasonable disagreement about morality's authentic requirements.

It also abandons the communitarian element of George's reinterpre-tation since interpersonal integration per se no longer appears to have *any* independent value. And even if it still does, the logical focal point for a conception of right reason that identifies *basic human goods* is much more cosmopolitan, and less narrowly nationalistic, than the intimacy suggested by George's marriage-partner/citizenship analogy. People may require interpersonal integration, but why must the scope of this cohesion coincide with national political communities? It can be both larger and smaller.[71]

We may, therefore, reject the Platonic ideal without embracing a self-defeating scepticism because the distinction between making moral judgements and coercively imposing them on others raises a new set of concerns related to the political uselessness of a perspectiveless notion of ethical truth. The disintegration thesis, then, cannot survive even under its modified communitarian format. But Devlin's democratic case for intolerance remains.[72] One of the more intuitively appealing justifications for democracy is the way in which it embodies the procedural expression of an underlying moral equality between human beings. Minority rights, however, appear to grant undue weight to relatively unpopular points of view by constraining the extent to which political majorities can exert influence over their society's moral ecology.

3.5 Conclusion

Liberals intent on resisting this conclusion must somehow demonstrate that minority rights follow from, rather than violate, procedural fairness as well explain why individual and collective self-determination are not straightforwardly analogous choice-situations. While Devlin's democratic argument is ingenious, liberals themselves have several resources at their disposal to meet this critique.

The first potential tactic in correcting the perception that liberal rights are inherently anti-democratic is to investigate some of the ways in which constitutional constraints on political power enhance, rather than simply limit, collective decision-making. For example, if majorities can act cohesively only *after* their constitutive political wills have been clearly identified, then liberalism is not obviously anti-democratic if minority rights are somehow procedurally instrumental in achieving such identification. In this view, the idea that liberalism is necessarily undemocratic 'reflects a common but one-sided understanding of what a constitution does.'[73] Clarifying this misconception would involve linking minority rights to the constitutional procedures in the absence of which popular government is meaningless.

A second strategy for rescuing liberalism from Devlin's democratic argument involves distinguishing *personal* from *political* autonomy. For Devlin, toleration is inherently inegalitarian and, thus, undemocratic because it appears to aggregate individuals' preferences for the ethical character of their community in a distorted or non-neutral way. But principled limitations on a community's ability to reinforce its constitutive morality may *expand*, rather than contract, choice in another, perhaps more vitally important sense from a liberal point of view. The area of personal autonomy established by minority rights provides a sphere of discretionary competence within which individuals are equally accountable to no one but themselves for their conduct and beliefs. If personal autonomy rather than collective efficacy is the underlying value that justifies majoritarianism in the first place, then liberalism and democracy no longer conflict because they both rest upon the same normative grounds.[74]

The final possible strategy derives, interestingly enough, from Devlin himself. Recall that the Clapham omnibus passenger charged with pronouncing upon, and ultimately enforcing, his community's public morality is described as the man in the jury box. This analogy is meant to draw attention to certain epistemic criteria that must be satisfied before Devlin's passenger can competently assess which breaches of his society's shared moral code are fit for punishment. As juries are asked to yield verdicts only after instruction, deliberation, and argument, Devlin's passenger must be similarly reflective. Until he is, any of his claims about the content of his society's public morality are purely speculative or hypothetical because its authentic requirements emerge *from* this deliberative process,[75] and this creates two problems. First, Devlin's epistemic requirements come perilously close to collapsing into Hart's idea of critical morality since both distinguish people's *actual* moral beliefs from those they *would* hold after rational scrutiny. And second, if instruction, deliberation, and argument are essential in the identification of the shared moral code, then it is difficult to see how democracy can be anything but liberal to the extent that intolerance impedes, rather than encourages, the reasonable inquiry that is the admission price for riding Devlin's Clapham omnibus.

As in chapters 1 and 2, we see here important building-blocks of any defensible liberal theory. Chapter 1 revealed that equality and pluralism combine to generate a contractual ideal of political justification, and also that the foundations of that ideal are quintessentially moral rather than epistemological. Chapter 2 illustrated how and why comprehensive character ideals are inadequate bases for liberal politics. In this chapter, we learned that any justifiable liberal theory will yield politics that are constitutional rather than purely majoritarian, and deliberative rather than purely aggregative. In part 3 of the book, we articulate and defend precisely such a theory. Before doing so, however, we turn to criticize the most influential alternative view of political morality.

PART TWO

Liberalism Today

4 Should Liberals be Perfectionists?

4.1 Introduction

When confronted with the task of having to make serious choices in our daily lives, the question we ask ourselves most often is not, What *do* I most want? but rather, Which of these options is most *worth* wanting? Our having goals or desires necessarily implies a belief that there is value in them independently of the fact that we now want to pursue them. In fact, the anxiety prompted by important questions that require practical solutions is intelligible only if the possibility exists for deciding wrongly; and deciding wrongly implies, in turn, that various options have an intrinsic value that precedes our current desires and choices, which the latter can fail to reflect. A desire or choice is unreasonable precisely when this is the case.

The reason-dependent character of wants and desires seems to have two consequences, one ethical, and the other political. First, because the achievement of any goal is good for the person whose goal it is only if that goal is itself worthwhile or valuable, his well-being is improved only through success in valuable activities. Second, to the extent that want-satisfaction is not intrinsically valuable, authorities do not necessarily help their subjects by assisting them in achieving or getting whatever they happen to want. When people want what is worthless or evil, they have reason not to have their wants fulfilled, and authorities may have reason to frustrate, or to alter, their existing desires.

The basis of this view is Millian, and its most fully elaborated contemporary version is offered by Joseph Raz in a series of books and articles[1] that impressively bring together discussions on the nature and source of value, its connection to practical reasoning, and the implications of both for liberal political morality. For Raz, 'It is the goal of all political action to enable individuals to pursue valid conceptions of the good and to discourage evil or empty ones.'[2]

In this chapter, we subject this claim to critical scrutiny. Section 2 explains Raz's conception of well-being and indicates how his particular ideal of personal autonomy is linked to it. Section 3 outlines the connections between value, practical reason, and authority that are implied by that character ideal. Section 4 explains how personal autonomy and moral pluralism combine in Raz's reinterpretation of J.S. Mill's famous harm principle. Section 5 evaluates the merits of this reinterpretation and shows that the Razian harm principle is the focal point for a host of interrelated problems. Section 6 examines Raz's subsequent attempt at resolving some of these difficulties. Raz ultimately fails to reconcile state action in pursuit of the good with a due regard for individual liberty, and this failure is symptomatic of perfectionist political moralities generally.

Showing why this is so is important for a number of reasons. First, perfectionism gains unwarranted credibility from its intuitive appeal or naturalness.[3] After all, what could be wrong with the requirement that governments promote what is good, and discourage what is bad? This alleged naturalness betrays several crucial defects, however, which are brought to light only through detailed philosophical analysis. Second, while perfectionism is currently very popular among philosophers and the voting public alike (partly because of its natural appeal), no one has set out the case for basing state power on ethical ideals with as much care and consideration as has Raz. If his theory fails, then, there are prima facie grounds for doubting that any such theory could succeed, and this finding would be important for law and public policy. Finally, state neutrality is everywhere under attack, from anti-liberal critics *and* those endorsing more popular autonomy-based forms of liberalism, so the more popular view should also have its day in court.

4.2 Well-Being and Personal Autonomy

According to Raz, government's main purpose is to assist people in leading 'successful and fulfilling lives, or, to put the same point in other terms, to protect and promote the well-being of people.'[4] He maintains that this is the 'pivotal ethical precept of public action.'[5] We therefore need to know much more about precisely what makes a life successful and fulfilling before we may reasonably assess the role of the liberal state in promoting it.

In general terms, well-being consists of everything that is good for a person. This is divided into two complementary aspects: that which makes her into a better person, and that which makes her life itself better or more successful. For Raz, the goodness of a life depends on the value of the activities it comprises, and their value, in turn, is revealed through understanding what a good life consists of. His formal characterization of well-being reflects this interdependency: 'Well-being consists in the 1) whole-hearted and 2) successful pursuit of 3) valuable 4) activities.'[6] Ultimately, how successful, fulfilled, or good a life[7] is depends essentially upon both the character of its possessor and the values that constitute it.

Rather than defending this claim by establishing the intrinsic value of particular virtues, goals, and actions on substantive ethical grounds, Raz invokes four general features of practical reasoning that influence and constrain the shape of any valuable or worthwhile life. While some commentators have understandably found this strategy evasive,[8] it is intended to shift the debate away from Raz's own ethical convictions (which may or may not be persuasive) toward the structural conditions of personal well-being that he thinks do not depend upon these convictions for their plausibility.[9]

Raz explicates the first condition by distinguishing well-being from self-interest. Self-interest is promoted by satisfying basic needs and associated desires that are primarily biological in their origin. Other things being equal, for instance, a person's self-interest is served and she is therefore better off when well fed, in moderate temperature, with adequate sensory stimulation, and in good health, *whether she adopts these things as her goals or not*. These are natural requirements that derive from certain contingent features of her biological make-up. She benefits from their satisfaction regardless of whether she recognizes their importance.

Well-being, on the other hand, is essentially a function of success and failure in the pursuit of our non-biologically determined goals.[10] Raz thinks that this, what we shall call Condition 1, is the major determinant of our well-being. By goals, Raz means both those that people adopt deliberately and those that they simply drift into or grow up with. In this category, he includes 'projects, plans, relationships, ambitions, commitments, and the like.'[11]

Goals such as these have several distinguishing and interrelated features. First, unlike biologically inspired needs and wants, these are ends that people have but could have avoided. They are consciously adopted or endorsed and, as such, play a formative role in shaping people's perceptions of their physical,[12] emotional, and intellectual environments.[13]

Second, because the connection of such goals to well-being is internal, or conceptual, we can normally improve the lives of others only *through* them: either by helping people achieve the goals that they actually have or, if these are valueless or depraved, by helping them to change them.[14] Finally, they are 'comprehensive'[15] or 'pervasive' goals that form 'nested ... hierarchical structures.'[16] Because people's immediate goals are nested in their larger projects, this yields an evaluative criterion for judging the relative importance of various courses of action: one does not measure the importance of an action by the number of goals it enables people to reach, but by its contribution to the highest goals it serves. Other things being equal, then, pervasive goals are more important determinants of personal well-being than are immediate or limited ones.

The second structural condition is an implication of the reason-dependent character of desires, wants, and preferences. For Raz, wanting something is not a reason for doing anything, nor can it render anything valuable. Value, by contrast, is what determines what agents have reason to do, and their goals, in turn, reflect their perception of what is reasonable. This dependence of reason on value, together with the dependence of goals on reason, yields the second formal condition of well-being, namely that only success in intrinsically valuable activities contributes to it (Condition 2):

> A person's well-being depends on the value of his goals and pursuits. A person who spends all his time gambling has, other things being equal, less successful a life, even if he is a successful gambler, than a live stock farmer busily minding his farm. Their self-interest may be equally served by their activities, but their well-being is not. The reason is that they engage in what they do because they believe it to be a valuable, worthwhile activity (perhaps but not necessarily because of its value to others). They care about what they do on that basis. To the extent that their valuation is misguided it affects the success of their life.[17]

As set out in Condition 1, success in comprehensive goals is the major determinant of personal well-being. However, comprehensive goals are no less reason-dependent than the more limited ones nested within them. This has the following result. Because comprehensive goals are pursued for reasons, and reasons are conditional upon value, valueless goals or projects are, by definition, unreasonable and their satisfaction therefore cannot logically contribute to personal well-being (Condition 2). A gambler succeeds in improving her life by quitting gambling for farming rather than by increasing her winnings.

The third structural condition of well-being is the primacy of 'action reasons'[18] (Condition 3). People adopting or endorsing comprehensive plans for their lives are often primarily concerned with what to *do*, what they will *do with themselves*, what they will *make of themselves*, how they will *conduct themselves*, and so forth. A great segment of their most important goals, then, is agency goals. Insofar as the major determinant of well-being is success in comprehensive goals (Condition 1), and these goals both provide, and are constituted by, action reasons, personal well-being is assessable largely by reference to people's success as *agents*.[19]

Raz's final condition of well-being is that 'a person can have a comprehensive goal only if it is based on 'existing social forms, i.e. on forms of behaviour which are in fact widely practiced in his society'[20] (Condition 4). This does not assume that whatever is practised with social approval is *for that very reason* valuable. Rather, it states a limiting condition on which comprehensive goals can be valuable for anyone – they can be valuable only if they can be goals, and they can be goals only *if* they are founded in social forms.[21]

Raz advances both a conceptual and an empirical argument to support this condition. The conceptual one points to the logical presuppositions of certain comprehensive goals. Simply put, some of them require social institutions for their very possibility. One cannot pursue a legal career, for instance, except in a society governed by law, nor can one practise medicine except where it is recognized as such. Lawyers, doctors, and even birdwatchers[22] all participate in complex social forms involving general recognition of their distinctive activities, their social organizations, along with their relative status in society. Resolving conflicts, curing illnesses, and tracking wildlife are activities that play different roles and have different meanings in the lives of individuals depending on the social practices and the attitudes that constitute them.

As a matter of empirical observation, people ultimately acquire comprehensive goals by habituation rather than explicit deliberation. They derive the goals by which they constitute their lives from exposure to 'the stock of social forms available to them, and the feasible variations on it.'[23] This does not preclude the possibility for innovation. People can, and often do, transcend existing social forms, as in the case of open marriages,[24] but, for Raz, the distance they have travelled away from the shared forms is the most significant aspect of their situation.[25]

Raz's view of personal well-being, therefore, consists of four key conditions:

Condition 1 Success and failure in the pursuit of non-biologically determined or comprehensive goals is the major determinant of our well-being.

Condition 2   Our well-being is increased only through success in intrinsically valuable activities.

Condition 3   Our well-being depends primarily on our success in following action reasons because of their connection to comprehensive goals.

Condition 4   Our well-being depends to a considerable extent on our success in socially defined and determined pursuits and activities.

But how, exactly, does liberalism flow from an ethical foundation such as this? Is there anything recognizably liberal in the general claim that people's preferences should be freely pursued only within the boundaries set by their own well-being, rather than within those circumscribed by the rights of others? In the end, how tolerant can a state be that is duty-bound to eliminate whichever activities, pursuits, and relationships it deems repugnant; and does it make any sense to speak of tolerance in relation to such a duty at all? Normally, one only *tolerates* the objectionable, but the activities within the range of options that the Razian state tolerates are intrinsically valuable, and it is difficult to imagine how one can reasonably object to them. What is left of liberal toleration if one must either abandon one's objections as unreasonable or persecute others in their name?

Perfectionist governments are duty-bound to promote valid conceptions of the good, and to discourage evil or empty ones. At least initially, Raz's contention that this requirement is not only consistent with, but actually flows from, a respect for individual liberty appears somewhat puzzling. How free can people really be in a state that allows them only to engage in (what it takes to be) valuable activities? For Raz this question misunderstands the implications of his four conditions of well-being. Successful or flourishing lives are those consisting of valuable *goals*, *activities*, and *commitments*. This focus on agency implies that people prosper by leading *autonomous* lives that are partially of their own making. Valuable activities contribute to well-being only when they are self-chosen and this is 'incompatible with any vision of morality being thrust down people's throats.'[26] In this way, the worry identified above is alleviated. Perfectionist ethics yield liberal politics because valuable lives are possible only under conditions of political freedom.

In its particular application to individuals, autonomy has several interrelated connotations: the *capacity* of an agent to govern herself, or the actual condition of self-governance; an agent's having an effective sense of justice – what is sometimes called *moral autonomy*; an agent's *moral right* to unlimited discretionary competence within what is thought to be her private domain; and, finally, an *ideal of character* derived from the virtues and capacities presupposed by, and associated with, the condition of self-governance. Raz's conception of personal autonomy is best understood as a (partial) character ideal. Let us see why he is committed to adopting this conception and to rejecting the others.

One way of understanding autonomy is in terms of a person's capacity to conceive of, and act upon, projects and values. This corresponds roughly with the first half of John Rawls's conception of moral personality.[27] Someone autonomous in this sense has the ability to 'form, to revise, and rationally pursue a conception of [her] rational advantage or good.'[28] As a project pursuer with the capacity to conceptualize and act upon projects and values that transcend her own immediate experiences, an autonomous individual in this sense is simply an agent. While agency is clearly presupposed by Raz's idea of personal autonomy, the two are necessarily distinct. Agency is but one important aspect of personal autonomy, and not all agents realize that ideal.

A second view is *moral autonomy*. A person is morally autonomous by having an effective sense of justice. To have an effective sense of justice, in turn, is to recognize other human beings as agents with projects and values of their own. The morally autonomous agent accepts that justice sometimes requires restraint in the pursuit of her own projects insofar as others have legitimate claims of their own. The mark of a person who lacks moral autonomy is an inability to think of others except in terms of objects available to be used for her own purposes. For Raz, personally autonomous individuals may or may not have an effective sense of justice. While the *value* of personal autonomy is threatened by immorality or injustice, autonomy itself is not. Even those who blatantly neglect morality's requirements may lead a self-chosen life.

There is, however, an idea related to moral autonomy nested within the ideal of personal autonomy, what we may call moral authenticity. The moral beliefs of an authentic individual are rooted in her own character, and not merely inherited from others. Her moral opinions and ideals are the product of rational self-evaluation. In this view, those who most conspicuously fall short of autonomy are not the wicked, but rather, as Mill might have said, those whose morality is a mindless reflex.

Another view of autonomy understands by that idea a *moral right* to

self-determination. On analogy from the political state, individual autonomy is thought of as a right to an inviolable discretionary competence
within an area of decisional space that is central to both agency and personal identity.[29] While this idea of personal sovereignty is a possible foundation for political morality, it is inconsistent with perfectionism because
it implies that when the exercise of a person's sovereign right conflicts
with what is truly good for her (well-being), her decisions are to be protected from interference nonetheless. There is no necessity that the free
exercise of an agent's autonomy will effectively promote her own good,
and even where individual self-determination is, on clear evidence, likely
to harm her, paternalistic interference is (almost never) justified.
Because Raz conceives of personal autonomy as an aspect of human well-
being, he rejects the idea that the two are competitive values. The value
of personal autonomy may justify giving individuals various rights to govern themselves in certain ways, but it is *itself* not a moral right.

Raz's notion of personal autonomy is essentially a character ideal that
links well-being to self-creation. Autonomous individuals shape their
characters in accordance with their own perception of what is valuable.
They do so by reflectively adopting projects, commitments, and relationships from a broad range of eligible alternatives. Through a series of self-
defining choices, they chart their own courses through life: 'The ruling
idea behind the ideal of personal autonomy is that people should make
their own lives. The autonomous person is a (part) author of his own life.
The ideal of personal autonomy is the vision of people controlling, to
some degree, their own destiny, fashioning it through successive decisions throughout their lives.'[30]

Raz's qualifications on the metaphor of authorship in this passage
('part' and 'to some degree') reveal two ways in which personal autonomy is only a *partial* character ideal. Although self-chosen goals and relationships are constitutive elements of well-being for Raz, he does not
specify precisely *which* of these a person must choose to flourish. The
autonomous life, we are told, 'is discerned not by what there is in it but
by how it came to be'; it may consist of 'diverse and heterogeneous pursuits ... and a person who frequently changes his tastes can be as autonomous as one who never shakes off his adolescent preferences.'[31] Clearly,
then, *pedigree* and not content is determinative of the autonomous life.

The second aspect of partialness relates to the fact that autonomy is
possible only within 'a framework of constraints.'[32] An autonomous personality can develop and flourish only against a background of biological
and social constraints that fix some of its needs. Many choices are inevi-

tably determined by such needs and because this is so, 'the ideal of the perfect existentialist with no fixed biological or social nature who creates himself as he goes along is an incoherent dream.'[33] Personal autonomy is not all or nothing, then, but rather a matter of degree.

Raz's ideal presupposes the existence of both internal capacities and external conditions for its possibility. Indeed, personal autonomy is ultimately a composite of three such distinct conditions: appropriate mental abilities, an adequate range of options, and independence. Clearly, if a person is to be the maker or author of her own life by choosing and pursuing projects (commitments, relationships, goals), then she must possess a range of cognitive skills. A project-pursuer requires at least a certain competence at practical reasoning that enables her to conceive of alternative options for choice. Additionally, she must have the mental abilities to form complex intentions as well as the capacity to comprehend the means required for the realization of her goals.

These capacities are only necessary, but not sufficient, conditions of personal autonomy. To be autonomous, a person must actually exercise them in a way such as to make her life her own. Because coercion and manipulation prevent their intended targets from doing this, autonomous individuals must be relatively free from both of them. For Raz, coercion 'invades autonomy by subjecting the will of the coerced.'[34] As he says, 'the contribution of autonomy to a person's life explains why coercion is the evil that it is, and why it provides an excuse to those who yield to it.'[35] Manipulation, on the other hand, rather than interfering with a person's options, 'perverts the way [a] person reaches decisions, forms preferences or adopts goals.'[36] Both are often also symbolic expressions of contempt or disregard toward their intended recipient who is thereby treated as a 'non-autonomous agent, an animal, a baby, or an imbecile.'[37] Independence from coercion and manipulation is, thus, Raz's second general condition of personal autonomy.

Alongside cognitive capacities necessary for project pursuit and independence, the final precondition of personal autonomy is an adequate range of options for choice. As we saw above, autonomous individuals shape their lives on their own terms and this self-creative activity is exercised primarily through choice. Yet clearly there must be an adequate range of options to choose from if one is to be author of one's life: 'the requirement of adequate choice is necessary to make sure that our control extends to all aspects of our lives.'[38] When is an option-set adequate, then, for personal autonomy?

The condition of adequacy is satisfied primarily through variety, and not number, of options. Because choices are guided by reasons, the options available for an autonomous individual must differ enough to rationally affect choice. A brief example illustrates why this is so. Consider two individuals, call them X and Y, presented with option-sets 1–3 and 4–10, respectively. Both have recently finished university and are (fortunately) in a position to choose where to work and live. Option 1 is a remote subtropical island with an agrarian economy; 2 is a North American city with a highly developed industrial sector; and 3 is a mid-sized English town populated largely by academics and researchers. Options 4, 5, 6, 7, 8, 9, and 10 are all subtropical islands with similar agrarian economies. Each of the three options in X's set differs geographically, climatically, socially, economically, and culturally. Y is presented with at least twice the number of options as X, but her 'choice' is insignificant insofar as 4–10 display little, if any, variety. With a smaller option-set, X has the possibility of choosing in accordance with her tastes, temperament, and talents, as well as of integrating her decision within her more comprehensive goals. Unless Y has, luckily, always aspired to cut sugarcane, her larger option-set contributes little to her personal autonomy, as 4–10 yield almost identical reasons for choice, none of which reflects her aims.

The contingency of option-set 4–10's adequacy on Y's goals suggests a further precondition. This is not a precondition that Raz, himself, spells out, but one implied by the three that he does. An autonomous individual's option-set must not only exhibit sufficient variety, but a person must have several options that are, *from her own point of view*, worthy of choice.[39] To be sufficient for personal autonomy, then, an option-set must satisfy four general conditions: it must contain (1) a plurality of options with (2) distinct opportunities that yield (3) significantly different reasons for choice and, of these, (4) at least one and ideally several[40] of them must be thought of as worthwhile by the agent in question.

Raz's view of personal autonomy links well-being to choice, and well-being is increased only through success in *intrinsically valuable* activities. The conjunction of both of these propositions yields the following dilemma: on the one hand, choice is somehow a constitutive aspect of well-being; on the other, well-being is rooted in the successful pursuit of intrinsically valuable activities (Condition 2) that do not depend upon choice for their value in any way. As Raz writes, 'Can anything we choose be good for us just because we choose it? ... we can only choose what we believe to be of value, and ... that value is independent of our choice.'[41] So while the contribution of options to our well-being is determined by their intrinsic value, and not by our choosing them, only our choosing them allows for them to contribute to our well-being.

At the core of Raz's ideal of personal autonomy, then, is this complex dynamic between choice and intrinsic value, and that ideal cannot be fairly evaluated without a subtler appreciation of the connection at work between these two elements. There are five[42] possibilities.

This first possible link entails a necessary correspondence between choice, intrinsic value, and well-being. In its stronger variant, it implies that the best way of promoting personal well-being is to allow people to choose for themselves because they are always the most reliable judges of their own interests. A weaker and more plausible version acknowledges that the correspondence between choice and well-being is contingent upon and subject to exceptions that are so infrequent – as, say, when one is about to cross a bridge known by others to be unsafe – that their connection should be treated as exceptionless for the purposes of legislation and public policy.

Raz's ideal of personal autonomy cannot sensibly rely upon such a connection for two reasons. First, that people either *never* or only *rarely* make self-destructive choices that adversely affect their well-being is patently false. Second, the necessary correspondence of choice and well-being is inconsistent with Raz's conception of authority. If people's well-being is always maximized by their choosing for themselves, then it is never reasonable for them to submit to the authoritative directives of others, including those of government. The first possible link, then, yields anarchism, not liberalism, and it renders the harm principle pointless to the extent that the latter is meant to guide authorities in the use of their coercive powers.

The second view entails a general correspondence between choice and well-being but privileges the latter in cases of conflict. That is, while people's well-being is normally improved through the unhampered exercise of their deliberative capacities, this is not always the case. Because, in this view, the value of choice is entirely derivative from its conduciveness to personal well-being, authorities may justifiably constrain people from making choices that are patently self-destructive. Raz maintains that people compromise their well-being by 'autonomously choosing the immoral'[43] and that, as such, they should be prevented from doing so within the limits set out in his revised harm principle. Tentatively at least, this suggests that his view of personal autonomy embodies a variant of this second possible link. Below, we shall see whether this is the case, or whether appearances are, in fact, misleading.

The third potential link is consistent with, but does not depend upon, a general correspondence between choice and well-being. However, it reverses the justificatory relationship between the core (well-being) and derivative (choice) values as set out in the second view above. The ideal of personal autonomy implied by this third connection regards choice itself as the most basic or foundational value. Even if voluntary choices *are* the most reliable indicators of which activities, goals, and relationships are conducive to well-being, authorities may not legitimately interfere with obviously self-destructive choices because personal autonomy itself is the most important moral value. Joel Feinberg adopts this position when he writes that the 'life that a person threatens by his own rashness is after all *his* life; it *belongs* to him and to no one else. For that reason alone, he must be the one to decide – for better or worse – what is to be done with it in that private realm where the interests of others are not directly involved.'[44] This is the idea of personal sovereignty as a moral right that we dismissed earlier as inconsistent with perfectionism to the extent that it abandons well-being as *the* foundational ethical value.

The fourth possible link between choice and well-being is unlike any of the others. It abandons both a necessary (link 1) and a general correspondence (link 2), as well as a lexical ordering (link 3) of the two values, in favour of a relatively unprincipled compromise. The value of personal autonomy is neither derived from, nor more basic than, people's well-being. This implies that when people pursue intrinsically worthless goals and relationships, authorities must balance the competing values of choice and well-being intuitively[45] because neither has general priority over the other. While this view accords well with Raz's commitment to value pluralism, that is, to the idea that 'there are various forms and styles of life which exemplify different virtues and which are incompatible,'[46] it is difficult to imagine how it, alone, could yield distinctively *liberal* conclusions. If choice is simply one among a plurality of competing values, then on what basis can Raz maintain the superiority of self-chosen lives?

The final possible connection between choice and intrinsically valuable lives is an internal or conceptual one. The contribution of valuable activities, goals, and relationships to people's well-being rests not simply in their intrinsic nature, but rather in their being chosen *because of that nature*. If this view is coherent, then intrinsically valuable activities such as friendship and athletic achievement, for example, are not competitors with autonomy; they presuppose it.[47] Only when intrinsically valuable things are pursued for the reasons provided by their value do they contribute to well-being.

4.3 Practical Reason, Value, and Authority

According to Raz, theoretical reason tells us what we may justifiably believe while practical reason tells us what we may justifiably do. A theoretical authority, in turn, is someone whose utterances are themselves reasons for believing that the propositions uttered are true; a practical authority is someone whose utterances yield reasons for acting in conformity with them. Because the exercise of coercive or any other form of power is no exercise of authority unless it includes an appeal for compliance by the person(s) subject to it, the typical exercise of authority is through giving instructions or commands of one kind or another. But when, precisely, can one person justifiably treat such instructions or commands of another as, themselves, reasons for believing or doing something? Put otherwise, what distinguishes legitimate authority from power?

Raz's answer to this question in *The Morality of Freedom* and elsewhere is complex and particularly dense. At bottom, however, the 'main justifying aim of authority is that it improves conformity with good reasons. It relies on its ability to achieve better consequences than any alternative for its justification.'[48] His argument for this proposition is found in three interrelated claims – what he calls the 'normal justification,' the 'dependence,' and, finally, the 'pre-emptive' theses.

The normal justification thesis stipulates that an authority is legitimate if the alleged subject of it is *'likely better to comply with reasons which apply to him (other than the alleged authoritative directives) if he accepts the directives of the alleged authority as authoritatively binding and tries to follow them, rather than by trying to follow the reasons which apply to him directly.'*[49] The dependence thesis, by contrast, is designed not to identify authorities, but rather to limit the types of reasons upon which they may legitimately rely in exercising their powers. It requires that all authoritative directives be based on 'dependent reasons'[50] – that is, on those that already independently apply to the subjects of the directives and are relevant to their action in the circumstances covered by them. Finally, because authorities do not have the right to impose completely independent duties on people, 'they have the right to replace people's own judgment on the merits of the case. Their directives pre-empt the force of at least some of the reasons which otherwise should have guided the actions of those people.'[51] Reasons for action or belief that are constituted by authoritative directives, then, are second-order exclusionary norms that summarize and ultimately displace the first-order ones upon which they depend. They are not simply to be added to the existing balance of reasons and weighted along with the rest, but pre-empt them.

The conjunction of these three claims yields the result that authoritative directives are binding and should be recognized as such even when they are (sometimes)[52] mistaken. This is because the advantage gained by accepting these directives would evaporate if they were ignored every time one of them failed to reflect right reason. Although the normal justification thesis assumes that the authority's judgements on a given issue or question are likely to be more reliable than those of its subjects, the subjects would be assessing the reasons upon which such judgements are based for themselves. Because the whole point and purpose of authorities, for Raz, is to pre-empt individual assessments on the merits of a case, evaluative independence of this kind would render them self-defeating.

The only limit that Raz places upon the scope of authority satisfying the normal justification thesis is an exemption clause that renders it inoperative when it is at least as important that people should choose for themselves as that they should choose wisely.[53] This constraint is one implication of what he calls the condition of subsidiarity, which says that 'governments have only as much legitimate power as it is necessary for them to have. Whenever adequate results can be achieved without governmental interference governments do not have the authority to interfere.'[54] The particular example he gives of something that satisfies this condition is the choice of one's friends.

Importantly, Raz's three theses apply to *all* types of practical authority. That authority is based on reason, and reasons are general guarantees that authority is, itself, essentially general. Governmental directives, that is to say, laws, are legitimate exercises of political authority, then, only to the extent that compliance with them satisfies the litmus test of practical authority generally – that they improve citizens' conformity with what reason antecedently requires. And because the epistemic, moral, and cognitive resources of individuals are likely to be radically different, this conception 'invites a piecemeal approach to the questions of the authority of governments.'[55] Governments will have varying degrees of authority across different individuals over the same substantive policy issues, depending upon how reasonable such people tend to be. As one commentator has perceptively observed, this 'most striking conclusion about political authority – that the scope of government's authority is likely to vary from citizen to citizen – merely serves to emphasize that political authority is *not* in a class by itself.'[56]

It is ultimately this foundational continuity between ethics and politics – between what reason demands of us and what we can rightfully demand from one another – that yields a perfectionist political morality in which value determines what is reasonable, and what is reasonable, in turn, establishes what is politically authoritative.

4.4 Moral Pluralism and the Harm Principle

Because autonomy is exercised through choice, and choice requires a plurality of reasons for action, it is possible only on the assumption that there exists a plurality of intrinsic values *other than autonomy* to yield such reasons.[57] For Raz, if autonomy is an ideal then we are committed to such a view of morality: 'Valuing autonomy leads to an endorsement of moral pluralism.'[58]

Although Raz appears to use the expressions 'value pluralism' and 'moral pluralism' interchangeably, there is also a sense in which they convey two different but related ideas. The first involves a conceptual claim about the relative commensurability of plural and conflicting values; the second embodies an ethical claim about the implications of the first one for comparative assessments of personal well-being.

For Raz, values are incommensurable if they do not appear on any common scale of ordering. His test for such value pluralism is a failure of transitivity. Thus, any two values are incommensurable if (1) it is not true that one is more valuable than the other or that they are of equal value *and* (2) there is or could be a third one more valuable than one but not the other.[59] The intransitivity that is indicative of incommensurable values is more easily grasped by distinguishing incommensurability with equality of value. By saying that two things are equally valuable, one is making a judgement about their relative value, namely, that they are the same; by saying that they are incommensurable, in contrast, one is rejecting the applicability of such a judgement to the values in question. Raz maintains that because incommensurability between intrinsic values is quite pervasive, reason often underdetermines which commitments, goals, and relationships people ought to choose.

While value pluralism constrains reason's ability to guide people in their choices, it neither renders such choices any less significant,[60] nor makes them arbitrary. Rationally under-determined choices are, or may be, non-arbitrary in two ways. First, they may still be based on reasons. For example, choice X may be incommensurate with its alternative Y because the reasons for each derive from values that are, themselves, incommensurate; however, this only negates the comparability, not the *value* of each of them. To the extent that they realize different values, both choices are reasonable ones. Second, value pluralism does not necessarily render rationally under-determined choices arbitrary because the latter may be in character. That is to say, 'the chooser is the kind of person who would choose thus in the prevailing circumstances.'[61] Because choices such as these exemplify, rather than compromise, personal autonomy, we see that incommensurability renders them neither trivial nor impossible.

Moral pluralism is the upshot of this value incommensurability for personal well-being. While only one of Raz's conditions of well-being refers explicitly to intrinsic value (Condition 2), the latter is clearly implicated in all three of the others. Comprehensive goals are the major determinant of our well-being (Condition 1), and these instantiate intrinsic value. The action reasons (Condition 3) that influence our well-being derive from these same comprehensive goals. Finally, social forms determine people's *access* to intrinsic value (Condition 4) – that is, they identify which particular valuable activities are available to people in any given society – but they are not the *source* of that value, which somehow inheres in the world itself. Value pluralism has a critical effect upon all four conditions, namely, that if intrinsic values cannot all be compared and ranked on one common scale, then obviously the lives of people that are constituted by such values must be similarly incommensurable. 'Moral pluralism' is Raz's expression for this ethical idea:

> Moral pluralism is the view that there are various forms and styles of life which exemplify different virtues and which are incompatible. Forms or styles of life are incompatible if, given reasonable assumptions about human nature, they cannot normally be exemplified in the same life. There is nothing to stop a person from being both an ideal teacher and an ideal family person. But a person cannot normally lead the life both of action and of contemplation, to use one of the traditionally recognized contrasts, nor can one person possess all the virtues of a nun and of a mother.[62]

Moral pluralism is a presupposition of autonomy from at least two separate perspectives. From the vantage point of autonomous agents, themselves, complete moral perfection is unattainable because 'the existence of more goods than can be chosen by one person, which are of widely differing character, speaks of the existence of more virtues than can be perfected by one person.'[63] No matter which form or style of life a person pursues, then, there are always other virtues that elude her because these are available only to those pursuing alternative and incompatible lifestyles.

This also creates a dilemma for us, the onlookers, in judging the relative success of autonomous lives. When we compare the lives of two moderately successful and equally content individuals who have very dissimilar comprehensive goals, it is often not the case that one person's well-being was greater, less than, or equal to the other's. Moral pluralism means that we simply lack any grounds for judging a career as a graphic designer, for instance, to be intrinsically better or worse for those engaged in it than a career as a livestock farmer or a gliding instructor.[64] The impossibility of identifying a single standard of perfection against which to measure relative levels of personal well-being stems from the plurality, not the paucity, of intrinsic value.

Moral pluralism is the argumentative hinge that links ethics to politics in Raz's defence of toleration. Somewhat paradoxically, the plurality and incommensurability of values both generates the need for a principle of political restraint, and also supplies that principle with its content.

Raz thinks that intrinsic values are not only incommensurable, but sometimes also competitive. He writes, 'The moral virtues associated with the diverse forms of life allowed by a morality which enables all normal persons to attain autonomy by moral means are very likely to depend on character traits many of which lead to intolerance of other acceptable forms of life.'[65] Because autonomy requires the availability of a plurality of intrinsically valuable options, and their pursuit presupposes, in turn, the possession of competitive virtues, respect for autonomy also establishes the necessity for toleration.

The competitive pluralism that prompts the need for toleration manifests itself in conflicts between incompatible as well as between rival ways of life. Incompatible lifestyles are those that cannot normally be adopted by the same people because of certain contingent limitations that inhere in either them or in their circumstances. For instance, 'the way of life of town dwellers is incompatible with the way of life of the inhabitants of the prairies or of remote mountains.'[66] Although nothing logically precludes urbanites from *valuing* rural comprehensive goals such as cattle ranching, town dwellers are unlikely to possess the requisite virtues for *succeeding* in them because towns provide their residents with few, if any, opportunities to develop these virtues. For Raz, the virtues that are a constitutive part of one of these incompatible lifestyles normally lead their possessors to be intolerant of limitations deriving from the distinctive virtues of the other.[67] People with *rival* ways of life, by contrast, are intolerant of one another for a different reason. Because rival forms of life such as, say, Islam and Christianity each contain attitudes, beliefs, and practices that the other *logically* excludes, one person cannot consistently endorse both of them.

Earlier, we said that Raz's view of well-being yields liberal conclusions because its focus on agency (Conditions 1–4) implies that intrinsically valuable lives must be self-chosen ones, and these are possible only under conditions of political freedom. Now, we have a second reason why perfectionist ethics entail liberal politics – moral pluralism. If disagreement, condemnation, and hostility are essential elements of valuable but rival ways of life, then a state committed to promoting well-being must somehow distinguish between disapproval that expresses and intolerance that violates the personal autonomy of its citizens. Raz believes that a modified version of Mill's harm principle is particularly well suited to achieving this discriminatory task.

Raz's harm principle differs from its historical predecessor – the one we encountered in chapter 2 above – in at least three important ways. Whereas Mill's version prevents both individuals and the state from coercing people to refrain from certain activities or to undertake others, on the ground that those activities are either valueless or objectionable, Raz's 'read[ily] embrace[s] ... various paternalistic measures.'[68] For Raz, the point of the harm principle is not to exclude perfectionist ideals from politics, but instead to guide political authorities in the proper way to enforce them. Because political authorities have a duty to promote well-being, the Razian harm principle allows them to use coercion both to prevent people from acting in ways that would diminish either their own or other people's autonomy, *and* in order to force them to take actions that are required to improve peoples' options and opportunities.

The second main difference is a direct result of the first. Raz collapses the self- versus other-regarding distinction at the heart of Mill's anti-paternalism. The overall plausibility of the putative link between perfectionism and liberalism, then, rests entirely upon Raz's notion of harm, a tactic that Mill's formulation carefully strives to avoid. If moral ideals may not be promoted coercively except when this is required to prevent harm, then the range of freedoms available to people under the authority of perfectionist governments can be established only once it is known precisely which activities, goals, commitments, and relationships are, in fact, harmful.

Because 'harm' implies that the action causing it is prima facie wrong, it is a thick or normative concept that acquires its meaning from the moral theory within which it is embedded.[69] If well-being provides the moral foundation for the harm principle as Raz contends, then we may reasonably infer that people harm themselves or others by doing one or more of the following four objectionable things: (1) by frustrating their success or inducing their failure in (non-biologically determined) comprehensive goals; (2) by deflecting them away from intrinsically valuable activities and/or by leading them to adopt worthless or immoral ones; (3) by inhibiting their success as agents; and, finally, (4) by limiting their participation and, thus, their likelihood of success in socially defined pursuits and activities. Ultimately, to inflict harm is to prevent either oneself or others from being autonomous.

The final difference between Raz's reinterpreted harm principle and Mill's is simply that Raz distinguishes between two things that Mill insists must be treated identically – physical versus moral well-being.

4.5 Raz's Harm Principle Examined

The harm principle's central purpose is to distinguish liberties that governments must always respect from others that may be legitimately circumscribed in order to advance a number of important collective goals. Raz's view of well-being provides the moral foundation for this principle. As a result, (negative) liberty is valuable because it is, and only to the extent that it is, a concomitant of the ideal of personal autonomy – of people creating their own lives through self-defining choices from a plurality of worthwhile options. But if the value of liberty derives exclusively from that of the activities, commitments, and relationships that it renders possible,[70] then precisely what does the harm principle imply for the legislation and public policy of a liberal perfectionist state?

Raz's view of well-being suggests three general guidelines for such policy. First, its primary aim should be the promotion and protection of 'positive freedom which is understood as the capacity for autonomy, consisting of the availability of an adequate range of options, and of the mental abilities necessary for an autonomous life.'[71] Second, it should actively promote personal autonomy through the creation and sustenance of a social, cultural, and economic environment conducive to that ideal rather than simply to protect against violations of it. Finally, no goal may be pursued politically by means that infringe on people's autonomy 'unless such action is justified by the need to protect or promote the autonomy of those people or of others.'[72]

Raz thinks that these guidelines produce, in turn, two main limitations on the autonomy-based freedom that a perfectionist state makes available to its citizens. Personal autonomy requires that people have an adequate range of options available to them so that their choices simultaneously embody both endorsements and rejections of different and potentially incommensurable reasons for action. However, nothing in this requirement tells conclusively in favour of protecting any one particular option: 'The autonomous life depends not on the availability of one option or freedom of choice. It depends on the general character of one's environment and culture.'[73] Because the barometer of option-adequacy is this general environment and culture rather than the particular components that constitute it, the state may justifiably eliminate particular options and replace them with others if it has undefeated reasons for doing so.

Clearly, the longer and the more deeply committed people are to their projects, the less willing and able they are likely to be to abandon them in favour of government-sponsored alternatives. The well-being of people who have been training all of their lives to play in the World Cup would be harmed by the elimination of, say, football (soccer) in ways that that of disinterested spectators or even fans would not. Because preventing people from carrying on with their chosen projects, commitments, and relationships hinders their ability to be autonomous, the harm principle requires that perfectionist-inspired changes in the options a society makes available be gradual so that they will not affect committed persons.

The second main limitation of autonomy-based freedom is that it does not extend to 'the morally bad and repugnant.'[74] To be autonomous, a person must pursue the good as she sees it, and she can do this only if she believes that she has several – and ideally many – valuable options to choose from. However, this is consistent with many of her options actually being bad or valueless. Autonomy is partially blind, then, to the relative quality of the options available for choice in the sense that one is no less autonomous for being actively depraved or immoral. But while autonomy is consistent with the presence of bad options, they contribute nothing to its value: 'autonomously choosing the bad makes one's life worse than a comparable non-autonomous life.'[75] Because autonomy is valuable only if exercised in pursuit of the good, it 'supplies no reason to provide, nor any reason to protect worthless let alone bad options.'[76]

Raz admits that what he calls 'full-blooded'[77] perfectionism is likely to arouse popular resistance in most countries, if not in all. Accordingly, he thinks that it should be confined to things that command a large measure of social consensus. For instance, perfectionist political action may be taken in support of social institutions that enjoy unanimous support in the community in order to recognize them formally, to harmonize them with various legal and administrative arrangements, as well as to encourage the belief in their value to future generations.[78] For Raz, the legal recognition of monogamous marriage and the prohibition of polygamy have this significance in many countries around the world.

This suggests that not all perfectionist-inspired legislation and public policy involves the coercive imposition of a lifestyle by dominant groups on other, less powerful, ones. Much of it could be 'encouraging and facilitating action of the desired kind, or discouraging undesired modes of behaviour.'[79] Examples of the former include conferring honours on creative and performing artists, and giving grants or loans to people who start community centres; with respect to the latter, certain types of leisure activities such as hunting could be taxed more heavily than others. In either case, political action in pursuit of conceptions of the good falls well short of the 'threatening popular image of imprisoning people who follow their religion, express their views in public, grow long hair, or consume harmless drugs.'[80]

For Raz, scepticism about the *tolerance* of a state duty-bound to eliminate or, more mildly, to discourage, whatever options it considers morally repugnant ignores the centrality of the normal justification and dependency theses to the overall argument for the liberal perfectionist state. Recall that reasons derive from intrinsic value, and that because political authority is not in a class by itself, states must act on the basis of dependent reasons – that is, on those that apply to their subjects anyway. As a result, the fact that the state *considers* anything to be valuable or valueless is no reason for action on the part of either the state or its subjects; only its *being* valuable or valueless is such a reason. So Raz's moral theory is both the foundation and the safety valve of the perfectionist state: people are not in danger of being persecuted in the name of false ideals because when governmental directives fail to track right reason, they cease to be authoritative. This is ultimately why Raz's harm principle differs so fundamentally from its historical predecessor. A strict inhibition against paternalism such as Mill's is dispensable because it is inconceivable that such a safeguard should ever be needed with Raz's view of authority already and securely in place.

Alongside the normal justification and dependency theses stands moral pluralism in Raz's overall case for the compatibility of state perfectionism and civil liberty. Political action in pursuit of conceptions of the good will not compromise personal autonomy, because intrinsic value is pluralistic. That is to say, even if, *per impossibile*, government managed to discourage or eliminate all of the repugnant options in society, a multiplicity of potentially incommensurable but intrinsically valuable options would remain to choose from. Because the harm principle promotes and protects *these* options, the resulting conditions are favourable to personal autonomy.

The next considerations meant to allay liberal worries about the seemingly unlimited powers of the perfectionist state are essentially pragmatic. In principle, morally repugnant options are not protected from coercive interference on the ground that they have been freely chosen, because the value of choice itself is parasitic upon the value of what is chosen, which, we are assuming in this case, has none. Nonetheless, 'the harm principle is defensible in the light of the principle of autonomy for one simple reason. The means used, coercive interference, violates the autonomy of its victim.'[81] It does so in two basic ways. First, coercion violates the condition of independence and 'expresses a relation of domination and an attitude of disrespect for the coerced individual.'[82] Second, criminal penalties are a 'global and indiscriminate invasion of autonomy.'[83] By imprisoning a person, for instance, the state prevents her from almost every conceivable autonomous pursuit. Admittedly, other less severe forms of coercion are available, but all of these still invade autonomy in a fairly indiscriminate way. Because there is no practical way of ensuring that coercion will restrict the victim's choice of repugnant options without also interfering with her other (valuable) choices, using coercion to promote well-being is necessarily self-defeating and, thus, illegitimate.

Raz's final claim has somewhat of a Kantian dimension to it. While the harm principle merely guides rather than rules out state paternalism, governments should not use coercion to discourage what Raz calls 'victimless immoralities' because measures such as criminalization interfere with people's 'general standing as autonomous beings.'[84] Coercive invasions of autonomy are sometimes required to protect the autonomy of others and they are justified when this is the case. Otherwise, respect for this general standing dictates a policy of toleration that goes beyond recognizing the plurality of intrinsic values.

Putting all of this together, Raz thinks that state perfectionism is compatible with a due regard for individual liberty because:

1 It is limited to legislation and public policy measures with nearly unanimous support;
2 It is primarily non-coercive;
3 It is authoritative only when reasonable;

4 It leaves a multiplicity of valuable options intact for people to choose from;
5 It tolerates (some) morally repugnant but autonomous choices because of the practical difficulties of coercively interfering with them;
6 It respects the general standing of autonomous beings by not interfering with victimless immoralities.

A cursory glance at this list reveals that it comprises two distinct sets of considerations. Items 1, 2, and 5 are largely pragmatic or political ones that explain why perfectionist public policy that has the advancement of well-being as its goal is unlikely to succeed when undertaken coercively. The other three items (3, 4, and 6) are ethical propositions meant to link Raz's moral theory directly to liberal toleration.

On the very last page of *The Morality of Freedom*, Raz concedes that full-blooded perfectionism is likely to arouse popular resistance leading to civil strife. Therefore it should be confined to public policies that command 'a large measure of social consensus.'[85] Elsewhere in the book, however, he introduces a different constraint when he writes that perfectionism should be limited to things enjoying 'unanimous support in the community.'[86] Raz's equivocation makes it difficult to see precisely what requirement he has in mind. Although 'large measure of social consensus' is unhelpfully vague, this obviously imposes much less stringent restrictions on state perfectionism than does unanimity. In either case, however, it is doubtful whether any perfectionist-inspired measures actually meet this condition. To my knowledge, Raz provides no examples of public policy satisfying the weaker formulation, and the only one that he does adduce as evidence of the stronger one is the legal recognition of monogamous marriage.[87] Unless monogamous marriage is interpreted loosely to the point of vacuity so that virtually any type of committed relationship qualifies, it is in fact a counter-example to the position it is designed to support. In the United States and Canada, for instance, two autonomy-supporting environments of the kind to which Raz's argument applies, Mormons, swingers, homosexuals, atheists, and unmarried parents, to mention but a few, all reject (though for different reasons) the predominant or orthodox view that a monogamous, heterosexual, and religiously inspired partnership should be officially enshrined as the state-sanctioned union of choice. If Raz's position safeguards liberty, then this is only because the pervasive ethical disagreement that renders it necessary actually rules out the very state perfectionism it is intended to guide.

Even if we concede, against our better judgement, that there *are* perfectionist public policy measures that command nearly unanimous support in a given political community, we can and should ask ourselves whether this ethical homogeneity is the result of informed and reasoned deliberation, and mindless conformity, or simply the product of coercion and manipulation. John Rawls, for instance, argues persuasively that the Inquisition's suppression of heresy during the Middle Ages was not a historical accident; it was necessary to preserve a shared belief in the Catholic faith.[88] Until we investigate the conditions under which consensus or unanimity obtain, then, Raz's first safeguard offers little protection for individual liberty. State perfectionism may be limited to public policy that receives a large measure of popular support, but this requirement threatens, rather than safeguards, individual liberty if such support itself is the product of intense social pressure or political bullying.

One important implication of Raz's view of authority that we discussed earlier is that consent has virtually no role to play in the justification of political coercion. This is so for two main reasons. First, consent is binding only if it meets certain conditions, but as per the normal justification thesis, these conditions are themselves roughly those that establish the legitimacy of an authority independently of consent. Second, to consent to coercion is ultimately to endorse a loss of independence. However, a complete loss of independence destroys one's autonomy altogether and makes a valuable life impossible as a result, while a partial loss diminishes it and renders one's life less successful and worthwhile. If the value of independence was conditional upon one's desiring it, then consent *could* possibly avert these consequences. However, because the value of independence for Raz is absolute, those who lack the desire for it lack self-respect and diminish their lives by this fact alone.

Tentatively, there appears to be, if not a contradiction, then at least somewhat of a tension between this view of consent and Raz's claim that state perfectionism is consistent with individual liberty because it will be limited to policy measures that command (nearly?) unanimous popular support. On the one hand, Raz's first safeguard appeals first and foremost to the actual distribution of ethical views in a given community – the scope of political perfectionism is determined by the relative level of consensus therein; on the other, consent plays no role in the justification of legitimate authority, which is based upon general reasons deriving from intrinsic value. Admittedly, the large consensus/unanimity requirement is a prudential calculation about when state perfectionism is likely to succeed, not about when it is legitimate. But there *is* something peculiar about this requirement to the extent that it arises against the backdrop of a moral theory that places virtually no weight at all upon what people actually believe in favour of what is objectively *true*. Below, we explain the basis of this peculiarity. Raz's last-minute shift away from what we may call the God's-eye view of truth at the core of his moral theory towards consensus is unsurprising: the latter is a remedy for the inevitable political problems that ethical pluralism creates for the former.

Finally, the large consensus/unanimity requirement inverts one of the oldest insights of the liberal tradition. Historically, liberals have argued that contingencies such as nationality, religion,[89] and socio-economic status,[90] for instance, should not be the basis of one's political entitlements in a just society committed to equal freedom. They have also maintained that minorities are most vulnerable to persecution and, thus, in need of stringent protections when majorities are overwhelmingly predominant and powerful. Yet Raz's first safeguard, if it can be so called, jettisons both of these ideas. The likelihood of being able to live according to one's own perception of what is ultimately valuable in life unimpeded by the state depends crucially upon one's relative popularity with one's co-citizens. The more unpopular one is, the more one is in need of protection, but according to Raz, this is precisely when full-blooded perfectionism should be undertaken by the state.

There are several reasons, then, why Raz's contention that the (near) unanimity requirement adequately safeguards personal liberty is problematic: no perfectionist public policy measures actually satisfy the requirement, so we are unsure what the standard in question ultimately is; unanimity alone tells us virtually nothing about the conditions under which it obtains, and these may be intolerably oppressive; it is difficult to square Raz's rejection of consent within his overall moral theory with the centrality that consensus assumes in his defence of perfectionism; and, finally, the unanimity requirement advocates full-blooded state perfectionism precisely when liberals traditionally have been most concerned with insulating minorities from its reach.

Raz's second reason for thinking that perfectionism is consistent with individual liberty is that the public policy of the liberal-perfectionist state is, or at least should be, primarily non-coercive. Does this claim fare any better than his first one? To begin with, we should remind ourselves of what non-coercive perfectionist measures amount to for Raz. The primary examples he gives of encouraging and facilitating rather than coercing are the conferring of honours on creative or performing artists, and giving grants or loans to people who start community centres. As for discouraging undesirable modes of behaviour, he cites taxing certain leisure activities such as hunting more heavily than others. Each of these strategies – subsidizing and taxing – influences people primarily by altering the opportunity costs of the activities to which they are applied. A subsidy decreases the opportunity costs to a person contemplating engaging in a given activity by transferring some of them onto others through the redistributive mechanisms of the state. For example, a person normally unwilling to forgo $150 to attend intrinsically valuable but capital-intensive artistic or creative events such as opera perhaps *would* be willing to do so if the cost was reduced to $50 through a government subsidy. A tax, on the other hand, operates in precisely the opposite direction by *increasing* the opportunity costs involved in participating in activities that the state considers for some reason valueless or morally repugnant. In contemplating whether or not to head for the woods and kill a deer, for instance, Raz's prospective hunter must not only assess the intrinsic merits of her controversial leisure activity, she must also decide whether it is still worthwhile *given* the additional resources and, thus, the other opportunities she will necessarily forfeit through taxation by doing so.

If the liberal perfectionist state is committed to 'moulding'[91] rather than satisfying the existing preferences of its citizens in this way, then this is highly problematic in light of Raz's own indictment of manipulation in *The Morality of Freedom*. As one critic[92] points out, Raz says virtually nothing about manipulation beyond the fact that, like coercion, it interferes with autonomy, that it is often endowed with a symbolic social meaning beyond its consequential impact, and that its use in politics should be restricted as the use of coercion is. Of interest to us, however, is the particular reason *why*, for Raz, manipulation violates autonomy: it 'perverts the way [a] person reaches decisions, forms preferences or adopts goals.'[93] This indictment of decisional perversion is puzzling because in the absence of a more detailed account of manipulation, this appears to be precisely what perfectionist subsidies and taxes would do. While all subsidies and taxes have inherent distributional effects to the extent that they render certain activities more or less costly, only perfectionist ones are *motivated* by the desire to encourage or discourage *specific* activities, rather than simply to finance those that people freely choose *ex post*.

To bring this distinction into clearer focus, consider the following. A tax for the upkeep of a provincial park, for instance, is not raised to discourage people from entering it, but rather to finance the provision of this public good for its users. A tax motivated by the intrinsic disvalue of hunting, on the other hand, *is* levied with the aim of reducing the likelihood that people will choose to kill animals for sport. It is difficult to see how artificially and intentionally altering the costs of various options in this way is consistent with the independence from manipulation that Raz thinks people require to be personally autonomous.

Subsidies are manipulative in a similar way when they are substantial enough to induce people to engage in activities they otherwise would not: 'we would then worry because people were responding, not to the nobility of the activity, but to the bribe that was being offered for pursuing it.'[94] Government can certainly make farming, for example, less costly and thus more attractive than gambling by handing out free land and increasing so-called sin taxes on flights to Las Vegas. Justifying this on perfectionist grounds is rather difficult, however, if Raz is correct in believing that people's well-being is improved only when they respond to intrinsic value *on their own*.

Raz's final claim concerns the indiscriminate effects of governmental coercion. Because of the putative difficulties involved in coercively interfering with morally repugnant or valueless choices without also restricting those that instantiate intrinsic value, Raz thinks that governments should err on the side of caution by tolerating immoral activities where these do not also harm others. One obvious and relatively easy way to discredit this blunt instrument argument for toleration is simply to sharpen it – that is, to provide a variety of counter-examples that illustrate the possibility of precise or narrowly tailored coercive measures that target what are thought to be morally repugnant options with minimal or non-existent spillover effect.[95] Consider the following laws:

1 Those that prohibit the production, distribution, and possession of 'obscene' materials
2 Those that prohibit the publication or dissemination of opinions that are critical of government policy and/or political leaders
3 Those that prohibit same-sex marriages
4 Those that prohibit the sale and/or the possession of contraceptives
5 Those that prohibit the production, possession, and consumption of drugs such as alcohol, tobacco, and marijuana

If the only sanction for violating laws 1, 4, and 5 is confiscation of the illicit materials in question, then they are clearly enforceable without greatly affecting people's other worthwhile choices. As long as there remains plenty of other valuable things to read, movies to watch, ways to have sex, and substances to ingest, Razian personal autonomy is intact. With respect to type-2 laws, social critics could be simply fined rather than jailed, and television and radio stations could have their licences revoked should authorities find their communications to be unreasonable. Similarly, under type-3 laws, homosexuals would not be prevented from cohabiting with their partners, but only from having such arrangements legally recognized and from obtaining whatever attendant (fiscal, social, or symbolic) benefits this recognition brings.

These examples illustrate three basic defects of Raz's argument. First, it has a limited utility, given its excessively narrow scope. As one critic points out, at best, it is 'an autonomy-based argument against the penalty of imprisonment for morally repugnant actions, but it is not sufficient to justify rejection of all coercive prohibitions of immoral (though harmless) behaviour.'[96] Second, Raz's argument trivializes the many ways in which people often have their life-prospects diminished – by being denied the legal recognition others are given, for instance – by reducing them all to either coercion or manipulation. Finally, it reintroduces, via our counter-examples, the ambiguity and thus the inadequacy of Raz's conception of manipulation. On the one hand, a view of manipulation that rules out as inconsistent with personal autonomy the sanctions (fines, confiscations, revocations of licences, etc.) implicated in laws 1–5 above also necessarily excludes perfectionist taxes and subsidies of the kind that Raz defends, for all of these measures simply make certain choices more difficult or costly, rather than impossible; on the other, to say that these are *not* inherently manipulative is scarcely plausible because they are specifically designed to alter people's choices.

The failure of each of Raz's three practical safeguards implies that if political intolerance is, in fact, objectionable, then this must be for reasons having to do with its injustice, not its impracticality. Because none of the considerations that we have surveyed so far adequately protects individual freedom in a perfectionist state, the argumentative burden of Raz's position falls squarely upon his three remaining ethical claims, which are equally unsuccessful.

Raz's first ethical safeguard is that political perfectionism will not unduly threaten individual liberty because, in the end, *it is authoritative only when reasonable.* One way of cashing this claim out is to test it against intolerant legislation of the kind outlined in 1–5 above. Perhaps laws criminalizing political dissent and homosexuality are illegitimate not because they are coercive or manipulative, then, but rather because they are unreasonable to the extent that the ongoing criticism of political leaders and same-sex relationships are, for differing reasons, intrinsically valuable activities after all. Seen from this perspective, Raz's first ethical safeguard is a reformulation of the normal justification and dependency theses applied to political authority – because people can only be made to abide by directives that reason antecedently requires, only unreasonable people are likely to have their wants, desires, and choices frustrated by perfectionist laws and public policies.

The problem is that value pluralism implies that reason underdetermines many, if not most, ethical controversies. We cannot simply appeal to what is reasonable in order to settle political disputes over the scope and content of perfectionist state action because, if Raz is correct, reason is partially what creates them. If intrinsic values are sometimes mutually exclusive because they make either incompatible or rival demands on what people should think or do, then reason licenses a plurality of inconsistent ethical beliefs and actions. A principle of political restraint that relies upon what is reasonable (in Raz's sense) for its content is therefore either incoherent or politically useless: if reason mandates only one determinate set of ethical beliefs, then moral pluralism is false as an account of what generates the need for a principle of toleration; but if moral pluralism is true, then that principle cannot sensibly rely upon it for its content because ethical disagreement arising from differing but equally reasonable perceptions of what is, in fact, intrinsically valuable is the very problem that liberal tolerance is meant to remedy.

Another way of stating this problem is to ask, Who will be the judge of what is reasonable for the purposes of perfectionist state action? This question clearly has two different senses that Raz's argument seems to elide. While personal autonomy implies that everyone will be the judge of what is intrinsically valuable and, thus, reasonable for herself, this diffusion of epistemic authority cannot survive unmodified in political form because conflicting perceptions of intrinsic value mean that an exercise in *adjudication* is required. Although each person will decide on her own what is reasonable or not, politically at least, *someone's* decision must be determinative or binding in cases of controversy. Because government itself will ultimately judge the reasonableness of its own policy, Raz's first safeguard embodies the very 'inconveniences'[97] of the Lockean state of nature to which liberal constitutionalism is meant to respond.

What about Raz's second ethical safeguard? State perfectionism need not be illiberal because it *leaves a multiplicity of valuable options intact for people to choose from,* even after political action has been taken to eradicate or discourage those that are morally repugnant or valueless. Assessing the plausibility of this claim requires that we examine the connections that Raz defends between moral pluralism, the social forms thesis, and toleration.

Recall that, for Raz, 'the moral virtues associated with the diverse forms of life allowed by a morality which enables all normal persons to attain autonomy by moral means are very likely to depend on character traits many of which lead to intolerance of other acceptable forms of life.'[98] If certain intrinsically valuable activities exclude others because they are not all realizable within the space of one human life, because they exemplify incompatible virtues (e.g., those of a nun vs those of a mother), or because they make rival truth claims (e.g., Christianity vs Islam), then each person's development will be bought at the cost of certain personal deficiencies that they would or at least could have avoided had they chosen a different life for herself. The political promotion of autonomy leads to intolerance, then, because the cultivation and perfection of virtues attendant to certain intrinsically valuable activities also tends to produce in their possessors hostility towards deficiencies that are largely inevitable by-products of other people's differing perfections.

It is notoriously difficult to explain why we should ever allow people to do, or believe in, things that we rightly disapprove of when we have the power to stop them. To disapprove of something is to judge it to be wrong. If our judgements express moral imperatives in this way rather than simply subjective preferences, then they imply, in turn, that the objects of our disapproval are properly preventable. But if our objections to others are indeed reasonable, then why should we be tolerant? Moral pluralism is Raz's answer. Autonomous people must be sensitive to a plurality of incompatible but genuinely valuable options eligible for choice. They can begin charting their own courses through life with a subtle appreciation for a wide range of goods and lifestyles very different from their own. And once people recognize that their intolerant inclinations are directed at limitations deriving from such different but intrinsically valuable beliefs or activities, they will curb their desires to restrain or coercively interfere with others.

For Raz, then, moral pluralism is both an explanation of the genesis of intolerance in autonomy-supportive environments, and also a putative remedy for it. Moral pluralism is an account of what Raz takes to be the objective structure of intrinsic value – namely its plurality and incommensurability. This is a philosophical claim whose truth is not dependent upon its being widely accepted; it is, as Hart would have said, a matter of critical rather than positive morality. However, before moral pluralism can serve as a remedy for intolerance, it *must* move beyond a controversial philosophical claim about the fragmentation of ethical value to a widely accepted idea that changes the way people's existing beliefs are held in society. The citizens of the liberal perfectionist state must be reflective moral pluralists, that is, they must endorse Raz's philosophical account of the structure of intrinsic value before it can supply *them* with a reason to tolerate other people's limitations. One obvious objection to this is that Raz clearly misrepresents how most people experience ethical controversy: what he depicts as a clash between plural and conflicting intrinsic values is normally thought of in terms of a confrontation between true (mine) and false (other people's) beliefs. This dichotomy between the perspectives of the citizen and that of the political philosopher has the following result. On the one hand, if citizens of the Razian state are *not* appreciative of the plurality and incommensurability of intrinsic values, then moral pluralism cannot serve as a foundation for justifying tolerance because it has no effect upon the beliefs of the only people who count – those tempted to persecute others through the coercive apparatus of the state. On the other, if they do endorse the philosopher's metaphysical thesis about the structure of value, then toleration becomes inappropriate because people cannot reasonably object to limitations that are logically inseparable from, or constitutive aspects of, intrinsically valuable activities.

One possible explanation for this dilemma is that while Raz's account of the genesis of intolerance relies upon *two* sets of concerns, the putative solution he advances focuses upon only one of them, and the wrong one at that. He tells us that people tend not to suffer limitations that are *incompatible* with their own virtues, and that people's valuable activities and beliefs often logically exclude the *rival* truth-claims of those of others. People are intolerant, then, both because they are insufficiently broad-minded to appreciate a plurality of valuable activities where these are different from those they themselves actually participate in, and because they believe in things that logically commit them to denying the beliefs of others. However, as we saw above, the moral-pluralist argument for toleration misrepresents how ethical conflict is most often experienced in assuming a widespread belief in a controversial metaphysical thesis about value incommensurability. While the problem that tolerance raises in its most acute form is the issue of how *rival* truth-claims can be adjudicated politically, in focusing on incompatibility, Raz's argument does not address this at all.

The Razian harm principle is symptomatic of this conceptual telescoping. The traditional Millian version precludes coercively interfering with individual actions on any other grounds than harm to others. The foundation of the Razian version, however, is a perfectionist ideal of personal autonomy whereby choice is valuable only to the extent that it is aimed at worthwhile activities. This strategy of justifying toleration on the basis of the incompatibility of intrinsic *goods* renders the harm principle (1) pointless because if only valuable or morally upright actions are protected from coercive interference, then there is nothing to tolerate; and (2) incoherent because, within Raz's own moral theory, people cannot reasonably object to what is intrinsically good.

So moral pluralism cannot serve as an adequate remedy for intolerance. Could the social forms component of Raz's view of well-being rescue his second ethical safeguard? Perhaps his contention that state perfectionism will respect individual liberty should be read within the context of his claim that personal well-being depends to a considerable extent on people's success in socially defined pursuits and activities. If liberty is a precondition of both participation and success in a society's social forms, then it appears as though a state committed to promoting well-being will have to be tolerant. Appearances are deceptive.

Raz maintains that what is required for individual well-being varies so that 'not everyone has an interest in personal autonomy ... [which] is a cultural value, i.e., of value to people living in certain societies only.'[99] These modern industrial societies are characterized by rapidly changing technologies and the free movement of labour which call for 'an ability to adjust, to acquire new skills, to move from one subculture to another, to come to terms with new scientific and moral views.'[100] Concern with autonomy is therefore concern with the environment in not one, but two, senses. The *content* of autonomous lives will vary across societies, depending upon the particular range of activities made available by the social forms therein, and the *value* of self-chosen lives will depend upon whether or not autonomy and, thus, liberty is a precondition for succeeding in these social forms.

Raz's second ethical claim is meant to establish that perfectionism will safeguard liberty because personal autonomy requires moral pluralism, that is, because it presupposes the availability of an adequate range of intrinsically valuable options for people to choose from. There is a serious problem with indexing the value of liberty in this way. If liberty is, in fact, valuable only because of its contribution to the sort of options available in modern industrial societies, then it cannot be a reason to promote or sustain those options should they change or decline – such transformations would merely signal that the importance of liberty itself had changed or declined.[101] Because Raz embeds the requirement of option-adequacy within the social forms thesis, the crucial link at the core of his argument between moral pluralism and toleration is severed: people will always be free enough to participate in their society's social forms no matter how few or how many options they actually have, because those social forms are precisely what *determine* how many options people *should* have.

Clearly then, Raz's second ethical argument does not adequately safeguard liberty within the very autonomy-supporting environments to which, for him, it applies. But there are also two further interrelated problems with the particular scope of Raz's contextual argument for the value of autonomy. First, if autonomy-supporting conditions are a prerequisite for defending liberalism, then liberal institutions and practices are justifiable only where they already exist. This means that arguing for the value of autonomy in pre-industrial or underdeveloped areas of the world where the need for tolerance is often most pressing is not only impractical, but illegitimate as well. Second, there is an inconsistency between Raz's universalist account of the genesis of ethical disagreement or conflict and the constricted scope of the remedy that he advances. It is true that Raz's view of moral pluralism is partly about how certain contingent limitations inherent in human lives prevent people from accommodating the entire range of valuable activities that are available to them. But the foundational incommensurability (value pluralism) upon which moral pluralism is partly based is *not* an empirical claim about the nature of people's current beliefs in any particular part of the world, but rather a metaphysical one that purports to describe the real structure of intrinsic value generally. If there are values that are plural and conflicting independently of the contingent beliefs or limitations of particular individuals or groups, then it seems to follow both that people are faced with pluralist choices whether or not they recognize them as such, and also that virtues such as personal autonomy necessary to make these choices will be important to *any* recognizably human life. To the extent that value pluralism implies that everyone should be personally autonomous, Raz's contextual argument for liberalism is unduly narrow in scope.

Raz's final argument to support his contention that state perfectionism need not be intolerant is that it *respects the general standing of autonomous beings by not interfering with victimless immoralities.* This putative safeguard on liberty raises two important questions: In what does such general standing consist, and how are we to understand victimless immoralities?

One obvious difficulty in making sense of Raz's notion of general standing comes from the particular qualifications that he places upon the
value of autonomy itself. While this notion relies implicitly on autonomy
as a general value, Raz's overall moral theory restricts the worth of a self-
chosen life exclusively to autonomy-supporting environments whose
shared social forms require it, and to morally respectable choices that
instantiate intrinsic value. As Donald Regan points out, this is incoherent: 'There is no inconsistency in saying that autonomy is autonomy even
when it chooses the bad, and saying also that autonomy is valuable only
when it chooses the good. But there is an inconsistency in asserting both
of these propositions and in supposing also (as Raz does) that autonomy,
tout court, is valuable. These three propositions taken together entail that
autonomy which chooses the bad both is and is not valuable.'[102]

Regan correctly identifies this problem, but not its source, which is
even more important. Raz must maintain that autonomy is intrinsically
valuable in order to explain the general standing that authoritative or
legitimate governments are bound to respect, because this standing is
what is supposed to exclude coercive state paternalism. Otherwise, this
status is foundationless and whatever respect is owed to people accrues
simply on account of the value of their particular choices – if people's
choices are directed at the good, then their autonomy should be
respected, if not, then not. This is an implausible basis for justifying
liberal tolerance because, first, only valuable choices are protected and
second, we cannot reasonably object to these. However, Raz *cannot* consistently maintain that choice per se is valuable to provide an ethical
foundation for the harm principle without also undermining his central
perfectionist claim that bad or immoral choices are worthless and, thus,
undeserving of protection from coercive state interference. Either Raz's
moral theory or the political conclusions it entails must be revised, then.

The idea of victimless immoralities fares little better. While all coercion violates the independence that is one of the main preconditions of
personal well-being, Raz allows that the state may justifiably coerce people to prevent them from harming others, that is, in order to prevent
injustice. But if injustice is wrong and, thus, coercively preventable
because of the detrimental impact it has on personal well-being, then on
Raz's own perfectionist assumptions, *all* immorality has a victim – by acting in unreasonable but nonetheless self-regarding ways, people damage, neglect, or short-change integral aspects of their own well-being.[103]
There is no reason of principle why a perfectionist state should be any
less concerned with vice than it is with injustice if both have a common

source in compromising personal well-being. Once the traditional harm principle's operative distinction between injustice and (self-regarding) immorality collapses, there are no remaining restrictions against state paternalism.

4.6 Perfectionism and Politics

The ultimate failure of Raz's argument for toleration is symptomatic of a more general problem that makes perfectionism a bad foundation for liberal political morality.

For Raz, the foundation of practical reasoning is intrinsic value. Generally speaking, people only have reasons to perform actions that are likely to realize value. Because governmental directives must be based upon dependent reasons, they are authoritative, in turn, only to the extent that they enable their subjects to think and to act on the basis of intrinsic values, that is to say, reasonably. At least within the context of modern industrial societies, this moral theory is meant to establish that state perfectionism must be liberal because intrinsically valuable lives are autonomous ones, and these can flourish only under conditions of political freedom.

Clearly, none of the arguments that Raz produces in support of this inference from perfectionism to liberalism is very persuasive. But perhaps these limitations derive from the six specific arguments in question rather than perfectionism more generally. An unsympathetic critic might plausibly ask: How can we be sure that Raz's ultimate failure to justify the harm principle on perfectionist grounds does not simply derive from the particular construction he gives it (in combining *valuable* autonomy and moral pluralism within the social forms thesis)? Could another formulation avoid the pitfalls that we discussed above?

One way of discounting this possibility is to assume that Raz's political safeguards on liberty will be effective and also to *concede* that his moral theory is sound, but deny that a principle of toleration is derivable from the claim that only reasonable conceptions of the good are legitimately enforceable in a perfectionist state. This would show that perfectionism is an implausible foundation for the harm principle, *no matter which account of personal well-being it contains.*

If a principle of restraint is to be politically implementable, then it must lead people with radically different and possibly incompatible ethical views to arrive at convergent conclusions when testing the validity of legislation or public policy against it. As we saw in chapter 1, it must satisfy certain conditions of publicity. The issue of tolerance arises only in a context characterized by *rival* truth-claims. But by now, it should be abundantly clear why perfectionism cannot be successfully deployed to justify mutually acceptable regulative principles in this context: it presupposes the truth or validity of the very propositions that give rise to ethically based political dispute – those that make toleration necessary in the first place. Pluralism ensures that incontestable truths of the requisite kind are unavailable for defending liberal tolerance.

Raz has recently advanced an intriguing and relatively novel argument[104] against coercive moral paternalism that links citizenship to political trust that may, if successful, possibly evade the problems faced by his reinterpreted harm principle. But this argument also fails, and this reinforces the suggestion that the problem with perfectionism is structural and foundational. Because the idea of trust that Raz relies upon to exclude coercive moral paternalism is a perfectionist one, the overall argument within which it is found is as weak as his reinterpreted harm principle.

In this recent formulation, Raz tells us that paternalistic coercion is justified when it meets two cumulative conditions: first, it is undertaken for a good reason, one sufficient to make reasonable a partial loss of independence; and second, 'barring emergencies, it comes from the hands of someone reasonably trusted by the coerced.'[105] This second condition explains the way that consent can be indirectly relevant to the justification of coercion by establishing or expressing a relationship of trust, one that involves a 'relaxation of the normal standards of vigilance (though, of course, not their complete abandonment).'[106] Paternalistic coercion, in this view, is normally justified only if used by friends or others whose good intentions are beyond doubt. How do we get from these two justificatory conditions to a principled inhibition *against* coercive *moral* paternalism?

Trust in government is a condition of its right to apply coercion against people for their own good. Full citizenship is normally a precondition of political trust, and it is shared by all those who reasonably believe that the state or its government recognizes them as 'people who matter in their own right, that their fate is a matter of intrinsic value.'[107] When people enjoy full citizenship, their government can use coercive paternalism against them as long as this is justified by right reason. On the other hand, those who either find it impossible to regard the government as *their* government, or to regard themselves as full citizens alongside everyone else are unable to trust the government, which is accordingly barred from adopting paternalistic measures.

For Raz, if a government pursues coercive *moral* paternalism against people by criminalizing vices such as sodomy, for instance, then, *by definition*, it is preventing those who would normally engage in them from participating in constitutive (sexual) aspects of their lifestyles. Coercive moral paternalism undercuts people's trust that they, and their interests, are seriously being taken into account in deciding public policy and thereby denies them full citizenship. Raz explains:

> A person who finds some of the essential aspects of his way of life, or some of his fundamental values or moral beliefs, rejected as base and worthless by the government cannot trust its ability to take his interests into account ... it is bound to seem to them as failing through moral blindness to take them and their well-being seriously, lacking the ability to give their interests the weight they deserve. *The people who feel like that may be wrong. Their beliefs and way of life may indeed be worthless. But it is reasonable for them to deny that and to feel that the government has forfeited their trust.*[108]

The eschewing of moral paternalism is therefore required to secure people full citizenship, because moral paternalism compromises the very trust that is one of its central preconditions.

But how, precisely, does moral paternalism undercut the relevant form of political trust? Raz's perfectionism commits him to the view that the state ought to promote the personal well-being of its citizens. Those who condemn sodomy as immoral or vicious, for instance, allege that it is incompatible with such well-being and wish to prevent it coercively on that basis through the institutions of the state. For them, securing people full citizenship mandates, rather than precludes, this measure. Given Raz's overall ethical theory, one would surely expect to find that whether or not a sodomite's distrust in a government intent upon eradicating his unconventional sexual practice is reasonable or not depends exclusively upon whether or not this practice is, in fact, valuable or worthless. But here, at the critical moment, Raz's moral theory undergoes a radical transformation. For the first time and without any explanation as to why, the subjective feelings of people are taken at face value – it is now reasonable for them to distrust others who condemn the fundamentals of their lives as base and worthless, *whether they are actually depraved or not.* This claim is required to sustain the view that coercive moral paternalism compromises full citizenship, but it is utterly inconsistent with the perfectionism that allegedly grounds it.

4.7 Conclusion

Raz's argument for the liberal perfectionist state is an eloquent and complex defence of a type of full continuity between values, reasons, and political morality. This argument, however, is defective at several points. The requirement that public policy in pursuit of the good be limited to measures commanding nearly unanimous support actually excludes, rather than guides, state perfectionism. The claim that state perfectionism is, or should be, primarily non-coercive fails because both taxes and subsidies artificially distort the opportunity costs involved in people's choices and, in a moral theory that has autonomy as a foundational ethical value, people should be responding to these costs on their own. The idea that (some) autonomous but morally repugnant choices will be tolerated because of the practical difficulties of coercively interfering with them overstates such problems, which are not insurmountable, as illustrated by our hypothetical laws against obscenity, political dissent, same-sex marriages, and the sale of contraceptives.

Raz's ethical safeguards on individual liberty in the perfectionist state are equally unsuccessful. The notion that perfectionism is authoritative only when reasonable renders its underlying conception of toleration either incoherent or politically useless: if reason mandates only one determinate set of ethical beliefs, then moral pluralism is false as an account of what gives rise to the need for the harm principle; but if moral pluralism is true, then the harm principle cannot sensibly rely upon it for its content because ethical disagreement arising from rival but equally reasonable perceptions of what is, in fact, intrinsically valuable is precisely the problem that liberalism is meant to remedy. The claim that state perfectionism need not be illiberal because it leaves a multiplicity of valuable options intact for people to choose from is unpersuasive for a similar reason. Either citizens of the perfectionist state are reflective moral pluralists in Raz's sense, in which case their objections to one another's limitations are unreasonable, and so tolerance is an inappropriate response, or they are not, in which case they have been given no reason to refrain from persecuting, when possible, others whose ways of life they condemn as worthless or base. Finally, the idea that some general standing of autonomous beings precludes coercively interfering with victimless immoralities introduces a conception of autonomy as a general value that is utterly inconsistent with Raz's overall moral theory where that value is restricted to morally respectable choices within autonomy-supportive environments.

The ultimate failure of this strategy directs our attention to an opposing one deeply embedded within the liberal tradition that conceives of ethics and politics as partially discontinuous[109] with one another. Rather than justifying toleration directly on the basis of views about worthwhile or flourishing human lives, it takes seriously the pervasiveness and depth of reasonable controversy regarding such matters. It does so by abandoning the idea of political morality as personal ethics simply writ large, in favour of a principled settlement that identifies, before perfectionist values enter into the picture, the political entitlements or ground rules that constrain how, and the extent to which, citizens can legitimately press such values upon one another through the institutions of the state. So far, I have not defended this view of political morality against its numerous and important criticisms. Rather, I have lent indirect support for it by showing what liberal political morality *cannot* be.

5 The Continuity Thesis

5.1 Introduction

In our daily lives, we have particular responsibilities toward those with whom we have special relationships: our selves, family, friends, and colleagues, among others. We rightly suppose that we need not, as individuals, treat our neighbour's children with the same concern as our own, or, for that matter, treat everyone that we meet with the same respect. Only ethical idiots, then, show equal concern for everyone by devoting, in their private lives, as much time, attention, and resources towards complete strangers as they do towards their own children.

Politically, however, a legitimate government *must* treat all of its citizens in this way – with equal concern and respect – and just citizens, in their political lives, should vote and work for candidates and programs that reflect this requirement. But if governments cannot legitimately distribute goods or opportunities unequally on the ground that some citizens are entitled to more because they are worthy of more concern, and if they cannot restrict basic liberties on the ground that one citizen or group's conception of the good life is nobler or superior to another's, then there appears to be a plain contradiction between the partiality of our most fundamental private ethical convictions, and the neutrality or impartiality of the liberal political perspective. Liberals must therefore explain why people who do not treat everyone else with equal concern in their personal lives both should and actually would nevertheless endorse equality from a political point of view.

There are two ways that they might do this. First, they could argue that the two perspectives are compatible because the political one is *artificial*, a social construction meant to embody a perspective that no one need

regard as the application of her full ethical convictions to political decisions, so that people with conflicting ethical beliefs can occupy it
together. Such a 'discontinuous' or 'ethically insensitive'[1] theory would
show that each person has reasons originating from within her respective and diverse ethical convictions for constructing and occupying the
artificial political point of view. Classical and contemporary social contract theories are canonical examples of this approach. Second, liberals
might effect the needed reconciliation of perspectives by showing that
the tension in question is ultimately misleading – the account of the
good life that allows for private partiality actually recommends, rather
than undermines, ethical neutrality and distributive equality in politics.

Recently, Ronald Dworkin has pursued this 'continuous' or 'ethically
sensitive' tack by connecting liberalism as a political philosophy with a
version of perfectionism that he calls the 'challenge model' of ethics. In
order to reconcile personal partiality and political equality, that model
must be

1 drawn from people's existing considered views of the good life, notwithstanding the fact that these allow for private partiality (otherwise,
   the ensuing political morality is 'discontinous');
2 sufficiently comprehensive so that its adherents come to endorse liberal equality and reject alternative theories of political and economic
   justice (otherwise, it fails in its stated objective because there is nothing distinctively liberal about it); and
3 sufficiently abstract so that different people with contested ethical
   convictions can all support it (otherwise, it is not ethically neutral).

Because these criteria pull in opposite directions simultaneously, the ethical foundations of liberal equality have to be structural and philosophical, rather than substantive in character, and this explains why Dworkin's
version of perfectionism has the shape that it does.

In this chapter, I assess the extent to which Dworkin's challenge model
of ethics provides a plausible foundation for liberal neutrality. In section
2, I lay out the central components of the challenge model. In section 3,
I examine that model directly and demonstrate that while it needs to be
less abstract for some purposes, and more abstract for others, it cannot
be both simultaneously. I explain the significance of this failure in terms
of Dworkin's key distinction between strategies of 'continuity' versus 'discontinuity.' Two conclusions emerge. First, the challenge model of ethics
leads to an endorsement of liberal equality only when it has already been

constrained in a variety of ways that call into question Dworkin's claim
that his argument is an instance of the strategy of continuity after all.
This suggests that abstract or subtler forms of perfectionism are no more
successful than comprehensive ones (such as Raz's) are in justifying a liberal egalitarian political morality. Because the challenge model is insuffi-
cient to do so, the burden of Dworkin's case for neutrality rests with a
different argument, one rooted in the distributive implications of equal
concern and respect, and that is modelled by a complex hypothetical
auction and counterfactual insurance scheme. In section 4, a closer look
at some of this strategy's simplifying counterfactual assumptions reveals
our second conclusion, which is that the hypothetical auction/insurance
scheme generates whatever ethical neutrality it does by means of a type
of implied or closet contractualism.

5.2 The Challenge Model of Ethics

Dworkin presents and contrasts two rival accounts of the character and
origin of ethical value to illustrate the kind of goodness or value that a
human life has when it is lived well, or fails to have when it is lived badly.
The first is the 'model of impact,' which holds that a life is good or valuable in virtue of the consequences that it has for, or the difference that it
makes to, the rest of the world. We admire the lives of Alexander Flem-
ing, Mozart, and Martin Luther King Jr, for instance, and explain our
doing so by pointing to penicillin, *The Marriage of Figaro*, and racial
desegregation.[2] The model of impact generalizes from these examples
so that the ethical value of a life is parasitic upon its consequences for
others or states of affairs in the world: 'A life can have more or less value,
the model claims, not because it is intrinsically more valuable to live
one's life in one way rather than another, but because living in one way
can have better consequences.'[3]

At first glance, the model of impact appears promising because it
seems to explain the basis of some ethical judgements that we confidently make within a limited range. But it is also unduly constricting of
ethical value, because it renders many of our other ethical intuitions and
judgements incoherent. It seems reasonable to suppose that the question of how we ought to live is, for virtually everyone, the most important
one that we will ever have to face. We agonize, for instance, about
whether and whom to marry, which career to pursue, and about how to
make something meaningful of our lives. Upon reflection, however, it
seems plainly obvious that most of us will do nothing so grand as discover

penicillin, create great art, or lead a civil-rights movement. On the model of impact, therefore, we worry very much about things (our lives) that matter very little from an objective point of view, given that we can exert only a very limited influence upon the world around us.

The 'model of challenge' by contrast, rejects the idea that lives can only go better in virtue of their impact on the objective value of states of affairs in the world. It adopts Aristotle's view that 'a good life has the inherent value of a skillful performance'[4] so that events, achievements, and experiences can have ethical value even when they have no impact beyond the life in which they occur:

> We admire a complex and elegant dive, for example, whose value persists even after the last ripple has died, and we admire people who climbed Mount Everest because, as they said, it was there. The model of challenge holds that living a life is *itself* a performance that demands skill, that it is the most comprehensive and important challenge we face, and that our critical interests consist in the achievements, events, and experiences that mean that we have met the challenge well.[5]

The model of impact convincingly explains why influential deeds bestow ethical greatness upon the rare individuals who carry them out. But it cannot explain how or why anyone else's life has objective value or significance. It makes most people's ethical convictions – those that presuppose that their lives matter – seem self-indulgent or delusional. Because the challenge model conceives of ethical value as the value of a performance rather than as linked to the independent value of a product and its consequences, it allows 'a further range of considerations and beliefs to enter ethical judgment, though it does not itself select among any particular set of these as more appropriate than others.'[6] Producing great art or reducing suffering by conquering disease can be plausibly interpreted as skilful responses to the challenge of living, so these examples (designed to lend intuitive support to the model of impact) do not actually violate or undermine our ethical convictions about great individuals. But skill at the challenge of living might sometimes conceivably require *avoiding* rather than embracing difficult endeavours in favour of others more suited to one's talents or situation. The model of challenge, but not the model of impact, can rescue us from ethical self-deception and incoherence by explaining why this is so.

Dworkin's central analogy to illustrate the ethical challenge that life poses is to art, because artistic achievement includes defining, as well as securing, success. Even in the most academic or conventionalized moments, that is, there is no settled view about what artistic achievement is: 'artists are not furnished with blueprints.'[7] They enter the history of art at a particular time, and in a particular place, and the political, technological, and social conditions of their age establish the traditions that they may continue, redefine, or defy. Since there is no timeless view about what good art is, and living well is analogously sensitive to context, we cannot define what a good life is per se – specific people in particular and varying circumstances must, like artists, reflectively define this for themselves.

Any ethical theory deployed to compare the objective goodness of different lives, or to help people improve their own by its standards, seems doomed from the outset if the metric that it relies upon must derive from people's subjective estimations of their lives' relative value. Indeed, if a component or aspect of someone's life is valuable simply because she thinks it is, then interpersonal comparisons of the objective goodness of lives are pointless because ethical beliefs are always self-validating. Asking which of two lives is better and which is more pleasant or strongly preferred come to the same thing.

On the one hand, then, the idea that there is only one timeless way to live a good life is highly implausible, and this seemingly precludes transcendent ethical standards; on the other, Dworkin insists that the ethical foundations of liberalism must be based upon what he calls 'critical,' as opposed to 'volitional,' interests, and this seems to *recommend* such transcendent standards:

> Sailing well and freedom from dentistry are part of my own volitional well-being: I want them both, and my life therefore goes better, in the volitional sense, when I have them. I take a different view of others things I want: having a close relationship with my children, for example, securing some success in my work, and – what I despair of attaining – some minimal grasp of the state of advanced science of my era. These I regard as critical interests because I believe that my life would be a less successful one if I failed to have, or wholly failed to achieve, these goals.[8]

People's volitional well-being is improved, therefore, when they have or achieve what they in fact want. Their critical well-being is improved by their having or achieving what makes their lives objectively better to want, that is, what they ought to want independently of whether they, in fact, actually do so. However, if the overarching goal of the continuity strategy is to show that people who take their critical interests seriously have that very motive for adopting the liberal political perspective, then an important difficulty emerges. Can the challenge model consistently disavow transcendent ethical standards while focusing on critical well-being in this way? Does that model's sensitivity to culture and context render liberalism's ethical foundations merely subjective and, thus, arbitrary?

No, because as the artistic analogy reminds us, evaluative standards can be indexed to changing circumstances while still posing categorical demands. This indexing is provided by what Dworkin calls 'parameters of challenge.'[9] His idea of a parameter is clarified by contrasting it with a limitation. On the model of impact, the ideal life is always the same because it is the one that creates as much independent value as is humanly possible. All the circumstances of a person's actual life therefore operate as limitations on its quality. Someone's ethical well-being is limited by her eighty-year lifespan, say, because it is plausible to assume that she would have created more value had she lived longer.

On the challenge view of ethics, by contrast, living well, like painting well, means sensing what the challenge one faces really is, and this requires 'a personal response to the full particularity of situation, not the application, to that situation, of a timelessly ideal life.'[10] To meet the challenge of living well, people must accurately distinguish between limitations such as, say, crushing poverty, that constrain their ability to lead good lives, and parameters, such as a normal lifespan, or being Canadian, that help them define what a successful performance of living would be for people in precisely those situations.

We are now better positioned to understand how ethics can be indexed to time and place while still posing categorical demands. Living well is not merely a matter of doing whatever we happen to want, because in pursuing what we want, we may have identified the wrong challenge (by confusing limitations and parameters, for instance), or failed at the right one. This should not mislead us however. Rather than judging the convictions it assumes we already have, the challenge model simply tells us that 'we will understand our ethical life better if we see [such convictions] in the way it recommends, as opinions about the skillful performance of an important self-assignment, rather than just as opinions about how we can change the world for the better.'[11] Dworkin's ethical theory is therefore thoroughly interpretive as opposed to judgemental: it simply interprets and organizes ethical convictions that precede it in order to give them greater coherence, instead of arguing for these from the ground up, as it were.

5.2.1 *From Ethics to Politics*

What kind of liberalism emerges from this view of ethics? The continuity strategy links ethics and politics so that they cohere to yield two different but related types of integrity, each having important political implications. 'Normative integrity'[12] mandates egalitarian principles of distributive justice that operate on the space of resources rather than welfare, and 'ethical integrity'[13] requires anti-paternalism and liberal neutrality.

Many of the parameters that help us to define the challenge of living we face are normative. That is, they define our ethical situation not in terms of how it actually is, but rather as we reasonably suppose it *should* be. Our lives may go badly, then, not just because we are unwilling or unable to respond to the circumstances that confront us, but because we confront the wrong circumstances. People denied the challenges they ought to have been permitted live worse lives for that reason alone, no matter what else they manage to do or to be.

Reasonable people choose what sorts of lives to lead against a background of assumptions about the type and quantity of resources that are or will be available to them. Some of these resources are personal – expected lifespan, talents, and health – while others are impersonal – wealth, liberties, and opportunities. Both kinds must sometimes figure as parameters, rather than limitations, because 'we cannot think that the ideally best life is the life of someone with all the resources available to him that imagination might conceive.'[14] Rather, good lives are those suited to circumstances of justice, and this is what Dworkin means when he says that the search for liberalism's ethical foundations is a search for normative integrity. Ethics and justice interpenetrate one another: liberal principles of justice tell us what kind of political community we should have; liberal ethics tells us how we should live within it. But if good lives are those that embody skilful performances in just circumstances, then precisely which circumstances are these?

Ethical thought – reflection about how well our lives are going – presupposes that we can accurately distinguish between the limitations and the parameters of our specific circumstances. We cannot do this, however, without having some prior notion of reasonable regret. For instance, while we can regret the fact that we would probably have achieved more and made something better of our lives if only we could have lived for an extra hundred years, or have had all of the world's resources to ourselves, we cannot *reasonably* regret this. Our inability to lead a certain type of valuable life is reasonably regrettable only if that life might have been possible except for the fact that we have been denied what justice entitles us to, that is, to a fair share of society's resources. Because reasonable regret is essential to distinguishing between accurate and spurious self-assessments of objective welfare, and this idea presupposes, in turn, an independent and antecedently justified idea of fair shares or resource equality, welfare or well-being is necessarily redundant as a metric of distributive justice – to avoid incoherence, welfarism inevitably collapses into a variant of resourcism. This is one of many reasons why welfare or well-being cannot be used to determine what people are owed as a matter of distributive justice without falling victim to the problem of expensive tastes.[15] Liberal equality therefore 'builds justice on the space of resources rather than well-being or welfare'[16] by defining the ideal society not in terms of the goodness of the lives people live but rather in terms of the share of resources each of them has available.

So resources rather than welfare should be the metric of distributive justice, and some theory of resource fairness is required to anchor the notion of reasonable regret. But precisely which distribution of resources enables people to face appropriate normative parameters? Because ethics and justice are continuous, the distribution of liberties, opportunities, and resources should reflect these foundational ethical assumptions. Circumstances of justice are therefore those in which resources are distributed equally, because only then does everyone have the opportunity to face and potentially succeed in life's challenges. Ethics and justice do not conflict, and liberalism's critics are deeply mistaken, then, because goodness and fairness thrive in the same soil.

In thinking about the value of other people's lives, we may ask two different types of questions. We can ask, first, how far their lives include whatever experiences, relationships, or achievements we count as good or valuable. We can ask, second, about the extent to which they endorse or identify with such components as serving their critical, as distinct from their volitional, interests. For Dworkin, two different views are possible as to how these questions can be combined. The '*additive view*'[17] holds that we can judge their lives to be good or bad without consulting their own opinions on the matter: if they endorse those components of their lives that are objectively valuable, then this increases their goodness; but if they do not, the ethical value of those components remains. People can still lead very good lives in virtue of experiences and achievements that they think are worthless, or at least that they fail to appreciate.

On any plausible interpretation of the challenge model, however, the connection between conviction and value is 'constitutive,'[18] because it is absurd to think that someone's life could be improved by some feature or component of it that she rejects as worthless. The art analogy helps us to understand why. In judging the value of a performance, for instance, we *must* consult the performers' intention – we do not credit them, that is, with some feature of a performance that they were struggling to avoid, or would not recognize, even in retrospect, as good or desirable. If the right motive is necessary to the right performance, then this means that critical paternalism – restricting people's liberty to enhance their critical well-being – is incoherent because self-defeating, rather than simply difficult. It implies that what Dworkin calls ethical integrity must take priority in all of the judgements we make about the goodness of people's lives: 'someone has achieved ethical integrity, we may say, when he lives out of the conviction that his life, in its central features, is an appropriate one, that no other life he might live would be a plainly better response to the parameters of his ethical situation rightly judged.'[19] Prioritizing ethical integrity in this way destroys the point of critical paternalism altogether – it makes the merger of life and conviction a parameter of ethical success so that 'a life that never achieves that kind of integrity cannot be critically better for someone to lead than a life that does.'[20]

Perhaps subtler forms of paternalism could circumvent this problem, though. If challenges are, in fact, richer, more valuable, when people are more likely to choose good over bad options, and the likelihood of this increases if the latter are antecedently screened out by wise rulers, then state paternalism would support rather than undermine ethical integrity by improving the deliberative context in which people decide for themselves how to lead valuable lives. This account of ethical reflection, however, profoundly misunderstands the challenge model by confusing parameters and limitations. It does so by assuming that there is some standard of what a good life is that transcends the question of what circumstances are appropriate for people deciding how to live, which can then be used in answering *that* question, by stipulating that the best circumstances are whichever ones most likely to produce the correct answer. For Dworkin, we cannot think that it would be better for people to choose how to live in ignorance of lives that other people disapprove of without begging the question.

So the ethical foundations of liberal equality imply that governments must eschew (most forms of)[21] critical paternalism. How do we get from those foundations to ethical neutrality, and in what sense must the liberal state be neutral between the competing ethical ideals of its citizens?

We saw above that governments must treat people with equal concern and respect, and this means that they cannot distribute goods or opportunities unequally on the ground that some citizens are entitled to more because they are worthy of more concern. Dworkin also thinks that they must not constrain liberty on the ground that one citizen's conception of the good life, or that of one group's, is, or is perceived to be, superior to that of another's. There are, in fact, two arguments for this latter requirement. One conceives of equality as a political ideal that cannot be specified without presupposing state neutrality between conceptions of the good life already in place. If treating people with equal concern and respect requires equalizing their circumstances, and liberty is plainly a part of those circumstances, then governments must be neutral on the question of the good life, because state perfectionism violates the best understanding of distributive fairness. The other argument derives from within the challenge model of ethics itself. Simply put, ethical liberals could not consistently support a government that relied upon a controversial account of human well-being in order to assess and influence the relative goodness of people's lives because, in doing so, it would necessarily 'usurp the most important part of the challenge people face in leading a life, which is identifying life's value for themselves.'[22] Ethical liberals will, therefore, accept state neutrality between conceptions of the good life as continuous rather than discontinuous with their own comprehensive ethical convictions.

5.3 The Challenge Model Examined

Dworkin thinks that living well involves responding skilfully to an appropriate challenge and also that this supports liberal equality. However, the challenge model lacks the discriminatory power required to exclude welfarism, perfectionism, and critical paternalism, and it is insufficiently abstract to accommodate the kind of ethical neutrality that he thinks follows from it. That it is simultaneously too abstract and not abstract enough suggests that there is something problematic with 'ethically continuous' justifications of the political positions that Dworkin endorses, and this is the central lesson of the challenge model's failure.

5.3.1 Challenge and Equality of Resources

Dworkin discusses the relative merits of challenge and impact as though these were exhaustive as competing models of ethical value. That is, he seems to imply that the model of impact's manifest inadequacy lends direct support for his challenge model. To begin with, however, it might be the case that neither of these, nor any combination of the two, accurately captures our pre-theoretical intuitions about what it means to live well. Consider the following two alternative accounts of ethical value,[23] both plausible, but neither fitting comfortably within Dworkin's binary framework. On a rational preference satisfaction view, a person's life goes well when she gets what she wants so long as her wants are not based on ignorance or cognitive error. This view is opposed to the model of impact because someone might conceivably lead a life that greatly influences the world without ever preferring or intending that this be the case. It is also opposed to the model of challenge because someone might skilfully respond to life's challenges without necessarily satisfying any of her important self-interested preferences. Next, think of an 'objective list' view of ethics with some of the following representative items: friendship and love, pleasure and the avoidance of pain, athletic attainment, meaningful work, systematic understanding of the natural world, ethical and moral wisdom, and creative artistic, cultural, and scientific accomplishments. With enough good luck or help compensating for a lack of talent, someone might attain several of the items on this list, and thereby manage to lead an objectively valuable life, without either having any substantial impact on the world or demonstrating any great skill at living. There is reason to believe, then, that Dworkin's challenge model is as constricting of ethical value as the impact model that he rejects.

For the sake of argument, however, let us grant that the model of challenge accurately and coherently organizes the ethical intuitions it assumes we already have. Does Dworkin's premise that justice is a normative parameter of ethics support his conclusion that liberal equality must operate on the space of resources rather than welfare, and be defined in ethically neutral, rather than perfectionist, terms? Living well involves responding in the right way to the right challenge. Since justice is a normative parameter of ethics, someone faces the wrong challenge, and her life accordingly goes worse, when and because she holds an unjust share of resources. Goods such as education, health, and money, for instance, can never fundamentally improve someone's welfare unless their acquisition is consistent with justice. Dworkin thinks that this rules out welfare-based and perfectionist egalitarian theories because these mistakenly suppose that people's interests can be comprehensively defined independently of what justice requires. But in the context of an ethically continuous political morality, why can't this be done? The parametric status of justice does not exclude a comprehensive and perfectionist account of welfare if the theory of justice that constrains it is understood in either access egalitarian[24] or equal opportunity for welfare terms.[25] To see this, consider the following outline of an ethically sensitive or continuous theory of justice conjoined with the challenge model of ethics:

1 Justice is a parameter of ethics, so the goodness of someone's life or, what amounts to the same thing, her welfare, cannot be improved through injustice.
2 Justice mandates distributive equality.[26]
3 In accordance with the challenge model of ethics, someone's welfare is improved *pro tanto* when she faces and skilfully succeeds at several, and ideally many, of the objectively valuable challenges that are in her critical interests.
4 *Therefore*, justice requires that people have equal opportunity or access to such valuable challenges.

This challenge-inspired argumentative structure allows for a perfectionist egalitarian metric of interpersonal comparison. It incorporates a substantive account of ethics that also respects the parametric status of justice by establishing the goods or opportunities that would improve people's welfare *if everyone enjoyed equal access to them*. At its existing level of abstraction, then, the challenge model does not prevent us from anchoring egalitarian distributive claims in a detailed and comprehensive account of human flourishing. Clearly, we can interpret our ethical intuitions as convictions about skilful responses to worthwhile challenges and still consistently reject the neutralist and resourcist components of liberal equality.

Dworkin concedes that lives can be 'more exciting, diverse, complex, and creative' when the challenges they contain are themselves 'more interesting and valuable'[27] and, on the continuity view, this tends to support rather than undermine the state's discouraging certain activities and lifestyles and subsidizing others in order to equalize people's opportunities to pursue such valuable challenges.[28] Of course, there may be other fairness-based or distributive objections to altering the opportunity costs of people's choices in this way, but these are independent of the challenge model, and so cannot be relied upon to bolster its connection to liberal equality.

Dworkin reinforces his case for equality of resources by highlighting what he perceives to be a basic flaw in any variant of its chief rival, equality of welfare. To recall, welfare egalitarian distributive principles require some antecedent notion of reasonable regret. Otherwise, equalizing welfare means compensating people for the frustration or unhappiness that derives from incredibly expensive but unsatisfied tastes. Reasonable regret, however, is utterly indeterminate unless it is anchored to some background theory that specifies when resources are fairly distributed, and so when welfare deficits are, in fact, reasonably regrettable. But if it is true that resources must be fairly distributed *before* interpersonal comparisons of welfare are possible and, absent this background fairness, compensable welfare deficits cannot be identified, then welfare egalitarianism must either collapse into some variant of equality of resources, or remain both redundant and vulnerable to the problem of expensive tastes.

Welfare or utility is simply a word for whatever makes someone's life intrinsically better; it is what someone pursues when she is being rationally prudent.[29] Dworkin's reasonable regret idea establishes only the incoherence of welfare egalitarian theories that straightforwardly identify welfare or well-being with simple contentment or preference-satisfaction. If X's estimation of how well her life is going is what determines her level of welfare, and she is intensely dissatisfied with an enormous bundle of wealth, then, other things being equal, a welfare-based theory of distributive equality is committed to transferring resources from already impoverished but (for whatever reason) happier Y until the point when the two of them are either equally satisfied or frustrated.

No such counter-intuitive results are forthcoming, however, if we adopt a perfectionist objective list account of welfare. Unless its items – pleasure and the avoidance of pain, meaningful work, athletic achievement, for instance – are completely incommensurable (something for which Dworkin offers no argument), we should be able to specify what weight any particular level of achievement has on any given dimension of achievement, and this allows for interpersonal comparisons of welfare without appealing to the notion of reasonable regret. The idea of reasonable regret is no longer required because the objective list account of ethics dispenses with the foundational distinction between parameters and limitations that gives it its force. If an individual's level of welfare depends upon the extent to which she obtains what is truly valuable and experiences what is authentically worthwhile, then what is good for her will not vary with her circumstances.[30]

5.3.2 Challenge and Anti-paternalism

Dworkin thinks that a person's life can *never* be better by virtue of containing some feature or component the she thinks is valueless. This does not mean that ethical value simply derives from endorsement. The constitutive view says only that her endorsement is a necessary – but not sufficient – condition of something's contributing to the goodness of her life. So whether or not a life in politics, for example, is intrinsically valuable is not for me to decide, but even if it is, my life does not go better because I am a politician unless I also share this conviction, and pursue such a career for this very reason. This merger of life and conviction is what Dworkin means by ethical integrity, which is destroyed whenever people fail to live up to their convictions about what it means to live well, either because of some weakness of will (what philosophers sometimes call *akrasia*) or because others forcibly prevent them from doing so.

Integrity amounts to a kind of fit, then, between a person's substantive ethical convictions, and her life as instantiated by her choices. The constitutive view establishes that restricting someone's liberty for her own good and against her convictions undermines integrity and *pro tanto* thereby diminishes the value of her life, all else being equal. But integrity is only one value among many, so all else is not likely to be equal. According to the challenge model, that is, the value of any given component in a person's life is established along two axes: the extent to which it is in her critical interests, and the extent to which she endorses it. Even if we accept that integrity as Dworkin describes it is good for a person, why can't small losses of integrity be outweighed by sufficient gains in critical value so that, on balance, her life is improved by being forced to abandon less valuable ends and being compelled to pursue more worthwhile ones, especially if what is in her critical interests is not up to her to decide? One reason for precluding such trade-offs would be if ethical integrity were lexically prior to all other values. Dworkin's claim that any life with integrity is better for a person than any other one without it[31] suggests that he endorses this weighting, but he provides absolutely no argument for it and, in any case, it does not actually support his blanket indictment of critical paternalism for a variety of reasons.

While some goods such as religion require endorsement to have any value, not all of them are of this type. Consider a person blissfully committed to a life of gluttony and slothfulness whose existing eating habits and lack of exercise are likely to result in her immanent death. A well-balanced and nutritious diet combined with a regular exercise regimen would improve her health (physical, mental, sexual) whether she cares about it or not. To the extent that such health would actually expand her capacity to shape the course of her life in a variety of previously unthinkable and largely unattainable directions, integrity is no barrier to improving her welfare by implementing a mandatory scheme that secured her these things. Consider also a person with a serious mental illness that will surely destroy her capacity to shape, revise, and ultimately implement any plan of life, in the absence of drug treatment and therapy that she rejects as unnecessary. Restricting her liberty to refuse such medical treatment may very well improve the value of her life.

And what if a person endorses *many* goods in varying degrees or, better still, if her life lacks integrity to begin with? Suppose, that is, that she is fanatically religious and only marginally interested in politics. Following one of Dworkin's examples, let us assume that religion is critically worthless, and that politics is critically valuable. By preventing her from entering religious orders and forcing her into a political career, we radically improve the goodness of her life without necessarily compromising ethical integrity, because she endorses both of them, albeit in varying degrees. As one critic points out, 'the constitutive view leaves it open that people's lives could be improved if they are forced to take the critically most valuable of all the options they endorse.'[32] Suppose, alternatively, that she desires a career in politics but also lacks the drive or ambition to achieve this. If her life lacks integrity because her choices do not reflect her convictions about what is ultimately worthwhile, then the priority of ethical integrity sanctions paternalistic intervention at virtually any cost to her other values, provided that it ultimately enables her to succeed politically.

Even if Dworkin convincingly explained why integrity takes strict priority in judgements we make about the quality of people's lives, and even if this priority established the self-defeating nature of all critical paternalism, there would still be something quite incongruous about it, given that the challenge model within which it is embedded is meant to be continuous with liberal equality. Recall that under liberal equality, unjust circumstances tarnish the quality of someone's life whether they benefit or harm her, and regardless of what she thinks about what political morality requires. Under the challenge model, by contrast, the lexical priority of integrity implies that her opinions about the relative value of different components of her life must be taken as authoritative from an ethical point of view. So, for example, if class relations in her society are unjust, this makes her life much worse, whether or not she knows or cares about this; but if she thinks that surfing is the best life for her, then surfing really is the best life for her, given that conviction, even if the conviction is wrong.[33] This is quite remarkable, because if liberal equality is continuous with the challenge model, then surely one would expect

to find either that injustice adversely affects the ethical quality of someone's life only if she has strong opinions about justice, or that the lexical
priority of ethical integrity is implausible because her subjective opinions are irrelevant to an assessment of how well her life is going, and so
there is no barrier to critical paternalism. There does not appear to be
any way of reconciling these two claims in an ethically sensitive political
morality.

5.3.3 Challenge and Ethical Neutrality

Dworkin thinks that a state that takes the challenge model seriously must
remain neutral on the question of the good life. That is, it cannot rely on
a controversial account of ethics to judge the relative success of people's
lives for purposes of distributive justice, or to restrict liberty to improve
people's welfare, because doing so would necessarily usurp the most
important part of the challenge people face in leading a life, which is
identifying life's value for themselves.

   It is unclear, however, what kind of usurpation perfectionist-based distributive or liberty-limiting principles actually embody on the model of
challenge. When a government subsidizes a particular activity to allow
more people access to it on the grounds that those who participate in it
lead better, more worthwhile lives for that reason, individuals are still left
with the task of deciding for themselves whether, upon reflection, they
wish to partake in what was previously an unavailable or prohibitively
costly pursuit. Similarly, when government taxes what it takes to be ethically impoverished options, individuals with a penchant for the latter
must still decide whether the increased opportunity costs associated with
such disincentives are ultimately worth paying, given their own estimation of their value. Subsidies and taxes do not necessarily impede people's deliberative capacities for reflective judgement about value and, in
some cases, may actually operate as stimuli (consider the case of smokers
who must decide for themselves whether cigarettes are worth smoking
under current tax rates in Canada). Altering the opportunity costs of
people's choices in these ways would diminish the ethical quality of their
lives only if personal autonomy was the most important component of a
good life so that choosing for oneself was always more important than
choosing correctly. But any such comprehensive view of the good is
excluded by liberal equality's commitment to state neutrality between
ideals of human flourishing.

   Restricting people's liberty to choose certain options on the ground that they are demeaning, corrupting, or otherwise bad for their authors, though not against justice, obviously *could* interfere with people's ability to identify life's value for themselves, but the model of challenge does not establish that this is necessarily and always so. Dworkin's challenge model is interpretive rather than judgemental, so it does not actually establish which particular options are interesting and complex, and thus valuable. However, understanding our pre-existing convictions about valuable options in terms of challenge rather than impact does not prevent us from also asking what would be better and worse responses to the challenge of living in any given circumstances, and this creates the following dilemma. On the one hand, other things being equal, people are better off to the extent that they face more valuable challenges, and challenges are more valuable when they include more options that are interesting and complex (this is why chess, say, is better than checkers). People choosing from a wider rather than narrower range of options clearly have greater room to tailor their choices according to their own estimation of what is ultimately valuable and, thus, according to their own plan of life. There is a prima facie reason, then, for allowing people the greatest possible range of choice. On the other hand, other things being equal, someone lives a better life when she chooses a critically better rather than worse option in response to a given challenge. And this means that there are actually two different values internal to the challenge model that must somehow be balanced or traded off against one another. That is, if someone would choose a worse option if presented with a wider range of choices, but choose better if presented with a narrower one, then it is conceivable that the worsening of her challenge by filtering alternatives paternalistically might be outweighed by the greater value of her better response to the smaller challenge.[34] Only the lexical priority of ethical integrity would preclude such counterbalancing but this ranking is implausible.

5.3.4 Whom Is the Challenge Model For?

So the challenge model lacks the discriminatory power to exclude perfectionist distributive principles, critical paternalism, and state action based on controversial views of the good. To see how it is simultaneously *too* abstract, consider the following three individuals:

Albert is an ethical liberal who finds that the challenge model fits well with most, if not all, of his convictions about how life should be led, and when it is going well. For him, a good life is one that skilfully responds to

normatively appropriate conditions, and such conditions include everyone having an equal share of society's resources, and a state that respects
the priority of integrity by remaining neutral on the question of what
gives value to life. He finds that there is no need to reconcile personal
partiality and political equality, because liberalism's critics are mistaken
in thinking that the two actually conflict in the first place.

Betty thinks that caring for the goodness of people's lives implies that
welfare rather than resources should be the metric of distributive justice,
and also that the best understanding of welfare is necessarily a perfectionist one. Embracing continuity leads her accordingly to believe that
governments are duty bound to provide people with equal opportunities
to lead what are, in fact, objectively valuable lives, and this makes state
neutrality between accurate and mistaken judgements about critical
interests a self-defeating strategy, both with respect to distributive and
liberty-limiting principles.

Charlie rejects the challenge model as altogether inconsistent with
what the best understanding of ethics requires. He thinks of life, not in
terms of a challenging self-assignment, but rather in terms of doing
God's will, and his life goes better to the extent that he can bring it about
that God's will is followed to a greater degree. For him, ethics and politics are purely continuous, which implies that 'good' people should be
rewarded with a greater than equal share of resources and liberties, and
that 'bad' people should have a lesser than equal share of both.

Is there a possible point along this spectrum of political beliefs where
the challenge model of ethics could make a difference in the sense that
those who endorsed it would also be more likely to embrace liberal
equality? The challenge model is not really addressed to Albert because
he has independent arguments for liberal equality grounded in considerations of distributive fairness. The best understanding of how government treats those under its authority with equal concern and respect
requires equality of resources and ethical neutrality and, to the extent that
justice is a parameter of ethics, there is no tension to be reconciled
between justice and ethics for which the challenge model needs to be
deployed. Betty accepts the challenge model, but its abstract characterization does not prevent her from also embracing the very positions it
was designed to exclude. Taking ethics seriously on the model of challenge actually leads her *away* from liberal equality, and nothing internal
to that model sufficiently explains why this would be objectionable.
Charlie rejects every aspect of liberal equality, and so the model of challenge is most naturally directed to him – Dworkin deploys his account of

the good first and foremost to answer liberalism's critics – but that model is *too* comprehensive to accommodate this understanding of what it means to live well. On the strategy of continuity, that is, the only way of persuading Charlie to embrace liberal equality is to convince him that his convictions about the good that lead him away from it are unsound, but this requires judgemental, not interpretive, ethics.

5.4 Desert Island Contractualism? The Auction and Neutrality

Dworkin's other argument for liberal neutrality is a distributive one that makes state neutrality between contested ethical ideals a presupposition of a hypothetical auction used to determine whether or not the allocation of a political community's resources is consistent with equal concern and respect for all of its members. This auction is incredibly complex, and it raises a number of very difficult issues in the areas of law, economics, insurance, and psychology, to mention but a few.[35] Fortunately, however, we can leave most of these troublesome issues aside, because our primary aim is to show that even if the auction does yield a secure place for liberal neutrality within equality of resources, Dworkin ultimately mischaracterizes this political morality as an ethically continuous or sensitive one. Within the auction that achieves distributive equality, justice ultimately constrains, rather than flows, from personal ethics.

Dworkin asks us to imagine a number of shipwreck survivors who have washed ashore upon a desert island with abundant resources that no one is antecedently entitled to. These immigrants accept that these resources shall be divided equally among them and also that 'no division of resources is an equal division if, once the division is complete, any immigrant would prefer someone else's bundle of resources to his own bundle.'[36] One of the immigrants is then chosen to divide the resources according to this envy test, but he is immediately confronted with a number of problems. He cannot achieve this egalitarian distribution by physically dividing the island's resources into *n* identical bundles, because some of them, like milking cows, are indivisible while others, like tracts of land, though divisible, would be unequally useful or productive for the same purposes, farming for instance.

Perhaps the divider could manage by trial and error, however, to create *n* bundles of resources and assign one to each immigrant so that, while each bundle was slightly different from the others, no one would envy anyone else's. This distribution might still fail as an equal distribution for a reason not caught by the envy test. Using Dworkin's example, let us assume that in order to achieve the distribution, the divider transformed all of the available resources into a very large stock of plovers' eggs and pre-phylloxera claret and divided this glut into identical bundles of baskets and bottles. After this allocation, everyone is thrilled except, say, Bob, who happens to detest plovers' eggs and pre-phylloxera claret. Now because Bob does not prefer anyone else's bundle to his own, the envy test is met, but he would still much rather that the divider had transformed the original bundle of resources into something else – say, pretzels and beer – prior to its distribution. The point should be obvious, which is that any possible combination of resources that composes each bundle the divider creates will favour some tastes over others, compared with different combinations he might have composed.

So the divider cannot satisfy the envy test by a simple mechanical division of resources, and there is no non-arbitrary way for him to select from among the many more complex divisions that could satisfy it. For Dworkin, the response to this problem lies in a constrained economic market in which the divider gives each of the immigrants an equal and large number of clamshells (100 – themselves valued by no one) to use as counters in the following auction. Each distinct item on the island is listed as a lot to be sold, unless someone notifies the divider, or auctioneer, that she wishes to bid for some part of that item, in which case the smaller part becomes, itself, a distinct lot. The auctioneer then proposes a set of prices for each lot and discovers whether there is only one purchaser at that price and all lots are sold. If this is not the case, then the auctioneer adjusts his prices until he reaches a set that does clear all markets. After this point, each of the immigrants remains free to change her bid, even when an initially market-clearing price is reached, or even to propose different lots.

Dworkin concedes that this process would be 'impossibly expensive of time'[37] if it could be made to work, but thinks that we can still imagine it coming to a close and goods distributed accordingly. At the end of this auction, no one would envy anyone else's set of goods because, *ex hypothesi*, she could have purchased that set with her clamshells instead of the one that she actually did, nor is the particular set auctioned off by the divider arbitrary, because each person played an equal role in determining its content through her purchases against an initially equal stock of clamshells. The auction therefore operationalizes what the envy test assumes, which is that 'the true measure of the social resources devoted to the life of one person is fixed by asking how important, in fact, that resource is for others.'[38]

Importantly, each immigrant begins Dworkin's auction with the same number of clamshells (100) to ensure that her hypothetical market transactions are conducted on fair terms. But while the auction is ultimately designed to test actual distributions in the real world,[39] the condition of equal bargaining power that it assumes is clearly falsified in that world. Furthermore, even if the immigrants somehow entered the auction on equal terms, and equality of resources obtained between them at its conclusion, this equality would be short-lived because the envy test would soon fail for a number of other reasons. Post-auction production and trading between the immigrants would reveal that some of them are obviously more skilful than others are at producing what others want, and would therefore trade to get. Some would enjoy working, or working in ways that would produce more to trade, while others would prefer leisure, or working in ways that produced less; some would remain healthy while others became sick: 'for any of these and dozens of other reasons some people will prefer the bundle others have in, say, five years, to their own.'[40]

The envy test assumes that people must pay the price of the life they have decided to lead, measured by what others give up in order that they may do so. This is what Dworkin means when he says that an egalitarian distribution of resources must be 'ambition-sensitive.'[41] But this also suggests a tentative solution to the post-auction instability problems sketched above: an egalitarian distribution must somehow be 'endowment-insensitive' so that people are *not* penalized for disadvantageous circumstances that are unchosen. These two desiderata working in concert explain why people are entitled to some form of compensation when they are handicapped or lack marketable talent, but not when and because their tastes or ambitions are expensive to satisfy.

The particular level of compensation that people are owed for inequalities in resource holdings that derive from natural disadvantage or bad fortune is established through a hypothetical insurance scheme that accompanies the auction. While there are, in fact, two such schemes – one for natural disabilities or handicaps, and another for unequal natural talents – the intricate details of each do not concern us here. What is important for our purposes is that, in both instances, we are asked to imagine that the immigrants are placed behind a 'modified veil of ignorance.'[42] In the case of natural disabilities, we are to assume, contrary to fact, that each immigrant shares the same risk of developing physical or mental handicaps in the future. We are also to assume, again contrary to fact, that none of the immigrants has already developed any of these disadvantages. Knowing what the total number of each handicap actually will be in the immigrant community, we must try to decide how much insurance coverage the average immigrant would purchase against developing any one of them. In the case of low marketable talent, we are to suppose, similarly, an imaginary world in which, while the distribution of skills over the immigrant community is in the aggregate what it actually is, each immigrant shares the same antecedent risk of suffering the consequence of lacking any particular set of these skills, and each is in a position to buy insurance against these consequences at the same premium structure.

With these assumptions in place, we are to ask ourselves, how much insurance would the average immigrant buy, and at what cost? Income tax in the real world would be used to collect the premiums that the immigrants had agreed to pay in the counterfactual one, as demonstrated by the number of clamshells each spent out of her initial 100 in both the disability and under-employment insurance markets, and the funds would then be transferred to those whose losses eventuated. Because everyone had the chance to insure against such losses from a position of equal bargaining power, within the same premium structure, and under conditions of equal antecedent risk, any remaining inequalities in peoples' resource holdings (how many remaining clamshells they have versus how much insurance coverage they have purchased) would stem from their differing choices, and so would be unobjectionable from a moral point of view.

Any conception of distributive equality requires some standard of interpersonal comparison to distinguish between people that are better from others who are worse off because, otherwise, there is no way of establishing who ought to be aiding whom, and with what. Most such metrics defended in the contemporary literature – Arneson's equal opportunities for welfare, Rawls's primary goods, and Sen's basic capabilities, for instance – require people to demonstrate that they lack, or have less of, some particular good that others already have, or have more of, which the metric in question assumes is in everyone's interest to possess. To be eligible for compensation as a matter of distributive justice (rather than simply charity or benevolence), that is, one must suffer relative deprivation along some substantive or concrete dimension of well-being that is authoritative from the point of view of justice. Someone is badly off and entitled to compensation because she lacks an itemized good that others have, then, or has less of it than others do, regardless of whether or not she actually values or desires it.

The envy test, by contrast, refrains from relying upon any such standard. It allows people's own judgements about well-being and self-interest, as expressed by their bidding and insurance behaviour, to determine whether they are disadvantaged and owed compensation as a matter of justice.[43] Equality of resources 'allows us to cite, as disadvantages and handicaps, only what we treat in the same way in our own ethical life.'[44]

So the envy test's reliance upon people's subjective preferences in order to determine whether or not a particular distribution of resources is an egalitarian one accommodates, and is thus neutral between, a variety of radically different ambitions and life-plans. Another way that the distributive argument yields neutrality between contested ethical ideals relates to the particular liberty-constraint baseline that the hypothetical auction uses to allocate resources equally.

Rather than make an ideal distribution directly depend upon some outcome such as welfare maximization, equality of resources depends, instead, on a process of coordinated decisions through which people belonging to a community of equal concern express this by appropriating only resources that are legitimately theirs. And a substantial degree of liberty is essential in the design of any institutions meant to identify which shares of resources people are justly entitled to, because 'the true cost to others of one person's having some resource or opportunity can be discovered only when people's ambitions and convictions are authentic and their choices and decisions reasonably well tailored to those ambitions and convictions'; for Dworkin, 'neither is possible unless liberty is ample.'[45]

Perhaps, then, liberty should be auctioned, so that people can, themselves, decide how much of it is needed to implement the rest of their projects and commitments. If such projects require ample freedom, people would have to pay for it out of their initial stock of clamshells, and its value then would depend upon how many other people also bid for it; anyone who did not value liberty as highly, or whose projects required less of it, would have additional clamshells remaining for other, less liberty-intensive pursuits. Dworkin rejects this possibility as resting upon an incoherent distinction between acquiring a particular resource and acquiring rights or opportunities to use it. These are not two independent transactions, because 'no one can intelligently, or even intelligibly, decide what to bid for in an auction, or what price to bid for it, unless he makes assumptions about how he will be able to use what he acquires.'[46] Any auction requires a background of parallel assumptions constituting a liberty-constraint system that stipulates what one acquires in acquiring something, that is, what one can and cannot rightly do with it.

If the envy test presupposes a liberty/constraint system, then clearly it cannot be used to yield one, and this creates a seemingly intractable problem. This is because the envy test, itself, is radically indeterminate to the extent that it is compatible with an indefinite number of distributions resulting from various auctions from equal initial resources with different liberty/constraint systems in place. Consider two auctions, A and B. The liberty/constraint baseline in A stipulates that no one is allowed, say, to sculpt clay into satirical figurines; in B, no such restriction obtains. In each auction, immigrants will adjust their bids to the liberty/constraint baseline in place in order to reflect the value of clay to their projects given that baseline, and the envy test will be met in both of them.

Auctions from different baselines produce different distributions, and unless we are able to discriminate between the myriad of these satisfying the envy test and identify the '*true* opportunity costs of a set of resources,'[47] liberal equality will remain hopelessly inadequate as a tool of social justice. Fortunately, however, there *is* a way of doing this. Liberal equality stipulates that each person should have an equal share of resources measured by the cost of the choices she makes, reflecting her own plans and preferences, to the plans and projects of others. This is its interpretation of how a community's scheme of private property treats everyone with equal concern. This suggests that we should select from among the possible liberty/constraint baselines whichever one provides the best 'bridge'[48] between the envy test and this abstract egalitarian principle: 'We select the baseline system that gives most plausibility to the claim that an auction from that baseline treats people with equal concern.'[49] This bridge strategy implies that an auction is fairer, in the sense of providing a more genuinely equal distribution, when it offers more discriminating choices and is accordingly more sensitive to people's plans and preferences.

The true opportunity cost of any transferable resource can be determined only, then, by figuring out what price others would be willing to pay for it in an auction where resources were offered in as abstract a form as possible. Any auction with a liberty/constraint baseline that compromises this principle of abstraction cannot secure distributive equality, because it does not allow the greatest possible flexibility in fine-tuning people's bids to their plans and preferences: 'an ideal distribution is possible only when people are legally free to act as they wish except so far as constraints are necessary to protect security of person and property, or to correct certain imperfections in markets.'[50] This is Dworkin's core argument for state neutrality between contested ethical ideals. If a neutral liberty/constraint baseline is a presupposition of any auction that successfully identifies the true opportunity costs of people's choices, then state neutrality between contested ethical ideals is required by the best interpretation of equal concern and respect. Any other baseline, one that relied upon perfectionist premises, for instance, would undermine, rather than secure, distributive equality, by compromising the principle of abstraction.

Does Dworkin's distributive argument fare any better than his challenge model? To begin with, we should notice something very peculiar about his characterization of it. For Dworkin, any liberal theory capable of reconciling personal partiality and political equality must be ethically 'continuous' or 'sensitive.' Its principles of justice, and political morality more generally, should be based upon the most attractive and persuasive account of how life ideally should be led. This is why he introduces the challenge model of ethics. It is true that the particular metric that equality of resources uses to identify an egalitarian distribution – the envy test – aims to be maximally sensitive to the goals and preferences that people actually have. In this sense, equality of resources makes justice and ethics continuous. But there is another more important sense in which equality of resources is maximally *insensitive* to people's differing and contested convictions about the good life – the point at which the hypothetical auction that secures distributive equality is *designed* rather than *held*.

To see this more clearly, let us reintroduce our cast of characters from the last section – Albert, Betty, and Charlie – and give them 100 clamshells each with which to bid on resources. Albert interprets his ethical convictions in the way that the challenge model recommends, so he has no problem accepting the auction's procedural constraints as continuous with them. But what about Betty and Charlie? Nothing in their personal ethics provides them with any reason to accept the auction, as Dworkin describes it, as a way of allocating things. Admittedly, once inside the auction house, they will make the most of their clamshells by bidding as their personal ethical convictions suggest they should, but those convictions exert absolutely *no* influence on the principles of justice that antecedently determine that goods should be distributed in as abstract a form as possible through a market that uses the metric of true opportunity costs to identify their price. Betty and Charlie, for instance, would prefer that the liberty/constraint baseline presupposed by the envy test *ignored* rather than *accommodated* people's mistaken ethical judgements, so that how ambition-sensitive the auction should be would depend crucially upon how sound people's convictions about living well actually are. And since the principle of abstraction is intended to allow for maximal ambition-sensitivity so that people's bids can be as fine-tailored as possible to their existing preferences, Betty and Charlie would reject that principle as well.

5.5 Conclusion

If Betty and Charlie's ethical convictions lead them running for the auction-house door, the question then becomes, On what authority can the auctioneer rightly keep them inside? For Dworkin, justice requires political institutions to accommodate people's competing interests through a pricing structure that is neutral among their differing ethical convictions, no matter how sound or unsound those convictions might be. This is because, as a matter of political morality, all individuals are antecedently entitled to an equal share of society's resources. Nothing in Albert, Betty, and Charlie's ethical beliefs can upset this requirement, and this makes sense only, it seems, within the context of the very kind of political morality that Dworkin officially disavows – discontinuity. In the end, the challenge model of ethics leads to an endorsement of liberal equality only when it has already been constrained in a variety of ways that call into question his claim that his argument is an instance of continuity after all.

The challenge model's failure to ground ethically neutral principles of justice shows that abstract or subtler forms of perfectionism are no better than comprehensive ones are in justifying liberalism. If ethical neutrality is an attractive feature of liberalism – as I think it is – then its justificatory foundations will have to lie elsewhere. In part 3 of the book, I argue that a version of contractualism supplies the needed starting point. In the next chapter, I clear a path for that argument by disposing of a number of recent critiques that imply that contractualism *cannot* supply the requisite foundations.

6 Contract Killing: A Critique

6.1 Introduction

Social contract theories distinguish legitimate from illegitimate uses of political authority by asking what reasonable people would and would not consent to under fair conditions. Contemporary liberal philosophers working within the social contract tradition defend the idea that this standard of legitimacy excludes principles of justice that presuppose the validity of any controversial views of human flourishing. Only principles that are neutral between the rival ethical doctrines that they are meant to adjudicate could, they claim, secure the reasonable consent of those who must live under them.

This alleged link between contractualism[1] and liberal neutrality[2] has prompted a torrent of criticism.[3] Some critics have rejected neutrality by denying the coherence of the argumentative structure that yields it. Even if people *would* only agree to neutral principles of justice from within the procedural constraints that contractualism recommends, this conclusion is worthless because such limitations are, themselves, implausible. Others have accepted reasonable agreement as an ideal of political legitimacy, if only for argumentative purposes, but have denied that neutralist principles would be chosen by citizens seeking reasonable agreement on constitutional essentials and matters of basic justice.

In this chapter, I consider three recent expressions of this second type of objection and conclude that none of them succeeds. My refutation of this argument – what I shall call the *reflexivity thesis* – should be of paramount importance to defenders of liberal neutrality. This is because unless the reflexivity thesis is mistaken, state perfectionism is unavoidable as well as legitimate *even from within their contractualist view of political legitimacy.* I will take no position (here) on the defensibility of either contractualism or of liberal neutrality but rather indicate why the claim that they cannot be linked is confused.

My argument proceeds as follows. In section 2, I briefly explain the contractual ideal of political legitimacy and the type of neutrality that it yields, before outlining the *reflexivity thesis* as presented by its three advocates.[4] These critics maintain that the contractual argument for neutrality is self-defeating because it cannot withstand its own epistemic presuppositions. In section 3, I distinguish moral from epistemic conceptions of reasonableness to illustrate that the reflexivity thesis gains whatever limited appeal it has from conflating the two. I then build upon this distinction and construct an alternative argument for neutrality that evades this critique. In section 4, I indicate how my argument usefully illustrates the flaws of several familiar objections to neutrality. If it does, in fact, avoid the type of self-defeating epistemic premises that some claim to have detected in contractualism, then perfectionist critics will have to go the hard way and attack the value of moral equality that recommends reasonable agreement as an ideal of political legitimacy.

6.2 The Reflexivity Thesis

For contemporary social contract theorists, only principles of political morality that can be the object of reasonable agreement are legitimate bases for the exercise of state power. This is the ideal of political legitimacy adopted by Brian Barry, Thomas Nagel, and John Rawls. Each of them argues that this criterion excludes principles of justice that presuppose the truth of controversial ethical, religious, or metaphysical premises. Legitimacy requires that adjudicative principles be somehow neutral between the conflicting ethical ideals that generate their need.

Precisely why, then, must states be neutral to secure the consent of those subject to them, and what form must this neutrality take to satisfy the contractual ideal of legitimacy? Perfectionist principles of justice are illegitimate because they are *reasonably* rejectable by hypothetical contractors selecting political ground rules from a position of equality. Contractualists argue that perfectionist values are unreasonable from a constitutional point of view. Barry's 'sceptical uncertainty,' Nagel's 'epistemic restraint,' and Rawls's 'burdens of judgement' are each an attempt to explain why this is so. While these ideas about the origins of ethical disagreement and the possibility and limits of moral knowledge differ, they have the same political implication: only principles of justice that do not presuppose the validity of any of the controversial ethical views they are meant to adjudicate are legitimate. This is widely referred to by both proponents and critics as *justificatory neutrality*. Political legitimacy is based upon reasonable agreement. Perfectionist principles – those that presuppose the validity of controversial views of human flourishing – are unreasonable. Therefore, legitimacy requires justificatory neutrality because reasonable people would consent only to neutral principles of justice.

At first glance, then, the inference from contractualism to neutrality is only as persuasive as the epistemic theory that is the argumentative bridge between them. Ultimately, whether something is politically legitimate or not depends upon whether it is reasonable or unreasonable, respectively, and controversial epistemic theories distinguish between the two.

Three critics have recently challenged this general argumentative strategy by pointing to the implausibility of the epistemic asymmetry it implies between perfectionist and neutral principles of justice. If perfectionist principles of justice are illegitimate because they can be reasonably rejected as a result of their epistemic status, then contractualism is self-contradictory unless, *per impossibile*, neutral principles do not share this same status. If they do and 'sceptical uncertainty,' 'epistemic restraint,' and the 'burdens of judgement' also apply to liberal neutrality, then the contractual position is self-defeating: the political conclusion (neutrality) that it seeks to justify is inadmissible on its own terms.

The idea that contractualism and neutrality, alone, escape the burdens of practical reasoning is dubious, to say the least. But unless this is so, they are, themselves, vulnerable to reasonable rejection and, therefore, illegitimacy. I call this argument the *reflexivity thesis*: it asserts that the contractual case for neutrality is self-defeating because it cannot withstand its own epistemic presuppositions.

Precisely how, then, do its proponents set forth their case? The reflexivity thesis takes slightly different forms, depending upon its target, but there are two principal versions of it. According to the first version,[5] the contractualist principle of political legitimacy is justified by arguments that, once thought through, call it into question. The basic idea is that contractualism must itself be justified in a way that is reasonably acceptable to all. But because the arguments commonly given for it are reasonably rejectable by some, contractualism is therefore self-defeating. According to the second one,[6] contractualist arguments for liberal neutrality are not self-defeating, but simply bad to the extent that they either exclude too much or too little.

Simon Caney has examined Rawls's position that legitimacy requires the liberal state to eschew the political pursuit of controversial ethical doctrines. He focuses on the second lecture of *Political Liberalism,* 'Powers of Citizens and Their Representation,' to assess Rawls's two 'aspects' of reasonableness. Caney begins with the second aspect because he takes it to be 'relatively unproblematic.'[7] Simply put, reasonable persons are those who recognize what Rawls calls the 'burdens of judgement.' These are the sources or causes of disagreement between reasonable persons; they are 'the many hazards involved in the correct (and conscientious) exercise of our powers of reason and judgment in the ordinary course of political life.'[8] Rawls's non-exhaustive list of them is as follows: (1) empirical and scientific evidence is often conflicting, complex, and thus hard to evaluate; (2) agreement regarding the considerations that are relevant to a particular issue does not preclude disagreement over the respective weight they are to be assigned; (3) moral and political concepts, among others, are indeterminate so that one must often rely upon judgement and interpretation within some range where reasonable persons may differ; (4) the ways in which reasonable deliberators assess evidence and weigh moral and political values are shaped by their total experiences, which must always differ; (5) there are often different kinds of normative considerations on both sides of an issue and it is difficult to make an overall assessment; (6) and, finally, people often face great difficulties in setting priorities and making adjustments among seemingly incommensurable values. The second aspect of reasonableness stipulates that reasonable individuals reject the idea that all ethical disagreement is reducible to either competing socio-economic interests or intellectual ineptitude. They see it as the inevitable result of the diligent exercise of reason within enduring free institutions rather than an unfortunate by-product of self-interest or stupidity.[9]

Caney examines three different possible interpretations of Rawls's first aspect of reasonableness. He dismisses one as circular, and another as logically incompatible with the idea of neutrality before settling on this one: 'Reasonable persons think that political decisions may not be based upon claims about which intelligent people disagree.'[10] In this view of reasonableness, Rawls's defence of neutrality takes the following form:

1 A state is fair if *reasonable* free and equal persons would accept it.
2 Because of the burdens of judgement, reasonable free and equal persons think that political decisions may not be based upon claims about which intelligent persons disagree.

3 Therefore, a state is fair if it eschews controversial ethical claims as the
   basis of principles of justice.

Caney finds this argument to be logically valid, but unconvincing nonetheless because the idea of reasonableness in premise 1 is 'unduly
strict.'[11] Since intelligent and reflective individuals hold radically dissimilar views about not only conceptions of the good, but also about issues of
distributive justice, affirmative action, and capital punishment, all of
these areas of public policy would be excluded as equally inadmissible.
For example, as a matter of basic justice, Rawls's difference principle
cannot legitimately rest upon controversial assumptions. However,
desert theorists and libertarians reject the idea that the distribution of
talents – the so-called 'natural lottery' – is arbitrary from a moral point of
view. Taking the idea of reasonableness seriously in premise 1 would thus
preclude the implementation of the difference principle. Rawls's contractual argument is, therefore, *too* successful because it renders unreasonable the very policies it purportedly justifies.
   Caney perceives Rawls's idea that people will share beliefs about
justice in a liberal political system 'especially puzzling given his account
of the causes of "the fact of reasonable pluralism."'[12] Because of the burdens of judgement, people will inevitably hold different but nonetheless
reasonable views about which conceptions of the good are attractive
unless coercion prevents this. But if this is so, a system of liberal rights
will presumably also produce different but reasonable views about the
most plausible theory of justice. Given Rawls's explanation of the fact of
reasonable pluralism, then, 'should this not also lead us to expect what
might be called the fact of reasonable pluralism *concerning the right?*[13]
   Joseph Chan has put forth a strikingly similar critique of Thomas
Nagel's most recent argument for liberal neutrality,[14] which he reconstructs as follows:

1 Conceptions of the good life are objects of reasonable disagreement.
2 We should respect people as ends (or we should never treat them
   merely as means).
3 Respecting people as ends implies that we should not force people to
   serve an end with which they may reasonably disagree.
4 Therefore, the state should not enforce conceptions of the good life.

Chan notices that if the argument for neutrality is rooted in the contest-
able nature of conceptions of the good, then Nagel's position faces a

serious internal challenge. As Caney also indicates, conceptions of the good are not the only things that are capable of arousing reasonable disagreement in connection with public policy. Education, national defence, as well as social and criminal justice are also highly controversial issues. Why, then, does the state's pursuit of perfectionist values, *alone*, but not of other controversial matters, lead to illegitimacy? Since the Kantian injunction contained within premise 3 appears to be equally violated by public policies on social justice with which reasonable people disagree, Nagel (who defends egalitarian redistributive policies) must explain his asymmetrical treatment of justice and perfectionist values. As Chan says, liberals 'must show us why a deep cut between the two types of issues is warranted.'[15]

Chan extrapolates Nagel's argument for this asymmetry, what he calls 'the argument of higher-order unanimity,'[16] from Nagel's treatment of national defence policy. For Nagel, everyone should recognize that some unified policy is absolutely necessary for national defence.[17] As such, they should be willing to allow the state to make authoritative decisions about it despite the existence of reasonable disagreements regarding particular decisions that are undertaken in its pursuit. The Kantian injunction in premise 3 above, then, is not actually violated by reasonable disagreements over the direction of national defence initiatives because such disputes are contained within a higher-order consensus on the need for a unified state policy in this area. Chan reconstructs Nagel's third premise into a general principle that incorporates this rule of exception: '*The principle of higher-order unanimity*: in situations where reasonable people have disagreements on how a problem should be resolved but nonetheless agree, or would agree, that the state should adopt a policy (even if the policy may turn out to be disputable), the state may legitimately make policy decisions dealing with the problem.'[18]

Practical necessity generates a reason for higher-order consensus on a unified national defence policy that every reasonable person should recognize. But in the case of the pursuit of the good life, Nagel contends that there is no similar necessity for coordinated collective action by the state.[19] There is no higher-order value of democratic control or pursuit of the good abstractly conceived that is capable of commanding reasonable agreement on the necessity of state perfectionism. Therefore legitimacy requires that individuals be left free to follow their own paths to excellence or perfection, consistent with the equal freedom of others to do the same.

Chan believes that Nagel's argument to justify this asymmetry is caught on the horns of a dilemma: either higher-order unanimity is so difficult to obtain that not only the state's pursuit of the good life but also its other traditional ones would be judged as illegitimate, *or* it is so easy to obtain that all of these pursuits, including perfectionist ones, are admissible. In order to justify many of the state's traditional pursuits such as military defence, education, and social justice, then, Nagel's account of political legitimacy requires a very broad version of higher-order unanimity, but this expansive version not only fails to reject perfectionism, it actually vindicates it.

Brian Barry's *Justice as Impartiality* is the final target of the reflexivity thesis. For Barry, scepticism supplies the premise that is required to get from the desire for agreement on reasonable terms to the anti-perfectionist conclusion that no conception of the good should be built into the constitution or the principles of justice.[20] By scepticism, Barry means that 'no conception of the good can justifiably be held with a degree of certainty that warrants its imposition on those who reject it.'[21] Therefore, this is not a view of human flourishing per se but rather an epistemological doctrine about the status of what constitutes it.

Barry thinks that secular and religious conceptions of the good are to be assimilated because they both give rise to conflicting practical implications and these conflicts cannot be resolved by rational argument. The possibility of arriving at a consensual basis for the ground rules of social life is equally undermined by both of them. The inherent uncertainty of all conceptions of the good precludes them from being the basis of agreement among those seeking terms of political justice that no one may reasonably reject. Liberal neutrality is, therefore, the only fair way of dealing with the 'unresolvability'[22] of disputes regarding human excellence.

To see the structural similarity of this argument to those of both Nagel and Rawls, let us represent it thus:

1 Political legitimacy requires reasonable agreement.
2 Arguments stemming from conflicting conceptions of the good cannot be resolved by rational argument.
3 Therefore, only neutral principles of justice are legitimate.

Simon Clarke echoes both Caney and Chan in rejecting the contractualist case for neutrality in all of its existing variants. He indicts Rawls and Nagel largely for the same reason that they do – neither of them adequately explains why their intuitions about reasonable disagreement do not also extend to principles of justice – and he identifies two major problems with Barry's position. First, the historical evidence that Barry points to in support of scepticism is inconclusive. Second, and more importantly, nothing appears to prevent the uncertainty thesis from being turned back upon contractualism itself: 'for the argument to work, uncertainty must knock out all conceptions of the good while leaving the contractarian procedure and the resulting principles intact.'[23] Clarke sees no reason why anyone should be any more certain about reasonable rejection as an ideal of political legitimacy than she should be about views of human flourishing. While Barry attempts to derive certain substantive principles such as freedom of religious worship from the reasonable rejection procedure, the distinction between what can be known with certainty and what cannot is unlikely to map neatly onto the distinction between justice and conceptions of the good. More plausibly, one can be certain about some but not all questions of justice and some but not all questions of the good. Barry's historical evidence comes nowhere close to establishing that the two distinctions do, in fact, coincide.

Each of these three critiques claims to have identified a key weakness at the core of the contractualist argument for liberal neutrality. The various epistemic premises designed to support the contention that perfectionist principles of justice cannot be reasonably agreed to also infect the contractual ideal of legitimacy itself. Because this ideal, and the neutrality that it is thought to generate, are also objects of reasonable disagreement, the entire argumentative structure within which they are embedded is self-defeating.

6.3 Two Concepts of Reasonableness

Ultimately, the reflexivity thesis fails because it mistakes a moral claim about what equality requires in a setting of ethical pluralism for various epistemic theories that explain how such disagreement may have originated. Properly understood, the contractual premise is admittedly controversial, but those who wish to dispute it are committed to rejecting a moral thesis about equality, not a view of the boundaries of human knowledge. The defence of moral equality does not necessarily presuppose any particular explanation of pluralism, and contractualists should remain agnostic about such issues, at least within the context of their arguments for liberal neutrality.[24]

Contractualism does not necessarily rely upon an implausible epistemic asymmetry between principles of justice and perfectionist values. Consider the following alternative argument for neutrality:

1 Moral equality recommends contractualism as an ideal of political legitimacy.
2 Because of pervasive ethical disagreement, this ideal cannot be satisfied unless a satisfactory strategy of exclusion is devised.
3 The contractual premise (1) supplies the criterion for this strategy of exclusion so that only views that are consistent with its (controversial) interpretation of moral equality are admissible to the hypothetical agreement.
4 The procedural constraints that model the criterion found in 3 rule out perfectionist principles of justice.

If these claims are coherent, then the reflexivity thesis collapses and its defenders must show either that moral inequality is the correct argumentative baseline for principles of political morality, or that the egalitarian procedural constraints that social contract theorists deploy are somehow defective.

6.3.1 Equality

The two most powerful statements of contractualism that are currently on offer differ somewhat in both the appropriate specification of the contractual situation and the principles of political morality that contractors would agree upon. In the Rawlsian version,[25] contracting parties maximize the interests of the least advantaged because certain informational constraints prevent them from knowing whether or not they, themselves, belong to this group. The Scanlonian version[26] replaces this combination of mutual disinterest and deliberative ignorance with a motivation of a different kind – the desire of contractors to find principles that others, insofar as they also have this aim, cannot reasonably reject. Under this version, we are directed to attend to the interests of the worst off, not because we might, in fact, *be* them, but because, if anyone has reasonable grounds to object to a proposed principle, it is likely to be them.

In both cases, however, the notion that political authority, to be legitimate, must be able to meet with the approval of everyone's reason attempts to capture a certain type of equality among human beings. Thomas Nagel provides a concise statement of this foundational contractual value as follows:

> The basic insight that appears from the impersonal standpoint is that everyone's life matters and no one is more important than anyone else. This does

not mean that some people may not be more important in virtue of their greater value to others. But at the baseline of value in the lives of individuals, from which all higher-order inequalities of value must derive, everyone counts the same. For a given quantity of whatever it is that's good or bad – suffering or happiness or fulfilment or frustration – its intrinsic impersonal value doesn't depend on whose it is.[27]

Social contract theorists develop various arguments to defend this moral idea. But whichever substantive criteria are singled out as the relevant justificatory grounds for it – we are all equally God's creatures; as free and equal citizens, we all possess the requisite capacities for the exercise of our moral powers – the implications of accepting it are constant. The reasonable agreement of every citizen is a necessary condition for the exercise of legitimate political authority, and the justification of higher-order inequalities must be undertaken from the perspective of free and equal citizens.

Moral equality is what gives the reasonable rejection criterion its content. Agent X, for instance, cannot reasonably reject principle P simply because its acceptance involves certain unwelcome burdens on her. The equal consideration of everyone's interests (howsoever specified) means that P is only *reasonably* rejectable by X if either there are other feasible alternative principles (Q, R, or S, say) whose acceptance will involve the imposition of no such burdens on anyone, including X, or other principles (T, U, say) the acceptance of which will entail lesser burdens on herself *and* no greater ones than those entailed by P on anybody else.

Moral equality thus enters the contractual argumentative strategy in two ways: it motivates the justificatory appeal to each person's reason in legitimating state power, and it helps (one would hope) to ensure the ongoing stability of liberal egalitarian institutions. This is because political decisions that satisfy the contractualist ideal of legitimacy are egalitarian in the sense that even those on the losing end of them are able to feel as though they have done as well as they could reasonably hope to.[28]

6.3.2 Plurality

Because ethical controversy is what creates the political problem, a distinction must be found between disagreements whose grounds make it legitimate for democratic majorities to use political power in the pursuit of their beliefs from others where it would be wrong for them to do so. Unless this can be done without relying on precisely the type of ethical values under dispute, contractualism is caught on the horns of a dilemma and straightforwardly self-contradictory. Either there is a consensus about the shape and character of a worthwhile human life, in which case the political problem has been misdiagnosed, or there is not, and then an ideal of legitimacy that has agreement at its core appears hopelessly misguided.

Paradoxically, this dilemma helps us to understand how the contractual diagnosis of the political problem influences the structure and content of the legitimating agreement. *Actual* agreement among individuals as they are cannot possibly be an appropriate solution to this problem because the straightforward application of personal ethics to political life is precisely what creates it. On the one hand, then, political morality must be ethically inventive and the contractual situation must be specified in hypothetical terms. Unless this is the case, narrow self-interest and unequal bargaining power threaten to produce, at best, a modus vivendi and, at worst, dissensus and, thus, both instability and illegitimacy. On the other hand, this ethical invention cannot simply identify the content of the hypothetical agreement with principles that are morally right by independent standards because the existence of such pre-political standards seemingly renders the need for agreement dispensable altogether.[29] The difficulty, then, is to make sense of a *via media* between these two positions that takes men as they are, and motives as they might be, as Rousseau might have said. How might this be done?

6.3.3 Abstraction

Pluralism complicates the problem of achieving political justification through contractual agreement. For this reason, we must develop a normative consensus by somehow abstracting from the actual views that are held by citizens in society. Otherwise, the social contract is little more than a compromise that accommodates diversity by conforming the principles of justice to the existing distribution of power. To some extent, narrow-minded or intolerant conceptions of the good will undoubtedly persist under free institutions. Yielding to them, however, would render liberalism 'political in the wrong way.'[30]

The ideal of public justification in a context of pluralism therefore raises the question as to how inclusive the social contract should be. To accommodate diversity and give normative content to the justificatory agreement, a strategy of exclusion[31] is needed. Two different strategies are possible to guide this abstraction.

We may call the first the 'reasonableness as valid argument' strategy.[32]

It asserts that only *views* satisfying certain stringent epistemic standards are justifiably held, and that only holders of such reasonable views are admissible to the hypothetical constitutional convention. According to one of its proponents, a view is reasonable 'just in case its adherents are stably disposed to affirm it as they acquire new information and subject it to critical reflection.'[33] Epistemic exclusionary criteria such as this one are meant to differentiate various types of ethical pluralism in order to identify a possible basis for an underlying normative, that is to say, justificatory, consensus.

As liberal-democratic societies demonstrate, the protection of deliberative liberties (conscience and speech) results in a plurality of conflicting ethical ideals. This is a basic and particularly uncontroversial claim about the correlation between permissive institutional arrangements and diversity. The 'reasonableness as valid argument' strategy incorporates this correlation but adds something crucially important to it. Because a subset of the controversial views that liberal institutions make possible satisfy the epistemic criterion identified above, they are also *reasonable* and 'permissibly taken by their adherents to be true.'[34] This factual claim leads to a prescriptive one. If some forms of diversity are the natural consequence of the free exercise of practical reason, then achieving a justificatory consensus by limiting the social contract to them does not make liberalism political in the wrong way. In this view, basic principles of justice accommodate reasonable pluralism, not the existing relative distribution of bargaining power among the citizenry.

This first strategy successfully distinguishes the contractual response to pluralism from a pragmatic truce, but it suffers from two fatal flaws. First, unless its advocates produce a defensible argument linking epistemic competence to the requirements of citizenship in democratic societies, 'reasonable pluralism' is an unnecessarily restrictive basis for toleration. While views that cannot be supported by good arguments may still be consistent with these requirements, the first strategy presupposes that epistemic and political unreasonableness track one another. It implies that people who hold ethical beliefs uncritically are, for this very reason, *necessarily* prone to violate the equal rights of others. Unless this doubtful claim can be supported, a conception of toleration that is limited to the philosophically enlightened is reasonably rejectable by free and equal citizens. Philosophical enlightenment should not be a precondition of moral status in a political society founded on the idea of a social contract.[35]

The second flaw is revealed by contrasting two different ways that epistemology can be related to principles of political morality. An epistemic hypothesis could explain the fact of ethical disagreement, but principles of political morality would not necessarily presuppose its validity because the *fact*, not the hypothesis, was thought to be politically significant because of the moral challenge that it poses for contractualism. Epistemology would, then, explain why people disagree, but the appropriate political response to this fact would be specified in relation to moral ideas such as equality.

The 'reasonableness as valid argument' strategy, by contrast, reverses the argumentative direction between epistemology and political morality. It transforms the epistemic hypothesis that explains why people disagree about ethics into the contractual premise for tolerating diversity. This needless extension exposes the liberal case for neutrality to the reflexivity thesis in the following way. If the burdens of judgement, sceptical uncertainty, or any other such epistemic theory is what grounds the proposition that perfectionist principles of justice are reasonably rejectable and, therefore, illegitimate, then *pace* Caney, Chan, and Clarke, we *do* need an explanation as to why the value of moral equality has an epistemic force or authority sufficient to overcome these limitations. For the asymmetry between neutralist justice and perfectionism to hold, it must be unreasonable, in an *epistemic* sense, not to endorse the contractualist's interpretation of equality.

Moral equality recommends contractualism as a justificatory device because submitting the exercise of political power to each person's assent is a procedural expression of everyone's equal share in it. This premise supplies the content of a second exclusionary strategy that ties reasonableness to moral equality. Call this 'reasonableness as fairness.' On this interpretation of reasonableness, the abstraction that is required to make agreement possible in a context of interpretive pluralism derives from a claim about the moral status of *agents* rather than a thesis about the relative epistemic adequacy of their *beliefs*. A brief look at how moral equality is modelled within the two most influential contemporary accounts of contractualism will help us to better understand this second strategy of exclusion.

Thomas Scanlon argues that we may establish the content of morality by asking questions about what it would be rational for individuals to choose or do, given certain background motivational assumptions that express the value of equality. His version of contractualism is as follows: 'An act is wrong if its performance under the circumstances would be disallowed by any system of rules for the general regulation of behaviour which no one could reasonably reject as a basis for informed, uncoerced general agreement.'[36]

What do these qualifications exclude? 'Reasonably' rules out rejections that would be unreasonable *given* the aim of finding regulative principles that could be the basis of informed, unforced general agreement. According to Scanlon, and by implication Barry and Nagel who rely on his version, moral argument about legitimacy concerns the possibility of agreement among persons who are all moved by this desire to the same degree. We must be very careful, however, about the limited scope of this counterfactual motivational assumption because it only characterizes the agreement through which the content of morality is explicated. As a result, it is no objection to Scanlon's view to point out that people are not primarily so moved because the counterfactual is not advanced as a psychological account of actual motivation, but rather as a moral claim about what equality requires of us when we disagree with one another. Political justification guided by the value of moral equality *should* conform to this motivational criterion.

Scanlon's last two criteria stipulate that, to be legitimate, the agreement must be both 'informed' and 'unforced.' The former rules out agreements that are based on superstition or false beliefs about the consequences of actions; the latter excludes those that result from either coercion or unequal bargaining power between contractors. Moral argument abstracts from such considerations and the only relevant pressure for agreement comes 'from the desire to find and agree on principles which no one who had this desire could reasonably reject.'[37]

Similar procedural constraints are found in the work of John Rawls. In *A Theory of Justice* and *Political Liberalism,* Rawls famously situates his hypothetical contractors behind a 'veil of ignorance.' They are prevented from knowing their respective socio-economic positions, comprehensive doctrines, race, ethnicity, and sex, as well as their natural endowments such as strength and intelligence. This deliberative ignorance models Rawls's settled conviction that these factors are arbitrary from a moral point of view and should, therefore, not influence the hypothetical agreement and basic principles of justice. The symmetrical positioning of the contractors behind the veil is a procedural manifestation of their moral status as free and equal citizens.

For Rawls, an ongoing and self-governing political community of equals is possible only if the procedural constraints that model its citizens' equality are somehow extended beyond the original constitutive agreement that establishes the basic principles of justice. This requires a 'companion agreement'[38] on the principles of reasoning and the rules of evidence with which citizens are to resolve interpretive disputes concerning the applicability of the principles of justice, the extent to which they are satisfied, and which laws and policies best fulfil them under existing social conditions. Accordingly, citizens acknowledge their equal moral status discursively by confining political argument over constitutional matters and questions of basic justice to ways of reasoning and inference that are, themselves, capable of securing general agreement.

The second strategy of exclusion should now be clear. We identify what is 'reasonable' by asking what fairly situated contractors would and would not choose as basic principles of justice. A moral thesis about equality specifies the constraints that make the choice-situation fair by distinguishing which considerations are, and which are not, relevant from a political point of view. Differential natural endowments and relative bargaining power advantages, for instance, are bracketed as irrelevant to the selection of principles of justice. Instead, an underlying juridical or Lockean equality that abstracts from such differences is the argumentative premise.

The reflexivity thesis maintains that reasonable disagreement about neutralist principles of justice renders the contractual argument self-defeating. If contractualism relies upon the first strategy of exclusion, then that argument is indeed incoherent in that way. However, the second strategy of exclusion is similarly incoherent only if we confuse procedural epistemic constraints with the moral propositions that these are designed to model.

Even though epistemology enters the argument for neutrality via procedural limitations on the information that is available to the contracting parties, moral equality, not epistemology, is the premise of the second justificatory strategy. Actual disagreement about the legitimacy of neutralist justice, then, does not threaten to render the contractual argument for it incoherent, because that argument does not assume that we are all moral egalitarians. The hypothetical contract is a heuristic device designed to yield a *normative* consensus. A consensus of this type demonstrates to us both why we *should* conform our reasoning about principles of justice to the constraints that moral equality generates, and also which particular principles we *would* select *if* we did. The reflexivity thesis misses this point because it conflates both ways that epistemology can be related to political morality (as explanatory hypothesis versus argumentative premise) and it reduces the second strategy of exclusion to the first one. It is this confusion that leads to the mistaken notion in the reflexivity thesis that contractualism must, itself, be contractually justified.

6.4 How to Defend Neutrality

We need not postulate an untenable epistemic distinction between the criteria of personal versus public justification to exclude perfectionism. Some have unsuccessfully tried to do this.[39] The relevant discontinuity is not between what one can justifiably believe and what one can justifiably impose on others as though the limits of toleration were identical with the limits of practical reason. For a contractual theory of the second stripe, that discontinuity is between *people*, not the epistemic status of their beliefs.

Perfectionist values are *reasonably* rejectable as the basis for principles of justice even if the ethical beliefs that underpin them are true because, for contractualists, *other people* who interpret these differently are equally entitled to enforce them. Moral equality means that political authority cannot be differentially distributed amongst citizens. All are to share equally in the community's political power, and varying degrees of moral virtue, intellectual competence, or business acumen, for instance, do nothing to upset this requirement. For this reason, pluralism renders perfectionist principles of justice 'unreasonable' because individual contractors would benefit from consenting to them only if they, alone, could successfully impose their interpretation of human flourishing on everyone else. This imposition is possible only by violating the procedural constraints that express moral equality.

The crucial distinction between epistemology and moral equality shows that neutrality can be defended without falling victim to the reflexivity thesis, but it also usefully illustrates the flaws of several other familiar critiques. One of them is as follows. Scanlon's motivational counterfactual and Rawls's veil of ignorance lead to neutrality because contractors have neither the bargaining-power superiority nor the relevant information to make perfectionism a reasonable choice. If all that the parties to the original agreement know is that people have different views, but not that some of these are more reasonable or likely to be true than others, then perhaps neutrality is, in fact, the only reasonable choice. But if there are ethical truths and these can be ascertained, would contractors contemplating the possibility that they may be holders of false views regard their interests as harmed by choosing that these should be repressed?[40] Interests are self-referential; they belong to *someone* and are normally valued by that person for that very reason. Beliefs, on the other hand, have independent content. People value their beliefs not simply because they are *theirs*, but because they hold them to be *true*. If truth is what beliefs are about,[41] and people have an interest in avoiding falsehood, then it appears as though neutrality is the reasonable response to ethical disagreement only if one cannot arrive at justified belief in these matters. Scepticism must underpin contractualism after all.

Scepticism cannot justify the procedural limitations that yield neutrality, because moral equality recommends them. If moral beliefs can never be justifiably held with a degree of certainty that warrants their imposition on those who dissent from them, then egalitarian principles of justice are unreasonable. While moral equality can be defended in a number of different ways, no sensible argument for it is consistent with scepticism unless one introduces the type of implausible epistemic asymmetry that the reflexivity thesis attacks. Unless it is recast, then, Barry's argument for neutrality is vulnerable to its perfectionist critics. As the second strategy of exclusion made clear, to get from pluralism to neutrality, we require moral arguments, not epistemic hypotheses.

Another criticism questions the (non) neutrality of contractual justice by rejecting the possibility of any stable position between a modus vivendi and political perfectionism. A contractual theory can avoid being 'political in the wrong way' only by developing a normative consensus that abstracts from the views that are actually endorsed in society. But this move renders any claim to ethical neutrality specious because this abstraction can be undertaken only in light of some moral value to guide it. As one critic writes, 'Liberalism cannot remain liberalism once it is defended on the basis of what is commonly accepted rather than what morality requires in a political context. One can only conclude that the growing literature purporting to develop a "neutral" form of liberalism is deeply misguided.'[42]

This worry is misplaced, because it misunderstands and overstates the scope and range of the neutrality that the contractual argument is intended to justify, which is admittedly limited. Justificatory neutrality applies only to the principles of justice and the basic institutions of a democratic society, and it is limited to permissible conceptions of the good where permissibility means consistency with the equal moral status of every citizen. Equality is what recommends reasonable agreement as an ideal of political legitimacy. This ideal, in turn, entails procedural constraints that rule out perfectionist principles of justice. As such, it is neither surprising nor problematic that the principles it actually defends *cannot* be neutral between views that endorse, and views that deny, moral equality. The neutrality that contractualists advocate is a type of impartiality between permissible conceptions of the good within a range bounded by a controversial ideal of equal freedom. Obviously, not everyone shares this ideal, and, contrary to the reflexivity thesis, the contractual argument *does not* presuppose that they do. Disagreement about moral equality may create problems for the ongoing stability of just institutions, but this does not affect the content of justice itself.

Finally, the distinction between two different strategies of exclusion helps to clarify some of the confusion surrounding Thomas Nagel's idea of 'epistemic restraint.' In 1987, he argued that a non-sectarian defence of toleration requires that appeals to truth in political argument be limited by reference to a mutually acceptable public standpoint.[43] However certain we may be that our ethical convictions are true, unless they can be justified from a more impersonal, or public, standpoint, they should be treated merely as beliefs that are inadmissible as legitimate bases for state action.

The distinction that Nagel wished to apply between beliefs simply justified from within and those shown to be justifiable from a more impersonal standpoint presupposed differing criteria for personal and public justification. For if one can have reasonable views that others may reasonably reject, then the standards of individual rationality must not only differ from but be less stringent than those of intersubjective justification. Only then can one have *personal* – but not *publicly* – justified beliefs.

Not surprisingly, this idea has been challenged as incoherent,[44] and Nagel has abandoned it in response to the criticism.[45] Recent commentators[46] have tried to rescue 'epistemic restraint' from its critics, while Nagel himself continues to defend the contractual argument for neutrality without it. However, if the argument of this chapter is sound, then the debate over 'epistemic restraint' is misconceived because the substantive political position that Nagel is trying to defend (liberal neutrality) need not presuppose the epistemic incoherence that critics such as Barry and Raz identify. The limits of public reason are moral,[47] not epistemic, ones, and the contractual case for neutrality does not sink with the ship of epistemic restraint.

6.5 Conclusion

The contractual argument for liberal neutrality is based upon a connection between moral equality and certain procedural constraints, rather than any specious link between epistemology and toleration, so there are only two possible avenues open to perfectionist critics wanting to further the debate. They could abandon equality as a premise for reasoning about principles of justice.[48] Alternatively, they could point out that there are competing conceptions of moral equality, and demand further justificatory support for the particular one(s) that contractualists rely upon. They might then ask what reason they have been given to accept *this* conception of equality in favour of others that may permit or even imply perfectionism. Because this question challenges the link between moral equality and the procedural constraints that are said to model it, a non-circular response cannot simply refer to those very constraints, but must also offer a substantive defence of moral equality itself to establish the plausibility of the requisite link.[49] We should notice, however, that in asking this question, perfectionist critics implicitly *concede*, rather than undermine, my central claim by shifting the argumentative terrain over liberal neutrality away from epistemology and towards the more promising issue of what equality means.

A particular conception of moral equality has been implied in this chapter, one that links the protection of certain vital interests to recognizing people as having equal standing as citizens in a self-governing political community. A full defence of this conception would explain why the political promotion of controversial perfectionist values compromises such a moral status while the promotion of other controversial policies does not. In doing so, such a defence would seek to demonstrate how state perfectionism runs the risk of denying this intuitively important link.

In the remaining chapters of this book, I elaborate on the four-part argument sketched here by establishing precisely what kind of *equality* grounds the contractual ideal of legitimacy; what type of *pluralism* is relevant to that ideal; the form of methodological *abstraction* required to render such contractual justification consistent with pluralism so understood; and, finally, the form of *neutrality* implied by these connections.

PART THREE

Defending Liberal Neutrality

7 Democratic Equality

7.1 Introduction

The failure of the reflexivity thesis implies that the contractual argument for liberal neutrality is neither incoherent nor self-defeating, and also that once we are committed to adopting reasonable agreement as an ideal of political legitimacy, we must reject perfectionist principles of justice. But this leaves a separate, residual, and perhaps more troubling possible objection entirely untouched – namely, that there might not, in fact, be compelling grounds for adopting contractualism in the first place.

Moral equality is what makes contractualism the appropriate test of political legitimacy, but this is a notoriously abstract idea, which can be rendered more concrete in a variety of different and potentially incompatible ways. The question naturally arises, then, as to whether any version of it can successfully ground neutralist principles of justice. Even those persuaded to abandon the reflexivity thesis might still rightly ask why they should accept *this particular* (contractualist) interpretation of equality in favour of other ones that would allow or even imply state perfectionism. Thus, there appears to be quite a large normative gap between claiming that moral equality is the correct premise for thinking about principles of justice, and concluding that those principles must be, because of that general premise alone, ethically neutral in some relevant sense. This gap must be narrowed.

On the one hand, then, we need to outline and defend persuasive intermediary reasons for linking equality and neutrality. On the other, we must do this in a way that avoids the opposite charge that the gap is entirely closed, because the contractual argument for neutrality would then be ultimately circular.[1] This problem – what we will call the *circular-*

ity thesis – is the most important objection to contractual theories of justice, and it goes as follows. Social contract theorists maintain that only principles of justice that can be reasonably agreed to or, equivalently, that cannot reasonably be rejected, are legitimate. In order for this method of justification to yield determinate results, however, certain motivational and/or informational constraints on the contracting parties must be introduced because, otherwise, there is no way of knowing precisely which principles it actually legitimates or excludes. Hypothetical contractors, after all, need to select and reject candidate principles on the basis of *something* – for instance, because such principles maximize their shares of 'primary goods,' or they respect certain basic liberties, rights that it is in their interest to have protected, or, finally, these give expression to their moral personality and sense of justice. An obvious way of discriminating between the many possible procedural constraints in question is to derive them from the underlying conception of equality that they model – the conception that makes reasonable agreement an appropriate test of legitimacy in the first place. But if the constraints that are ultimately introduced are selected on the basis of their according with some given conception of what political morality antecedently requires, then the idea of hypothetical 'agreement' at the core of the contractualist justificatory strategy seems entirely redundant. Ronald Dworkin expresses this point of view in a classic discussion of the original position's function in Rawls's social contract argument for the two principles of justice:

> It may be that I would have agreed to any number of ... rules if I had been asked in advance ... It does not follow that these rules may be enforced against me if I have not, in fact, agreed to them. There must be reasons, of course, why I would have agreed if asked in advance, and these may also be reasons why it is fair to enforce these rules against me even if I have not agreed. But my hypothetical agreement does not count as a reason, independent of these other reasons, for enforcing the rules against me, as my actual agreement would have.[2]

For example, some acts are wrong because they involve wanton killing or treasonous deception. *Because* they are wrong, it would be reasonable to reject any principle permitting them. This is a plausible explanation, but one that is unavailable to a contractualist, because it specifies the content of justice independently of, and prior to, the idea of the social contract – the notion of reasonableness that is supposed to test the legitimacy of principles actually depends upon them for its content. Thus, the circularity thesis – contractualist principles of justice are supposed to be derived from reasonable agreement, but such agreement, so the objection runs, is instead actually and tautologically derived from justice.

This chapter undertakes to explain why we *do* have compelling reasons for adopting contractualism as our standard of political legitimacy, and does so in a way that refutes the charge that the case for liberal neutrality is either foundationless or circular. Section 2 explains the idea of moral equality that commonly underlies contractualism's commitment to *public justification*. Section 3 defends a variant of that idea and shows that if we take it seriously, along with certain Lockean insights about disagreement and the nature of politics, we are logically committed to a form of democracy very broadly defined. Section 4 explains why contractualism is the political morality of democratic citizenship. This lays the foundation for the argument in the remaining three chapters that state neutrality between controversial ethical ideals is a requirement of the best understanding of liberal democracy.

7.2 Moral Equality

What does it mean, then, to say that moral equality is the premise of contractualism? By virtue of what property or properties are human beings entitled to the form of equal treatment that this view of political legitimacy says they are?

At bottom, moral equality is the view that all human beings have the same basic moral status. This means that they have the same fundamental moral rights, and that the comparable interests of every person should be equally weighted in the calculations that determine public policy, as well as in the justification of the constitutional structures that ultimately direct and constrain it. At this level of abstraction, this formulation is primarily negative – its main purpose is to exclude whatever actions, goals, and principles are inconsistent with it. It does not tell us what interests people actually have, nor does it specify the particular constitutional structures that are required to weight such interests equally. It does not assert that human beings are equally virtuous, or that their aims and aspirations are all equally praiseworthy. It simply amounts to the denial that things such as skin colour, sexual orientation, ethnicity, intelligence, and the ability to make money, for instance, are normally good or relevant reasons for treating some people better than others in the distribution of whatever it is that is taken to be valuable.

Contractualism's ideal of *public justification* is a way of modelling and working out the practical (political) implications of the equal primary importance of everyone's life. Before explaining this link we must first address several difficulties with this familiar characterization of moral equality. Underneath the indisputable and obvious differences between people – in strength, intelligence, beauty, and health, to mention but a few – social contract theorists sometimes maintain that we possess a certain capacity, or set of capacities, that distinguishes us all from other animals and inanimate objects. By virtue of these capacities, we, and only we, are members of a moral community – the community of rights-bearers to whom equal justification is owed. Three prominent recent candidates for such capacities are the following: the capacity to conceive, revise, and rationally pursue a coherent system of final ends; the capacity to understand, apply, and act from principles of justice that specify fair terms of social cooperation;[3] and the capacity to assess, and act upon, reasons and justifications.[4] These examples are representative cases of a more general problem that afflicts *any* such strategy of tying egalitarian distributive claims to empirical capacities such as these (or of any other kind, for that matter). Importantly, this problem recurs no matter what the theory in question requires that we distribute equally on the basis of such capacities – say, primary goods,[5] basic capabilities,[6] property rights,[7] access to advantage,[8] opportunity for welfare,[9] or resources.[10]

The argument moves from empirical claims about the possession of distinctively human capacities (C) to normative prescriptions about how people should be treated in light of their having them. There are two interrelated problems with this line of argumentation. First, as Hume famously pointed out, it is unclear how an 'ought' can be derived from an 'is' – that is, how moral requirements simply follow from natural facts alone. Setting this worry aside for the moment, a larger problem remains, however, because the factual premise itself appears false independently of its connection to the normative conclusion that it is designed to support. For in the above argument, possession of C is what distinguishes members (human beings) from non-members (plants, animals?) of the moral community: it is because all human beings have C that they are alleged to have the same moral rights, and so must all accordingly be treated in ways that could be justified to bearers of C. But any C that we specify as the basis of distributive entitlements – rational agency, the capacity for a sense of justice, benevolence – will admit of degrees. Some people, for example, are more effective at setting goals for themselves and implementing strategies to attain them than are others; some people set better goals than others do; and some people behave more justly than others. The question naturally arises then: if having C is the ground of one's having rights, so that only possessors of C have them, then why doesn't having *more* or *less* C also imply differential entitlements that are proportional to one's stock of it? Richard Arneson illustrates the point nicely: 'It is just as true that a creative genius has richer and more complex interests than those of an ordinary average Joe as it is true that a human has richer and more complex interests than a baboon. If the principle of equality is interpreted as equal treatment for equal interests, then the beings with fancier interests should get fancier treatment.'[11]

The very argument introduced to justify the special treatment that is owed to human beings (as agents, or reasoners, or whatever) seems simultaneously to undermine the claim that they should be treated equally, however we interpret this requirement.

There are at least two possible strategies for dealing with this problem, neither of which is very compelling. First, one could rest the argument for equal basic moral status on some threshold capacity: one could claim that while only possessors of C beyond a specified level are beings to whom justification is owed, their inequalities of C beyond that level would be morally insignificant. Rawls, for instance, seems to have something like this in mind when he argues that there is nothing inherently problematic about making natural capacities such as acting from a sense of justice the basis of equality: 'While individuals presumably have varying capacities for a sense of justice, this fact is not a reason for depriving those with a lesser capacity of the full protection of justice. Once a certain minimum is met, a person is entitled to equal liberty on par with everyone else.'[12]

The idea that all those who can give justice are owed justice is intuitively appealing, but how are we to identify the relevant threshold non-arbitrarily, given that there are obviously many such possible thresholds, and each one that we select will include and exclude a different range of beings? Perhaps this problem could evaded if some property or capacity was found such that, while it was normatively significant enough to ground basic moral status, it also did not vary from person to person by degree. It is very difficult to imagine, however, what such a capacity could be.

Over the last twenty-five years or so, egalitarian thinking in moral, legal, and political philosophy has taken what might be called a distributive turn. Egalitarian justice, that is, has often been understood primarily as a matter of ensuring that certain goods – welfare, resources, and rights, for instance – are distributed and, when necessary, redistributed, so as to correspond with favoured patterned results. Commonly, both the items thought to be particularly relevant to egalitarian theorizing, and the various distributional patterns that are favoured, are linked to metaphysical and ontological claims about the nature of human beings and their distinctive capacities.

What has recently been called 'luck egalitarianism'[13] is a case in point. Luck egalitarians maintain that inequalities in the advantages that people enjoy are morally legitimate only if they derive from the choices that people have voluntarily made; any inequalities deriving from unchosen features of people's circumstances are unjust. Some defenders of this view such as Ronald Dworkin, Eric Rakowski, Philippe Van Parijs, and John Roemer favour an egalitarian distribution of resources, while others such as Richard Arneson and G.A. Cohen maintain that some variant of welfare, or access to advantage, should be equalized. Different versions of the theory offer opposing views about what amounts to a choice, and what counts as a circumstance, but they all claim that the central point of egalitarian justice is to compensate people for involuntarily incurred bad luck.

Intramural luck egalitarian writings are concerned mostly with the question of *how* to implement the choice/circumstance distinction in practice. Some critics, however, reject both the metaphysical and the moral implications that luck egalitarians infer from that distinction altogether. Samuel Scheffler, for instance, thinks that the contrast between choice and circumstance cannot bear the degree of weight that luck egalitarians place upon it because it is both philosophically dubious and morally implausible:

> Some luck egalitarian writings seem implicitly to suggest that whatever is assigned to the category of unchosen circumstance is a contingent feature of the causal order, which is not under the individual's control and does not implicate his or her personhood, whereas voluntary choices are fully under the control of individuals and constitute pure expressions of their agency. But this contrast is, of course, untenable. In any sense of identity that actually matters to people, unchosen personal traits and the social circumstances into which one is born are importantly, albeit not exclusively, constitutive of one's distinctive identity. And, in any ordinary sense of 'voluntary,' people's voluntary choices are routinely influenced by unchosen features of their personalities, temperaments, and the social contexts in which they find themselves.[14]

This explains why there are often cases where unchosen personal attributes such as ugliness are disadvantageous, but we *do not* think that people afflicted by them are legitimately entitled to compensation from others simply by virtue of that fact. It also explains other cases where people's urgent medical needs such as surgery, for instance, can be directly traced to their own negligence or idiocy, but we *do* continue to think that they are still legitimately entitled to the medical care that they require.

Luck egalitarianism also raises in acute form all of the C-based difficulties identified above. If the capacity for voluntary choice is the basis of moral standing, then why should people exercising that capacity in varying degrees be treated the same? At one level, the luck egalitarian has an answer. She might say, 'Treating people as equals implies treating them differently when the number and quality of their choices are different. This just *is* what equal treatment requires.' At another more crucial level, however, this answer is radically defective, because the aim of ensuring that everyone's choice-sensitive entitlements are respected *presupposes* rather than explains why people should be treated as equals in the first place. We still need some explanation as to why people should matter equally from the moral point of view.

There is a more promising route that avoids this puzzle. As commonly understood by many social and political movements throughout history, equality is not, in the first instance at least, a distributive ideal. Rather, it is a normative conception of human relations, a moral ideal whereby social and political life should be conducted on the basis of an assumption that everyone's life is equally important. The ideal of democratic equality thus understood obviously has important distributive implications, but those implications derive their importance from the overarching theory of human relations that contains them. In this view, the core of the value of equality does not consist, then, in the idea that there is something that must be distributed equally, and that the chief philosophical task is figuring out *what* that something is; instead, equality is a relational ideal and the relevant normative question is about which principles of justice are most consistent, in modern conditions, with it.[15]

This relational ideal clearly needs to be defended, but its defence will take a very different form, and focus on very different factors, if one locates the value and point of egalitarianism in human arrangements, rather than in ontological claims about features of the natural world. Whereas elitists believe that collective life should be ordered to mirror a presumed natural hierarchy of human beings, ranked according to their intrinsic worth on the basis of class, caste, ascribed identity, and so on, egalitarians assert the irrelevance of individual (natural) differences of these kinds for social and political purposes. And once equality is understood in this way – as a relational rather than a distributive value – it is clear that egalitarianism's real enemy is not bad cosmic luck, but instead oppression, which is, by definition, socially imposed. So the general worries about 'C-based' arguments for moral equality might not apply to an argument for adopting contractualism on the basis of equality as a social and political ideal. If democratic citizens are entitled to make claims on one another simply by virtue of their status *as* equal citizens, then their fundamental rights and obligations are specifiable without reference to things such as their differing talents at choosing comprehensive goals, or their varying capacities for behaving justly. Ensuring that the exercise of coercive political power be capable of securing the reasonable consent of everyone subject to it might then be seen as a way of respecting this equal status, and spelling out some of its practical implications.

Of course, in order for this claim to be persuasive, there must be grounds for endorsing the idea of democratic equality, for thinking that political life must be conceived of as a set of relations among civic equals. In fact, there are good reasons for thinking this – reasons distinct from, and irreducible to, the problematic C-based strategy criticized above.

7.3 Democracy

Towards the beginning of *A Theory of Justice*, Rawls claims that the traditional theory of the social contract 'best approximates our considered judgments of justice and constitutes the most appropriate moral basis for a democratic society.'[16] In *Political Liberalism*, he re-emphasizes this connection in describing justice as fairness as a 'conception suitable for the basis of democratic citizenship.'[17] What makes social contract theory, then, an appropriate tool for thinking about justice *for a democratic society*?[18] For Rawls, the answer lies partly in the fact that pervasive disagreement about moral, religious, and philosophical ideals is a permanent and inevitable feature of such a society. A democratic regime grants all of its citizens, for instance, the right to vote and to be eligible for public office, it extends to them freedom of speech and assembly, as well as liberty of conscience and freedom of thought. These deliberative liberties both protect and foster pluralism, and Rawls thinks that the commitment to public reasoning implicit in the social contract tradition is the most appropriate response to that pluralism.

Historically, however, it is very doubtful that serious ethical controversy has been limited to constitutional democratic regimes, so one wonders why the pluralist argument for adopting contractualism should depend upon the *prior* existence of democratic institutions. While the European wars of religion and the Reformation made it abundantly clear that full-blooded state enforcement of religious orthodoxy was disastrous as a response to religious pluralism, that pluralism certainly predated the existence of democratic institutions. So if Rawls is correct to think that democratic institutions take pluralism more seriously than any of the available alternatives, and if such pluralism is, in fact, an enduring feature of any conceivable political life, then there is a powerful reason for bringing democratic institutions into being, even where they presently do not exist. There is accordingly no reason to limit the scope of contractualism as Rawls does to political communities with pre-existing democratic constitutions. He argues that contractualism is the political morality 'for a democratic society,' but this leaves it entirely open that justice might actually require something radically different in, for example, an aristocratic one, or a theocratic one united in affirming a common religious faith. Even if, *pace* Rawls, reasonable agreement *is* the most appropriate moral basis of a democratic polity, we still need to know why politics should assume a democratic form[19] in order for this claim to have critical bite.

As we saw in chapter 1, the Locke-Proast controversy highlighted two basic facts about politics. First, there is the *fact of pluralism* – that is, the fact that political principles operate in a context characterized by a multiplicity of conflicting interpretive claims about the nature of ethical truth.[20] It is the existence of ethical disagreement that generates the need for adjudicative principles or, as Locke calls them, settled 'standing rules.' Second, there is the *fact of coercion* – membership in a political community is largely[21] involuntary, and political principles are moral principles with which people can be legitimately *forced* to comply. Clearly, this is distinctive since not all moral principles are of this kind. For the violation of some moral norms – the keeping of one's promises, for instance – the appropriate sanction is the expression of disapproval, contempt, and outrage, but not compulsion. Putting these two facts together, the question becomes how ethical disagreements should be resolved politically, given that any political settlement will be coercively imposed. Neither of these descriptive claims about politics, it should be noted, implicates 'C-based' individual properties of the kind criticized above, for ethical disagreement is an emergent property of *groups* of people. If this is an ontological claim at all, then it is one of shared or social life that can be explicated in the absence of any claims at all about natural human capacities and variations among them.

The conjunction of both facts (disagreement/coercion) implies that under any conceivable political settlement, some views that make up this emergent property of the political association will win, while others will lose. And it immediately excludes one potential range of answers to the question about how disagreements are going to be resolved, Proastian answers of the kind 'Let the right view win.' For all of the reasons canvassed in chapter 1, perfectionist principles such as this are incoherent and inoperable unless we presuppose exactly what we do not have – an uncontroversial, antecedently correct, and independent standard of ethical rightness or truth. If we had this, then both the brute fact of ethical disagreement, and the need for political (adjudicative) principles, would be incomprehensible: so whatever the answer is, it cannot be based upon substantive rightness.

If ethical disagreement means that we cannot have a political system that begins in substantive claims of rightness, then we must look elsewhere, and the only alternative is to adopt rules and procedures that can adjudicate between the competing views. Could we, however, adopt a rule that weighted competing views differently? The only conceivable reason we might have for weighting views differently is that some of them are actually better than others, and so we simply revert to the problem identified immediately above. Taking the facts of pluralism and coercion seriously, then, logically drives us to adopt some form of procedural equality – to resolving political disputes democratically, in some minimal sense of that term.

But it is just that minimalism, it may be objected, that poses a problem. Perhaps, in abandoning problematic C-based views for a relational one, we can arrive at a basic idea of democracy that bridges equality and contractualism. But is not that idea *too* basic then? Do not contractualists require more? In Rawls's view, for instance, contractualism is the political morality of a *constitutional* democracy, one in which the political power of democratic majorities is subjected to principled limits: there are certain things such as violating individual rights, that is, that even democratic majorities can never legitimately do. Clearly, the argument in this section has shown only that *some form* of democratic equality is a requirement of taking ethical disagreement seriously, so nothing up to this point appears to exclude unconstrained majoritarianism of the kind that Devlin, for instance, would endorse.

We address this concern shortly by explaining how a particular (contractualist) view of justification emerges from the idea of democratic equality. Spelling out this notion of justification allows us to see that it involves additional constraints on political argument that ultimately yield a distinctively liberal (neutralist and non-majoritarian) conception of democracy.

7.4 Democracy and Contractualism

Certain basic features of politics[22] give us compelling reasons for adopting the social and political ideal of democratic equality as a relational rather than a distributive value. The general idea of moral equality with which we began was obviously attractive as a foundation of contractualism, but it raised a number of significant difficulties. Democratic equality, on the other hand, converges with the general moral egalitarian thesis in requiring that the interests of human beings must somehow be equally taken into account, but in focusing on citizenship and certain facts about politics rather than quintessentially human capacities, it renders the grounds for that thought far less mysterious. Taking ethical disagreement seriously implies giving each *citizen* an equal share in the collective power of her political community, because any other solution to the political problem reintroduces the perfectionism that effectively ignores that problem altogether.

Importantly, this implies that political morality must begin with adjudicative principles and procedures, not substantive claims of rightness. Because the politics directed by such principles and procedures is necessarily coercive, majority views will often be *imposed* upon every member of the community, and this raises a problem of legitimacy. If political life must be understood as a set of relationships between civic equals, as the model of democratic equality requires, then how can such coercive impositions ever be justified? Pluralism necessitates thinking of people as civic equals, but the democratic procedures that institutionalize that understanding seem to violate their own egalitarianism by coercing political losers.

Traditionally, the task of discovering the conditions of political legitimacy is understood as that of finding a way to justify a particular political system to everyone who is required to live under it. This justificatory problem connects the democratic conception of persons as civic equals with contractualism as a political morality by delineating the shape that any potential solution to it will have to take. Democratic political institutions will have to be regulated by principles of justice or, as Locke calls them, 'standing rules,' general in form and universal in application, that can be publicly recognized as a final court of appeal for ordering the conflicting claims of civic equals. Democracy itself, that is, will have to be constrained in a number of important ways in order to respect the underlying rationale for adopting it in the first place. The central guiding idea underlying social contract theories of legitimacy is that the principles of justice that serve this role must, themselves, be the object of a hypothetical agreement if political legitimacy is to be secured.[23] Because ethical pluralism rules out substantive unanimity on precisely *what* gets decided politically, democratic equality requires unanimity of another kind – unanimity in connection with the constitutional framework that sets out *how* such decisions are to be made. The contractualist test of political legitimacy both expresses *and* develops the specific implications of a *particular* democratic understanding of political equality – that in subjecting the coercive power of the state to each citizen's reasonable assent, contractualism politically expresses her status as a civic equal to whom justification is owed.

It might be tempting to conclude that the democratic argument for contractualism is incoherent, because the very procedural limits on political argument about constitutional essentials that democratic equality requires – Rawls's veil of ignorance, or Scanlon's motivational assumption, for example – ultimately destroy the idea and practice of democratic politics altogether. Contractualism requires a hypothetical choice situation to be specified in a particular way before any principles of justice ensue from it, but any specification of that situation will predetermine the scope and content of the politics that it legitimates. Maybe once procedural limits of these kinds have already been introduced, there is nothing much left to argue about politically, and no room left to legitimately argue for or against it. We are left with a set of foregone political conclusions, and the argument for contractualism that begins with democratic equality ultimately ends in the death of democracy. In subordinating the give-and-take of actual democratic politics to idealized constitution and lawmaking, then, hypothetical contract theories of political legitimacy simply decide *too much* in advance.

This objection comes both from deliberative democrats broadly sympathetic to the liberal project, and from hostile anti-liberal critics. Jürgen Habermas, for instance, levels precisely this type of objection when he writes that Rawlsian citizens, whose political life is regulated by contractually generated principles of justice,

> cannot reignite the radical democratic embers of the original position in the civic life of their society, for from their perspective all of the *essential* dis-

courses of legitimation have already taken place within the theory; and they find the results of the theory already sedimented in their constitution. Because the citizens cannot conceive of the constitution as a *project*, the public use of reason does not actually have the significance of a present exercise of political autonomy but merely promotes the nonviolent *preservation of political stability.*[24]

In effect, this is simply the political manifestation of the conceptual problem that the *circularity thesis* purports to unmask. That is, the tautological strategy of claiming simultaneously that (1) what can be reasonably agreed to *depends upon* what is antecedently and independently just, and that (2) what justice requires *derives* from reasonable agreement, results in a political situation in which actual citizens have their real deliberations about the content of justice predetermined by an idealized constitution that they have only hypothetically consented to.

Glen Newey[25] has recently advanced a more far-reaching critique, which purports to establish that contemporary analytical political philosophy (especially in its Rawlsian guise) is inherently *anti-political* in at least two interrelated senses. First, it has no deliberative content, to the extent that the ground rules governing participation in procedures such as Rawls's Original Position and Habermas's Ideal Speech Situation are fixed pre-politically and by philosophical fiat: 'the procedures' resemblance to actual decision-making processes is misleading: they replace and do not merely model them.'[26] Second, it adopts a purely instrumental view of political reasoning. Once political objectives are determined extra-politically in this way, individual practical reasoning can then be substituted as an adequate model for collective decision-making. While, in reality,[27] politics is the public forum within which disagreement plays itself out, *including disagreement about what counts as political*, political liberalism, in focusing on idealized or hypothetical consensus, envisions a world 'after politics' where such disputes are implausibly set aside. For example, Rawls argues that the content of public reason emerges from the deliberations of people in the Original Position but (1) only one person occupies that position and, more importantly, (2) she does not *choose* the moral/epistemic constraints that regulate their deliberations. In the end, constrained monologue ultimately masquerades as the give-and-take of real deliberative politics.[28]

To begin with, principles of justice are ultimately general conclusions about the status and propriety of various kinds of reasons for acting collectively through social and political institutions. Such principles tell us which considerations are, and which are not, especially relevant for deliberating from the political point of view. Admittedly, the procedural constraints that operationalize these general conclusions will often rule out some political proposals by excluding the reasons upon which they would be based,[29] but they also leave wide room for interpretation and judgement. As Scanlon points out, if 'a principle is taken to be a rule that can be "applied" to settle quite a wide range of questions with little or no room left for the exercise of judgment, then there are very few moral principles at all, and it would certainly be false to claim that every judgment about right and wrong must be backed by one.'[30] Contractualism is the best political morality for a pluralistic society precisely because it addresses itself to the question of *how* legislation and public policy can be framed consistently with democratic equality, while remaining as silent as possible on the question of *what* the specific content of that legislation and public policy should be.[31] Since there is no independently describable condition of society that democratic political institutions must produce and subsequently conform to, the contractually generated principles of justice that regulate these institutions cannot plausibly be said to be undemocratic. Once we understand that contractualism is an ongoing requirement of political morality, we see that it leaves ample room for a collectivity of civic equals to govern itself democratically, and both the conceptual and the political dimensions of the circularity thesis begin to unravel.

Rawls himself may be partly to blame for encouraging the misunderstanding at the heart of this democratic objection to contractualism, and seeing why is instructive in explaining why the circularity thesis might be appealing at first glance. In *A Theory of Justice*, he simultaneously argues for two seemingly incompatible things. On the one hand, he presents the hypothetical social contract as the engine of justice, as it were – the equal basic liberties and difference principles are just, we are told, *because* idealized agents would agree to them. On the other hand, he calls the social contract, and the notion of hypothetical consent that allegedly yields these principles, heuristic or expository devices. But this characterization makes sense only if there is some *other* self-sufficient argument for the two principles, and if this argument would likely be better understood and more clearly appreciated through the metaphor of the social contract. Of course, if the social contract is interpreted metaphorically in this way, this simply reinforces the *circularity thesis*, since Rawls's argument then reduces itself to the claim that idealized agents would agree to the two principles only because they are antecedently and independently just.[32] Since this is *not* Rawls's argument, he should abandon the characterization of the social contract as simply an expository or heuristic device, and so should we.

In sum, there is nothing inherently anti-political or undemocratic about the contractual argument for liberalism. What about the other worry, then, namely, that it is inherently non-deliberative, even if it *is* sufficiently democratic? We can alleviate this worry from both ends, as it were, by showing, first, how a contractual theory is deliberative and, second, taking Habermas's discourse ethics as an example, how putatively more 'radical' deliberative views *also* constrain political outcomes, as they must if they are to be at all plausible.

As with any other collective or individual agent, a political society has a way of setting an agenda, proposing alternative solutions to its problems, supporting those putative solutions with reasons, and ultimately settling on an alternative. The way it does this is its reason.[33] Broadly understood, 'deliberative democracy'[34] is the idea that this reason, in the form of law and public policy, should emerge from the free and informed public deliberation and participation of equal citizens.

Is the contractual argument for liberalism consistent with this ideal or, stronger still, implied by it? The answer to both questions is a qualified yes, and the qualifications are important. Consider the act of voting in a democracy. A vote takes place, all else being equal, when something must be done about a problem or issue, and time constraints prohibit continued discussion, or render it unduly costly. Even within the context of a deliberative democratic ideal in which the process of public deliberation is meant not only to register, but to *transform*, individual preferences thereby rendering them less selfish and more civic-minded, differences of opinion will surely remain. Because any set of preferences short of unanimity will still require a social choice mechanism to aggregate them, 'deliberative democracy,' at best, can only ever supplement the aggregation of preferences, rather than replace it altogether.[35] At least initially, then, we seem stuck with a form of brute majoritarianism that has the potential to subvert its own egalitarian foundations. If public deliberation and participation are both necessary *and* sufficient conditions of political legitimacy, then we seem committed to the view that a law or public policy, however oppressive or unjust, is legitimate, provided that it has the right deliberative and procedural pedigree.

But while public deliberation is often[36] a necessary condition of respecting people's status as civic equals, it is never a sufficient condition of political legitimacy alone. Consider several ways that a democratic citizen might exercise her voting rights. First, she might conceive of voting as does Joseph Schumpeter in the economic theory of democracy, that is, as a purely private or personal matter, and consistently vote on the basis of her narrow self-interest, however she conceives of it. In this market theory of politics, voting is like buying and selling.[37] Second, she might vote by appealing to whichever controversial ethical, religious, or metaphysical doctrines she endorses. Finally, she might reason *publicly* such that her vote sincerely expresses her opinion as to which of the alternatives best advances the common good in light of political values and, if none do, by proposing others for consideration. While the first two strategies are objectionably sectarian, violating as they do our duties of civility and reciprocity, the last one is implied by the contractual justificatory norm itself – majoritarian outcomes are democratically legitimate, then *if* (1) they could be the object of reasoned agreement among free and equal citizens and (2) they result from practical public reasoning of the kind just described. The political values constitutive of the common good are *not* made up of interests that are antecedent to deliberation. Rather, the interests, ideals, and goals that comprise the common good are those that survive deliberation, the ones that, on reflection, democratic citizens think are legitimate to appeal to in making claims on social resources.[38] Aside from egalitarian principles of justice that exclude a range of impermissible practices, then, the contractual argument for liberalism also generates additional moral and institutional requirements. Morally, citizens must do their fair share in reasoning publicly about the content of law and public policy for a democratic society, and vote accordingly.[39] Institutionally, democratic citizens must be furnished with the forums and also with whatever economic, legal, political, social, and cognitive resources and conditions they require to do so responsibly.

On the one hand, then, a contractual liberal theory will be 'deliberative' in the sense that the content of public reason emerges and evolves piecemeal through the exchange of reasons as citizens reflect on and debate, say, the nature of distributive justice, the boundaries between the public and private spheres, the balance between liberty and equality, and so on. On the other, it will *not* be deliberative if by this one means that everything is up for democratic grabs, such that political outcomes emerging from the democratic process are legitimate, whatever they turn out to be. This view is scarcely coherent, and clarifying why democratic self-rule does *not* have this kind of normative force further bridges the gap between 'liberal' and 'deliberative' democracy.

So far, I have been arguing that liberal contractualism is deliberative.

In what remains, I explain why any allegedly more 'radical' conception of deliberative democracy must be liberal.[40]

Jürgen Habermas contrasts liberalism with 'radical democracy' primarily in terms of how each conception of political morality prioritizes individual rights and collective self-rule.[41] In his view, liberals begin with the institutionalization of equal liberties, and these liberties enjoy normative priority over the will of the democratic legislature. Radical democrats, by contrast, interpret equal freedom in terms of sovereign will formation. The equal liberties, institutionalized in a scheme of individual rights, are themselves the expression of the sovereign will of the people, and mechanisms such as a constitutional separation of powers and judicial review that protect those liberties *emerge* from the enlightened will of the democratic legislature. Locke and Rousseau are the respective patron saints of each approach.

For Habermas, the radical character of modern democracy is lost on us if we continue to adhere to the classical notion of a normative hierarchy whose apex is occupied by independent moral principles to which collective decision-making must defer. In subordinating democratic self-rule to a scheme of individual rights, liberal thought does precisely this. Instead, we should move beyond a liberal conception of political life to one where political principles have their basis in the autonomous will of democratic citizens who are fully the authors of the rules that bind them.[42]

As the 'theory of communicative action' makes clear, we are to locate the norms of reason in the idealizations we necessarily make in speaking with one another, rather than in an ideal realm that exists independently of ourselves: 'a battery of philosophical arguments, assembled under the title of *discourse theory*, aims to bring out the necessity of this post-metaphysical shift in our conception of reason and to explain the idealized form of discussion (Diskurs) to which reason refers.'[43] Not surprisingly, however, Habermas's own theory does not satisfy the conditions he assigns to the notion of collective autonomy, because the sort of normative hierarchy that he dismisses as pre-modern actually shapes his own thinking. Unless there is some norm that is binding on us independently of our will as citizens, and that enjoys a moral authority that we have *not* fashioned ourselves, there is no conceivable reason why our political life should assume the democratic, that is to say, consensual shape that Habermas thinks it must. This norm is what Larmore calls 'respect for persons,' or what I have been calling democratic equality, and it undermines Habermas's claim that popular sovereignty is the ultimate basis on which our political life should be organized, and so the true source of individual rights. And since an egalitarian ideal of individual rights motivates, precedes, and defines the exercise of collective self-rule, 'Habermas's notion of radical democracy is not really so radical that it differs materially from the idea of liberal democracy to which he imagines himself opposed. Failing to note the moral basis of his own commitment to democratic self rule, he slips past the fact that he too assumes, if only implicitly, the antecedent authority of individual rights.'[44]

7.5 Conclusion

A contractualist political morality is one in which principles of justice are justified because they are the result of a certain form of reasoning, one that involves deliberating about what hypothetical agents would and would not do under certain conditions. Democratic equality, together with certain basic features of politics, leads us to adopt this type of political morality, and the form of reasoning embedded within it. Once we do so, the circularity thesis unravels, because there are no self-sufficient arguments for principles of justice that can be separated from the notion of hypothetical consent, and that notion does not predetermine legislative settlements to controversies in a democratic society – it simply specifies what constitutional and deliberative procedures must be like if such settlements are to be consistent with equality.

8 Against the Epistemic Turn

8.1 Introduction

The previous chapter contrasted distributive and relational understandings of equality in order to distance contractualism from a number of important, pervasive criticisms associated with the recent distributive turn in contemporary liberal theories of social and political justice. This refinement allowed us to locate the premise of the contractual argument in a particular ideal of democratic citizenship. We now turn our attention to the next steps in the argument to establish precisely which *kind* of pluralism is especially relevant to the contractual argument for liberalism; *how* this relevance manifests itself; and, finally, what type of methodological abstraction this pluralism necessitates. Pluralism complicates the task of achieving political justification through contractual agreement by raising the complicated question of how inclusive the social contract should ultimately be. A mutually acceptable distinction must be found between disagreements where the grounds make it legitimate for democratic majorities to use coercive political power in the pursuit of their convictions and others where it would clearly be wrong for them to do so, but there is no immediately obvious way to do this. Because the straightforward application of personal ethics to political life is precisely what generates the need for toleration, actual agreement among individuals as they are cannot possibly be the basis of such a distinction. Somehow, then, we must develop a normative consensus that abstracts from the particular ethical convictions that divide democratic citizens, in order to establish a publicly shared basis of political justification to adjudicate their claims against one another and the state.

Earlier, we outlined two such strategies of exclusion. Recall that on the first 'reasonableness as valid argument' view, only *beliefs* satisfying certain stringent epistemic standards are justifiably held, and only holders of such reasonable views are admissible to the hypothetical constitutional convention where principles of justice are selected. Because a subset of the rival ethical doctrines likely to persist under democratic institutions are the product of the free exercise of practical reason, rather than, say, symptomatic of unbridled self-interest or stupidity, a public basis of political justification can be found that accommodates pluralism without simultaneously collapsing into a modus vivendi. As the reflexivity thesis makes clear, however, as long as reasonableness is understood in a purely epistemic sense, the alleged asymmetry that the contractualist asserts between perfectionist and neutralist principles of justice is implausible, and this means that contractualism, itself, may be reasonably rejected.

The alternative 'reasonableness as fairness' strategy evades the reflexivity thesis because the underlying value animating our contractual justificatory framework is democratic equality, not an epistemic explanation of either the conditions of justifiably held belief, or of the origins of ethical disagreement. There is a sense, however, in which the contrast between these two approaches is somewhat overdrawn. Over the last decade or so, there has been what might be called an epistemic turn in liberal theorizing about justice, even among adherents of the reasonableness as fairness approach to contractualism.[1] Rawls, its most influential and sophisticated defender, now maintains that it is the fact of 'reasonable pluralism,' not the fact of pluralism per se, that justice as fairness must accommodate so that a well-ordered democratic society regulated by it is stable over time. In *Political Liberalism*, a whole family of new ideas – public reason, an overlapping consensus of reasonable comprehensive doctrines, a free-standing political conception, and so on – is introduced to rectify what Rawls considers to be serious deficiencies in the argument of *A Theory of Justice*, most, if not all of which, stem from his failure to fully appreciate the significance of the distinction between simple and *reasonable* pluralism, and the problems created by the latter for the stability of a democratic society. Coercively imposed political principles, to be legitimate, must be capable of securing the agreement of all *reasonable* persons who, among other things, endorse only *reasonable* comprehensive doctrines, and recognize the 'burdens of judgment,' that is, the 'many hazards involved in the correct (and conscientious) exercise of our powers of reason and judgment in the ordinary course of political life.'[2] These burdens are allegedly of central significance for the democratic understanding of toleration, because they limit what can be contractually justified through the public use of reason.

In *Political Liberalism*, epistemic and moral notions of reasonableness are subtly interwoven, making the precise connections at work between the two argumentative strands quite difficult to discern. As one commentator has recently noticed, 'Beginning with "Kantian Constructivism," Rawls explicitly marks a distinction between "the Reasonable" and "the Rational." But he still does not ever try to define the concept of "reasonableness." This can be frustrating for the reader, since the concept is so crucial to Rawls's argument and is used by him in several different ways.'[3]

We must try to make sense of these ways, and assess their respective influence on Rawls's overall position, however, because if 'reasonable pluralism' has the significance for contractualism that Rawls thinks it does, then the integrity of our fundamental distinction between the two general strategies of exclusion (a distinction upon which the success of our refutation of the reflexivity thesis rests) is undermined. While the premise of Rawls's contractual argument is a conception of society as a fair system of cooperation among civic equals, epistemology clearly plays an important role in how that (normative) conception of society is specified. It is worth considering, then, whether, or to what extent, contractualism actually requires an epistemology of the kind that Rawls offers us, and if one is needed, whether this, in fact, reopens the door to the reflexivity thesis. The two strands of the 'reasonable' must therefore be disentangled.

Our discussion in this chapter proceeds as follows. Section 2 briefly reviews Rawls's contractual argument for the two principles of justice in *Theory*, and explains how the primary modifications of that argument in *Political Liberalism* are connected to the fact of reasonable pluralism. This is a natural way to proceed, given Rawls's claim that the content of the reasonable, itself, can be best specified through a political conception of justice that relies on the idea of a social contract. Section 3 assesses these modifications by focusing on the overlapping consensus account of stability. It concludes that (1) Rawls's reasoning underlying that account is circular, and (2) the epistemic ideas that generate this circularity are actually dispensable to the contractual argument for liberalism, which can be more persuasively defended without them. We establish these claims, in part, by recasting the contractual situation: we leave the hypothetical contractors' motivational characteristics intact – those derived from the moral ideal expressed in Rawls's 'first aspect' of reasonableness – but replace the explanation of pluralism that they accept, the 'burdens of judgement,' with an alternative epistemic hypothesis, the 'stupid people' account, to show that, as trustees for actual democratic citizens, they would select the same two principles in either case. Once the original position is specified to model the ideal of democratic equality, only the fact of simple pluralism is relevant to the reasoning of hypothetical contractors selecting principles of justice. Aside from reinforcing an account of political stability that is viciously circular, then, there is simply no work left for an epistemic theory of pluralism to do. This suggests that the epistemic turn at work in Rawls's recent writings is a mistake. Section 3 explains what these findings imply about the type of methodological abstraction that a contractual theory of political morality must rely upon, and suggests that there are persuasive reasons for favouring Scanlon's formulation of contractualism over Rawls's.

8.2 Society as a Fair System of Cooperation

The fundamental organizing idea of justice as fairness, within which all of the other basic ideas are systematically connected, is that of 'society as a fair system of cooperation over time, from one generation to the next.'[4] This idea has two essential aspects – an ideal of social cooperation, and a normative description of persons as free and equal. Each of these ideas, in turn, leads directly to Rawls's claim that, of the traditional views, it is the theory of the social contract that best approximates our considered judgements[5] of justice and constitutes the most appropriate moral basis for a democratic society.[6]

Social cooperation has three distinctive elements.[7] First, unlike collective activity that is simply guided by orders issuing from some central authority, social cooperation presupposes the existence of publicly recognized rules and procedures that those cooperating under them endorse as properly regulating their conduct. Second, these publicly recognized rules and procedures, once fully worked out, specify an ideal of reciprocity that is fair to everyone whose interactions are regulated by them. As Rawls says, 'All who are engaged in cooperation and who do their part as the rules and procedures require, are to benefit in an appropriate way as assessed by a suitable benchmark of comparison.'[8] The final element in the ideal of social cooperation is this 'benchmark' itself – the notion of each participant's rational advantage, or good, that specifies what those engaged in cooperation – individuals, families, associations, or nations, for instance – are trying to achieve, when the regulative framework is viewed from its point of view.

Rawls's fundamental idea of the person is derived from this view of social cooperation. This means that it is decidedly *not* an account of human nature given by natural science or social theory, but rather a normative (moral) conception whose content depends upon the role it plays within justice as fairness. What, then, are the distinguishing features of persons[9] within Rawls's cooperative scheme? They are characterized as equal and free, reasonable and rational. The basis of their equality lies in their possessing, to a requisite degree, what Rawls calls the 'two moral powers':[10] first, they are able to form, revise, and rationally pursue a conception of their rational advantage or good, as specified by what Rawls now calls a 'comprehensive doctrine,' and second, they have a sense of justice. This means that they have both the ability and the willingness to moderate their rational aims to accommodate those of other moral persons through the application of reasonable principles, that is, by understanding, applying, and acting from the conception of justice that defines the fair terms of social cooperation.

8.2.1 *The Social Contract: The Argument for*[11] *the Original Position*

The argument for Rawls's two principles begins, then, with an ideal of fair social cooperation between free and equal persons. But how, exactly, are such persons to determine when the rules and procedures that regulate their cooperation are actually *fair,* given that the fair terms of cooperation could be specified in a variety of different ways? Should they appeal to an authority distinct from those cooperating, that is, to God's law? Perhaps they should identify the content of fairness intuitively by reference to an alleged prior order of moral values as specified by, say, a theory of natural law?

Rawls's answer derives from his ideal of social cooperation together with the functional role that the principles of justice play in regulating it. Principles of social and political justice assign rights and duties in the basic institutions of society and define the appropriate distribution of the benefits and burdens of social cooperation. The basic concept of justice, then, involves a proper balance between the competing claims of various individuals to these benefits and burdens. *Conceptions* of justice are particular interpretations of this function that differ primarily in the specific considerations that they identify as especially relevant in determining this balance. Returning to the question above, how are the fair terms of cooperation to be specified? Through a mutual agreement of all the cooperators from an original position of equal freedom:

The idea of the original position is proposed, then, as the answer to the question of how to extend the idea of a fair agreement to an agreement on principles of political justice for the basic structure. That position is set up as a situation that is fair to the parties as free and equal, and as properly informed and rational. Thus any agreement made by the parties as citizens' representatives is fair. Since the content of the agreement concerns the principles of justice for the basic structure, the agreement in the original position specifies the fair terms of social cooperation between citizens regarded as such persons. Hence the name: justice as fairness.[12]

Two things should attract our attention here. First, the general appropriateness of deploying the social contract device to settle conflicts about how the benefits and burdens of social cooperation should be divided is linked to an ideal of *reciprocity*. We are faithful to this ideal by justifying our claims to the fruits of social cooperation by reference to mutually acceptable regulative principles, ones that ultimately express our shared nature as free and equal, reasonable and rational beings.[13] Second, given that we disagree profoundly about what constitutes our rational advantage, or good, we are unlikely to satisfy this ideal of reciprocity unless our arguments for the principles of justice that we favour are sufficiently *public*.[14] Because 'it is characteristic of contract theories to stress the public nature of political principles,'[15] this makes the social contract tradition particularly well-suited to elaborating the ideal of reciprocity at the foundations of justice as fairness. This ideal implies that the reasons we have for rightly endorsing principles of justice must also be reasons for other people to do so as well. As a result, those principles must be grounded in a shared point of view, and this point of view is the original position.

8.2.2 The Social Contract: The Argument from the Original Position

The principles of justice that express Rawls's ideal of reciprocity, then, are to be the object of an agreement between rational persons concerned with furthering their own interests; these principles are 'to regulate all subsequent criticism and reform of institutions.'[16] However, in order for them to be fair to all the contracting parties, they must be agreed to under certain carefully specified conditions. In ordinary life, for instance, agreements reached through force and coercion, deception and fraud, are normally (and rightly) thought to be invalid. Surely the social contract, and the original position itself, will have similar provisions. But ordinary agreements are very different from the one that we are now contemplating, because they arise through the bargaining of specific people in determinate situations, and the particular features of those situations affect the terms agreed to in a number of important ways. Ordinary contracts, that is, operate against the backdrop of the very social, economic, and political conditions that a theory of justice must test. Unless the principles of justice that are agreed to abstract from this backdrop, they will simply mirror and reinforce the status quo, that is, the existing distribution of social, economic, and political power in the community. So in addition to ruling out agreement on principles through force, deception, and fraud, for example, we must also somehow specify a point of view sufficiently removed from the actual bargaining advantages that have arisen over time. As Rawls says, 'To persons according to their threat advantage' (or their de facto political power, or wealth, or native endowments) is not the basis of political justice. Contingent historical advantages and accidental influences from the past should not affect an agreement on principles that are to regulate the basic structure from the present into the future.'[17] The social contract, then, must be both hypothetical and ahistorical, but how is the original position shaped to reflect these requirements?

In answering this question, we should keep in mind that there are three different justificatory points of view in justice as fairness: that of free and equal democratic citizens reasoning publicly to justify political proposals to one another about constitutional essentials and matters of basic justice within the constraints allowed by the principles chosen in the original position; that of hypothetical trustees who must protect and advance the rational interests of such citizens by selecting principles that do so at a constitutional convention under certain constraints; and finally, that of you and me, charged as we are with devising those constraints – the constraints of 'the reasonable' – by subjecting both our considered judgements of fairness and the putative principles that best explicate them to the method of reflective equilibrium.[18]

Working through this process reveals one of our firmest considered judgements about justice, namely, that the fact that we occupy, for instance, a particular socio-economic position is not a good reason for us to accept, or to expect others to accept, a conception of justice that favours those in that position. To model this conviction, the hypothetical trustees for democratic citizens are situated behind a 'veil of ignorance': contractors know general facts about human society, political affairs, economic theory, and human psychology, but they are ignorant of their race, ethnicity, sex, and relative natural endowments such as strength and intelligence, and they must select principles of justice on this basis. The symmetrical positioning of contractors behind the veil achieves three essential objectives: first, it models the equal freedom of the citizens for whom they are trustees; second, it effectively nullifies the influence of historically accumulated differences in bargaining power – no one can tailor principles of justice to her advantage at the expense of others; and finally, it makes possible a unanimous choice on a particular liberal conception of justice that now reads as follows:

a Each person has the same indefeasible claim to a fully adequate scheme of equal basic liberties, which scheme is compatible with the same scheme of liberties for all; and

b Social and economic inequalities are to satisfy two conditions: first, they are to be attached to offices and positions open to all under conditions of fair equality of opportunity; and second, they are to be to the greatest benefit of the least-advantaged members of society (the difference principle).[19]

These two principles, Rawls maintains, are a special case of a more general conception of justice in which all social values or 'primary goods' – liberty and opportunity, income and wealth, and the social bases of self-respect – are to be distributed equally unless an unequal distribution of any, or all of them, is to everyone's advantage.[20] Both the equal basic liberties and the distribution of primary goods regulated by the difference principle, then, are expressly designed to reflect Rawls's ideal of social cooperation and its constitutive value of reciprocity. When the basic institutions of a democratic society satisfy these principles, everyone is better off, not relative to her respective level of welfare in some actual and historical pre-political state of nature, but relative to an initial baseline of equal freedom that precludes some people benefiting from social cooperation at others' expense.[21]

8.2.3 Stability for the Right Reasons, and the Idea of a Well-Ordered Society

Hypothetical contractors situated behind the veil of ignorance are choosing principles of justice for what Rawls calls a 'well-ordered society.' Such a society is designed to advance the good of its members, and it is effectively regulated by a public conception of justice. This means two things: (1) everyone accepts, and knows that everyone else accepts, the same principles of justice; and (2) the constitution and basic social institutions satisfy, and are generally known to satisfy, these principles.[22] Now the trustees who must unanimously agree to such principles may assume that, formally at least, the democratic citizens they represent have an effective sense of justice, that is, that they will comply with the principles that are eventually chosen. So much is clearly stipulated by the idea of a well-ordered society. However, as we saw above, the trustees are also aware of certain general facts of human psychology and principles of moral learning, and they are to take such things into account in selecting between rival conceptions of justice. Since the decision to adopt one conception over another is binding in perpetuity, and since that conception is to regulate the basic structure of society, one that radically affects everyone's overall life prospects, the parties must agree only to principles that people could honour even if it turned out to be the case that they fared worse than anyone else once the veil was lifted. Otherwise, in exceeding the 'strains of commitment,' they will not have acted in good faith.[23] Indeed, one of Rawls's central objections to both utilitarianism and perfectionism as systematic alternatives to justice-as-fairness is that they fail this test.[24]

The question of a conception of justice's stability, then, is ultimately a matter of assessing the extent to which it is consistent with psychological and social theory, as well as with certain fixed conditions of collective life. Rawls thinks that if a well-ordered society effectively regulated by justice-as-fairness is to be realistically possible, then it must be able to secure the ongoing support of most, and ideally of all, of its (living) members. This implies that the argument for the two principles developed within the original position has not one, but two stages. At the first stage, the two principles are chosen from within the reasonable constraints that model Rawls's ideal of social cooperation, together with its attendant notion of reciprocity between free and equal persons. The principles specifying the fair terms of social cooperation are worked out from these ideas independently from, and prior to, the issue of stability, because Rawls is interested in stability for the right reasons, rather than stability per se, which might conceivably be achieved, for example, in a society effectively regulated by fascist principles that are coercively imposed on its members against their wishes. Because justice-as-fairness is a *liberal* theory – that is, its stability must derive from the willing compliance of its members – it must generate its own support in a suitable way by addressing their *reason*. At the second stage, then, Rawls must show that those taking part in presumptively just arrangements regulated by the equal basic liberties and difference principles also 'acquire the corresponding sense of justice and desire to do their part in maintaining them.'[25] Otherwise, hypothetical deliberators in the original position would continue searching for other principles of justice more stable in this normative sense. The last two hundred pages of *Theory* are accordingly devoted to showing that justice-as-fairness would, in fact, be stable for the right reasons, because it is 'perspicuous to our reason, congruent with our good, and rooted not in abnegation but in affirmation of the self.'[26]

8.2.4 Reasonable Pluralism and Stability

Rawls now concedes that many of the arguments initially adduced in *A Theory of Justice* to support justice-as-fairness actually contradict the account of stability set forth in the last third of that book. The problem concerns the way that reasonable pluralism renders the idea of a well-ordered society unrealistic even under favourable conditions.

A modern democratic society effectively regulated by the two principles must guarantee its members, among other things, freedom of thought, conscience, and association, and it must also provide them with the all-purpose means required to secure the fair value of these basic liberties. If the actual political practices of contemporary liberal-democracies are any indication, these conditions of deliberative freedom – those recommended by justice-as-fairness – will not only permit, but also encourage, people to *reasonably* disagree about the nature of the good life. As presented in *A Theory of Justice*, however, the stability of justice-as-fairness depends essentially upon widespread agreement about the value of one particularly controversial conception of the good – a distinctively Kantian, and thus liberal, conception of moral agency. Rawls thinks that we express, rather than violate, our nature as free and equal rational beings only by acting from the principles of justice, and by assigning them regulative priority over all of our contingently held actual ends: 'It is acting from this precedence that expresses our freedom from contingency and happenstance ... in order to realize our nature we have no alternative but to plan to preserve our sense of justice as governing our other aims.'[27] All of the ideas developed in part 3 of *Theory* intended to establish the congruence of justice and goodness and, thereby, the stability of a society well-ordered by justice-as-fairness – Rawls's view of autonomy as self-realization, his argument that justice is intrinsically good because of its connection to moral autonomy, as well his constructivist understanding of moral objectivity – depend upon this Kantian view of practical reasoning.[28]

So the original position may be interpreted as a procedural manifestation of Kant's conception of autonomy and the categorical imperative. Under the conditions of deliberative liberty that justice-as-fairness recommends, however, there will obviously be people who reject this Kantian conception of moral personality (if they can manage to understand it), and anyone who does so will then also reasonably reject justice-as-fairness, thus undermining its stability. If a stable society effectively well-ordered by Rawls's two principles is to be realistically possible, that is, if a constitutional democracy is not to be hopelessly utopian, then its justification must lie elsewhere.

8.2.5 Political Liberalism: Basic Ideas

The central problem with justice-as-fairness, then, is its internal inconsistency: in order for a society well-ordered by it to be stable, everyone would have to endorse the same Kantian conception of the good, but reasonable pluralism means that a consensus of this kind could arise only through the oppressive use of state power,[29] and this is explicitly forbidden by the equal basic liberties.

In *Political Liberalism,* Rawls addresses this problem by recasting the argument for justice-as-fairness so that it no longer depends upon the Kantian account of practical reason and moral agency, because a society profoundly divided by incompatible but *reasonable* moral, religious, and philosophical doctrines, will be stable only if its principles of justice abstract from, and are thus neutral between, the various ethical ideals that give rise to these disagreements. To achieve this abstraction and accommodate reasonable pluralism, Rawls applies 'the principle of toleration to philosophy itself'[30] and introduces three new interrelated ideas in an attempt to purge justice-as-fairness of the doctrinal intolerance originally found in *Theory*.

First, he now distinguishes between the plurality of moral, religious, and philosophical 'comprehensive doctrines' that will likely persist under free democratic institutions, and a 'free-standing political conception' of justice.[31] Both are quintessentially normative (moral) notions, but each has vastly different grounds and scope. A comprehensive doctrine (religious or secular), that is, 'includes conceptions of what is of value in human life, and ideals of personal character, as well as ideals of friendship and of familial and associational relationships, and much else that is to inform our conduct, and in the limit to our life as a whole.'[32] A political conception, by contrast, is worked out for a specific, limited, and clearly defined subject, namely, the main political, social, and economic institutions of a democratic society as they form a unified system of social cooperation from one generation to the next. A political conception also specifies how its principles and standards are to be expressed in the character and attitudes of the members of society who realize its ideals. When both these principles and ideals are presented as not derived from, or as parts of, a comprehensive doctrine, the political conception they constitute is 'free-standing' in Rawls's sense.

One of the most important manifestations of this distinction between comprehensive doctrine and political conception is the transformation that we see in justice-as-fairness from the idea of the person as having moral personality with the full capacity of moral agency to that of the citizen. In *A Theory of Justice*, the basis of our equality lies in the two moral powers. We are entitled to equal justice, that is, by virtue of our capacity for practical reasoning. Furthermore, the basis of the interpersonal comparisons presupposed by the implementation of the difference principle, and also of the deliberations of hypothetical contractors – what Rawls calls primary goods – are singled out because of how important they are to our exercising this capacity. In the end, we need primary goods to satisfy a (Kantian) comprehensive ideal of human flourishing.

In *Political Liberalism*, however, primary goods specify what we require as free and equal citizens of a constitutional democracy: we are legitimately entitled to them as a matter of basic justice, not as moral agents in every sphere of life no matter what we do (they may, in fact, be useless to us in satisfying a number of our important comprehensive aims), but in our more restricted role as citizens, a role that is specified by a political conception of justice and the public political culture of a democratic society.

After he introduces the idea of a free-standing political conception, Rawls's second main innovation is the idea of an 'overlapping consensus' of reasonable comprehensive doctrines on such a conception. Leaving aside for now the troubling issues of precisely *which* comprehensive doctrines are reasonable, and exactly *how* we are to identify them, let us focus our immediate attention on the nature of the consensus that Rawls has in mind, which is easily misunderstood.

Each citizen of a stable constitutional democracy has, as it were, two points of view: first, the political conception of justice that she shares with her fellow citizens and that she appeals to in settling disputes about constitutional essentials and matters of basic justice, and second, the particular (partial or fully) comprehensive doctrine that organizes and orders her other substantive values and ends. Rawls must somehow explain how these two perspectives are related and, more importantly, why widespread reasonable disagreement from the second vantage point does not destroy the possibility of consensus at the first.

It might be tempting to conclude that stability and reasonable pluralism can be reconciled only if the political conception that is to be the focus of an overlapping consensus is adjusted to accommodate the content of the particular comprehensive doctrines that actually exist in society. Primary goods, for instance, would then be identified by striking a compromise between permissible conceptions of the good – those not excluded by the political conception. This cannot be what Rawls intends, however, for at least two reasons: first, so understood, justice-as-fairness would be indistinguishable from a modus vivendi and, thus, political in the wrong way; and second, its justification would then depend essentially upon various comprehensive doctrines, and this would prevent it from serving the practical role that Rawls assigns it, because it would be neither political nor freestanding.

For these reasons, in working out the fair terms of social cooperation, 'we leave aside the comprehensive doctrines that now exist, or have existed, or might exist'[33] and rely instead on ideas implicit in the public political culture of democracy. *Political Liberalism* therefore reproduces the two-stage argument for stability found in *A Theory of Justice*, albeit in modified form. At the first stage, the principles of justice are still chosen in the original position subject to reasonable constraints *before* the question of stability arises; at the second stage, however, citizens now affirm the same principles of justice, but for *different* reasons, those stemming from their respective and potentially conflicting comprehensive doctrines. Consequently, overlapping consensus 'does not mean the derivability of common principles of justice from all the comprehensive views in the pluralistic bouquet but rather the *compatibility* of each of those comprehensive views with a free-standing political conception that will permit them all to co-exist.'[34] Because justice-as-fairness does not depend for its justification upon the truth of any particular comprehensive doctrine, that is, because it is 'free-standing,' it allows for the 'overlap' required to ensure that a well-ordered democratic society effectively regulated by it will remain stable.

Rawls's final innovation in recasting his presentation of justice-as-fairness is the idea of public reason. If the principles of justice are to act as a public basis of justification between free and equal citizens, then the hypothetical agreement on those principles must also be supplemented by a 'companion agreement on the guidelines of public inquiry and on the criteria as to what kind of information and knowledge is relevant in discussing political questions'[35] when these involve constitutional essentials and matters of basic justice. Answers to questions such as Who has the right to vote? What religious beliefs should be tolerated? Who is to be assured fair equality of opportunity, or to hold private property? are coercively imposed upon everyone by the state. Appealing to comprehensive values in order to reach conclusions about such matters is a kind of discursive partiality that is inconsistent with the spirit of reciprocity animating the equal basic liberty and difference principles. As such, these questions should be settled by *political* values alone.[36] To show our fellow democratic citizens respect is to deliberate about such matters within a framework that we sincerely regard as the most reasonable political conception of justice, one which expresses political values that they, as free and equal, might also reasonably be expected to endorse.

8.3 The 'Reasonable' in Rawls

For Rawls, three conditions must obtain if a society well-ordered by justice-as-fairness is to be possible given the existence of a plurality of *reasonable* comprehensive doctrines: first, everyone must accept, and know that everyone else accepts, the same principles of justice; second, the main social, political, and economic institutions of society must be publicly known, or with good reason believed, to satisfy these principles; and, finally, citizens must have a normally effective sense of justice that enables them to comply with society's basic institutions, which they regard as just. The principles of justice must establish a shared point of view so that citizens' claims can be adjudicated from within the bounds of public reason.

Both the reasonable and the rational are basic and complementary conception-dependent ideas – their content depends upon the particular ideal of social cooperation that justice-as-fairness articulates and develops – but they differ in the range of agents to which they apply. Rational principles apply to a single, unified agent exercising her powers of judgement and deliberation in pursuing her own ends and interests. Examples of rational principles include the requirements that a person: adopt the most effective means to her ends; select the more probable alternative available to her, other things being equal; prefer the greater over the lesser good; and, finally, prioritize her objectives when these conflict with one another.

Reasonable principles, by contrast, regulate a *plurality* of agents and are, thus, public in ways that rational principles are not. As Rawls says, 'It is by the reasonable that we enter the public world of others and stand ready to propose or accept, as the case may be, reasonable principles to specify fair terms of cooperation.'[37] Such principles emerge from the original position, and this is why they are conception-dependent – by regulating our behaviour in light of them, we are expressing our desires to live up to an ideal of reciprocity.

The overlapping consensus of reasonable comprehensive doctrines cannot amount to a simple convergence of existing ethical views on the political conception, because this would render justice-as-fairness a mere modus vivendi that was stable for the wrong reasons. But if an overlapping consensus is specified in abstraction from the particular content of the existing comprehensive views that make it up, then on what basis can the relative reasonableness of those views be ascertained? How do we know which views are reasonable, and which ones are not? Rawls *does* briefly describe the structure of a reasonable comprehensive doctrine, but this description proceeds mainly via the idea of a *reasonable person* – one who holds such a doctrine. The overlapping consensus argument for the stability of justice-as-fairness is thus framed so that the central question is whether or not every *reasonable person* has grounds to endorse the political conception, regardless of her particular comprehensive views.

Rather than defining the reasonable, Rawls elaborates its content through the constraints required to situate citizens' representatives symmetrically in the original position, once they are represented solely as free and equal, and without their particular native endowments, social attachments, and conceptions of the good. In its application to persons, Rawls divides the idea of the reasonable into two primary aspects, but a careful reading of *Political Liberalism* reveals a much more complex picture. For the purposes of a political conception of justice, reasonable persons have the following distinguishing characteristics:

The first aspect:

1 They share the form of moral sensibility that underlies the desire to engage in fair cooperation. This means that they are 'ready to propose principles and standards as fair terms of cooperation and to abide by them willingly, given the assurance that others will likewise do so. Those norms they view as reasonable for everyone to accept and therefore as justifiable to them; and they are ready to discuss the fair terms that others propose.'[38]

The second aspect:

2 They are willing to recognize the burdens of judgment and to accept the consequences of such burdens for their attitudes toward other comprehensive doctrines.[39]

3 They affirm only reasonable comprehensive doctrines.[40]
4 They refuse to politically repress reasonable comprehensive doctrines that they reject as false or unsound, even if and when they have the opportunity to do so.[41]
5 They are willing to reason publicly about constitutional essentials and matters of basic justice, and to appeal only to political values when these issues are at stake.[42]

To complete this characterization, we need to identify the burdens of judgement, and the structure of reasonable comprehensive doctrines.

The burdens of judgement are meant to explain how ethical pluralism or disagreement is consistent with the correct and conscientious exercise of our powers of reason in the ordinary course of political life. Rawls's non-exhaustive list of these hazards is the following: the empirical and scientific evidence that confronts us is complex, conflicting, and difficult to evaluate; complete agreement about the kinds of considerations that are relevant to any particular question is consistent with disagreement about the respective weight that we should assign them; because moral and political concepts are vague and thus subject to hard cases, we must rely on judgement and interpretation within some indeterminate range where reasonable persons may differ; we assess evidence and weigh moral and political values in light of our total experiences, and such experiences always vary; there are often different kinds of normative considerations on both sides of an issue and all-things-considered assessments are hard to reach; and, finally, we face great difficulties in setting priorities and making adjustments between seemingly incommensurable values and objectives.[43]

What about reasonable comprehensive doctrines? They have three essential features. First, they order and articulate the major religious, philosophical, and moral dimensions of human life in a relatively coherent and consistent fashion through the use of theoretical reason. Second, they identify a certain subset of values as especially significant and balance these when they conflict through the use of practical reason. Finally, they normally belong to, or draw upon, a tradition of thought and doctrine that, while stable over time, tends to evolve gradually in light of what, from its own point of view, counts as good and sufficient reasons.[44]

This formal or structural characterization must be compatible with pluralism, and this means that it cannot be the case that anyone is *required* to endorse any particular comprehensive doctrine simply because it is reasonable – Rawls takes great care to point out that there are, in fact, many reasonable comprehensive doctrines. But the conjunction of the third and fourth features of reasonable persons noted above *does* imply that a reasonable comprehensive doctrine cannot reject the essentials of a democratic regime. Reasonable persons, then, have two further distinguishing characteristics that must be added to Rawls's official list:

6 They are democrats, to the extent that they conceive of their society as a fair system of cooperation among civic equals.
7 They endorse one of a family of political conceptions that specifies the fair terms of cooperation to model the democratic ideal, each member of which a) has a list of basic rights, liberties and opportunities easily recognizable from existing democratic polities; b) assigns special priority to these relative to utilitarian and perfectionist values; and c) guarantees all of its citizens the all-purpose means required for them to make effective use of their freedoms.[45]

Reasonable pluralism does not render the stability of a society effectively well-ordered by justice-as-fairness impossible, then, because *reasonable* people must be political liberals, regardless of the actual content of their respective comprehensive doctrines. The burdens of judgement ensure the existence of continuing ethical and political disagreement, but such disagreement, at least among reasonable people, extends only to rival claims about the most appropriate way of *interpreting* the three requirements found in a through c. To simplify matters, let us assume two things: first, that the choice situation in the original position has a determinate solution; and, second, that the equal basic liberties and difference principles *are* that solution as tested by our considered judgements in reflective equilibrium. Both are admittedly controversial, but neither one of them affects the substance of our argument in this section, which is concerned with showing two things: (1) that the moral ideas associated with the 'first aspect' (characteristics 1, 3, 4, 5, 6, 7) render Rawls's revised stability argument circular; and (2) that the epistemic ideas associated with the 'second aspect' (characteristic 2)[46] are dispensable to the argument for the two principles, but only once stability is understood in

a way that differs significantly from the way that Rawls himself understands that idea.

If the 'reasonable' is understood morally as specified by the first aspect
of reasonableness, then *reasonable* comprehensive doctrines are any and
all of those that are compatible with the free-standing political conception that emerges from the original position, that is, from the first stage
of Rawls's two-part argument for justice-as-fairness. Remember that,
within a social contract view, the moral facts are determined by the principles that would be chosen in the original position, and that the content
of the reasonable is explicated via the constraints that are required to
allow such a choice between rational agents to be possible, unanimous,
and fair. The issue of the stability of a society effectively well-ordered by
such principles arises at stage two, *after* the principles have been chosen
at stage one. This makes the question of stability, however, quite peculiar,
at least within the context of a well-ordered society. It is tautologically
true that the political conception would secure an overlapping consensus of all reasonable comprehensive doctrines, and that a society well-
ordered by that conception would be stable for the right reasons,
because a defining characteristic of such doctrines is precisely that they
accept that conception. An overlapping consensus is a thoroughly normative idealization whose content is specified by the very political conception that it focuses on. The idea of a well-ordered society, therefore,
assumes a consensus on the political conception of justice, so the issue of
stability is antecedently settled.

What work is actually done by the epistemic ideas of reasonableness
associated with the second aspect? Does the overlapping consensus argument for stability fare any better once we shift from the ideal setting of a
well-ordered society to the actual daily political lives of democratic citizens? Initially, it might be tempting to conclude that the burdens of
judgement are central to establishing the stability of justice-as-fairness
for the right reasons, insofar as these burdens purport to explain why
people who disagree profoundly in their comprehensive doctrines might
still be willing to propose and abide by fair terms of cooperation, given
the reasonable assurance that everyone else would do so as well. To show
that this is mistaken, and that the burdens of judgement are actually dispensable to Rawls's argument for the two principles, let us retain his first
aspect of reasonableness but replace the second with an alternative
explanation of pluralism – the Stupid People account. The two aspects
now read as follows:

The first aspect:

1 Reasonable people share the form of moral sensibility that underlies the desire to engage in fair cooperation. They are ready to propose principles and standards as fair terms of cooperation and to abide by them willingly, given the assurance that others will likewise do so. These norms they view as reasonable for everyone to accept and therefore as justifiable to them, and they are ready to discuss the fair terms that others propose.

The second aspect:

2 Reasonable people do not equate the fact of ethical pluralism with an unwillingness to behave as the first aspect requires, because the fact that others endorse comprehensive doctrines inconsistent with their own shows that they are simply stupid. Stupid people
   a oversimplify empirical and scientific evidence;
   b insist that there can be only one set of relevant considerations to any given issue, and that there is only one correct weighting of them;
   c believe that moral and political concepts apply themselves automatically and mechanically in the absence of interpretation and judgement;
   d regret that people's total experiences must differ, because if everyone could have lived as they did, then they, too, might have recognized the truth;
   e see issues from only their points of view; and finally,
   f think that all values are commensurable, so that setting priorities and adjusting goals should never require sacrificing anything.

How would this alternative epistemic hypothesis about the origins of ethical disagreement affect our reasons for endorsing the two principles at the first stage? By Rawls's own admission, not at all, because the parties to the original position must select the equal basic liberties and difference principles to regulate the social cooperation of democratic citizens, *regardless* of whether pluralism per se, or reasonable pluralism obtains:

> *The same principles of justice are selected in both cases.* The parties must always guarantee the basic rights and liberties of those for whom they are trustees. If they suppose reasonable pluralism obtains, they know that most of these liberties may already be secure as things are, but even if they could rely on that, they would for reasons of publicity select the two principles of justice, or similar principles. Besides, they must express in their selection of princi-

ples the political conception they find most congenial to the fundamental interests of the citizens they represent. On the other hand, if they assume pluralism as such to obtain, and hence that there may be comprehensive doctrines that would suppress, if they could, liberty of conscience and freedom of thought, the preceding considerations become all the more urgent.[47]

So the (moral) notion of reasonableness and the ideal of reciprocity that it articulates render epistemology dispensable to the argument for the two principles at the first stage, where only the fact of simple pluralism is relevant.

What about at the second stage? Is epistemology also useless there? One thing that suggests that the answer might be no is that hypothetical contractors in the original position must, themselves, assess the relative stability of rival candidate principles, so we should perhaps avoid placing too much emphasis on the distinction between the two stages. This means that even if epistemology is irrelevant to the *derivation* of principles in the original position, it might still be vital to their *stability* once we move from ideal theory to the ongoing political life of an actual democratic society. Something like this is probably what Rawls has in mind. And while the introduction of the modified second aspect (the Stupid People hypothesis) exerts no influence on the reasoning of trustees in the original position, it might not be similarly innocuous in its implications for *our* daily behaviour as real democratic citizens. For example, if we sincerely believed that others who disagreed with us were stupid for that very reason alone, then it is quite unlikely that we would continue to act towards them in the manner required by justice-as-fairness. To the extent that this was the case, our faith in the political conception would be undermined, and the overlapping consensus would unravel. Of course, it might always be possible to *enforce* the political conception against those too stupid to recognize its value but, for Rawls, this would make justice-as-fairness stable for the wrong reasons.

This worry begins to dissipate once we see that epistemic and moral unreasonableness are different things, which do not necessarily track one another. In the context of the first aspect, reasonable pluralism means that there is a multiplicity of comprehensive doctrines that are compatible with the political conception, because that conception does not depend upon those doctrines for its derivation. Being politically unreasonable, then, means endorsing a comprehensive doctrine outside of this relatively permissive range, one that has illiberal or intolerant political implications that violate fundamental democratic ideals. Saying that a particular action or proposal is politically reasonable and, thus, publicly justified, amounts to claiming that symmetrically situated and ideally rational agents constrained in a variety of ways would agree to a principle authorizing its performance. Politically unreasonable persons are those who reject such principles, or are willing to act on other ones that cannot be justified in this way.

Being epistemically unreasonable, on the other hand, means believing things for what ultimately turn out to be bad reasons, or because we have not sufficiently examined the evidence, or done so under the wrong circumstances – say, because we are inattentive to alternative explanations, drunk, distracted, excessively dogmatic, and so on. While these are two very different notions of reasonableness, with very different justificatory criteria, this is sometimes obscured by Rawls's contention that the first and second aspects of reasonableness are complementary.[48] In any event, Rawls requires only the first notion for an overlapping consensus of reasonable comprehensive doctrines to obtain, and any further epistemic requirements are unnecessarily exclusionary. As long as people endorse the political conception and respect each other's rights, the epistemic adequacy of their beliefs should have no bearing upon their equal claims to the benefits and burdens of social cooperation.

We can reinforce this point from the opposite point of view. Imagine, for example, that it turned out to be the case that a racist political ideology was vindicated by the best social, scientific, and genetic research: would we then abandon liberal democracy simply because this alternative withstood epistemic scrutiny? The case for Rawlsian liberal democracy lies in the attractiveness of its ideal of reciprocity, and epistemology has nothing to do with this.

Even if Rawls *is* right, however, to think that people whose comprehensive doctrines are epistemically unreasonable – Stupid People – are necessarily more likely to violate the democratic ideal of reciprocity, his particular conception of stability should be jettisoned as implausible. Whether or not a well-ordered society effectively regulated by a political conception of justice is stable for the right reasons depends, not upon whether general compliance with its principles necessitates the use of coercion, but upon the *content* of those principles. There is no reason to think that reasonable principles – those selected from an original position of equality that abstracts from considerations deemed irrelevant to political justice – can, or will have, the kind of motivational force that Rawls sometimes implies they will. A just society may be unstable; an unstable society may be just. The task of the political philosopher is to explain how political justification should proceed, what principles are ultimately justified, and on the basis of which considerations. The question of whether or not acting justly is congruent with our good is, indeed, a deeply philosophical question, and one at least as old as Socrates. *That*, however, is not Rawls's question, which is about whether antecedently justified principles that are congruent with our good *will be freely complied with*. Simply put, philosophy cannot settle this matter, which is probably best left to national myths, courts, and the police.[49]

8.4 Scanlon's Contractualism

Rawls tells us that, in setting out justice-as-fairness, 'we rely on the kind of motivation Scanlon takes as basic.'[50] According to Scanlon, 'an act is wrong if its performance under the circumstances would be disallowed by any set of principles for the general regulation of behavior that no one could reasonably reject as a basis for informed, unforced general agreement.'[51] Scanlon's hypothetical contractors are assumed to be willing to modify their personal demands in order to find a shared basis of justification to others that they also have reason to accept. Thinking about right and wrong, then, is thinking about what could be justified to others on grounds that they, if appropriately motivated, could not reasonably reject. Because this is so, the framework used to elaborate the content of political morality should reflect the question, What general principles of action could we all will? rather than simply, What would I want if I were in another's shoes?[52] One of Scanlon's main reasons for calling his view contractualist is to emphasize the centrality of this idea, one that has its roots in the classical social contract tradition beginning with Rousseau and Kant.

Scanlon thinks that the moral motivation that contractualism appeals to – that of being able to justify our actions to others on grounds they could not reasonably reject – is very similar to what Mill in *Utilitarianism* calls the 'social feelings of mankind; the desire to be in unity with our fellow creatures.' But while Mill is describing a natural feature of human psychology meant to explain how people could be motivated to act in accordance with utilitarianism on some basis other than social conditioning, Scanlon's notion of this unity appeals instead to the value and attractiveness of the kind of community that is made possible when people act on the basis of the moral reasons that contractualism provides: 'This relation, much less personal than friendship, might be called a relation of mutual recognition. Standing in this relation to others is appealing in itself – worth seeking for its own sake.'[53]

Justification that expresses this motivational base proceeds in the following way. In order to assess whether or not it would be wrong (or unjust) to do X in circumstances C, we must propose and consider possible principles governing how one may act in those circumstances. We must then ask ourselves whether any principle that permitted one to do X in such instances could, for that reason, be reasonably rejected. To ascertain whether this is so, we have to establish an idea of the burdens that would be imposed on some people in such a situation if others were permitted to do X. Scanlon calls these the 'objections to permission.'[54] Next, we need to consider the ways in which others would be burdened by a principle forbidding one to do X in these circumstances, in order to compare these to the 'objections to permission.'[55] On the one hand, then, if, compared to the objections to permission, the objections to prohibition are insignificant, then the action is wrong (or unjust) according to the contractualist formula, because it is reasonable to reject any principle permitting it under the circumstances in question; on the other hand, if there were some principle regulating behaviour in such situations that permitted X and that it would not be reasonable to reject, then doing X would not be wrong (or unjust).

But to whom are we to address such justification, and what are the relevant points of view that we must consider? While it is natural to think that we should concern ourselves with the specific individuals affected by our proposed action, we must also take a broader and more abstract perspective when deciding whether a given principle allowing it is one that could be reasonably rejected:

> General prohibitions and permissions have effects on the liberty, broadly construed, of both agents and those affected by their actions. But the acceptance of principles also has implications beyond these effects. Because principles constrain the reasons we may, or must, take into account, they can affect our relations with others and our view of ourselves in both positive and negative ways.[56]

Assessments of the rejectability of a principle must take into account the consequences of its acceptance in general, and not merely the particular case that we, as individuals, may happen momentarily to be concerned with. However, since we obviously cannot foresee which particular individuals will be affected by its acceptance in what particular ways – as an agent required to act in a certain way, as a potential victim, as a bystander, etc. – we must rely on commonly available information about what people generally have reason to want, rather than on the particular aims, preferences, and other characteristics of specific individuals. Scanlon calls this informational basis 'generic reasons.'[57]

Scanlon's version of contractualism has one important advantage over the one that Rawls develops in the overlapping consensus argument for stability. The equal moral status of the hypothetical contractors is modelled via certain motivational stipulations directly linked to an ideal form of community. A democratic ideal of social cooperation also animates justice-as-fairness at the deepest levels but, as we saw above, that ideal is mediated by a number of epistemic ideas – the veil of ignorance, and the burdens of judgement, for instance – that obscure its quintessentially moral underpinnings. If Scanlon's generic reasons could be specified to reflect the basic interests of free and equal democratic citizens engaged in a fair scheme of cooperation, then perhaps his reasonable rejection procedure might yield an attractive set of liberal principles without raising difficult epistemological questions. Once we understand that public reason is *public* by virtue of the shared interests it articulates, there are grounds for thinking that this project might succeed.

8.5 Conclusion

In this chapter, our recasting of the Rawlsian contractual situation has established two things: (1) Rawls's reasoning underlying the overlapping consensus account of stability is circular and, more importantly for our purposes, (2) the epistemic ideas that generate this circularity are actually dispensable to the contractual argument for liberalism, which can be more persuasively defended without them. As trustees for actual democratic citizens, Stupid People would select the same two principles of justice as Rawlsian contractors would when deliberating under the burdens of judgement. Once the original position is specified to model the ideal of democratic equality, only the fact of simple pluralism is relevant to the reasoning of hypothetical contractors selecting principles of justice. Aside from reinforcing an account of political stability that is viciously circular, then, there is simply no work left for an epistemic theory of pluralism to do. This suggests that the epistemic turn at work in Rawls's recent writings is a mistake. Ultimately, it is the fact of pluralism per se, rather than reasonable pluralism that is especially relevant to contractualist thinking about justice in democratic societies. Reasonable pluralism simply means that many ways of life are permissible in a society well-ordered by liberal principles, and this is a quintessentially *moral* rather than an epistemic idea. If an ideal of democratic equality implies that contractualism is the best framework to guide our deliberations about political justice, then the various substantive and methodological abstractions that it deploys to characterize our interests and model reasonable constraints should reflect this.

9 Beyond the Basic Structure

9.1 Introduction

Our argument for liberal neutrality is almost complete. An egalitarian ideal of human relations combined with certain basic facts of political life lead us to embrace a form of procedural democracy. This ideal and those facts, in turn, make contractualism the most appropriate test of political legitimacy, because collective self-determination is compatible with equal freedom only when democratic decision-making is, itself, tempered by principles that are reasonably acceptable to everyone. State neutrality between comprehensive and contested ethical ideals emerges as a central feature of liberal political morality, because pluralism ensures that the social contract that yields these regulative principles cannot proceed without it.

While some of liberalism's most illustrious contemporary defenders adopt one or another variant of this last claim – Barry, Dworkin, Larmore, Nagel, and Rawls – many critics reject the idea as incoherent in principle, unworkable in practice, or both. A recent book[1] on liberal neutrality concludes that it is utterly indefensible as a political and philosophical doctrine, and one of the book's reviewers is almost certain that its publication signals the end of neutralism.[2] Other articles, with titles such as 'Liberal Neutrality on the Good: An Autopsy,'[3] imply that the doctrine now is, or at least should be, dead.

Such dismissals are premature, however, if the argument of this book is sound. Sher, for example, considers and rejects four distinct sets of reasons, which he regards as exhaustive as to why the liberal state must remain neutral between the competing ethical ideals of its citizens: in order to respect the value of personal autonomy; in order to respect people's *capacity* for autonomously pursuing *other* intrinsically valuable ends; in order to protect people from the dangers of state tyranny and political abuse; and, finally, because claims about how we should live, or of what gives life its value, are always epistemologically dubious.

But our argument has appealed to none of these reasons. In chapters 2, 3, and 4, we rejected the idea that autonomy-based (perfectionist) claims could successfully yield liberal principles of political morality. In chapters 6–8, we explicitly distanced the argument for liberalism from epistemic considerations that might give us reasons for thinking that we should be more sceptical about the nature of the good life than we are about principles of right, or justice. And we have not relied on straightforwardly prudential or strategic calculations that might underscore the dangers of political perfectionism.

Arneson's critique, like Sher's, is also unwarranted, and basically for the same reason. His 'autopsy' of neutralism proceeds via a rejection of (1) Ronald Dworkin's challenge model of ethics, (2) Barry and Nagel's epistemic arguments, and (3) a broadly Kantian argument about neutrality following from respect for moral persons. But we rejected Dworkin's perfectionist argument for neutrality in chapter 5, Barry and Nagel's epistemic ones in chapter 6, and Rawls's broadly Kantian one in chapter 8. Unless the positive case developed over the last few chapters is reducible to any or all of these – something that neither Sher's nor Arneson's argument shows – neutrality is not only off the operating table, but showing up for work.

Over the last several chapters, we have explained why state neutrality between competing ethical ideals is a requirement of liberal democracy. In this chapter, we outline the form that this neutrality must take in light of that explanation. We proceed in three parts. Section 2 briefly recapitulates the overall structure of the four-part argument first sketched in chapter 6, and subsequently developed in chapters 7–8. This argument was quite complex, so it is worth clarifying and emphasizing how all of its components fit together. Section 3 answers the following important questions about the scope and breadth of the neutrality requirement: *Who* or *what* is to be neutral, about *what*, and, finally, *why?* Section 4 considers the place of neutrality within liberal political morality as a whole: Is neutrality, itself, a fundamental liberal value, an instrumental one, or a constraint on the pursuit of other traditional liberal values, and what is the connection between neutrality and justice?

9.2 The Argument Revisited

Moral equality is generally thought to be the norm that makes contractualism singularly appropriate for reasoning about principles of justice. This is the view that human beings – as moral agents, or reasoners – have the same fundamental moral rights, which implies that the comparable interests of each should be equally weighted in the calculations that influence public policy, as well as in the justification of the constitutional structures that direct and constrain it. Contractualism's ideal of public justification is a way of modelling and working out the practical political implications of this equal primary importance of everyone's life.

The most common defences of moral equality, however, proceed via appeals to what are allegedly distinctive human capacities that render their possessors exclusive members of the moral community – the community, that is, of rights-bearers to whom equal justification is owed. All such defences confront the same two problems: first, they purport to derive moral norms from natural facts alone; and second, they introduce a series of problems related to the threshold level at which the relevant egalitarian status-conferring capacity is set: if possessing some particular capacity is the ground of moral status, and people inevitably possess this capacity to varying degrees, then why do their moral or political entitlements not reflect this variability? Capacity-based arguments introduced to justify the special treatment that is owed to human beings appear simultaneously to undermine the claim that their interests should count for the same. 'Luck egalitarianism' is symptomatic of this general problem.

While we have accepted (or at least not rejected) the idea of moral equality, we relied on a different but related premise in arriving at contractual justification. For us, *democratic* equality is what has led to the social contract. Politics, that is, must be conducted on the assumption that everyone's life is equally important, not by virtue of metaphysical or ontological claims about human nature, but rather in light of the attractiveness of the ideal of interpersonal relations that this assumption makes possible. This is what Rawls calls 'civic friendship' or 'reciprocity,' what Scanlon calls 'mutual recognition,' and what Larmore calls 'equal respect.' Because democratic equality is primarily a relational rather than a distributive ideal, the central philosophical task is not to identify some particular item – resources, or welfare, for instance – that must be distributed equally, but instead to determine which principles of justice, in modern conditions, are most appropriate to the normative conception of human relations at its core. The key question is what kind of politics allows people to stand in relations of equality to one another, and the answer is a democratic politics tempered by contractually generated principles of justice.

Pluralism has been especially relevant to our elaboration of contractualism, but our characterization of this condition has been quite different from those commonly found in many recent arguments for liberalism. The two critical differences have been the contrasts between (1) epistemic versus moral notions of reasonableness, and (2) simple versus reasonable forms of pluralism.

Disagreement about the nature of religious salvation and the human good complicates the project of justifying regulative principles through consent. Actual agreement between individuals as they are – thickly constituted with their substantive ethical convictions and religious doctrines – is implausible as a response to disagreements of these kinds, because pluralism is effectively what creates the problem that political life must accommodate. Somehow, then, political morality must be ethically inventive and the contractual situation must be specified in hypothetical terms. But this ethical inventiveness must proceed very carefully: we cannot establish the content of the principles derived through contractual agreement by simply appealing to moral norms thought to be morally justified by (contract) independent standards, because the existence of such pre-political standards renders the social contract dispensable altogether. Proast appears to adopt one version of this claim in his rejection of Locke's contractual argument for toleration, and it finds its contemporary expression in what we called the *circularity thesis*.

There are two different ways of abstracting from the contested ethical beliefs that generate the need for mutually acceptable principles of justice – the reasonableness-as-valid-argument and reasonableness as fairness responses to pluralism. On the reasonableness-as-valid-argument view, only a subset of the ethical beliefs likely to persist under democratic institutions actually satisfy certain stringent epistemic standards and are, thus, justifiably held by their adherents. By limiting admission to the hypothetical constitutional convention to people whose views satisfy these epistemic standards, we are, in effect, accommodating the inevitable by-product of the free exercise of practical reason – that is to say, *reasonable* pluralism – rather than simply endorsing a modus vivendi between reasonable and unreasonable ethical doctrines alike.

Unfortunately, when liberal neutrality is contractually justified on the basis of epistemic hypotheses such as Barry's sceptical uncertainty,

Nagel's theory of epistemic restraint, or Rawls's burdens of judgement, it is unnecessarily exposed to the *reflexivity thesis*. If perfectionist principles are illegitimate because they can be reasonably rejected as a result of their (dubious) epistemic status, then contractualism is self-contradictory, unless, *per impossibile*, neutralist principles do not share this same status. Unless there are persuasive reasons, that is, for thinking that questions about human perfection or flourishing (the good) raise deeper epistemological difficulties, and are therefore more difficult to answer correctly, than questions about justice are (the right), the very epistemic hypotheses that neutralists deploy to criticize state perfectionism also appear to undermine their own position.

The epistemic asymmetry at the core of this strategy is indeed untenable, but our alternative approach does not rely upon it, so it escapes the reflexivity thesis unscathed. The content of the reasonable is best elaborated by asking which principles of justice fairly situated hypothetical contractors would choose to regulate the democratic institutions of the civic equals for whom they are trustees. Epistemology plays no role in the contractual derivation of reasonable principles – Rawls's equal basic liberty and difference principles, for instance, were robust vis-à-vis the shift between the burdens of judgement and Stupid People explanations of pluralism. Once the moral constraints of the reasonable are in place, only the fact of pluralism per se is relevant to the deliberations of the contracting parties. It *is* of course true that a multiplicity of ethical beliefs and lifestyles are compatible with reasonable principles so understood, and we might want to retain the term 'reasonable pluralism' to emphasize this attractive feature of liberalism. Provided that the reasonable is disassociated from epistemic claims about the origins of pluralism, and also from the burdens and limits of human knowledge, there is no harm in this.

9.3 The Scope of Neutrality

We can now directly address a series of related fundamental questions that any purportedly neutralist version of liberalism must confront, questions that will have occurred to readers as early as chapter 6. (1) *Who* or *what* is to be neutral: the constitution that sets out the basic structure of democratic government; legislation pursued within that structure; the reasoning of legislators as they vote for or against various bills; judicial verdicts interpreting the constitutionality of democratic legislation; the educational system; the deliberations of individual citizens in their private lives as well as those of the many voluntary associations that comprise civil society? (2) What exactly must those to whom the neutrality injunction applies be neutral *about* or *in relation to*: ethical beliefs, the individual persons adhering to such beliefs, or collectivities of such persons? Finally, (3) *why* must those to whom the injunction applies (a) adopt that form of neutrality, and (b) what liberal values or goals are secured in this way? The general point underlying all three questions is that the meaning, purpose, and practical consequences of adopting one or another conception of neutrality will clearly change, depending upon the particular context in which it is invoked. Because the appeal of the liberal political morality that we have been developing cannot be fairly assessed without some sense of these consequences, we must proceed to answer these questions carefully in light of our overall argument.

9.3.1 Who or What Is to Be Neutral?

The stringency of the neutrality constraint (howsoever understood) depends, in part, upon how extensive its scope of application is. The obvious starting point in answering the question of scope is that the neutrality injunction applies first and foremost to the state, because it, alone, acts as representative, trustee, and agent, for the entire community of free and equal citizens. But while this is important, it does not actually tell us very much, because a liberal-democratic state is institutionally diverse and highly complex – it includes the constitution, the legislative, executive, and judicial branches of government, the armed forces, the police, the (publicly funded) educational system and media, to mention only a few of its constitutive parts – so we also need to know exactly how far down the line, as it were, the neutrality constraint applies within the context of various state agencies, and whether or not it extends beyond the state to civil society more generally.

Neutrality or impartiality about what is intrinsically valuable in the world, and about what to do in order to live a good or ethical life is clearly not, in general, a moral or intellectual virtue that we must or should all strive for in all situations. If liberalism actually demanded this, then we would have a decisive reason for rejecting it, because it would be utterly inconsistent with human life as we recognize it – after all, we *do* routinely assess the relative value of different goals, relationships, and activities, and, if we are rational, we try to act on the basis of such discriminations to make decent lives for ourselves. The more reflective among us also worry about whether or not these evaluations might be mistaken and, when we think they are, we modify our goals, sometimes at great emotional and/or financial expense.

While ethical neutrality in everyday life makes nonsense of this familiar picture, neutrality as a distinctively *political* requirement does not, and unlike courage or honesty, for example, neutrality is not a virtue whose estimation in the case of political actors is explained as a special case of its estimation in the world at large.[4] There is something special about politics that distinguishes it from ordinary life, and this uniqueness also helps to explain the scope of state neutrality. The coercive nature of political power and the existence of widespread ethical disagreement are the most important of these distinguishing features.

Barry, Nagel, and Rawls all argue that the particular conceptions of neutrality that they endorse apply only to constitutional essentials and matters of basic justice. Only the constitution that sets out the basic framework and powers of government, assigns liberties and rights, and regulates how the benefits and burdens of social cooperation are to be allocated, must be justified independently from comprehensive and controversial ethical beliefs about human flourishing. Importantly, this implies that democratic majorities may legitimately impose perfectionist values on minorities through legislation and public policy, provided that the procedural framework that produces electoral results and legislative outcomes is, itself, fair, which is to say, contractually justified. There is a critical and fundamental contrast, then, between the constitution that sets out the basic rules and principles of democratic decision-making, on the one hand, and the particular legislation and public policies adopted under those rules, on the other. If Barry, Nagel, and Rawls are right, then the neutrality constraint *does not* apply to non-basic issues.

However, this restriction of the neutrality injunction is untenable, because the features of politics that underlie the democratic argument for contractualism – the coercive nature of political power, and pluralism – do not track the distinction between basic (constitutional) and non-basic political issues, and so that distinction is groundless. For Rawls, it is primarily because political power is coercive that its exercise must be justified to all reasonable people in order to respect the liberal principle of legitimacy. Consider the following very brief example that usefully illustrates how the acceptance of this proposition undermines the basic versus non-basic distinction that it is intended to support. In many areas of Canada, the Catholic separate school system receives public funds raised through compulsory taxation. Imagine that a group of ultra-conservative Roman Catholics, whose religious convictions condemn both premarital sex and homosexual activity of any kind as travesties of the proper value of sexual expression, manage to gain majority control of a local school board. The board, in turn, decides to transform the school curriculum to reflect its ethical convictions, and encourages principals to expel students who contravene the ultra-conservative interpretation of what Catholicism requires by way of sexual conduct. Since the neutrality constraint applies only to permissible conceptions of the good, that is, to those not antecedently excluded by the principles of justice, it does not condemn this use of political power, unless, impossibly, the exact content of local public school curricula is something required by justice. Here, coercive political power is deployed non-neutrally to penalize students with unconventional sexual practices, but because it occurs at a local level, it escapes the neutrality constraint when the latter is confined to the basic structure.

The point generalizes: state-run media, public health agencies, rent-review boards, military disciplinary committees, and police commissions, to mention but a few, all exercise coercive power that can radically affect people's life-prospects, for better or for worse. To the extent that this is so, the democratic argument for contractualism that we have been developing over the last few chapters suggests that the neutrality constraint must exclude sectarian values *whenever* citizens' interactions with one another are mediated through state agencies, at every level, and not only when constitutional questions are at stake.

Sometimes the argument in favour of restricting the scope of neutrality to constitutional essentials and matters of basic justice is linked to the alleged practical impossibility of extending it any further. Brian Barry, for instance, maintains that 'decisions about what the publicly run schools are going to teach must obviously involve a view about the value of learning some things rather than others'; accordingly, he concludes that the suggestion that there is some way of determining a school curriculum that is neutral between all conceptions of the good is 'absurd.'[5] As long as the relevant form of neutrality is a justificatory rather than a consequential one (a distinction we explore below), however, there is no reason to think that a neutral curriculum would be impossible to devise.[6]

9.3.2 What Kind of State Neutrality, and Why?

The democratic argument for contractualism yields a neutrality requirement at two different levels. At what we shall call level 1, neutrality operates as a constraint, or filter, on arguments for liberal principles of

justice, that is, for the contractually generated rules that settle the basic
terms of political association among civic equals – what Rawls calls 'constitutional essentials and matters of basic justice.' At level 2, neutrality is
more a matter of public ethos[7] rather than of rules, which regulates
the kinds of justifications that democratic citizens should offer to one
another for discretionary laws and public policies *not* required by basic
justice. Level 2 must supplement level 1 because the reasons that
contractualists such as Barry, Nagel, and Rawls deploy to establish the
distinctiveness of political morality – those required to fend off the suggestion that liberalism absurdly requires a kind of comprehensive sus-
pension of ethical deliberation not only in politics, but in everyday life –
also undermine the idea that the neutrality injunction can consistently
be restricted to the latter.

Moral principles can be divided into two general analytical categories
– that of the good, and that of the right.[8] Propositions about goodness
specify what is intrinsically valuable in the world, and which human
goals, activities, and relationships are ultimately worth seeking. When
numerous such propositions are systematically combined, as they often
are in various particular cultural (both religious and secular) traditions,
they define a complete, comprehensive theory about how people should
live[9] or, in the contemporary jargon, a 'conception of the good.' Propositions about rightness, on the other hand, do not constitute a single,
coherent plan of life; rather, they are moral principles that regulate the
interactions of a plurality of agents pursuing different conceptions of the
good by specifying what people can and cannot fairly demand of one
another.

Perfectionist and neutralist political moralities are normally distinguished in terms of the way that each connects the principles of the right
to those of the good. A perfectionist political morality requires that the
state promote a particular conception of the good, or range of such conceptions, within the bounds of its competency, while a neutralist political
morality requires that the state take no position on the question of the
good life, and that it restrict itself to enforcing principles of right. In a
very familiar expression, a neutralist political morality, that is, prioritizes
the right over the good.

But this priority can take two different forms. In the stronger version,
the priority of right means that the reasonable rejection procedure that
establishes the fair terms of social cooperation must be, itself, justified
independently of *any* propositions about intrinsic value or goodness.
Obviously, our argument for contractualism is not neutral in this stron-

ger sense, because it has appealed to a variety of substantive and not only procedural ideals – democratic equality, civic friendship, reciprocity, and mutual respect, for example. Hypothetical contractors selecting principles to regulate the scope of democratic decision-making must deliberate in light of interests that they must secure and protect, and since such interests can scarcely be identified and explicated without goodness-based claims altogether, this stronger version of the priority claim is implausible. Indeed, critics sometimes allege that liberal neutrality is a sham because if the argument for neutrality does presuppose claims about the human good, then it reproduces the very central feature of the perfectionism that it opposes – coercive state power deployed to bolster and privilege a set of controversial ethical convictions not shared by the citizenry as a whole.

The weaker version of the priority claim, however, is much more plausible. It simply requires that the values or ideals of the good that are presupposed by the reasonable rejection procedure must, themselves, be grounded in public reason. In this view, the priority of the right over the good does not mean that democratic citizens can never legitimately appeal to considerations of goodness in justifying the use of coercive political power; it means that in order for them to do so, they must base their arguments on generalizable interests[10] that supply everyone with what Scanlon calls 'generic reasons.'[11]

A neutral state prioritizes the right over the good, then, in accordance with the weaker of the two interpretations of this ordering, and democratic citizens, in their capacities as political agents, might interpret and act upon this priority by adopting one of the following three neutrality principles:

N1 Political agents must not do anything that has the *effect* of advantaging or disadvantaging any particular conception of the good.
N2 Political agents must *not* aim at advantaging or disadvantaging any particular conception of the good.
N3 Political agents must not rely on the supposed superiority of any particular conception of the good in *justifying* (or opposing) legislation, public policy, and various other state-sponsored initiatives.[12]

Which of these principles follows from the democratic argument for contractualism that we have been exploring?

N3 is the form of state neutrality that follows from the democratic argument for liberalism, and both N1 and N2 should be rejected. Now,

N1 is an outcome-based principle that requires that the constitution, as well as legislation and public policy, be neutral in the sense of helping or hindering its citizens' differing conceptions of the good to an equal degree. A neutral law satisfying N1 would not, for example, increase the likelihood that a free-thinking experimental lifestyle such as the one advocated by Mill would come to displace more traditional or conservative ones as found in orthodox Christianity or Islam. There are both practical and theoretical reasons for rejecting this interpretation of the neutrality principle, and virtually all of the contemporary defenders of liberal neutrality, in fact, do so.[13]

To begin with, it is often clearly difficult, if not impossible, to anticipate precisely what consequences any particular law or public policy will have on the distribution of ethical convictions, and thus the relative popularity of various lifestyles, that obtain in society. It is, therefore, unreasonable to assume that governments could ever satisfy N1 even if we wanted them to. Furthermore, respect for the civil liberties that are required by liberal principles of justice will necessarily have non-neutral consequences.[14] Freedom of speech and association, for instance, permit various groups to pursue and also to advertise their favoured ways of life. Liberal justice allows individuals to choose freely between these competing lifestyles, and the popularity of any given conception of the good will depend, among other things, upon the kinds of goods that it can offer its adherents. Mill, we may recall, thought that intrinsically valuable and worthwhile ways of life would drive out those that are worthless under conditions of deliberative and political freedom, but even if this conjecture is unduly optimistic – because it confuses the claim that freedom allows people to choose what they prefer with the different claim that they usually prefer what they ought to when given a choice – many groups will have a hard time attracting and maintaining adherents when liberal principles forbid them from persecuting dissenters or apostates.

Aside from these practical difficulties, the main conceptual problem with N1 is that its implementation by the state presupposes some ethically neutral baseline against which deviations may be measured and, thus, corrected. But the very ethical pluralism that makes contractualism the correct test of political legitimacy implies that such a baseline is unavailable, at least as long as we are thinking of neutrality as a kind of average of the actual ethical convictions in the community.

What about N2? At first glance, it might appear more promising than N1, because it is consistent with democratic legislation and public policy having (inevitable) non-neutral consequences, provided that those consequences are not intended. Borrowing an example of Locke's, the state might legitimately prohibit the slaughter of animals even though such a prohibition would differentially affect the religious practices of various groups in society, depending upon whether or not those practices required the ritualistic sacrifice of animals, provided that the ban aimed at public health rather than religious conversion. In this case, we have a situation where legislation with non-neutral consequences is consistent with N2 *and* N3, because both its goal – the suppression of infectious disease, say – and its justification – public health – do not rely on controversial ethical convictions. Are N2 and N3 indistinguishable then, and should the liberal state strive to satisfy both?

Appearances are deceptive: N2 and N3 are actually inconsistent. It *cannot* be the case that the liberal state may never legitimately *aim* at encouraging or discouraging its citizens from adopting certain ethical convictions rather than others, because some of those convictions – sexist, racist, and anti-social ones, for instance – violate the principles of justice that are required by N3. Unlike N1 and N2, that is, N3 is a critical perspective that does not take people's actual ethical convictions as self-validating. The liberal state must be neutral only between *permissible* conceptions of the good, and permissible conceptions are those that are consistent with principles that would be freely chosen by democratic citizens (or their hypothetical trustees) from an original position of equality. More than this, it must positively encourage the dispositions and virtues that strengthen support for such principles through the creation and maintenance of a democratic ethos.[15] While N2 and N3 may be contingently compatible from time to time, then, they will often conflict, and N3 is ultimately the correct interpretation of the neutrality principle.[16]

9.4 Conclusion: The Place of Neutrality

N3 requires that the hypothetical agreement that specifies the principles that settle constitutional essentials and matters of basic justice not presuppose the truth or superiority of controversial perfectionist values. This does not mean, however, that contractualism eschews ideas of the good altogether. This is impossible because hypothetical trustees cannot select between candidate principles without some view of the interests that must be protected and advanced through their deliberations. At level 1, then, democratic equality requires that the ideas of the good presupposed by the reasonable rejection procedure be themselves publicly justifiable. At level 2, democratic citizens *also* owe one another neutral justifications for discretionary laws and public policies not required by the principles of justice, that is, whenever their dealings with one another are mediated through state agencies, and not only when constitutional essentials and matters of basic justice are at stake.

This implies that the neutrality requirement at the core of the liberal political morality we have been exploring occupies a somewhat peculiar position. On the one hand, neutrality is clearly a fundamental or core liberal value – it enters into the picture at the deepest level (level 1) where the principles that specify the basic terms of political association are being justified. The egalitarian vision of political community that contractualism expresses cannot be explicated without N3, so we cannot plausibly characterize this form of neutrality in purely instrumental terms. On the other hand, neutrality is not, itself, a goal or aim of the liberal state, but a constraint on the pursuit of whichever goals free and equal democratic citizens wish to pursue (at level 2) through their shared social, political, and economic institutions.[17]

Recently, feminist and socialist critics have challenged the institutional focus of liberal justice in a way that might imply that the neutrality requirement must be extended, on pain of inconsistency, even further than level 2, into the personal choices that structure and inform citizens' daily lives. Like any other aspect of political morality, N3 would then have to constrain not only constitutional essentials and ordinary legislation and public policy, but also individual choices about, say, what job to take, whom to marry, and what hobbies to pursue. This would give us a decisive reason for rejecting liberalism – we cannot, after all, imagine deciding such things without relying on perfectionist judgements about what is ultimately worthwhile in life and how we best lead it – so let us now see whether or not the anti-institutional critique forces this upon us.

10 How Political Is the Personal?

One of the thornier problems facing us in moral life is the familiar tension between equality and partiality. On the one hand, if our political values are decent, then the institutions that reflect them are supposed to treat all human beings, simply because they are human beings, with equal concern and respect – our spouses, friends, and family members no better than strangers; our compatriots no better than foreigners. As occupants of the political perspective, we have 'agent-neutral'[1] reasons deriving from the constitutive values of democracy, and these reasons apply to us independently of our particular identities, allegiances, and commitments, which they accordingly constrain. On the other hand, both common-sense morality and philosophical ethics tell us that, sometimes, we may justifiably devote more of our affection, time, and money to people we know and care about than we are normally ready to give others. As occupants of the personal perspective whose lives are deeply influenced by those allegiances and commitments, we have 'agent-relative' reasons for *limiting* the demands of the political perspective. Indeed, many of our significant personal attachments appear to depend essentially on forms of partiality that would be undermined by a requirement that we treat everyone equally in our day-to-day affairs. We also (rightly) value our freedom to shape those attachments by our own lights.

This duality of perspectives raises both normative and practical puzzles: how should we interpret the relationship between equality and partiality; what weight should be attached to each value in cases of conflict; and if we are not required to treat people with equal concern and respect in our daily lives, why, morally and practically speaking, should we be expected to support political parties, legislation, and public policies that effectively constrain our partiality towards our associates? Matters worsen in cases where morality appears not only to license but also *require* that we prioritize their interests over the wants and even the needs of strangers. So unless we are ready to abandon political equality, or, less likely, the personal ties that make our lives worth living, we must somehow explain how these putatively incompatible values are, in fact, mutually sustaining. If this integrative task proves too demanding, then we should at least establish whether the incompatibility in question is genuine or illusory, and, if genuine, what (if anything) can be done about it.

The strategy implicit throughout this book adopts a moral division of labour between institutions and personal conduct. The basic idea is that once background institutions and the rules that regulate them are designed to promote equality, people can pursue partial aims and attachments in their daily lives with a clear conscience. In this chapter, I defend this strategy against two recent challenges: the socialist critique of economic incentives and the feminist critique of gender inequality. Both reject as untenable any sharp distinction between institutions and personal choice, on the grounds that 'the personal is political.' Therefore justice is said to require not only egalitarian institutions, but also a widely shared ethos, or set of equality-supportive attitudes and beliefs, to guide personal choices that are neither mandated nor forbidden by institutional rules. In section 2, I explain the motivation behind, and the implications of, the moral or institutional division of labour. In section 3, I set out the substance of the socialist/feminist critiques. In section 4, I argue for distinguishing between various senses in which the personal is political, between various ways that political principles might apply to personal conduct and, finally, between different forms of partiality. Once we do, we can see that while some of the personal is indeed relevantly political, egalitarian justice

1 does *not* require strict equality as a norm of personal conduct;
2 condemns the greed of economic high-fliers and the sexism of misogynists entirely from within the institutional approach, so there is accordingly no need to abandon it; and, finally,
3 has as its real enemy not partiality per se, but only those sub-forms of special concern for associates that lead to hierarchy, subordination, and, ultimately, oppression.

This position embodies a midway point, then, between stronger forms of egalitarianism that apply political principles directly to personal choices in everyday life,[2] and weaker ones that mostly insulate those choices from the demands of equality once background institutional justice has been secured.[3] In my view, some personal choices are political, others are not, and political institutions are, themselves, indispensable in figuring out the difference. The real question then is not, Is the personal political? Of course it is. The real question is, *How* political is the personal? And the answer to *that* question does nothing to undermine the case for liberalism.

10.1 The Moral Division of Labour

We might try to reconcile the personal and political perspectives by contrasting equality-violating and equality-consistent forms of partiality. While this distinction *would* yield a principled balance between the demands of justice and those stemming from our private pursuits and attachments, it could not be drawn from within the confines of the personal perspective alone, for the following reason. Whether or not a certain type of partial concern is politically reasonable (consistent with equality) ultimately depends, among other things, on judgements about the collective results of everyone's following candidate principles that allow or forbid it.[4]

Because politics raises a special kind of normative problem, the reconciliation we seek cannot be achieved via a direct application of individual practical reason to political institutions.[5]

But if political philosophy is *not* simply personal ethics writ large, the worry presently occupying us may have been overstated just now. That is, if the normative principles applying to institutions are importantly different from those applying to individual persons, and if equality is a distinctively *political* value, then our two perspectives might be only contingently, rather than fundamentally, competitive. To see this, consider the following example. While it would remain true that money spent on my spouse would be unavailable for improving the lives of the homeless, this expenditure would not violate any justice-based obligation of *mine* to improve their plight, unless we also assumed either that I, in fact, have this duty, or that they have rights *against me* to money that I would rather spend in this, or other non equality-promoting ways.

The institutional approach to justice's 'moral division of labour'[6] builds on this insight by assigning the realization of agent-neutral values to background social, political, and economic institutions, allowing people to pursue partial attachments and goals in their day-to-day lives. In this view, we are to look for 'an institutional division of labor between the basic structure and the rules applying directly to individuals and associations and to be followed by them in particular transactions. If this division can be established, individuals and associations are then left free to advance their ends more effectively within the framework of the basic structure, secure in the knowledge that elsewhere in the social system the necessary corrections to preserve background justice are being made.'[7] In effect, the position distinguishes between equality as a justificatory point of view and equality as a norm of interpersonal fairness, and it claims that acting partially is often permissible and sometimes even required, but only *when partial principles of interpersonal conduct, themselves, can be justified from the impartial point of view.* The central implication is this: while justice requires equality in the design of the basic institutional structure of society, and the rules that apply to it, it does not require equality in people's choices within that structure, beyond the non-optional choice to comply with the structure itself. People therefore have justice-based obligations to create and support egalitarian political institutions that treat everyone with equal concern and respect, but no analogous duty falls on them individually. As such, they 'are free to take up partisan aims and attachments in their private lives with complete conviction, if and because politics has secured a distribution that is egalitarian publicly.'[8]

In this way, partiality is tolerated but some of its more unacceptable manifestations are regulated through egalitarian institutional design. This normative partitioning has two primary effects that help explain the attractiveness of the institutional approach as a solution to the problem we are considering: (1) it allows people to lead self-chosen lives by freeing them from the mentally oppressive and economically burdensome task of continuously monitoring and readjusting their personal conduct for the sake of maximizing the prospects of the worst off in society (which is likely what would be required by equality as a consequentialist norm of personal conduct, at least until everyone was brought up, or reduced, to the same level), and, as explained below, (2) by subtly distinguishing between acceptable and unacceptable forms of equality-subverting partiality, it balances several otherwise seemingly incompatible goods – freedom, equality, *and* solidarity. A just society will not seek to undermine the strong affective ties found between lovers, spouses, families, friends, church members, and compatriots, for instance, because political equality is consistent with many of the forms of partiality that such valuable relationships depend upon. Tragic choices between equal freedom and loyalty are thereby evaded, or so it is hoped.

10.2 The Socialist and Feminist Critiques

Some maintain, however, that it is inconsistent for people to demand equality in politics while condemning it in ordinary life because, in the words of a familiar slogan, 'the personal is political.' This claim has motivational, conceptual, and political dimensions.

From a psychological point of view, the institutional approach's partitioning of motives between institutions and people seems deeply problematic. Once egalitarian institutions are in place, we are supposed to be concerned primarily with our own interests, broadly construed. But how can we then be expected to support the institutions that often limit our pursuing those interests? The moral division of labour absolves us from always having to worry about how well other people's lives are going, and from being personally responsible for fixing those lives when they go badly. But it also *assumes* that we *will* be so concerned in demanding that we create and support just institutions, sometimes at large personal cost, particularly, say, when we are rich. This combination of egalitarian public values and partial personal aims therefore appears to lack the character of an integrated moral outlook.[9] While it is good that justice gives us the right to pursue our private goals and develop our relationships within designated limits, it is bad that the sense of entitlement that we get from that right erodes those limits and, thus, undermines our support for egalitarian politics.

A related concern is the effect that institutional redistributive mechanisms – as opposed to interpersonal acts of private charity – are likely to have on the linkages between communal self-identification, solidarity, and equality. The worry is essentially the flip side of the freedom-based claim at the core of the institutional approach. Suppose for the moment, for whatever reason you like, that it *is* both liberating and fairer to have a fixed portion of your income taxed and then redistributed to the poor according to public principles than it is for you to contribute the same amount through multiple acts of private charity. Setting practical considerations aside, *ex hypothesi*, the poor receive the same amount of money in each case, but the mediated character of the welfare state's tax and transfer system walls you off from the people that your money goes to help. In an important sense, then, you are responsible for them, but not *to* them.[10] Even if a bureaucratized transfer of funds is more liberating for contributors and dignified for beneficiaries than private charity is, it also ensures that, aside from brief and uncomfortable encounters on the street, you and the poor remain total strangers. But strangers are normally less likely than associates are to identify often and strongly enough with others to trigger a willingness to help them – intimacy grounds solidarity, solidarity grounds equality, and the remoteness of institutionally mediated relationships threatens to undermine all three.

The symmetry between the institutional and charity-based approaches exemplified above is therefore taken to be illusory, and the illusion is sustainable only when we focus on a particular time-slice. At any arbitrarily selected time, that is, institutional transfers can be used to mimic private ones, but, over time, their mediated quality undermines solidarity, and this makes it less likely that individuals will personally support political parties, laws, and public policies that defend those transfers in the first place.

Unless the empirical assumptions about the importance of communal identification to egalitarian concern underlying these claims are false, the institutional approach is threatened by psychological incoherence and, thus, political instability.[11] A further, conceptual, worry is that the normative foundations of the approach render its institutional focus arbitrary and ultimately self-defeating. Recall that people are individually obligated to create and support political institutions that satisfy the correct principles of egalitarian justice, even though they may act partially in their daily lives. Suppose, for the sake of argument, that Rawls's difference principle, or something like it, is one such principle of justice. People therefore have a duty to create and support background social, political, and economic institutions that, taken together as a system, permit inequalities if and only to the extent that they maximally benefit the least advantaged members of society. But if maximin is the goal,[12] there are surely plenty of other non-institutional ways we could achieve it, such as forgoing the latest fashions, expensive meals, good wine, and luxury vacations and donating the proceeds directly to the poor, or to non-governmental agencies acting on their behalf.[13] Given this, it seems both odd and arbitrary to limit our justice-based duties to the creation and sustenance of egalitarian institutions. As one critic asks, 'If people have a duty to promote just institutions, why do they lack a duty to promote whatever it is that just institutions are *for*?'[14] The strategy's overly narrow focus is the upshot of an implausibly strong view about the normative significance of institutions, and a correspondingly weak view about personal responsibility: if institutions are supposed to aim at equality, then people should be as well.[15]

The motivational and conceptual worries just described imply that the institutional approach is incoherent, self-defeating, or both, because its moral division of labour is untenable. Recently, socialist and feminist critics have concluded that because 'the personal is political,' the approach is also morally unacceptable, condoning as it does both equality-subverting selfishness in daily life and misogynistic personal attitudes about gender.

Marx[16] famously argued that bourgeois politics necessarily fosters anti-communal behaviour, because it encourages people to see themselves first and foremost as private members of civil society, whose antecedently defined interests the state exists to protect, as opposed to equal participants in a collective emancipatory project. In sharply separating the public and private spheres, liberalism defends and magnifies our egoism by insulating many areas of life from political intervention.

Recently, G.A. Cohen[17] has directed a particular version of this critique at Rawls's difference principle. Recall that, for Rawls, inequalities in overall life-prospects are legitimate only when they are to the advantage of the worst off, in the sense that further equalizing measures would actually worsen their prospects by diminishing the productivity of the better off, whose economic surplus funds redistributive policies.[18] The justification therefore presupposes a choice that marketable people – those who, for whatever reason, command a high salary and can vary their level of productivity depending upon how high it is – make about how long, how hard, and where to work. Talented people can be expected to produce more than they otherwise would if, but only if, they are paid higher than average wages, and without these incentives, reduced productivity on their part means fewer resources are available to help the poor.

Cohen thinks that this creates the following dilemma. On the one hand, if the talented, themselves, do not affirm the difference principle, then their society is unjust because a just society is not only governed in accordance with the right principles; it is also one in which those principles are sufficiently *public* – each citizen accepts, and knows that everyone else accepts, the same (correct) principles of justice. On the other hand, if the talented *do* accept the difference principle, that is, if they affirm and act from it in everyday life, then they can be asked why 'in light of their own belief in the principle, they require more pay than the untalented get, for work which may indeed demand special talent but which is not especially unpleasant.'[19]

Incentive-based inequalities that are required to induce high-fliers to improve the prospects of the worst off are made 'necessary' only because the talented are unwilling to work at the same level of productivity for less. If the personal choices of the talented about work and leisure were more thoroughly informed by the difference principle – if they lacked the acquisitive and selfish attitudes that the incentives argument attributes to them – then hardly any inequalities in life-prospects would be justified under it.

Because the motives that influence how hard individuals work ultimately dictate how much inequality the institutional approach tolerates, personal choices not regulated by the law clearly must fall within the primary purview of justice. Specifically, this means that (1) distributive principles must apply, wherever else they do, to people's legally unconstrained/optional choices; and (2) an egalitarian society will require not only just coercive *rules*, but also an *ethos* of justice to inform and guide legally unconstrained choices within those rules. The motivations that inform people's choices in everyday life must be adequately infused with egalitarian concern. Otherwise, we will be forced to tolerate inequalities that are, strictly speaking, unnecessary to improve the prospects of the worst off. Because the personal is political in ways that clearly undermine the moral division of labour, equality requires not 'mere politics, but a moral revolution, a revolution in the human soul.'[20]

This point also appears to be nicely illustrated by the family. As feminists convincingly argue, gender neutrality in various aspects of family law is perfectly consistent with, say, an unfair distribution of domestic labour between husbands and wives. Even though unfairness of this kind has unmistakable and devastating consequences for women's autonomy and equality, it flies under the institutional radar, as it were, because it is mostly socially reinforced. On the one hand, then, it is the *social* definition of sex – gender – that enforces the hierarchical attitudes that subordinate women to men; on the other, there are virtually no sex equality laws applicable anywhere in civil society except in the workplace and at school. So except for at work and school (and sometimes even there), women are at the mercy of the rules of everyday life. These rules

> have never been legislated or adjudicated. They have not had to be. They effectively prescribe what girls can be, what the community encourages and permits in a woman, what opportunities are available and hence what aspirations are developed, what shape of life is so expected that it is virtually never articulated. These rules go under the heading of socialization, pressure, religion, popular culture, masculinity and femininity, everyday life. The rules of everyday life, in this sense, are that law which is not one, the law for women where there is no law.[21]

Informal social pressures of these kinds are powerful enough to sustain gender inequality without being enacted formally as sex classifications in the law. But the state *is* nonetheless complicit in enforcing the rules of everyday life, because it often *refuses* to interrogate the misogynistic attitudes and practices that underlie them in the name of individual rights to privacy.

Hierarchical gender expectations in civil society undermine women's access to all sorts of social, economic, educational, and political goods, in two interrelated ways. First, women's exclusion prevents them from shaping the institutional rules that distribute these important goods. Second, the boundaries that divide the personal and political spheres that determine how much and what kinds of things are subject to political control are, themselves, the result of a complex interaction between social norms and institutional rules. The family is a case in point. Gendered family structure profoundly affects women's life chances, but it does so partly via the choices that they make in response to gender-based expectations, which their choices in turn sustain.[22] This is at once coercive and voluntary, institutional and personal. It is no wonder, then, that the moral division of labour has trouble responding to it.

In limiting the application of egalitarian principles to institutions, then, the moral division of labour takes the content of a society's dominant ethos at face value, even *when that ethos is objectionably selfish and sexist.* While any acceptable theory of justice must also subject the ethos to normative scrutiny, liberalism interprets it – with all of its greed and misogyny – as part of the fixed social background that institutional rules are forced to accommodate.

10.3 The Institutional Approach Defended

The institutional approach therefore leaves us with a paradox. On the one hand, we are *not* required to be strictly egalitarian or impartial in our daily lives because this requirement, if generally acted upon, would destroy most of what is valuable in life. After all, we cannot imagine treating, say, our own spouses, children, and projects as of no greater importance than anyone else's. But on the other hand, if the personal sphere is beyond egalitarian norms, then we seem unable to condemn forms of greed and misogyny that are inconsistent with the democratic values underlying the institutional approach in the first place.

Let me begin my attempt at rescuing the institutional approach from this paradox by noting a peculiar feature of the current debate. Both critics and defenders of the moral division of labour reduce virtually *any* kind of equality-subverting behaviour to a morally problematic form of partiality. In essence, 'partiality' is synonymous with selfishness. Nagel, for example, implies that when two people are both interested in 'the last éclair on the dessert tray' or each 'wants the last life jacket for his child as the ship goes down,'[23] the key difference is how much more psychologically demanding equality is on the personal perspective in the second case. It is harder to give up your child than an éclair for the sake of others but equality requires both, and the 'partiality' that subverts it is not qualitatively different in each case. Cohen, unlike Nagel, rejects the institutional approach, but his indictment of the incentives argument trades on a similar ambiguity. In the economic context, being selfish 'means desiring things for oneself, and for those in one's immediate circle, and being disposed to act on that desire, even when the consequence is that one has (much) more than other people do, and could otherwise have had.'[24]

This conflation misleads us into thinking that the economic incentives and family examples illustrate the same point – namely, that because the personal is political, equality must also apply to our personal choices in daily life, and this undermines the institutional approach. Actually, the two cases are strikingly different, and they lead to no such conclusion.

In the case of personal choices regarding occupation and wages, equality requires that we refrain from pressing certain economic demands that, if met, disadvantage others in ways that undermine their equal status. But the attitudes and motives that lead to this kind of restraint are, strictly speaking, irrelevant to the distributive outcome, which is achievable by institutional means such as tax and transfer. In the case of the family, however, partial motives are often inseparable from the valuable relationships in question that they constitute, so some other response that takes those motives directly into consideration is required. Think of typical spousal or parent–child relationships. It matters not only what intimates do – say, spending more time and money on people they love than on strangers; it matters *why*, namely, that this pattern of expenditures partly symbolizes and reinforces devotion, love, affection, and respect . This is one reason why personal choices that sustain social institutions like the family are unlike economic choices about how hard to work and for what wages.

Another reason is that the family appears to be a special kind of social form, one that often exerts far greater influence on both private and public life than many personal economic choices do.[25] Individual choices about whether to work hard for less money are also clearly influenced by the effects of other people's economic choices in a market economy, but this process is significantly different from the one that obtains when, say, husbands and wives 'decide' to divide domestic labour unequally and along gender-based lines, or parents regularly favour sons over daughters when budgeting for higher education. In the latter cases, unevenly distributed expectations are reinforced in ways that make individual dissent from the resulting dominant patterns of behaviour much more costly. When this happens in ways that undermine people's status as free and equal citizens, it seems perverse to suggest that such decisions, even if fully voluntary (which is often doubtful), are 'personal' and thus beyond the reach of egalitarian justice. Some personal choices, then, must clearly be brought within the ambit of collectively enforceable norms, so we need some way of distinguishing between these and others that, because benign, are immune from political control.

A growing body of scholarly writing, mostly in defence of Rawls and in connection with the difference principle,[26] claims that this can be done entirely from within the institutional approach. These exegetical and interpretive disputes are important, but I want to leave them behind and argue, in general terms, that the paradox identified above dissolves once we differentiate between various (1) senses in which the personal is political, (2) ways that political principles apply to personal conduct, and, finally, (c) forms of partiality. These refinements are suggestive and schematic rather than exhaustive of all of the possibilities but, taken together, they are enough (I think) to disarm the socialist/feminist critiques. After briefly laying them out, I return to the incentives argument for inequality and the family examples to illustrate how.

10.3.1 Three Ways That 'The Personal Is Political'

10.3.1.1 INSTITUTIONAL SALIENCE

Surely we can disagree about how badly off the badly off have to be before equality overrides what are otherwise reasonable forms of partiality towards compatriots, spouses, lovers, friends, and children, for instance. But a line obviously has to be drawn *somewhere* because it is implausible that there are no agent-centred prerogatives that allow for deviations from strict equality.[27] And wherever we draw this line, one of its effects is that some individuals will end up having less than they otherwise could have had under a more equal distribution of concern and resources, and this can raise issues of justice.

For example, any plausible theory of distributive justice will make people's economic entitlements sensitive to considerations of personal responsibility – that is, what and how much they end up with will be indexed to what they have *done*. People who choose to respond to economic incentives designed to benefit the least advantaged by working longer, harder, and at more arduous tasks than others do are legitimately entitled to the greater rewards associated with them. For adults with equal opportunity, there is nothing objectionable about this. In fact, there *is* something unfair about correcting *ex post* for inequalities between adults when these result from voluntary trade-offs that they have made between labour and leisure, or various forms of labour.[28]

What happens when we introduce children into this picture? Political philosophers have mostly[29] ignored this complication. Parents, in normal cases, tend to favour their own children over those of others. In general, there is nothing objectionable about this. Wealthy parents, however, can and do spend more money on private education, better health care, culturally enriching holidays, and social/leisure activities that prepare their children for life in the ruling classes. Most parents would do this if they could, but many cannot, so there is a conflict between the justice-based entitlements of adults, and those of their children. If our entitlements should be sensitive to our choices, this also implies that we should *not* be economically disadvantaged by circumstances beyond our control, and being born into a poor family is clearly one such circumstance. More progressive inheritance and estate taxes alone will not solve this problem because the benefits of wealth accrue long before children reach maturity, and equality of opportunity is subverted *intra-generationally* as well.

This example reveals that the personal is institutionally salient because there are many areas of domestic or quotidian life in which strict equality has little (if any) place, but that also interact with the public domain to generate inequalities that raise serious issues of social justice: 'Individual choices and efforts and personal attachments which are in themselves unexceptional combine on large scale and over time to produce effects that are beyond individual control and grossly unequal.'[30] There is no default political response to these inequalities that does not require justification – every public choice, from laissez-faire to radical egalitarianism, must be defended against the possible alternatives.

10.3.1.2 JUSTIFICATORY LINKAGE
Some theories of justice interpret political equality to mean that, as individuals, we should aim directly at equalizing the distribution of resources either by specifically adopting this as our personal goal, or by developing personal goals and attachments that are at least instrumental in realizing

it. In entirely subordinating the personal perspective to the demands of justice, this transforms us all into simple agents of impartial concern.

On the liberal view, however, the *point* of state neutrality between competing conceptions of the good is that people are equally entitled to pursue, within the bounds of justice, those relationships and projects that matter to them. Stronger forms of egalitarianism that imply that not only institutions but people should be optimally designed to maximize equality remember the 'equally' and forget the 'matters.' As Rawls puts it, 'Justice draws the limit ... the good shows the point, [and] justice cannot draw the limit too narrowly.'[31]

Somehow, then, the importance of what matters to us must be directly taken into account by the rules that specify how the basic social, political, and economic institutions of society distribute the benefits and burdens of social cooperation. A contractual theory makes reasonable agreement between free and equal citizens the appropriate test for the legitimacy of those rules. Principles of justice can be reasonably rejected, that is, when they leave us too badly off compared to other people, or when they require too great a sacrifice of our interests and attachments by comparison with feasible alternatives that impose no such burdens on us, or on anyone else. Political justification therefore presupposes an account of the types of personal projects and attachments that people have reason to value, not in specific detail, but in broad outline. Even if we have very different substantive ends, we can still agree that certain constraints on personal partiality are legitimate while others are not. For example, the value of familial intimacy is undermined by laws preventing parents from reading to their children at night (which may place them at a competitive advantage relative to the children of parents who do not do this) but not by laws stopping parents from buying their children scarce and lucrative jobs for which they may be otherwise unqualified.

10.3.1.3 RECIPROCAL IDENTITY FORMATION AND JUSTICE
The personal and political perspectives are inter-penetrative in the additional sense that each shapes how we conceive of our status and role in the other. There are two aspects to this. The first concerns the pedagogical role of the family as the original school of political justice. The basic idea should be instantly recognizable to anyone who has read her J.S. Mill. In *The Subjection of Women*, Mill argues,

All the selfish propensities, the self-worship, the unjust preference, which exist among mankind, have their source and root in, and derive their principal nourishment from, the present constitution of the relation between men and women. Think what it is to a boy, to grow up to manhood in the belief that without any merit or any exertion of his own, though he may be the most frivolous and empty or the most ignorant and solid of mankind, by the mere fact of being born a male his is by right the superior of all and every one of an entire half of the human race ... Is it imagined that all this does not pervert the whole manner of existence of the man, both as an individual and as a social being? It is an exact parallel to the feeling of a hereditary king that he is excellent above others by being born a king.[32]

Mill is saying that domestic arrangements such as marriage can and should be evaluated using the same terms that have traditionally been deployed in connection with the state – tyranny versus liberty, hierarchy versus equality. There is also a causal link: marriage is not simply *like* a state; the power relations within it also *affect* the kind of state that we end up having. Because the family is the primary school of social and moral development, the subjection of women is not simply one injustice among others, but the basis of *all* injustice. Unless and until marriage and family life more generally is reformed, there is little hope that children will grow up to become citizens who demand justice in all relationships, including political ones. Democratic states concerned with reproducing themselves over time therefore have direct interests in the processes of identity formation whereby people come to see themselves as one another's equals.[33]

The second aspect is a corollary of the first. Domestic life shapes our identities in politically significant ways, but a society's institutional structure will also likely influence how, as individuals, people conceive of and carry out their personal goals and attachments. People decide where to work, whom to marry, and whether to have children, for example, partly on the basis of expectations that are, themselves, encouraged by institutional rules that announce what benefits and burdens are associated with various courses of action in these contexts. This means that political institutions and the rules that regulate them not only satisfy existing preferences, they create new ones.

10.3.2 Applying Political Principles to the Personal: Three Sites and Modes

So the personal is institutionally salient, foundational in contractual justification, and pedagogically vital to the stability and permanence of democratic communities. Socialist/feminist critics, then, are right to claim that an egalitarian society cannot ignore the personal perspective.

While their premise ('the personal is political') is sound, their inference (people must directly aim at equality in their daily lives) is not, because there are at least three different sites and three possible modes of subjecting the personal perspective to egalitarian scrutiny, with multiple combinations thereof. Many strategies are therefore available. I now set them out before returning to the economic incentives and family examples, which show that the most appropriate one in a given case depends upon both the *type* of partiality and the equality interests at stake. The institutional approach to justice incorporates this insight, while stronger forms of egalitarianism implausibly ignore it.

10.3.2.1 SITES

10.3.2.1.1 Ethos An ethos is a set of beliefs, sentiments, and attitudes that (implicitly or explicitly) shape and sustain the conventional practices and informal pressures of a group of people who share it. So understood, an ethos has three interrelated levels: values, principles, and practices.[34] In order to establish whether, and how strongly, any particular individual shares a target group's ethos, we must determine how much her practices internalize its values and principles.

Applying equality to a society's ethos means ensuring that (1) enough people have internalized whichever interpersonal attitudes are needed to secure general compliance with egalitarian law and public policy, and (2) its informal practices and conventions mirror rather than undermine our status as one another's civic equals. While this ethos is beyond immediate legislative control – after all, the state cannot dictate how we feel about one another – the state might try indirect measures to cultivate it. For example, civic education starting in early childhood might counterbalance a popular culture too intent upon glorifying economic dominance and sexual inequality at the expense of the poor and women. It is not clear whether this would work unless it was also compulsory, and a mandatory scheme may subvert other aspects of the egalitarian ethos.

10.3.2.1.2 Personal Choices Equality might be applied to legally unconstrained personal decisions involving, say, career choice, salary negotiations, marital status, and parenting, instead of only regulating the background culture of justice that is supposed to inform them. People would then decide where to work, whom to live with, and on what terms, in light of how each of the available options was comparatively equality-optimizing. The informational/epistemic burdens of this requirement are enough to discredit it, but it is also implausibly demanding from a moral point of view: it subordinates self-interest, affective ties, and personal projects to the standards of society-wide equality. It is little wonder that its advocates place such a heavy emphasis on the unconscious internalization of the egalitarian ethos.

10.3.2.1.3 Institutional Rules Finally, equality might be applied to institutions. By 'institutions' I mean public systems of rules that create frameworks within which personal choices are made, rather than particular choices or actions themselves. These frameworks set out the rights and duties attached to various social, legal, and economic positions, they permit and forbid different forms of action, and they impose antecedently defined penalties for violations of the rules.

Applying equality to institutions means designing them so that general compliance with their rules yields patterns of social behaviour that ultimately improve the prospects of the worst off.

10.3.2.2 MODES
There are (at least) three different ways of applying equality to each or all of these sites.

10.3.2.2.1 Direct Application Direct application requires that people, informal social practices and conventions, and institutions adopt equality as their primary goal. In this view, the relationship between the entities in question – people, practices, institutions – and equality is an instrumental one, and the instrument, in each case, can be related to its supposed goal either performatively or inspirationally.[35] That is, either they ought to be shaped so that equality is, in fact, optimally promoted, or, alternatively, they ought to be inspired and motivated by it. As we know from the history of utilitarian thought, these two often do not track each other.

10.3.2.2.2 Lexical Constraint Most of the time, people adopt goals and participate in relationships that have little or nothing to do with equality. Lexical constraint envisages equality as externally constraining, rather than being instrumentally related to, these goals. That is, personal choice, ethos, and institutions need be neither performatively nor inspirationally egalitarian, as long as their effects are consistent with whatever distributive outcome is required by justice. Of course, if deviations from strict equality are *never* just, then the lexical constraint view is incoherent, because the distinction between it and the direct application view collapses – aiming at equality and having permissible goals and relationships would always amount to the same thing.

10.3.2.2.3 Mutual Constraint Fortunately, however, justice cannot require this because, as I explain below, selfishness is only one form of equality-subverting partiality, and there are others that any defensible political morality will have to accommodate. This yields a third mode of applying equality to the personal perspective – mutual constraint. Remember, the second mode, lexical constraint, is ecumenical in permitting a multiplicity of different goals. But it is also quite restrictive in condemning *any* goal that subverts what would be an otherwise more egalitarian outcome. The mutual constraint view, by contrast, conceives of the relationship between equality and partiality in a reciprocal fashion. In deciding how to weight each value in cases of conflict, it considers (1) the value or importance of the goal or attachment in question; (2) the extent to which that value or importance is partiality-dependent; (3) the costs, in terms of that value, of imposing egalitarian constraints of varying stringency; and, finally (4) the costs, in terms of equality, of shielding partiality to varying degrees.

10.3.3 Three Different Types of Partiality

Partiality is essentially bounded concern that is expressed attitudinally, behaviourally, or, in normal cases, both. If we focus on the potential objects of people's limited concern, the options are basically endless – beginning with ourselves and expanding outward to include a growing circle of friends, family, compatriots, and perhaps eventually humanity at large. Focusing instead on the *motives* leading us to care about some things more than others, we notice three non-exhaustive and non-mutually exclusive classes. The last two, in particular, seem inextricably linked.

10.3.3.1 SELF-REFERENTIAL PARTIALITY
The most familiar kind of partiality is self-referential, whereby people care disproportionately more about their goals, projects, and commitments *because* they are theirs. It is a mistake, however, to confuse this with selfishness or greed, where this means being unconcerned with others or wanting, as a goal in itself, more than they have. Of course, people sometimes do pursue what matters to them in selfish or callous ways, but then the problem is selfishness or callousness, not partiality per se. The point is that every person has a right to exercise agent-centred prerogatives to

some reasonable extent, and even when doing so makes things worse than they need be for the badly off. Even Cohen concedes that only 'an extreme moral rigorist'[36] would deny this.

10.3.3.2 ALTRUISTIC PARTIALITY

Another form of partiality consists of other-regarding dispositions and actions that are altruistic, benevolent, or paternalistic. Think of volunteers in charitable organizations such as Big Brothers or Big Sisters who serve as role models for only a subset of needy kids from a bad neighbourhood. Hopefully, the extra time, energy, and affection spent helping these Little Brothers and Sisters will improve their prospects relative to children living in safer parts of town. But it will *also* distance them from friends in the bad neighbourhood without Big Brothers or Sisters of their own. Altruistic partiality will compete with equality, but any plausible moral view must accommodate it. So there is yet another reason why, even if the personal *is* political, we should expect the best theory of justice to endorse some *indirect* strategy of applying egalitarian principles to personal choice. Otherwise, we are not allowed to help anyone unless, *per impossibile*, we somehow manage to help everyone. Surely, nothing could be worse for the badly off.

10.3.3.3 CONSTITUTIVE/AFFECTIVE PARTIALITY

Finally, we have what might be called constitutive/affective partiality. We cannot *be* someone's spouse, friend, or parent, for example, without also understanding that these social forms often require us to accord their wants and needs certain kinds of priority over those of non-associates, at least absent special or extenuating circumstances. The intimacy, solidarity, and trust that this kind of limited concern makes possible is crucial to the emergence and flourishing of several of life's most wonderful interpersonal ties. It is therefore highly unlikely that justice demands that we abandon such attachments even for a weighty goal such as improving the prospects of the worst off.

On the other hand, giving constitutive/affective partiality free rein would likely operate as 'the moral equivalent of a tax shelter'[37] for the rich, who could then lavish great resources on their friends and family while reminding the poor that morality requires that they take care of their own. Clearly, then, the strength of our associative duties in any given situation depends on variables of the sort identified above in connection with the *mutual constraint* view. But as long as justice allows *some* room for associative priority (as it surely must), then we have a third and final equality-subverting motive.

What light does this taxonomy shed on the anti-institutional critique? We now return to the economic incentives and family examples to determine what (if anything) the institutional approach can say about corporate greed and sexism.

10.4 Justice and Economic Incentives

It is well known that the ratio of executive to production worker salaries is much higher in the United States, but lower in some of the Scandinavian countries. Assuming that less inequality in Scandinavia does not adversely affect its productivity, there are grounds for thinking that an ethos friendlier to equality there caused the worst paid to be better remunerated than their American counterparts living under a different and more selfish culture of reward.[38] On the one hand, then, we should say that a principle, such as Rawls's, allowing only inequalities that benefit the least advantaged was (1) *better* satisfied in Scandinavia than in the United States; and that (2) Scandinavia's distribution of income was accordingly more *just*, at least in light of that egalitarian principle. On the other hand, the socialist critique alleges that, in focusing on institutions, a liberal theory *cannot* say this, because the smaller Scandinavian wage dispersion was the result of ethos, not law, and so accordingly beyond the direct reach of such a theory.

Now, if the *institutional salience* and *reciprocal identity formation* theses are correct, liberalism does not have to abstain from judgements of this kind, because an ethos of corporate greed is likely to have institutional roots. The incentives that liberals defend are supposed to operate against the backdrop of a number of further institutional guarantees, particularly equality of opportunity. The talented are entitled to greater rewards for work that benefits the badly off, that is, only when *everyone* has had fair and equal access to that work. But the selfish ethos leading executives to (successfully) demand astronomical salaries may ultimately be the product of a number of political (institutional) failures. If this is right, indirect measures can be taken to alter that ethos, because this is how institutional change is likely best effected. For example, the state might transform the culture of entitlement among the executive elite by increasing the supply of talents they currently monopolize; it could do this through more funding for educational and training programs that now artificially restrict access to positions of prestige and power. Real equality of opportunity throughout society might also alter people's manifest unwillingness to tax high levels of market compensation. Finally, labour law might be reformed to make collective action on the part of less skilled workers more effective. In short, unless selfishness and greed are unalterable natural facts,[39] liberalism does *not* have to take them at face value, and it can introduce institutional reforms to correct what are ultimately institutional failures.

The *institutional salience* and *reciprocal identity formation* theses postulate a symbiotic relationship between institutions and ethos – rules shape people's personal character and motivations, and the resulting ethos strongly influences how (and whether) those rules work. So, in an important sense, 'the personal is the political.' But *how* political is the personal in the economic context that we are now considering? In some cases, self-interest, altruism, and affection will be decisive reasons for shielding personal choices regarding, say, career and income from egalitarian inspection; in others, these forms of partiality must give way to the claims of the worst off. Where do we draw the line? The general answer[40] is this: individual choices that have direct implications for the kinds of institutions that can be established or supported are not *personal* in the sense of immune from political control. In this case, we have to look at variables 1–4 described under *mutual constraint* to see where/how equality should temper partiality. Personal choices, by contrast, that are *not* institutionally salient in this way are exempt from the demands of egalitarian justice. In this case, individuals may act partially so long as they do not violate basic institutional rules (*lexical constraint*).

The three valuable forms of partiality identified above undermine the socialist critique's fundamental assumption, which is that absent strategic and greedy behaviour on the part of the talented, inequality-generating economic incentives are dispensable. Consider the following rationale for Rawls's difference principle.[41] If aggregate economic productivity was fixed, then equality would maximize the smallest distributive share. This output, however, is variable and affected by all sorts of things such as innate talent, trained ability (education), and career choice. These are shaped, in turn, by the various packages of rewards that firms offer employees for different kinds of economic performance. An economy regulated by Rawls's principle will accordingly tolerate differences in after-tax income to the extent that the resulting inequalities maximize the lowest ones. Of course, people with the lowest incomes could do even better than they would under this tax and transfer scheme if the talented chose to produce at the same levels *without these incentives* – this is the key point about ethos – but it is unreasonable to *demand* this from them for the following two reasons.

First, personal choices about where to work, on what, and for how much, may sometimes be based upon selfish greed, a lust for economic power, and mindless consumerism. But they are even more likely to reflect complex trade-offs between the different activities, interests, preferences, goals, and tastes that constitute alternative lifestyles. People have incredibly diverse employment preferences and these are integrated within their other projects and commitments in multiple ways. This pluralism, together with the fact that some work contributes far more to the social product than other work does, also explains much economic inequality. It is therefore a mistake to reduce the need for incentives to selfishness, and forcing people into occupational roles on the grounds that doing so will maximize their overall contribution to society clearly violates their freedom indefensibly. As Kok-Chor Tan points out, 'It is not unreasonable for self-interest to play a role in deciding how to spend one's time – that is, in making decisions about occupational choice – and so not unreasonable for individuals to demand some incentives for performing work that brings large benefits to the less well off but that they would otherwise prefer not to do.'[42]

Second, it is hard to say precisely how large an incentive any person can reasonably demand, given that so much of her inequality-generating behaviour will probably be motivated by concerns about, say, her family and friends' well-being, rather than by brute self-interest.[43] Constitutive partiality competes with the requirement to benefit the badly off so, again, we need to do the moral philosophy implicated by the *mutual constraint* view. We should not assume (as the socialist critique does) that whenever people respond to inequality-generating incentives they are, for that reason alone, blind to the claims of others. Incentives are a useful way of reconciling social justice with the partiality of the personal viewpoint.

10.5 Justice and the Family

The family is 'a crucial case'[44] for testing the adequacy of the institutional approach, and it actually raises two different sets of questions: (1) whether equality can be achieved without undermining forms of partiality indispensable to family life, and (2) whether respecting familial partiality undermines equality between women and men.

10.5.1 Familial Partiality

I assume rather than defend the claim that family life is valuable, so I rely on what I take to be a relatively uncontroversial account of what a family is: a stable social group consisting of at least two adults and sometimes also children linked together by a special history and by strong senti-ments of mutual affection.[45] So understood, families play a variety of important roles: they (1) secure a context for the development of emo-tional and physical intimacy; (2) shape personal identity; (3) transmit ethnic, religious, and cultural values and practices between generations; (4) produce and distribute basic resources; (5) influence the cognitive, emotional, and moral capacities of children; (6) identify and respond to the specific needs of distinct individuals, often in ways impossible for larger and less intimate social groupings; and, finally, (7) engender feel-ings of mutual affection and concern between parents and children that, hopefully, lead to reciprocal care during the inevitable dependencies of infancy and old age.

Even a cursory glance at this list reveals that partiality is differently related to its various items. Partiality is constitutive of some of these familial goods, particularly 1, 2, and 7, which cannot be successfully pro-vided without it. After all, we cannot become emotionally or sexually inti-mate with our spouses if we care no more for them than we do for strangers; our children are unlikely to share our cultural values and prac-tices if they spend only as much time with us as they do with anyone else. For other familial goods, such as specific need identification (6), partial-ity enhances their value without being essential to them. It might be more intimate and thus satisfying for a child to have her parents read to her at night but, in principle, her distinctive literary needs could also be identified and met by competent educational professionals. Finally, there are some familial goods that are mostly if not entirely partiality-independent. Notable among these are basic resources such as food, shelter, and clothing whose value to people is *not* plausibly diminished when partiality does not supervene on their provision.

Now, the tension between equality and partiality is particularly acute in connection with the family, whose members can reap its many benefits mostly to the extent that they downplay the needs and preferences of outsiders relative to their own. On the one hand, then, familial goods are so important that justice *must* make some room for them by shielding the family from the direct application of egalitarian principles. We should *not* have to spend as much time, affection, and money on other people's families as we do on our own. On the other hand, the practical effect of this will be that some of us – the spouses and children of the rich – will have access to many more resources than others do. This is particularly objectionable in the case of children, who are not responsible for their economically disadvantageous positions.

Children therefore pose difficulties for a theory of justice that indexes distributive entitlements to people's choices, because the responsibility-grounded entitlements of adults will often conflict with equal opportunity for children.[46] My parents worked harder than yours did, so, *ceteris paribus*, they should have more money than yours do. Fine. But we're both five years old and haven't worked a day in our lives, so why should *I* have a better doctor, teacher, and tricycle than you do?

There are three general solutions to this dilemma, two bad ones and one good one. First, we might follow Plato's suggestion by abolishing the family and charging the state with educating and rearing children. Since no *liberal* theory could countenance this and it would also be disastrous, we can set it aside. Second, we might follow up on one implication of the socialist critique by purging our theory of any choice-sensitive distributive principles. This would guarantee equal opportunity for children by entitling their parents to identical economic resources no matter what (if anything) they did throughout the course of their lives. Without having an argument for this claim here, this secures an important goal at too great a price. Finally, we might reconcile equality, familial partiality, and responsibility through the institutional division of labour.

In this view, children's equality of opportunity would be guaranteed through the political provision of basic resources and opportunities, such as housing, health care, and education, at least up to the undergraduate university level (*direct application*). In order for these goods to be provided to children on a fair and equal basis, some portions of the social product generated through market transactions would be treated as public rather than privately held resources.[47] Beyond whatever taxation such programs would require, parents would not have to spend privately held resources in equality-maximizing ways. But they *would* be forbidden from spending in ways that subverted the egalitarian objectives just mentioned (*lexical constraint*). That is, they would be allowed to buy their child, and only their child, a new tricycle, but not a better education or hospital bed. At least until real equality of opportunity is in place, and we can also operationalize the distinction between adults, who *should* be allowed to trade off net income for health care, and children, for whom such trade-offs are authoritatively made, justice seems to condemn two-tier health care and education.[48]

The system just described carefully balances political equality, familial partiality, and personal responsibility: it guarantees equal access to basic resources on fair terms; it regulates the effects of familial partiality through institutional design rather than destroying it altogether; and, finally, it tolerates choice-based inequalities between adults so that economically successful parents can share their prosperity with their children, but only in the realm of non-basic resources. When all works out well, the line dividing basic from non-basic resources will, itself, be drawn so that the respective weights attached to equality and partiality are in reflective equilibrium with judgements emerging from the *mutual constraint* procedure.

10.5.2 Justice and the Family

Many familial goods require levels and kinds of intimacy that are easily threatened by state interference. Sometimes, even simple exposure to outside monitoring and inspection can undermine them.[49] Aside from clear cases of spousal abuse or the neglectful treatment of children, then, the threshold for political interference with a family's internal affairs is normally and rightfully held to be quite high.

But this kind of privacy also shields families from serious inequalities that are socially, not politically, reinforced, through the guise of tradition, culture, and religion. Gender expectations requiring women to do most domestic tasks even when they also work as hard as their husbands do in the paid labour force are one notable instance of these. Must the institutional approach condone sexism simply because it is perpetrated largely by non-state actors, in this case, families? After all, gender expectations are surely among the important values and practices connected with identity formation, the intergenerational transmission of culture and religion, and a variety of other partiality-dependent familial goods. The answer is a loud no, however, which we reach by distinguishing partiality from *hierarchy*.

At least since Aristotle wrote his *Nicomachean Ethics*, 'distributive justice' has essentially meant a kind of proportionality – that is, to be the same is to be entitled to the same; to be different is to be entitled to different treatment. This idea – one applied to race and nationality over the centuries with depressingly familiar results – presupposes a benchmark of normality relative to which deviations are measured, and in light of which differential treatment is accordingly justified. The tautology here should be obvious: we are justified in treating someone less well who is 'different' by virtue of being already less well off than we are.

This sameness/difference model has been applied to gender in many areas of law and public policy: 'society defines women as such according to differences from men: hence the sex difference, as gender is customarily termed. Then equality law tells women that they are entitled to equal treatment mainly in the degree they are the same as men.'[50]

In the institutional approach, the *institutional salience* and *reciprocal identity formation* theses trigger a response to gender analogous to the one we saw in connection with corporate greed. A customary expectation that women perform a disproportionately large share of household work, even when they also work for wages outside of the home, subverts at least two important democratic rights – the freedom to choose one's occupation, and equality of opportunity. Constitutive partiality is therefore no bar to reforming an ethos that undermines women's status as full and equal members of a democratic community.

Because families require a certain measure of privacy, however, the state must proceed indirectly to eradicate the social, political, and economic influence of gender. For example, rather than dictating a uniform and society-wide blueprint for intra-familial relations, it should impose instead a variety of basic constraints that are never permissibly breached. Aside from guaranteeing the same rights, liberties, and opportunities for husbands and wives, the state should effectively prosecute spousal abuse, coercion, and rape; safeguard the voluntariness of religious and cultural practices; and guarantee women and their children economically safe options for divorce, among other things. Constraints such as these (if actually enforced) would ensure that any remaining division of labour along gender lines was voluntary.

Identifying gender with *hierarchy* rather than difference is particularly appropriate in the context of a liberal theory committed to state neutrality between competing ethical ideals. A perfectionist theory of equality must identify the sameness/difference benchmark by relying on substantive moral judgements about right and wrong. A neutralist theory focuses instead on a requirement of non-hierarchical treatment. Rather than asking whether attitudes or practices are right or wrong, good or bad, it asks, Do they subordinate some people to others, or not?

The institutional approach to justice has two central virtues. First, it avoids appealing to both essentialist notions of the public and private spheres, and also to an allegedly natural or pre-political location of the boundary between them – things of which liberalism is often accused. Ultimately, whether something is 'private' or, better, personal and thus beyond the reach of collectively enforceable norms is, itself, the upshot of a democratic ideal of equal citizenship. The operative distinction is between self- and other-regarding actions, not between public and private ones. Limitless greed and misogyny are social practices that inflict

264 Defending Liberal Neutrality

tangible harm, and it hardly matters *where* they are perpetrated. Second, the institutional approach relies on a non-reductive account of affective ties; it does not trivialize their significance by reducing them all to instruments of impartial justice. The *point* of social forms such as the family is the kind of interpersonal communion that they make possible. Institutional rules simply identify how far we can go in expressing the partiality that constitutes them. Beyond living within and supporting those rules, then, we need not further explain ourselves.[51] So in the end, we are back to Locke, and the distinction that he made famous – between how we think we ought to live and what we can reasonably *demand* from one another through the state.

Conclusion

Respecting equal freedom in the face of widespread disagreement leads to a distinctive and radical political form, namely, a liberal-democratic state whose authority is justified independently of the contested ethical values dividing its citizens. This reverses an idea at least as old as Plato, in which how we organize our collective life follows directly from a philosophical (most often religious but, over the last several hundred years, increasingly secular) account of how we should live. In the conventional view, shared by many on both the political Left and Right, ethics and politics are seen as purely continuous with one another.

Taking pluralism seriously, however, requires that we abandon the conventional view, and seek instead a distinctive *political* morality that adjudicates fairly between both our conflicting personal interests and our rival understandings of the common good. The liberal hope is that the appeal to minimal and therefore potentially sharable premises (equality and freedom) will render the necessarily coercive aspects of state power as consensual as possible. In a democracy, where unanimity is rarely to be had, coercion is inevitable, because there must be political winners and losers. But as long as that coercion is limited to the pursuit of civil interests, no one is asked to accept a lesser liberty for the sake of values that contravene her deepest ethical convictions. A procedural understanding of democracy and its attendant account of public reason allows us to identify the types of interests that both should and should not be submitted for public deliberation and judgement.

While this view is minimal, it is also radical, because there is nothing weak in the demand for ethical neutrality that it generates, from either the individual or the collective points of view. It requires that, as individuals, we forsake feel-good clichés about holistic ethical/political integration, and that we learn to see politics as a bounded sphere that will not and *cannot* coincide with our deepest convictions about our place in the universe, and with accounts of human flourishing.[1] This point is hardly just academic. The real-world costs of failing to exercise this restraint are simply too high – in the early modern era, the price was religious warfare; today, we have sectarian violence and global terrorism. Economic prosperity, social stability, and tolerance are not collective goals as lofty as are national glory, ethnic purity, or religious salvation, but they are no less worthy of pursuit for that reason, and certainly less costly in human terms.

Equality makes democracy the only acceptable way of translating personal preferences and convictions about the common good into social choices, but unconstrained majoritarianism betrays liberalism's egalitarian promise, so we must find another way to interpret political autonomy. Ultimately, we can reconcile collective self-rule with personal independence only if minorities are not bullied simply because they, or their views, are unpopular with their fellow citizens. Democracy must be limited, then, by a scheme of individual rights justified on ethically neutral grounds to preserve an area within which we are each free, as far as possible, to live by our own lights.

Reforming law and public policy to conform to this ideal would likely[2] bring about radical changes in a number of areas. As far as the economy is concerned, aside from financing public goods and rectifying distributive injustices, the tax and transfer system would correct for negative externalities, but it would never express dominant or conventional attitudes about the relative propriety or impropriety of, say, various recreational, consumptive, or cultural activities.[3] For example, if taxes on cigarettes exceed the aggregate costs (however this should be calculated) that smoking imposes on the health care system, such punitive taxes should be lowered accordingly. Also, it is doubtful that either the current Canadian practice of funding and perhaps of even permitting, separate school systems, or tax exemptions/credits for religious organizations would survive scrutiny on the neutralist view. State funding for specialized and capital-intensive arts that only a few directly enjoy – opera and ballet come to mind – is also suspect, to the extent that familiar 'trickle-down' arguments for justifying these as public goods seem quite implausible.

Socially, we would also have to move towards a more purely contractual approach to family law. Over the last several years, the public debate about same-sex marriage and polygamy in Canada, the United States, and elsewhere, has tended to obscure a more interesting and potentially troublesome question, which is this: What business, if any, does the state have in defining and regulating *any* interpersonal relationships between consenting adults? That is, why should the state have *anything* to do with defining (rather than simply enforcing) the rights and obligations that the participants, themselves, voluntarily assume?

People would then be free to structure these relationships any way they wish, subject to the usual caveats about voluntary and informed consent. Two objections to this approach are that (1) it subjects people with less bargaining power to the manipulation, exploitation, and oppression of those with more by sanctioning and compounding pre-existing socio-economic inequalities with the force of law; and (2) it fails to safeguard the rights and interests of children and other dependents (the elderly, the ill, for example). The second is a very difficult case. Rather than undermining neutrality, however, it only shows that, like any other view, it has its limits. But the first is not really an objection to neutralism per se, but rather to distributive injustice or, if they are different, to inequality. Accordingly, the solution might be to distinguish between ideal and non-ideal cases. In a world in which inequalities of bargaining power were eliminated or at least greatly mitigated, the contractual approach to family law would express the state's commitment to ethical neutrality. In our world, however, where those inequalities are all too familiar, and unlikely to disappear anytime soon, the goal should be to supplement and constrain pure contractualism in ways *as least damaging as possible to the neutralist ideal* in order to protect the rights and interests of the vulnerable. That is, rather than using inequality as an excuse to abandon the neutralist ideal, we should rely on that ideal as yet another reason for mitigating inequality. Our existing law and public policy on the family still falls afar short of this modified neutralist ideal, defining, as it does, all sorts of immunities and privileges for traditionally approved arrangements. In fact, in some cases, those immunities and privileges are themselves partly responsible for harming the vulnerable,[4] so the inequality-inspired objection actually gets things backwards.

There is, however, no doubt that liberal neutrality's chief rival – perfectionism – has great intuitive appeal. What could be plainer and simpler than that governments should help people lead ethically valuable lives, and prevent or at least discourage them from leading worthless ones? If we are at least minimally reflective, each of us cannot help but formulate convictions about living well rather than badly, about what amounts to seizing rather than wasting the opportunities that we are given, and perfectionism seems like a natural consequence of those convictions. Indeed, it is the neutralist view that is initially likely to strike us as strained and implausible. After all, why should we pledge our allegiance, pay our taxes to support, and, at the limit, die fighting for a state that is expressly committed to neutrality between ourselves and those with whom we disagree?

In fact, some of the most influential contemporary liberal political philosophers have joined anti-liberal critics, past and present, in claiming that state power must be based upon the whole truth about the good life, either directly by incorporating ethical premises into their accounts of political justification, or indirectly by conceiving of neutrality as a fallout or consequence of our epistemic limitations.[5] Both paths are perilous. Strong or comprehensive forms of perfectionism develop full accounts of ethical flourishing, and base political principles directly on them. The problem is that these accounts do not take the fact of pluralism seriously enough, and they do not supply an adequately secure foundation for the civil and political liberties that we, as democratic citizens, have reason to value. Weak or thinner forms of perfectionism are cognizant of these failings, so they develop instead a structural ethics that is supposed to be, at once, comprehensive enough so that its adherents are led to endorse liberalism, and abstract enough so that people from different and conflicting ethical perspectives all come to share it. This see-saw, however, cannot support the burden that this strategy places upon it, and it ultimately snaps – that is, in order for the argument to yield liberal neutrality, it must strengthen its ethical premises, but this is insufficiently attentive to pluralism and therefore self-defeating; in order to respect pluralism, it must weaken its ethical premises, but then nothing distinctively liberal remains. There are many ways of either blurring or ignoring this problem but none of them works.

We evaded the horns of this dilemma by adopting a different, better approach, that of the social contract. Moral equality is generally thought to be the norm that makes contractualism singularly appropriate for reasoning about principles of justice. This is the view that human beings – as moral agents, or reasoners – have the same fundamental moral rights, which implies that the comparable interests of each should be equally weighted in the calculations that influence public policy, as well as in the justification of the constitutional structures that direct and constrain it. The social contract models and works out the practical political implications of this equal primary importance of everyone's life.

Because the most common defences of moral equality, however, proceed via appeals to what are allegedly distinctive human capacities that render their possessors exclusive members of the moral community – the community, that is, of rights-bearers to whom equal justification is owed – they confront a variety of intractable problems.

While we have accepted (or at least not rejected) the idea of moral equality, we relied on a different but related premise in arriving at contractual justification. For us, *democratic* equality is what has led to the social contract. Politics, that is, must be conducted on the assumption that everyone's life is equally important, not by virtue of metaphysical or ontological claims about human nature, but rather in light of the attractiveness of the ideal of interpersonal relations that this assumption makes possible. Because democratic equality is primarily a relational rather than a distributive ideal, the central philosophical task is not to identify some particular item – resources, or welfare, for instance – that must be distributed equally, but instead to determine which principles of justice, in modern conditions, are most appropriate to the normative conception of human relations at its core. The key question is what kind of politics allows people to stand in relations of equality to one another, and the answer is a democratic politics tempered by contractually generated principles of justice.

Pluralism has been especially relevant to our elaboration of contractualism, but our characterization of this condition has been quite different from those commonly found in many recent arguments for liberalism. The two critical differences have been the contrasts between (1) epistemic versus moral notions of reasonableness, and (2) simple versus 'reasonable' forms of pluralism.

Disagreement about the nature of religious salvation and the human good complicates the project of justifying regulative principles through consent. Actual agreement between individuals as they are – thickly constituted with their substantive ethical convictions and religious doctrines – is implausible as a response to disagreements of these kinds, because pluralism is effectively what creates the problem that political life must accommodate. Somehow, then, political morality must be ethically inventive and the contractual situation must be specified in hypothetical terms. But this ethical inventiveness must proceed very carefully: we cannot establish the content of the principles derived through contractual agreement by simply appealing to moral norms thought to be morally justified by (contract) independent standards, because the existence of such pre-political standards renders the social contract dispensable altogether. This claim first emerged in early modern critiques of liberal demands for religious toleration, and it finds its contemporary expression in what we called the *circularity thesis*.

We surveyed two different strategies of exclusion, or ways of abstracting from the contested ethical beliefs that generate the need for mutually acceptable principles of justice – the 'reasonableness-as-valid-argument' and 'reasonableness as fairness' responses to pluralism. Recall that, on the reasonableness-as-valid-argument view, only a subset of the ethical beliefs likely to persist under democratic institutions actually satisfy certain stringent epistemic standards and are, thus, justifiably held by their adherents. By limiting admission to the hypothetical constitutional convention to people whose views satisfy these epistemic standards, we are, in effect, accommodating the inevitable by-product of the free exercise of practical reason – that is to say, *reasonable* pluralism – rather than simply endorsing a modus vivendi between reasonable and unreasonable ethical doctrines alike.

Unfortunately, when liberal neutrality is contractually justified on the basis of epistemic hypotheses, it is unnecessarily exposed to the *reflexivity thesis*. The epistemic asymmetry at the core of this strategy is indeed untenable, but the alternative approach that we have taken in this book does not rely upon it, so it escapes the reflexivity thesis unscathed. We elaborated the content of the reasonable by asking which principles of justice that fairly situated hypothetical contractors would choose to regulate the democratic institutions of the civic equals for whom they are trustees. Epistemology played no role in the contractual derivation of reasonable principles – once the (moral) constraints of the reasonable are in place, only the fact of pluralism per se is relevant to the deliberations of the contracting parties. Those deliberations, we argued, yield a form of state neutrality between competing ethical ideals as the best interpretation of democratic equality.

As critics have noted, the 'personal is political,' and this fact undermines both much traditional political philosophy and practice in general, which has relied upon an unduly constricted view of the state's responsibilities, and liberal political theory in particular, whose commitment to principled boundaries between the public and private spheres has variously resulted in the oppression of women, children, the disabled, the elderly, and foreigners, among others. There is great insight in the famous feminist slogan, but also much peril. The insight is that if liberalism is to be defensible, the scope of public reason must be expanded to include people and issues hitherto thought beyond the reach of democratic equality. Justice demands no less. The peril is that, in the face of that demand, politics will come to include *too much*: 'The liberal idea, in society and culture as in politics, is that no more should be subjected to the demands of public response than is necessary for the requirements of collective life. How much this is will depend on the company and the circumstances. But the idea that everything is fair game and that life is always improved by more exposure, more frankness, and more consensus is a serious mistake.'[6]

We should actively resist attempts to expand the scope of politics so that it includes everything – for example, how and upon whom or what we spend our after-tax income, with whom and how often our politicians sleep, whether or not people like and wish to associate with, or to avoid, members of other ethnic or religious groups. We want political and economic equality, but we should also value personal freedom and choice; we want transparency and accountability in our politicians, but we should also retain a commitment to privacy; we want basic equality, but we should learn to put up with those who exercise their associative freedoms in ways that we never would ourselves, and that we might find especially repugnant. Equal freedom requires that we do so.

This book began by defending the paradox of anti-perfectionism, that is, the Lockean and seemingly contradictory idea that there are quintessentially (politically) moral reasons why the state should not enforce contested ethical values. It ends by noting another one, what might be called the stringency of minimalism. On the one hand, the neutralist state is minimal in the sense that its normative foundations are ecumenical – justifying political authority on the basis of equal freedom is less sectarian than doing so by appealing to ideals of human flourishing. After all, whom does equal freedom exclude? Admittedly, people who think that they are for some reason better and therefore should have more rights than others do. I am not troubled by this exclusion in the least. On the other hand, if the neutral state is to emerge and remain stable, its citizens must learn to view themselves and their institutions in a distinctive way. In settling disagreements about, say, the allocation of public resources, the content of the criminal law, and the structure of the family, citizens of the neutralist state must be prepared to appeal to the constitutive values of democracy that they share, rather than to the whole ethical truth that so often divides them. This will be difficult, but justice often is.

Notes

Introduction

1 See, for example, Charles Larmore, 'Political Liberalism,' in *The Morals of Modernity* (Cambridge: Cambridge University Press, 1996), 121; and John Rawls, *Political Liberalism* (New York: Columbia University Press, 1993), xxiv.

2 This is one prominent usage of the contractual device, but there are also others. For distinctions between contract theories of political sovereignty, consent theories of political obligation, and recent attempts to account for moral authority in terms of hypothetical agreements, see Paul Kelly, 'Contractarian Ethics,' in *Encyclopedia of Applied Ethics* (San Diego: Academic Press, 1997), 1:631–43, and Paul Kelly and David Boucher, 'The Social Contract and Its Critics,' in *The Social Contract From Hobbes to Rawls*, ed. Paul Kelly and David Boucher, 1–34 (London: Routledge, 1994). For a recent, though sympathetic, critique of the social contract, see Martha Nussbaum, *Frontiers of Justice: Disability, Nationality, Species Membership* (Cambridge, MA: Harvard University Press, 2006). While persuasive, her critique is actually much less damaging than she takes it to be: it is true that deriving political principles from actual agreements between people as they are not only permits but *compounds* existing inequalities of bargaining power, thus privileging, say, the healthy over the ill, compatriots over foreigners, and humans over non-humans, but no contemporary political liberal that I can think of (certainly not Barry, Larmore, Nagel, or Rawls) actually relies on this *mutual advantage* conception of contractualism. For political liberals, the agreements in question are doubly hypothetical – both the contractors and the contracting situations are idealized in various counterfactual ways. For a version of contractualism that *is* vulnerable to Nussbaum's critique, see David Gauthier, *Morals by Agreement* (New York: Oxford University Press, 1986).

3 The neutrality thesis is adopted by, among others, Bruce Ackerman, Brian Barry, Ronald Dworkin, Charles Larmore, Thomas Nagel, John Rawls, and Thomas Scanlon.

4 See Michael Freeden, *Ideologies and Political Theory: A Conceptual Approach* (Oxford: Clarendon, 1996), 3.

5 See, for example, Jeremy Waldron, *God, Locke and Equality: Christian Foundations in Locke's Political Thought* (Cambridge: Cambridge University Press, 2002).

6 Paul Kelly writes, 'This model of political society is much more widespread than the endorsement of the idea of a hypothetical contract as an explanatory tool, and one can misunderstand the significance of the contractualist turn prompted by Rawls, by focusing narrowly on the structure of decision-making behind the veil of ignorance.' *Liberalism* (Cambridge: Polity, 2005), 39. As we see in chapter 8 below, people should probably wonder more than they do *why* Rawls's political theory takes the contractual form that it does – when he writes in *Theory* that his 'aim is to present a conception of justice which generalizes and carries to a higher level of abstraction the familiar theory of the social contract as found, say, in Locke, Rousseau, and Kant,' he is *not* simply paying homage to his intellectual heroes or articulating conventional pieties. *A Theory of Justice* (Cambridge, MA: Harvard University Press, 1971), 11. This particular conception of political community leads directly to the social contract device, which in turn yields the requirement of justificatory neutrality. This is why Locke, but not, say, Bentham, is the beginning of neutralist liberalism.

7 Kelly, *Liberalism*, 2.

8 Joseph Raz, *The Morality of Freedom* (Oxford: Clarendon, 1986), 1.

9 Jürgen Habermas, 'Popular Sovereignty as Procedure,' in *Deliberative Democracy: Essays on Reason and Politics*, ed. James Bohman and William Rehg (Cambridge: MIT Press, 1997), 44.

10 The Disintegration Thesis is also an important precursor to recent anti-liberal criticisms that challenge the possibility of a political community stably 'well-ordered' by Rawlsian principles of justice, something examined in chapter 8.

1. Putting Up with Heresy

1 John Dunn, *The Political Thought of John Locke: An Historical Account of the Argument of the Two Treatises of Government* (Cambridge: Cambridge University Press, 1969), 208.

2 For interpretations of Locke based in the history of ideas, see John Dunn,

'What Is Living and What Is Dead in the Political Theory of John Locke,' in *Interpreting Political Responsibility*, 9–25 (Princeton: Princeton University Press, 1990); Quentin Skinner, *The Foundations of Modern Political Thought*, 2 vols. (Cambridge: Cambridge University Press, 1978); Quentin Skinner, 'Meaning and Understanding in the History of Ideas,' in *Meaning and Context: Quentin Skinner and his Critics*, ed. James Tully (Princeton: Princeton University Press, 1988); and James Tully, *An Approach to Political Philosophy: Locke in Context* (Cambridge: Cambridge University Press, 1993). For a concise discussion of some of the problems associated with this approach to understanding Locke, particularly in connection with the links between Locke and contemporary egalitarianism, see the 'Introduction' to Jeremy Waldron's *God, Locke, and Equality: Christian Foundations in Locke's Political Thought* (Cambridge: Cambridge University Press, 2002).

3 John Locke, *A Letter concerning Toleration*, in *Political Writings*, ed. David Wootton (London: Penguin, 1993), 402.

4 Ruth Grant, *John Locke's Liberalism* (Chicago: University of Chicago Press, 1983), 198. For a discussion of Locke's views on mathematics, see P. Cicovacki, 'Locke on Mathematical Knowledge,' *Journal of the History of Philosophy* 28 (1990): 511–24.

5 '*Moral knowledge* is as *capable of real certainty* as mathematics. For certainty being but the perception of the agreement or disagreement of our *ideas*, and demonstration nothing but the perception of such agreement by the intervention of other *ideas* or mediums, our moral *ideas*, as well as mathematical, being *archetypes* themselves and so adequate and complete *ideas*, all the agreement or disagreement which we shall find in them will produce real knowledge, as well as in mathematical figures' (1690; repr. in *An Essay concerning Human Understanding*, ed. John Yolton [London: Dent, 1996], 325–6).

6 Grant, *John Locke's Liberalism*, 5.

7 Readers interested in Locke's life and times, his possible intellectual influences, and the initial reception of his writings, should consult Richard Ashcraft, 'John Locke's Library: Portrait of an Intellectual,' *Transactions of the Cambridge Bibliographical Society* 5 (1969): 47–60; H.R. Fox Bourne, *The Life of John Locke*, 2 vols. (London: Knight, 1876); Maurice Cranston, *John Locke: A Biography* (London: Longmans Green, 1957); John Harrison and Peter Laslett, *The Library of John Locke* (Oxford: Oxford University Press, 1965); Peter King, *The Life of John Locke, with Extracts from His Correspondence, Journals, and Common-Place Books* (London: Colburn, 1829); and, finally, Martyn P. Thompson, 'The Reception of Locke's *Two Treatises of Government*,' *Political Studies* 24 (1976): 184–91.

8 Locke, *A Letter concerning Toleration*, 420.

9 Ibid., 393.

10 In the literature, the term *perfectionism* has no settled or canonical meaning.
Nonetheless, we may usefully contrast three different but related classes of
perfectionist views. The first are perfectionist theories of value, which deny
that what is intrinsically valuable for people is reducible to desire or preference-satisfaction. In this sense, perfectionism is synonymous with objectivism.
The second are perfectionist ethical theories that identify what a good or
flourishing human life consists of. The third class, which presupposes the
first two, comprises perfectionist political moralities of the kind to be examined in this book.

11 Ian Harris, for example, maintains that 'there remains a suggestion, which
Locke did not foresee, but which was levelled some years later against his *Epistola de Tolerantia* by Jonas Proast. Proast suggested that whilst force could not
effect a change of heart, a moderate application of it might encourage people to take seriously arguments which otherwise they would ignore. *The
answer to that is that Locke had "premised" that the magistrate's power could not
extend legitimately to purely ecclesiastical opinions: however useful force might be it was
illegitimate.* He rested his case on the magistrate's limited field of jurisdiction.'
The Mind of John Locke (New York: Cambridge University Press, 1994), 113;
emphasis in original. The 'premise' in Locke's argument for the magistrate's
limited field of jurisdiction is a particular conception of natural freedom and
equality. Harris gets things backwards by confusing Locke's conclusion – 'the
magistrate's limited field of jurisdiction' – with his 'premise' – natural freedom and equality.

12 Locke, *A Letter concerning Toleration*, 394.

13 Important and illuminating discussions of Locke's contractualism include
Joshua Cohen, 'Structure, Choice, and Legitimacy: Locke's Theory of the
State,' *Philosophy and Public Affairs* 15 (1986): 301–24; John Dunn, 'Consent in
the Political Theory of John Locke,' *Historical Journal* 10 (1967): 153–82;
John Dunn, 'Justice and the Interpretation of Locke's Political Theory,' *Polit-
ical Studies* 16 (1968): 68–87; Kirstie M. McClure, *Judging Rights: Lockean Poli-
tics and the Limits of Consent* (Ithaca: Cornell University Press, 1996); Patrick
Riley, 'On Finding an Equilibrium between Consent and Natural Law in
Locke's Political Philosophy,' *Political Studies* 22 (1974): 432–52; Patrick Riley,
'Locke on "Voluntary Agreement" and Political Power,' *Western Political Quar-
terly* 29 (1976): 136–45; Paul Russell, 'Locke on Express and Tacit Consent:
Misinterpretations and Inconsistencies,' *Political Theory* 14 (1986): 291–306;
A.J. Simmons, 'Tacit Consent and Political Obligation,' *Philosophy and Public
Affairs* 5 (1976): 274–91; and, finally, Jeremy Waldron, 'John Locke: Social
Contract versus Political Anthropology,' *Review of Politics* 51 (1989): 3–28.

14 Locke, *A Letter concerning Toleration*, 394.
15 Ibid.
16 John Locke, *The Second Treatise of Government*, in *Political Writings*, ed. David Wootton (London: Penguin, 1993), 262.
17 Ibid.
18 Ibid.
19 Ibid., 263.
20 For excellent discussions of Locke's state of nature and the law that obtains there, see Hans Aarsleff, 'The State of Nature and the Nature of Man in Locke,' in *John Locke: Problems and Perspectives*, ed. John W. Yolton, 99–136 (Cambridge: Cambridge University Press, 1969); Richard Ashcraft, 'Locke's State of Nature: Historical Fact or Moral Fiction?' *American Political Science Review* 62 (1968): 898–915; A.J. Simmons, 'Locke's State of Nature,' *Political Theory* 17 (1989): 449–70; and, finally, John W. Yolton, 'Locke on the Law of Nature,' *Philosophical Review* 67 (1958): 477–98.
21 Locke, *Second Treatise*, 306.
22 Ibid., 325.
23 For discussions of the natural right to freedom, and natural rights generally, in Locke, see Margaret Macdonald, 'Natural Rights,' in *Theories of Rights*, ed. Jeremy Waldron, 21–40 (Oxford: Oxford University Press, 1984); A.J. Simmons, 'Inalienable Rights and Locke's *Treatises*,' *Philosophy and Public Affairs* 12 (1983): 175–204; A.J. Simmons, *The Lockean Theory of Rights* (Princeton: Princeton University Press, 1992); and Richard Tuck, *Natural Rights Theories: Their Origin and Development* (Cambridge: Cambridge University Press, 1979). On the associated natural right to property, see Matthew Kramer, *John Locke and the Origins of Private Property: Philosophical Explorations of Individualism, Community, and Equality* (Cambridge: Cambridge University Press, 1997); Alan Ryan, 'Locke and the Dictatorship of the Bourgeoisie,' *Political Studies* 13 (1965): 219–30; Alan Ryan, *Property and Political Theory* (Oxford: Blackwell, 1984); James Tully, *A Discourse on Property: John Locke and His Adversaries* (Cambridge: Cambridge University Press, 1980); Jeremy Waldron, 'Enough and as Good Left for Others,' *Philosophical Quarterly* 29 (1979): 319–28; and, finally, Jeremy Waldron, *The Right to Private Property* (Oxford: Clarendon, 1988).
24 Locke, *Second Treatise*, 325.
25 Ibid.
26 Ibid.
27 Ibid., 304.
28 Ibid., 327.
29 'It cannot be supposed that they should intend, had they a power to do so, to give any one, or more, an absolute arbitrary power over their persons and

estates, and put a force into the magistrate's hands to execute his unlimited and arbitrary will upon them. *This were to put themselves into a worse condition than the state of nature, wherein they had a liberty to defend their right against the injuries of others, and were upon equal terms of force to maintain it, whether invaded by a single man or many in combination. Whereas by supposing they have given up themselves to the absolute arbitrary power and will of a legislator, they have disarmed themselves, and armed him to make a prey of them when he pleases.*' Locke, *Second Treatise*, 332; emphasis mine.

30 Ibid., 394.

31 John Locke, *A Third Letter for Toleration*, in *Works* (London: Tegg, 1823), 6:212; emphasis mine.

32 John Locke, *An Essay concerning Toleration*, in *Political Writings*, ed. David Wootton (London: Penguin, 1993), 188.

33 Locke, *A Letter concerning Toleration*, 408.

34 Ibid.

35 Grant, *John Locke's Liberalism*, 95.

36 Locke, *A Letter concerning Toleration*, 390.

37 Jeremy Waldron, like Proast, thinks that, politically, a plausible and operative distinction can be drawn between ethical beliefs that individuals merely *think* are true, but are false, and those that are *actually* true: '[Locke's] is a good argument only against the following rather silly principle: (P1) that the magistrate may enforce *his own* religion or whatever religion *he thinks* is correct. It is not a good argument against the somewhat more sensible position (P2) that a magistrate may enforce the religion, whatever it may be, which is *in fact* objectively correct.' *Liberal Rights: Collected Papers, 1981–1991* (Cambridge: Cambridge University Press, 1993), 99. (P2) presupposes, however, that we have what we do not – an independent standard to distinguish between itself and the 'silliness' of (P1). If there are such standards, how does one explain continued ethical disagreement? If (P2) is less 'silly' than (P1), I am unsure why that is so.

38 Richard Vernon, *The Career of Toleration: Locke, Proast and After* (Montreal: McGill-Queen's University Press, 1997), 107.

39 Locke, *A Letter concerning Toleration*, 395.

40 Locke does overestimate the 'impertinence' of penalties at altering beliefs, but many of his critics have conflated this argument with the other two and believe that its refutation destroys Locke's entire case for toleration. Jeremy Waldron, for example, takes what he calls the 'argument from belief' as 'the main line of argument in the *Letter concerning Toleration*,' and asserts that 'an argument based on a concern for the moral interests of the potential victims of intolerance would differ considerably from Locke's argument. Not being

an argument about rational agency, it would not merely be a principle of restraint on reasons, but would generate more strenuous and more consequentially sensitive requirements for political morality.' 'Locke, Toleration, and the Rationality of Persecution,' in *Liberal Rights: Collected Papers, 1981–1991* (Cambridge: Cambridge University Press, 1993), 114. Like Proast, Waldron conflates (and confuses) the internal argument about legitimacy with the external claim about the impertinence of penalties. If I have characterized the contractual argument accurately, this is precisely what Locke offers: an argument about the moral interests of citizens and how these influence the internal constitution of any political community. Waldron, like Proast, sees only one argument when, in fact, Locke has three: 'Again; if it be true, that "magistrates being as liable to error as the rest of mankind, their using of force in matters of religion, would not at all advance the salvation of mankind," *allowing that even force could work upon them, and magistrates had authority to use it in religion, then the argument you [Proast] mention is not "the only one in that letter, of strength to prove the necessity of toleration"* ... *For the argument of the unfitness of force to convince men's minds being quite taken away, either of the other would be a strong proof for toleration.*' *A Second Letter concerning Toleration*, in *Works* (London: Tegg, 1823), 6:67; emphasis mine.

41 Locke, *A Letter concerning Toleration*, 95.
42 Ibid., 394.
43 Ibid., 410.
44 Ibid., 395.
45 'I desire nobody to go further than his own bosom for an experience whether ever violence gained anything upon his opinion, whether even arguments managed with heat do not lose something of their efficacy, and have not made him the more obstinate in his opinion, so chary is human nature to preserve the liberty of that part wherein lies the dignity of a man, which would it be imposed on would make him but little different from a beast.' Locke, *An Essay concerning Toleration*, 204.
46 Ibid., 402–3.
47 Ibid., 205.
48 Ibid., 405.
49 For a fascinating discussion of this idea's pervasive influence on contemporary art, social and natural science, law, philosophy, politics, and educational policy, among other things, see Steven Pinker, *The Blank Slate: The Modern Denial of Human Nature* (New York: Penguin, 2002).
50 Locke, *An Essay concerning Human Understanding*, 45.
51 Ibid., 3.
52 Ibid., 4.

53 Ibid., 41.
54 For discussions of Locke's epistemological theory, see Peter H. Nidditch, 'Introduction,' in *Essay concerning Human Understanding*, ed. Peter H. Nidditch, vii–x (Oxford: Oxford University Press, 1975); and John W. Yolton, *Locke and the Compass of Human Understanding: A Selective Commentary on the* Essay (Cambridge: Cambridge University Press, 1970).
55 Locke, *A Letter concerning Toleration*, 395; emphasis mine.
56 David Wootton, 'Introduction,' in *John Locke: Political Writings* (London: Penguin, 1993), 104.
57 My refutation of the *reflexivity thesis* in chapter 6 unfolds this Lockean insight by distinguishing between various ways that pluralism might be relevant to the social contract argument for neutrality.
58 Locke, *A Letter concerning Toleration*, 395–6.
59 Wootton, 'Introduction,' 101.
60 *A Third Letter for Toleration*, 356.
61 *A Letter concerning Toleration*, 396.
62 For discussions of Locke's thoughts on religion, see John Passmore, 'Locke and the Ethics of Belief,' *British Academy Proceedings* 64 (1980): 185–208; and Nicholas Wolterstorff, *John Locke and the Ethics of Belief* (Cambridge: Cambridge University Press, 1996).
63 *A Letter concerning Toleration*, 407.
64 Ibid.
65 'If you can make it practicable that the magistrate should punish men for rejecting the true religion, without judging which is the true religion, or if true religion could appear in person, take the magistrate's seat, and there judge all that rejected her, something might be done. But the mischief of it is, it is a man that must condemn, men must punish; and men cannot do this but by judging who is guilty of the crime which they punish.' *A Third Letter for Toleration*, 428.
66 'For, if I understand this *Letter*, the whole Strength of what it urgeth for the Purpose of it, lies in the Argument: *There is but one Way of Salvation, or but one True Religion. No man can be saved by this Religion, who does not believe it to be the True Religion. This Belief is to be wrought in men by Reason and Argument, not by outward Force and Compulsion. Therefore, all such Force is utterly of no use for the promoting True Religion, and the Salvation of Souls* ... This, upon a careful perusal of this *Letter*, I take to be the single Argument by which the Author endeavours in it to establish this Position.' Jonas Proast, *The Argument of the Letter concerning Toleration, Briefly Consider'd and Answer'd*, in *Letters concerning Toleration*, ed. P.A. Schouls (New York: Garland, 1984), 4.
67 Ibid., 14.

68 Ibid., 15.
69 Ibid., 16.
70 Ibid., 23.
71 Ibid., 78.
72 Ibid., 23.
73 See Harry Frankfurt, 'Freedom of the Will and the Concept of a Person,' *Journal of Philosophy* 68 (1971): 5–20.
74 Charles Taylor, *Sources of the Self: The Making of the Modern Identity* (Cambridge, MA: Harvard University Press, 1989).
75 Ibid., 19.
76 H.L.A. Hart, *Law, Liberty and Morality* (Oxford: Oxford University Press, 1963), ix.
77 'The Scripture ... has for at least these sixteen hundred years contained the only true religion in the world.' *A Third Letter for Toleration*, 356.
78 John Rawls, *A Theory of Justice* (Cambridge, MA: Harvard University Press, 1971).
79 As I hope to make clear at the end of this section, Locke and Proast operate from radically different methodological assumptions. Proast thinks that truth can be appealed to politically because it is self-evidently found within the historical community to which he belongs. Locke, on the other hand, is interested in the problem of toleration from a wider perspective. Hence, his repeated discussions in later *Letters* of the problem of religious minorities.
80 'For if my Church be in the right; and my religion be the true; why may I not all along suppose it to be so? ... For 'tis obvious enough that there can be no other reason for this assertion of yours, but either the equal Truth, or at least the equal Certainty (or Uncertainty) of all Religions.' *The Argument of the Letter*, 47.
81 Locke remarks to Proast, 'If you will add but one more to your plentiful stock of distinctions, and observe the difference there is between the ground of any one's supposing his religion is true, and the privilege he may pretend to by supposing it true, you will never stumble at this again; but you will find, that though, upon the former of these accounts, men of all religions cannot be equally allowed to suppose their religions true, yet in reference to the latter, the supposition may and ought to be allowed or denied equally to all men. *And the reason of it is plain, viz. because the assurance wherewith one man supposes his religion to be true, being no more of an argument of its truth to another than vice versa, neither of them can claim by the assurance, wherewith he supposes his religion the true, any prerogative or power over the other, which the other has not by the same title an equal claim to over him.' A Third Letter for Toleration*, 420; emphasis mine.
82 Proast, *The Argument of the Letter*, 52.

83 'Proast and Waldron try to escape the whole issue that Locke is raising – can I trust the government to decide on my behalf – by saying that of course the state should not compel people to believe a false religion, only the true one.' Waldron, *The Right to Private Property*, 72. Both Locke and Bayle thought that this was the most transparent and ridiculous equivocation, for it presumes that we have the answer to what we are trying to find out, that we know that the state will make the right choice.' Wootton, 'Introduction,' 102.

84 John Dunn, *The Political Thought of John Locke: A Historical Account of the Argument of the Two Treatises of Government* (Cambridge: Cambridge University Press, 1969), 101.

85 Locke, *Second Treatise*, 287.

86 Ibid., 263.

87 'When Locke emphasizes the decision of each to join with others into a community for their mutual protection as the distinguishing characteristic of civil society, the society does seem to take priority over government both temporally and theoretically. Its temporal priority is evident in that the creation of the government is the act of the society.' Grant, *John Locke's Liberalism*, 103.

88 Nature and artifice are distinct but related concepts. Equal freedom originates from God's purposes and is, therefore, natural, but political institutions, like churches, are created by *men* as effective means for the fulfilment of pre-existing natural obligations.

89 Locke, *An Essay concerning Human Understanding*, 231.

90 Ibid.

91 Ibid., 236.

92 Ibid., 233.

93 Ibid., 269.

94 Ibid.

95 Vernon, *The Career of Toleration*, 44.

96 Locke, *An Essay concerning Human Understanding*, 269.

97 Ibid., 272.

98 Locke, *A Third Letter for Toleration*, 77.

99 Locke, *A Letter concerning Toleration*, 403.

100 Ibid., 402.

101 This is not the place to discuss Locke's cosmopolitanism, but his preoccupation with minorities clearly suggests that the perspective of political justice must be global.

102 Much attention has been drawn to the fact that Locke denied the right of toleration to both atheists and Catholics – the former because, without God, nothing binds oaths and covenants; the latter because of their divided

loyalty. The focus on *whom* Locke excludes often comes at the expense of obscuring the moral reason for his doing so: 'Papists are not to enjoy the benefit of toleration because where they have power they think themselves bound to deny it to others. For it is unreasonable that any should have a free liberty of their religion who do not acknowledge it as a principle of theirs that nobody ought to persecute or molest another because he dissents from him in religion.' *An Essay Concerning Toleration*, 202. Compare this with Rawls's view of the 'reasonable': 'People are unreasonable ... when they plan to engage in cooperative schemes but are unwilling to honor, or even to propose, except as a necessary public pretense, any general principles or standards for specifying fair terms of cooperation. They are ready to violate such terms as suits their interests when circumstances allow.' *Political Liberalism*, 50. Even if Locke misjudged Catholics and atheists, the norms of reciprocity and fairness to which his judgement appeals are sound.

103 'Locke's domicile on the continent was part of the process that elicited a general theoretical statement from him. His *Epistola* was written with a new audience in mind. Where Locke's English writings were concerned primarily with the question of indifference, here a broader statement was appropriate. To write in Latin was to write for an audience spanning Europe and whose mutual divergences were more marked than those amongst English Protestants.' Richard Ashcraft, *Revolutionary Politics & Locke's Two Treatises of Government* (Princeton: Princeton University Press, 1986), 185.

104 'My aim is to present a conception of justice which generalizes and carries to a higher level of abstraction the familiar theory of the social contract as found, say, in Locke, Rousseau, and Kant.' Rawls, *A Theory of Justice*, 11. As the argument of part 3 will make clear, unlike Locke, neither Rousseau nor Kant is a plausible building block for the theory of neutrality defended in this book – Rousseau, because the unconstrained majoritarianism he endorses violates the ideal of reciprocity that is expressed through constitutional limits on the exercise of state power; Kant, because the comprehensive ideal of personal autonomy at the foundation of his moral theory is inconsistent with pluralism. Rawls ultimately concedes the latter point. See his *Political Liberalism*, and our discussion in chapter 8 below.

105 Charles Larmore, 'Public Reason,' in *The Cambridge Companion to Rawls*, ed. Samuel Freeman (Cambridge: Cambridge University Press, 2003), 369.

2. Freedom for Eccentrics

1 For comprehensive biographies, see Nicholas Capaldi, *John Stuart Mill: A Biography* (Cambridge: Cambridge University Press, 2004); and John Robson

and Jack Stillinger, eds., *John Stuart Mill: Autobiography and Literary Essays* (Toronto: University of Toronto Press, 1981).

2 Isaiah Berlin, *Four Essays on Liberty* (Oxford: Oxford University Press, 1969), 201.

3 Important critical discussions include Alexander Bain, *John Stuart Mill: A Criticism* (London: Longmans, 1882); Richard Bellamy, 'T.H. Green, J.S. Mill, and Isaiah Berlin on the Nature of Liberty and Liberalism,' in *Jurisprudence: Cambridge Essays*, ed. H. Gross and R. Harrison, 257–85 (Oxford: Clarendon, 1992); Maurice Cowling, *Mill and Liberalism*, 2nd ed. (Cambridge: Cambridge University Press, 1990); Gerald Dworkin, ed., *Morality, Harm, and the Law* (Boulder: Westview, 1994); Ronald Dworkin, *Taking Rights Seriously* (Cambridge, MA: Harvard University Press, 1977); Joel Feinberg, *The Moral Limits of the Criminal Law*, 4 vols. (Oxford: Oxford University Press, 1984–8); H.L.A. Hart, 'Are There Any Natural Rights?' *Philosophical Review* 64 (1955): 175–91; Gertrude Himmelfarb, *On Liberty and Liberalism: The Case of John Stuart Mill* (New York: Knopf, 1974); J.C. Rees, *John Stuart Mill's* On Liberty (Oxford: Oxford University Press, 1985); Alan Ryan, *The Philosophy of John Stuart Mill* (London: Macmillan, 1990); Samuel Scheffler, *The Rejection of Consequentialism*, rev. ed. (Oxford: Clarendon, 1994); C.L. Ten, *Mill on Liberty* (Oxford: Oxford University Press, 1980); and Bernard Williams, 'A Critique of Utilitarianism,' in *Utilitarianism: For and Against*, ed. Bernard Williams and J.J.C. Smart, 77–150 (Cambridge: Cambridge University Press, 1973).

4 John Stuart Mill, *On Liberty and Other Essays*, ed. John Gray (Oxford: Oxford University Press, 1993), 21.

5 Jeremy Waldron, 'Locke, Toleration, and the Rationality of Persecution,' in *Liberal Rights: Collected Papers, 1981–1991* (Cambridge: Cambridge University Press, 1993), 120.

6 Mill, *On Liberty*, 5.

7 Ibid., 7.

8 Ibid., 8.

9 Ibid.

10 Ibid.

11 Ibid., 94.

12 Ibid., 9.

13 This link is persuasively suggested by Rees in *John Stuart Mill's* On Liberty.

14 Mill, *The Subjection of Women*, in *On Liberty and Other Essays*, 495.

15 *On Liberty*, 65.

16 Ibid., 9.

17 Ibid., 10.

18 Ibid.

19 Ibid.

20 Mill's argument seems to partially conflate two argumentative lines that are kept separate in Bentham. Bentham indicts the principle of 'sympathy and antipathy' to illustrate the inadequacy of intuitionism as an epistemic basis for moral judgements. The principle is essentially a failure of individual (moral) rationality. Mill's critique of 'custom,' however, seems to encompass both an individual and a collective dimension: custom not only licenses the intuitionism that Bentham ridicules by preventing the critical examination of one's beliefs, but it also makes the fact of consensus a legitimate basis for the prescriptive force of conventional normative rules. My thoughts on Bentham have greatly benefited from conversations with Professor Douglas Long at the University of Western Ontario. See his *Bentham on Liberty: Jeremy Bentham's Idea of Liberty in Relation to His Utilitarianism* (Toronto: University of Toronto Press, 1977).

21 Mill, *On Liberty*, 68.

22 Ibid., 11.

23 Ibid., 13.

24 Ibid., 13–14.

25 Ibid., 14.

26 Ibid., 15.

27 Ibid., 17.

28 Ibid.

29 Ibid.

30 Ibid.

31 Ibid.

32 The search for a principled limitation on the power of states to interfere with individual liberty logically implies that such interference is sometimes justified. Otherwise, why bother developing a principle?

33 On the connections between utility and liberty, see Fred Berger, *Happiness, Justice and Freedom: The Moral and Political Philosophy of John Stuart Mill* (Berkeley: University of California Press, 1984); Isaiah Berlin, 'John Stuart Mill and the Ends of Life,' in *Four Essays on Liberty*, 173–206 (Oxford: Oxford University Press, 1969); D.G. Brown, 'Mill on Liberty and Morality,' *Philosophical Review* 81 (1972): 135–58; Feinberg, *The Moral Limits of the Criminal Law*; and, finally, Robert W. Hoag, 'Happiness and Freedom: Recent Work on John Stuart Mill,' *Philosophy and Public Affairs* 15, no. 2 (1986): 188–99.

    For general discussions of utilitarianism as a moral and political theory, see Larry Alexander, 'Pursuing the Good – Indirectly,' *Ethics* 95 (1995): 315–32; Richard B. Brandt, *A Theory of the Good and of the Right* (Oxford: Clarendon, 1979); Brandt, *Morality, Utilitarianism and Rights* (Cambridge: Cambridge

University Press, 1992); David O. Brink, 'Mill's Deliberative Utilitarianism,' *Philosophy and Public Affairs* 21 (1992): 67–103; Jonathan Glover, ed., *Utilitarianism and Its Critics* (London: Macmillan, 1990); James Griffin, *Well-Being: Its Meaning, Measurement, and Moral Importance* (Oxford: Oxford University Press, 1986); Griffin, *Value Judgment: Improving Our Ethical Beliefs* (Oxford: Oxford University Press, 1996); R.M. Hare, *Moral Thinking: Its Levels, Method and Point* (Oxford: Oxford University Press, 1981); Paul Kelly, *Utilitarianism and Distributive Justice: Jeremy Bentham and the Civil Law* (Oxford: Clarendon, 1990); David Lyons, 'Mill's Theory of Morality,' *Nous* 10 (1976): 101–20; Philip Petitt, 'Consequentialism,' in *A Companion to Ethics*, ed. Peter Singer, 230–40 (Oxford: Blackwell, 1991); Jonathan Riley, *Liberal Utilitarianism: Social Choice Theory and J.S. Mill's Philosophy* (Cambridge: Cambridge University Press, 1988); Samuel Scheffler, ed., *Consequentialism and Its Critics* (Oxford: Oxford University Press, 1988); Amartya Sen and Bernard Williams, eds., *Utilitarianism and Beyond* (Cambridge: Cambridge University Press, 1982); and Henry Sidgwick, *The Methods of Ethics* (London: Macmillan, 1907).

34 'The supposition of complex, heterogeneous, and rank-ordered pleasures thwarts the ambition, characteristic of Bentham's utilitarianism, to reduce moral and political questions to a simple calculus of pleasure and pain; at the same time, it subverts the equally characteristic dream to construct an unambiguous decision rule for governance of the moral life.' Peter Berkowitz, 'Liberty, Virtue, and the Discipline of Individuality,' in *Mill and the Moral Character of Liberalism*, ed. Eldon J. Eisenach (University Park: Penn State Press, 1998), 27.

35 Mill, *On Liberty*, 15.
36 Ibid.
37 Ibid., 21.
38 Ibid.
39 Ibid.
40 See Jeremy Waldron, 'Mill and the Value of Moral Distress,' *Political Studies* 35 (1987): 410–23; and 'Locke, Toleration, and the Rationality of Persecution.'
41 Mill, *On Liberty*, 39.
42 Ibid.
43 Ibid., 41.
44 Ibid., 59.
45 Ibid.
46 Ibid.
47 'Unnecessary offence,' 'unmeasured vituperative,' 'want of candour,' 'malignity,' 'bigotry,' and 'intolerance of feeling' are all violations of what Mill calls 'the real morality of public discussion.' *On Liberty*, 61.

48 Ibid., 54.
49 Ibid., 63.
50 Mills, *Utilitarianism*, in *On Liberty and Other Essays*, 137.
51 Ibid., 138.
52 Ibid., 139.
53 Ibid., 140.
54 Mills, *On Liberty*, 63.
55 Ibid., 64.
56 Ibid.
57 Ibid., 65.
58 Ibid.
59 Ibid., 75–6.
60 Ibid., 75.
61 On this distinction, see John Gray's *Mill on Liberty: A Defence* (London: Rout-ledge and Kegan Paul, 1983). Since the two pull in opposite directions, Gray believes that 'this distinction between a criterial and an evidential view of the relations between autonomy and the higher pleasures fails to capture the spirit of Mill's view of the matter' (73).
62 Mill, *On Liberty*, 67.
63 See H.L.A. Hart, 'Natural Rights: Bentham and John Stuart Mill,' in *Essays on Bentham*, 79–104 (Oxford: Clarendon, 1982).
64 Mill, *Utilitarianism*, 168.
65 Mill, *On Liberty*, 66.
66 Stephen Holmes, 'The Positive Constitutionalism of John Stuart Mill,' in *Passions and Constraint: On the Theory of Liberal Democracy* (Chicago: University of Chicago Press, 1995), 195.
67 James Fitzjames Stephen, *Liberty, Equality, Fraternity* (Chicago: University of Chicago Press, 1991), 264.
68 Mill, *The Subjection of Women*, 491.
69 Stephen, *Liberty, Equality, Fraternity*, 70.
70 Ibid., 71.
71 Ibid.
72 Ibid.
73 Ibid., 21.
74 Ibid., 29.
75 Ibid., 44.
76 Ibid., 75.
77 Ibid., 85.
78 Ibid., 54.
79 Ibid., 55.

80 Interestingly, Stephen's reply to Mill is *identical* to Proast's response to Locke. For both critics, political authority is conditional upon empirical observations about the effects and limits of coercion, and a direct and unmediated consequence of normative truth.
81 Stephen, *Liberty, Equality, Fraternity*, 145.
82 Ibid., 28.
83 Doing so is legitimate since Stephen's argument is a response to one of Mill's within which this extension is intentionally made.
84 Stephen, *Liberty, Equality, Fraternity*, 91.
85 'English legislation in England is neutral as to Mahommedanism and Brahminism. English legislation in India proceeds on the assumption that both are false. If it did not, it would have to be founded on the Koran or the Institutes of Manu' (ibid.).
86 Ibid., 50.
87 Ibid., 105.
88 Ibid.
89 We address the question of the stability of neutralist institutions in connection with Rawls in chapter 8.
90 Stephen, *Liberty, Equality, Fraternity*, 84.
91 Ibid., 79.
92 Ibid., 81.
93 Ibid.
94 It should be obvious that Mill's sophisticated version of utilitarianism *defines* utility in a way that makes utility-maximizing intolerance conceptually and empirically impossible. Since utility is inseparable from autonomy, coercion can only have disutility. One wonders, however, what role, if any, utility plays in this argument. Why not dispense with it altogether and appeal directly to the perfectionist value of autonomy?
95 Stephen, *Liberty, Equality, Fraternity*, 86.
96 Mill, *The Subjection of Women*, 471.
97 Mill, *Utilitarianism*, 165.
98 For a parallel critique in connection with perfectionism, see my 'Should Egalitarians Be Perfectionists?' *Politics* 25, no. 3 (2005): 127–34.
99 Stephen, *Liberty, Equality, Fraternity*, 185.
100 Ibid., 85.
101 Mill, *On Liberty*, 83.
102 Mill, *Utilitarianism*, 195.
103 Stephen, *Liberty, Equality, Fraternity*, 122.
104 Mill, *On Liberty*, 107.
105 Ibid.

106 Ibid., 112.
107 Ibid.
108 Ibid., 116.
109 Dworkin, *Taking Rights Seriously*, 263.
110 Gray, *Mill on Liberty*, 5.
111 Hart, 'Natural Rights,' 90.
112 Ibid., 95.
113 Berlin, *Four Essays on Liberty*, 191.

3. Is Prostitution Unpatriotic?

1 H.L.A. Hart, *Law, Liberty and Morality* (Oxford: Oxford University Press, 1963), 14.
2 Committee on Homosexual Offences and Prostitution, *Report of the Committee on Homosexual Offences and Prostitution [Wolfenden Report]* (London: Her Majesty's Stationery Office, 1957).
3 For the communitarian position see Alasdair MacIntyre, *After Virtue: A Study in Moral Theory* (London: Duckworth, 1981); Michael Sandel, *Liberalism and the Limits of Justice* (Cambridge: Cambridge University Press, 1982); Charles Taylor, *Philosophy and the Human Sciences*. Vol. 2 of *Philosophical Papers* (Cambridge: Cambridge University Press, 1985); and Michael Walzer, *Spheres of Justice: A Defence of Pluralism and Equality* (Oxford: Blackwell, 1983). Two of the most influential statements of liberal egalitarianism are found in the works of Ronald Dworkin and John Rawls. See Dworkin, *Taking Rights Seriously* (Cambridge, MA: Harvard University Press, 1977); Dworkin, 'Liberalism,' in *Public and Private Morality*, ed. Stuart Hampshire, 113–43 (Cambridge: Cambridge University Press, 1978); Dworkin, *Sovereign Virtue: The Theory and Practice of Equality* (Cambridge, MA: Harvard University Press, 2000); and Rawls, *A Theory of Justice* (Cambridge, MA: Harvard University Press, 1971); Rawls, *Political Liberalism* (New York: Columbia University Press, 1993); Rawls, *Justice as Fairness: A Restatement* (Cambridge, MA: Harvard University Press, 2000).
4 This contrast in methodological approaches is nicely represented in Dworkin's review of *Spheres of Justice* entitled 'What Justice Isn't,' in *A Matter of Principle*, 214–20 (Cambridge, MA: Harvard University Press, 1985).
5 Stephen Holmes, 'Precommitment and the Paradox of Democracy,' in *Passions and Constraint* (Chicago: Chicago University Press, 1995), 134.
6 Will Kymlicka, *Contemporary Political Philosophy*, 2nd ed. (Oxford: Oxford University Press, 2002), 257.
7 I investigate this question in chapter 8.

8 Patrick Devlin, *The Enforcement of Morals* (Oxford: Oxford University Press, 1965), 8.
9 Ibid., 10.
10 Ibid.
11 Ibid.
12 Ibid., 14.
13 See, for example, Thomas Nagel, 'Moral Conflict and Political Legitimacy,' *Philosophy & Public Affairs* 16, no. 3 (1987): 215–40; Nagel, *Equality and Partiality* (Oxford: Oxford University Press, 1991); Rawls, *A Theory of Justice*; Rawls, *Political Liberalism*; Rawls, *Justice as Fairness*; and Thomas Scanlon, 'Contractualism and Utilitarianism,' in *Utilitarianism and Beyond*, ed. Amartya Sen and Bernard Williams, 103–28 (Cambridge: Cambridge University Press, 1982); Scanlon, *What We Owe to Each Other* (Cambridge, MA: Harvard University Press, 1998).
14 Devlin, *Enforcement*, 114.
15 Ibid., 89.
16 Ibid.
17 Ibid.
18 Ibid.
19 Ibid., 90.
20 Ibid.
21 Ibid.
22 Ibid.
23 Ibid.
24 Ibid., 17.
25 Ibid.
26 Ibid., 100.
27 Ibid.
28 Ibid., 93.
29 Ibid.
30 Ibid.
31 Hart, *Law, Liberty and Morality*.
32 Many of the essays collected in *The Enforcement of Morals* are devoted to showing the extent to which tort, marriage, and contract law in England already do, in fact, enforce a positive (Christian) morality.
33 Several critics follow Devlin in rejecting the possibility that liberal states are, can be, or should be neutral between rival conceptions of the human good as these are enshrined in various positive moralities. See, for example, William Galston, *Liberal Purposes: Goods, Virtues and Duties in the Liberal State* (Cambridge: Cambridge University Press, 1991); Joseph Raz, *The Morality of Freedom*

(Oxford: Clarendon, 1986); George Sher, *Beyond Neutrality: Perfectionism and Politics* (Cambridge: Cambridge University Press, 1997); and Stephen Wall, *Liberalism, Perfectionism and Restraint* (Cambridge: Cambridge University Press, 1998).

34 Hart, *Law, Liberty and Morality*, 55.
35 Ibid., 51.
36 Ibid., 52.
37 Ibid., 70.
38 Ibid.
39 Ibid.
40 Ibid., 19.
41 Ibid., 72.
42 Ibid.
43 Ibid.
44 Ibid.
45 Ibid., 79.
46 Ibid.
47 Ibid., 81.
48 Ibid., 79.
49 For a recent discussion and defence of the epistemic approach to democratic authority, see David Estlund, 'Beyond Fairness and Deliberation: The Epistemic Dimension of Democratic Authority,' in *Deliberative Democracy: Essays on Reason and Politics*, ed. James Bohman and William Rehg, 173–204 (Cambridge, MA: MIT Press, 1997).
50 'When therefore the opinion that is contrary to my own prevails, this proves neither more nor less than that I was mistaken, and that what I thought to be the general will was not so.' Jean-Jacques Rousseau, *The Social Contract*, ed. G.D.H. Cole (1762; London: Dent, 1973), 278).
51 Ronald Dworkin himself is not a utilitarian, but he presents the case for this justification of democratic decision-making very clearly. See the contrast between internal and external preferences in his celebrated essay 'Liberalism.' Majoritarianism allows more people to get more of what they happen to want (internal preferences), but this decision-rule must be constrained by a scheme of liberal rights that exclude objectionable (external) preferences for others having less, in virtue of their being less virtuous, or popular, and so on.
52 H.L.A. Hart, 'Between Utility and Rights,' in *The Idea of Freedom*, ed. Alan Ryan, 77–98 (Chicago: University of Chicago Press, 1979); Rawls, *A Theory of Justice*.
53 For a recent justification of democracy as procedural fairness, see Thomas

Christiano, 'The Significance of Public Deliberation,' in *Deliberative Democracy*, ed. Bohman and Rehg, 243–78.

54 Dworkin, *Taking Rights Seriously*.
55 Ibid., 248.
56 Ibid., 254.
57 Ibid., 255.
58 Robert P. George, *Making Men Moral: Civil Liberties and Public Morality* (Oxford: Oxford University Press, 1993).
59 Ibid., 1.
60 Ibid.
61 Ibid.
62 Ibid., 65.
63 Ibid., 68.
64 Ibid.
65 Ibid., 69.
66 Ibid., 5.
67 Ibid., 29.
68 Devlin, *Enforcement*, viii.
69 In recognizing the legislative uselessness of the distinction between these two principles, Devlin anticipates contemporary objections to Thomas Nagel's idea of 'epistemic restraint' in 'Moral Conflict and Political Legitimacy.' See also Brian Barry, *Justice as Impartiality* (Oxford: Oxford University Press, 1995); Joseph Raz, *Ethics in the Public Domain: Essays in the Morality of Law and Politics* (Oxford: Oxford University Press, 1994); and T.L. Price, 'Epistemological Restraint – Revisited,' *Journal of Political Philosophy* 8 (2000): 401–7, on the coherence and viability of distinguishing between belief and truth in justifying the use of coercive political power.
70 George, *Making Men Moral*, 77.
71 See Charles Jones, *Global Justice: Defending Cosmopolitanism* (Oxford: Oxford University Press, 1999); and Jeremy Waldron, 'Minority Cultures and the Cosmopolitan Alternative,' in *The Rights of Minority Cultures*, ed. Will Kymlicka, 93–119 (Oxford: Oxford University Press, 1995).
72 As one anonymous referee from *Contemporary Political Theory* perceptively pointed out, the circularity of the disintegration thesis apparently precludes the possibility of ever legitimately conducting moral dispute at all – for Devlin, social cohesion depends upon shared moral convictions and anything that weakens moral consensus is therefore opposed to cohesion. While this is undoubtedly true, the democratic argument, once detached from this tautological claim, appears to avoid this circularity by focusing on a principle for politically *resolving* moral dispute. It may be vulnerable to other objections, but it does not seem to rule out the possibility of moral dispute *tout court*.

73 Holmes, *Passions and Constraint*, 6.
74 Richard Vernon, 'Liberals, Democrats and the Agenda of Politics,' *Political Studies* 46 (1998): 295–308.
75 Joshua Cohen puts the point thus: 'The deliberative conception holds that free expression is required for *determining* what advances the common good, because what is good is fixed by public deliberation, and not prior to it. It is fixed by informed and autonomous judgments, involving the exercise of the deliberative capacities. So the ideal of deliberative democracy is not hostile to free expression; it rather presupposes such freedom.' 'Deliberation and Democratic Legitimacy,' in *Deliberative Democracy*, ed. Bohman and Rehg, 83.

4. Should Liberals be Perfectionists?

1 See, in particular, Joseph Raz, *The Authority of Law* (Oxford: Oxford University Press, 1979); *The Morality of Freedom* (Oxford: Clarendon, 1986); *Ethics in the Public Domain: Essays in the Morality of Law and Politics* (Oxford: Oxford University Press, 1994); and *Engaging Reason: On the Theory of Value and Action* (Oxford: Oxford University Press, 2000). Raz's important articles include 'Professor Dworkin's Theory of Rights,' *Political Studies* 26 (1978): 123–37; 'Liberalism, Autonomy and the Politics of Neutral Concern,' *Midwest Studies in Philosophy* 7 (1982): 89–102; 'Right-Based Moralities,' in *Theories of Rights*, ed. Jeremy Waldron, 182–200 (Oxford: Oxford University Press, 1984); 'Authority and Justification,' *Philosophy & Public Affairs* 14 (1985): 3–29; 'Autonomy, Toleration, and the Harm Principle,' *Issues in Contemporary Legal Philosophy*, ed. R. Gavison, 313–33 (Oxford: Oxford University Press, 1987); 'Liberating Duties,' *Law & Philosophy* 8 (1989): 3–21; 'Liberalism, Skepticism and Democracy,' *Iowa Law Review* 74 (1989): 761–86; 'Facing Diversity: The Case of Epistemic Abstinence,' *Philosophy & Public Affairs* 19 (1990): 3–46; and 'Liberty and Trust,' in *Natural Law, Liberalism and Morality*, ed. Robert P. George, 113–129 (Oxford: Oxford University Press, 1996).
2 Raz, *Morality of Freedom*, 133.
3 See Raz's defence of the 'natural case' for perfectionism in his 'Facing Up: A Reply,' *Southern California Law Review* 62 (1989): 1153–1235, at 1230.
4 Raz, 'Liberty and Trust,' 113.
5 Raz, *Ethics in the Public Domain*, vi.
6 Ibid., 3.
7 'Evaluation of people's well-being involves judgments about their lives, or periods of their lives, and the degree to which they do or did do well, were good or successful' (Ibid.).
8 As Jeremy Waldron observes, Raz says 'almost nothing about what makes an option or an individual's conception of the good repugnant or immoral,

even though the central thrust of his argument is to establish the government's right, indeed its duty, to extirpate options of this sort.' 'Autonomy and Perfectionism in Raz's *Morality of Freedom*,' *Southern California Law Review* 62 (1989): 1130.

9 'The intuitions I referred to matter not as particular intuitions as to what is right in one case or another. We automatically read them as instances of certain general features of reasoning, which exemplify valid argument even while it is conceded that each of the chosen examples may not in itself carry conviction.' Raz, *Morality of Freedom*, 288.

10 Ibid., 297.

11 Ibid., 291.

12 'The value to me of living near open country depends on whether among my pursuits there are any which make use of the country' (ibid., 290).

13 '[Goals] contribute to a person's well-being because they are his goals, they are what matters to him. Since I never wanted to be a concert violinist I am none the worse for not being one. Someone whose ambition it is or was to become a concern violinist is, other things being equal, worse off if he is not one than if he is' (ibid., 292).

14 'When we serve others' interests in ways which are independent of any service to their goals this is likely to be by advancing some biologically determined interest of theirs. What we cannot do is make someone who does not wish to see a Bogart film enjoy watching it without also making him want to watch it. By way of contrast, we can benefit people by improving the room temperature, providing adequate sensory stimulation, etc., even while they continue to protest against such measures. The reason is conceptual, rather than empirical, though the conceptual connection is loose and allows certain exceptions' (ibid).

15 'A comprehensive goal is not a long-term goal. I may desire to visit Venice on my sixtieth birthday, and I may have been working to save for it ever since I was twenty-five. It is still not a comprehensive goal. To be that it itself (not merely its means) must have ramifications which pervade important dimensions of my life. This also entails that it does not consist merely of a repetition of one kind of activity. Going bell-ringing every Sunday is not a comprehensive goal in itself, but when it is conceived as a complex activity with social, sightseeing, architectural, and other interests and when it assumes a significance which pervades other times than those when one is actually on a bell-ringing outing, then it is a comprehensive goal' (ibid., 308–9).

16 Ibid., 292.

17 Ibid., 299.

18 Ibid., 305.

19 'Our notion of a successful life is of a life well-spent, of a life of achievement, of handicaps overcome, talents wisely used, of good judgment in the conduct of one's affairs, of warm and trusting relations with family and friends, stormy and enthusiastic involvement with other people, many hours spent having fun in good company, and so on' (ibid., 306).
20 Ibid., 308.
21 Ibid., 310.
22 'Activities which do not appear to acquire their character from social forms in fact do so. Bird watching seems to be what any sighted person in the vicinity of birds can do. And so he can, except that this would not make him into a bird watcher. He can be that only in a society where this, or at least some other animal tracking activities, are recognized as leisure activities, and which furthermore shares certain attitudes to natural life generally' (ibid., 311).
23 Ibid., 319.
24 'An open marriage is a relation combining elements of a conventional marriage and of a sexual pursuit which is kept free of emotional involvement. It is a combination of elements of two socially recognizable forms' (ibid., 309).
25 Ibid., 313.
26 Raz, *Ethics in the Public Domain*, 120.
27 See John Rawls, *A Theory of Justice* (Cambridge, MA: Harvard University Press, 1971); *Political Liberalism* (New York: Columbia University Press, 1993); and *Justice as Fairness: A Restatement* (Cambridge, MA: Harvard University Press, 2000).
28 Rawls, *Political Liberalism*, 19.
29 Joel Feinberg defends such a conception in *Harm to Self* (New York: Oxford University Press, 1986), and *Harmless Wrongdoing* (New York: Oxford University Press, 1988).
30 Raz, *Morality of Freedom*, 369.
31 Ibid., 371.
32 Ibid., 156.
33 Ibid.
34 Ibid., 155.
35 Ibid., 377.
36 Ibid., 377–8.
37 Ibid., 157.
38 Ibid., 374.
39 See Steven Wall's *Liberalism, Perfectionism and Restraint* (Cambridge: Cambridge University Press, 1998), for an argument that defends this presupposition of personal autonomy.

40 'A choice between good and evil is not enough. (Remember that it is personal, not moral, autonomy we are concerned with. [Even concentration camp inmates are moral agents] and fully responsible for [their] actions ... but they do not have personal autonomy.' Raz, *The Morality of Freedom*, 379.

41 Raz, *Engaging Reason*, 324.

42 The first four originate from Joel Feinberg's discussion of the relation between personal autonomy and what he calls 'personal good' in *Harm to Self* (58). Feinberg maintains that there 'are only four standard ways of treating the relation between' between the two, but there are, in fact, five – the fifth being Raz's.

43 Raz, *Ethics in the Public Domain*, 123.

44 Feinberg, *Harm to Self*, 59.

45 Feinberg's example of this 'balancing strategy' is the following: 'If the legislator must decide ... whether to vote for a bill requiring drivers to buckle their seatbelts on pain of penalty, he must balance against one another such considerations as the magnitude of harm prevented, on the one hand, and the degree to which the motorist's liberty is restricted on the other, and generalize over the whole class of motorists.' *Harm to Self*, 62.

46 Raz, *Morality of Freedom*, 395.

47 For such a connection, see George Sher, *Beyond Neutrality: Perfectionism and Politics* (Cambridge: Cambridge University Press, 1997), 58.

48 Raz, 'Liberty and Trust,' 123.

49 Raz, *Morality of Freedom*, 53.

50 Ibid., 47.

51 Ibid., 59.

52 'There is no point in having authorities unless their determinations are binding even if mistaken (though some mistakes may disqualify them)' (ibid., 8).

53 Raz, 'Liberty and Trust,' 119–20.

54 Ibid., 119.

55 Raz, *Morality of Freedom*, 80.

56 Donald Regan, 'Autonomy and Value: Reflections on Raz's *The Morality of Freedom*,' *Southern California Law Review* 62 (1989): 1033.

57 'Because one cannot respond to a reason unless there is some value that gives rise to that reason, it is inconsistent to hold that autonomy is responsiveness to reasons and that autonomy is the only thing with value.' Sher, *Beyond Neutrality*, 57.

58 Raz, *Morality of Freedom*, 399.

59 Ibid., 325.

60 'Incomparability ... marks the inability of reason to guide our action, not the insignificance of our choice.' Raz, *Morality of Freedom*, 334.

61 Ibid., 339.

62 Ibid., 395.

63 Ibid., 399.

64 Ibid., 343.

65 Ibid., 406.

66 Raz, *Ethics in the Public Domain*, 166.

67 'The traits of character which make for excellence in chairing committees and getting things done, when this involves reconciling points of view and overcoming personal differences, those very traits of character also tend to make people intolerant of single-minded dedication to a cause.' Raz, *Morality of Freedom*, 404.

68 Ibid., 422.

69 Ibid., 414.

70 'Any assessment of degrees of liberty depends on the importance of various actions for the protection or promotion of values other than freedom. If so then the value of freedom depends on the other values which the freedom to perform some actions serves. It would seem plausible that the freedom to perform some actions is valueless. For it is plausible to assume that there are some actions such that neither their performance nor the ability not to perform them has any value, unless the freedom so to choose is by itself independently valuable' (ibid., 17).

71 Ibid., 425.

72 Ibid.

73 Raz, *Ethics in the Public Domain*, 391.

74 Raz, *Morality of Freedom*, 412.

75 Ibid. Raz also emphasizes this point when he asks, 'Is the autonomous wrongdoer a morally better person than the non-autonomous wrongdoer? Our intuitions rebel against such a view. It is surely the other way around. The wrongdoing casts a darker shadow on its perpetrator if it is autonomously done by him. A murderer who was led to his deed by the foreseen inner logic of his autonomously chosen career is morally worse than one who murders because he momentarily succumbs to the prospect of an easy gain. Nor are these considerations confined to gross breaches of duties. Demeaning, or narrow-minded, or ungenerous, or insensitive behaviour is worse when autonomously chosen and indulged in' (ibid., 380).

76 Ibid., 412.

77 Ibid., 429.

78 Ibid., 161.

79 Ibid.

80 Ibid.

81 Ibid., 412.

82 Ibid., 419.

83 Ibid.

84 Raz, *Ethics in the Public Domain*, 124.

85 Raz, *Morality of Freedom*, 429.

86 Ibid., 161.

87 Raz, *Morality of Freedom*, 161.

88 Rawls, *Political Liberalism*, 37.

89 See my discussion of John Locke's *Letter concerning Toleration* in chapter 1.

90 See my discussion of Rawls's *A Theory of Justice* and *Political Liberalism* in chapter 8.

91 Raz, *Ethics in the Public Domain*, 337.

92 Jeremy Waldron, '*Ethics in the Public Domain* in Raz's *The Morality of Freedom*,' *Southern California Law Review* 62 (1989): 1118.

93 Raz, *Morality of Freedom*, 377–8.

94 Waldron, 'Autonomy and Perfectionism,' 1147.

95 Wojciech Sadurski, 'Joseph Raz on Liberal Neutrality and the Harm Principle,' *Oxford Journal of Legal Studies* 10 (1990): 133.

96 Ibid.

97 In the absence of both a mutually acceptable 'standing rule,' viz., a regulatory principle established by common consent, and an indifferent judge to interpret it, there is no impartial basis for resolving disputes politically. See *The Second Treatise of Government*.

98 Raz, *Morality of Freedom*, 406.

99 Ibid., 189.

100 Ibid., 369–70.

101 See David McCabe, 'Joseph Raz and the Contextual Argument for Liberal Perfectionism,' *Ethics* 111 (2001): 493–522.

102 Regan, 'Autonomy and Value,' 1084.

103 See Robert P. George, *Making Men Moral: Civil Liberties and Public Morality* (Oxford: Oxford University Press, 1993) for an argument of this type.

104 Raz, 'Liberty and Trust.'

105 Ibid., 122.

106 Ibid.

107 Ibid., 124.

108 Ibid., 127; emphasis mine.

109 This distinction between strategies of continuity vs discontinuity is taken from Ronald Dworkin's 'The Foundations of Liberal Equality,' in *The Tanner Lectures on Human Values* (Salt Lake City: University of Utah Press, 1990).

5. The Continuity Thesis

1 Ronald Dworkin, 'The Foundations of Liberal Equality,' in *The Tanner Lectures on Human Values* (Salt Lake City: University of Utah Press, 1990). This lecture is abridged and reprinted in *Sovereign Virtue: The Theory and Practice of Equality* (Cambridge, MA: Harvard University Press, 2000). Pages references in this chapter are to *Sovereign Virtue*.
2 Dworkin, *Sovereign Virtue*, 250.
3 Ibid., 251–2.
4 Ibid., 253.
5 Ibid.
6 Ibid., 257.
7 Ibid., 258.
8 Ibid., 242.
9 Ibid., 260.
10 Ibid.
11 Ibid., 254.
12 Ibid., 245.
13 Ibid., 270.
14 Ibid., 264.
15 In Dworkin's example, 'Louis' deliberately cultivates tastes for things like plovers' eggs and pre-phyloxera claret, opera, and skiing, all of which are expensive in the sense that once he has these preferences, he will not have as much welfare as he previously had unless he also acquires enough additional wealth or resources to satisfy them. Any government intent upon equalizing welfare will then be committed to transferring resources from someone else that is perfectly satisfied consuming, say, malt liquor or beer. Even if we wish to distinguish people like Louis who voluntarily decide to cultivate expensive tastes and so should be responsible for bearing the additional costs associated with satisfying them, from others who simply come to discover that they have these preferences, 'the distinction is less important than is sometimes thought, because that decision is rarely if ever voluntary all the way down' (ibid., 52).
16 Dworkin, 'Foundations of Liberal Equality,' 91.
17 Dworkin, *Sovereign Virtue*, 248.
18 Ibid., 268.
19 Ibid., 270.
20 Ibid.
21 'The challenge model does not rule out the possibility that the community should collectively endorse and recommend ethical ideals not adequately supported by the culture. Nor does it rule out compulsory education and

other forms of regulation which experience shows are likely to be endorsed in a genuine rather than manipulated way, when these are sufficiently short-term and noninvasive and not subject to other, independent objection. All this follows from the central, constitutive role the model of challenge assigns to reflective or intuitive *judgment* (ibid., 273).

22 Ibid., 277.

23 See Richard Arneson, 'The Cracked Foundations of Liberal Equality,' in *Ronald Dworkin and His Critics*, ed. Justine Burley, 79–98 (Oxford: Blackwell, 2005).

24 Matthew Clayton, 'Liberal Equality and Ethics,' *Ethics* 113, no. 1 (2002): 8–22.

25 Richard Arneson, 'Perfectionism and Politics,' *Ethics* 111, no. 1 (2000): 37–63.

26 If justice is a normative parameter, then people cannot sensibly claim that they would be better off if they were to be awarded a larger than just share of resources. It is unclear, however, how Dworkin's claim about the parametric status of justice either affects or relates to the very different proposition that *equal shares are just*, and it is this latter proposition that grounds his critique of perfectionism as a distributive principle.

27 Dworkin, *Sovereign Virtue*, 265.

28 Matthew Clayton maintains that offering 'access to education, art or culture, or opportunities for the development and exercise of various virtues might enhance people's well-being if the government ensured that all enjoyed equal access to goods related to human flourishing.' 'Liberal Equality and Ethics,' 21.

29 Richard Arneson, 'Equality and Equal Opportunity for Welfare,' *Philosophical Studies* 56 (1989): 77–93.

30 'If what would be good for me to get if I could get it does not vary with my particular circumstances, then a fortiori it does not vary depending on circumstances that should determine what in my life I can reasonably regret. There is no temptation whatsoever to suppose that a welfarist ideal with this yardstick of individual welfare needs anything like the fatal "reasonable regret" idea that Dworkin proposes in order to carry out interpersonal comparisons.' Richard Arneson, 'Welfare Should Be the Currency of Justice,' *Canadian Journal of Philosophy* 30, no. 4 (1999): 477–524.

31 Dworkin, *Sovereign Virtue*, 270. Dworkin concedes that it is sometimes better if people do not lead certain lives – those devoted to fascism, for instance – at peace with themselves but this is because such lives are bad for other people.

32 Martin Wilkinson, 'Dworkin on Paternalism and Well-Being,' *Oxford Journal of Legal Studies* 1, no. 3 (1996): 436.

33 The example is Richard Arneson's. See 'Cracked Foundations,' 85.

34 Richard Arneson suggests this possibility in 'Cracked Foundations.'

35 See the symposium on *Sovereign Virtue* in *Ethics* 113, no. 1 (2002): 8–22; Colin M. MacLeod, *Liberalism, Justice, and Markets: A Critique of Liberal Equality* (Oxford: Clarendon, 1998); the exchange between Dworkin and Scheffler in *Philosophy & Public Affairs*: Samuel Scheffler, 'What Is Egalitarianism?' *Philosophy & Public Affairs* 31, no. 1 (2003): 5–39, and Ronald Dworkin, 'Equality, Luck and Hierarchy,' *Philosophy & Public Affairs* 31, no. 2 (2003): 190–8; and, most recently, the collection of critical essays found in Justine Burley, ed., *Ronald Dworkin and His Critics* (Oxford: Blackwell, 2005).

36 Dworkin, *Sovereign Virtue*, 67.

37 Ibid., 68.

38 Ibid., 70.

39 'A fully developed description of an equal auction, adequate for a more complex society, might provide a standard for judging institutions and distributions in the real world. Of course, no complex, organic society would have, in its history, anything remotely comparable to an equal auction. But we can nevertheless ask, for any actual distribution, whether it falls within the class of distributions that might have been produced by such an auction over a defensible description of initial resources, or, if it does not, how far it differs from or falls short of the closest distribution within this class. The device of the auction might provide, in other words, a standard for judging how far an actual distribution, however it has been achieved, approaches equality of resources at any particular time.' Ibid., 72.

40 Ibid., 30.

41 Ibid., 89.

42 Will Kymlicka, *Contemporary Political Philosophy*, 2nd ed. (Oxford: Oxford University Press, 2002), 77.

43 This explains why even though regal 'Louis' is frustrated by having to spend so much money satisfying his expensive preferences for things like plovers' eggs and pre-phylloxera claret, he cannot, at least with a straight face, demand compensation on that account. Because these things are *valuable* to him, his life would be a *worse* one if he became the kind of person who no longer wanted them, so, at least for him, they are not *disadvantages* that justify compensation but, rather, convictions that establish what living well is.

44 Dworkin, *Sovereign Virtue*, 294.

45 Ibid., 123.

46 Ibid., 114.

47 Ibid., 149.

48 Ibid.

49 Ibid., 148.

50 Ibid.

6. Contract Killing: A Critique

1 Brian Barry, *Justice as Impartiality* (Oxford: Oxford University Press, 1995); Thomas Nagel, 'Moral Conflict and Political Legitimacy,' *Philosophy & Public Affairs* 16, no. 3 (1987): 215–240; Nagel, *Equality and Partiality* (Oxford: Oxford University Press, 1991); John Rawls, *A Theory of Justice* (Cambridge, MA: Harvard University Press, 1971); Rawls, *Political Liberalism* (New York: Columbia University Press, 1993); Rawls, *Justice as Fairness: A Restatement* (Cambridge, MA: Harvard University Press, 2001); Thomas Scanlon, 'Contractualism and Utilitarianism,' in *Utilitarianism and Beyond*, ed. Amartya Sen and Bernard William, 103–28 (Cambridge: Cambridge University Press, 1982); and Scanlon, *What We Owe to Each Other* (Cambridge, MA: Harvard University Press, 1998).

2 For discussions of the idea of liberal neutrality, see Barry, *Justice as Impartiality*; Ronald Dworkin, 'Liberalism,' in *Public and Private Morality*, ed. Stuart Hampshire, 113–43 (Cambridge: Cambridge University Press, 1978); Peter Jones, 'The Ideal of the Neutral State,' in *Liberal Neutrality*, ed. Robert Goodin and Andrew Reeve, 9–38 (London: Routledge, 1989); Charles Larmore, *Patterns of Moral Complexity* (Cambridge: Cambridge University Press, 1987); Larmore, 'Political Liberalism,' in *The Morals of Modernity*, 121–51 (Cambridge; Cambridge University Press, 1996); Larmore, 'The Moral Basis of Political Liberalism,' *Journal of Philosophy* 96 (1999): 599–625; Alan Montefiore, *Neutrality and Impartiality* (Cambridge: Cambridge University Press, 1975); Nagel, 'Moral Conflict and Political Legitimacy'; Nagel, *Equality and Partiality*; Rawls, *A Theory of Justice*; Rawls, *Political Liberalism*; and Rawls, *Justice as Fairness*.

3 William Galston, *Liberal Purposes: Goods, Virtues, and Diversity in the Liberal State* (Cambridge: Cambridge University Press, 1991); Thomas Hurka, *Perfectionism* (Oxford: Oxford University Press, 1993); Joseph Raz, *The Morality of Freedom* (Oxford: Clarendon, 1986); Raz, *Ethics in the Public Domain: Essays in the Morality of Law and Politics* (Oxford: Oxford University Press, 1994); George Sher, *Beyond Neutrality: Perfectionism and Politics* (Cambridge: Cambridge University Press, 1997); and Stephen Wall, *Liberalism, Perfectionism, and Restraint* (Cambridge: Cambridge University Press, 1998).

4 Simon Caney, 'Anti-perfectionism and Rawlsian Liberalism,' *Political Studies* 42 (1995): 248–64; Joseph Chan, 'Legitimacy, Unanimity and Perfectionism,' *Philosophy & Public Affairs* 29, no. 1 (2000): 5–42; and Simon Clarke, 'Contractarianism, Liberal Neutrality and Epistemology,' *Political Studies* 47, no. 1 (1999): 627–42.

5 Caney, 'Anti-perfectionism'; Clarke, 'Contractarianism.'

6 Chan, 'Legitimacy.'

7 Caney, 'Anti-perfectionism,' 251.

8 Rawls, *Political Liberalism*, 56.

9 Ibid., 37.

10 Caney, 'Anti-perfectionism,' 256.

11 Ibid., 257.

12 Ibid., 258.

13 Ibid.

14 Nagel, *Equality and Partiality*.

15 Chan, 'Legitimacy,' 21.

16 Ibid.

17 Nagel, *Equality and Partiality*, 164–5.

18 Chan, 'Legitimacy,' 23.

19 'That is not true of religion and other basic choices regarding what life is about and how it is to be led. There the argument of necessity does not supply a common standpoint capable of containing the centrifugal force of diametrically opposed values.' Nagel, *Equality and Partiality*, 24.

20 Barry, *Justice as Impartiality*, 173.

21 Ibid., 169.

22 Ibid., 13.

23 Clarke, 'Contractarianism,' 635.

24 Although contractualists are clearly free to advance controversial explanations of pluralism as well, their argument for neutrality does not depend essentially upon the truth of any of them, and, as such, doing so unnecessarily reinforces the conflation of morality and epistemology at the core of the reflexivity thesis.

25 See Rawls, *A Theory of Justice*; and Rawls, *Political Liberalism*.

26 See Scanlon, 'Contractualism and Utilitarianism'; and Scanlon, *What We Owe to Each Other*.

27 Nagel, *Equality and Partiality*, 11.

28 Barry, *Justice as Impartiality*, 7.

29 Ronald Dworkin, 'The Original Position,' in *Reading Rawls*, ed. Norman Daniels, 16–52 (Oxford: Blackwell, 1975); and Jean Hampton, 'Contracts and Choices: Does Rawls Have a Social Contract Theory?' *Journal of Philosophy* 87 (1980): 315–38.

30 Rawls, *Justice as Fairness*, 188–9.

31 Joshua Cohen, 'Moral Pluralism and Political Consensus,' in *The Idea of Democracy*, ed. David Copp, Jean Hampton, and John Roemer, 270–91 (Cambridge: Cambridge University Press, 1993).

32 Joshua Cohen is the source of this proposal, but John Rawls's thoughts on the need for an 'overlapping consensus' on liberal principles of political justice

have popularized it in academic quarters. It is an open question as to what extent Rawls's arguments for anti-perfectionism actually depend upon this view. See Rawls, *Political Liberalism.*

33 Cohen, 'Moral Pluralism and Political Consensus,' 280–1.

34 Ibid., 282.

35 Erin Kelly and Lionel McPherson, 'On Tolerating the Unreasonable,' *Journal of Political Philosophy* 9 (2001): 55.

36 Scanlon, 'Contractualism and Utilitarianism,' 110.

37 Ibid., 111.

38 Rawls, *Justice as Fairness*, 89.

39 Nagel, 'Moral Conflict and Political Legitimacy.'

40 Gerald Dworkin, 'Non-neutral Principles,' *Journal of Philosophy* 80, no. 14 (1974): 491–506.

41 Peter Jones, 'Liberalism, Belief, and Doubt,' *Archiv für Rechts und Sozialphilosophie* 36 (1989): 67.

42 Jean Hampton, 'The Moral Commitments of Liberalism,' in *The Idea of Democracy*, ed. David Copp, Jean Hampton, and John Roemer (Cambridge: Cambridge University Press, 1993), 312.

43 Nagel, 'Moral Conflict and Political Legitimacy.'

44 See Barry, *Justice as Impartiality*; and Raz, *Ethics in the Public Domain.*

45 See Nagel, *Equality and Partiality.*

46 T.L. Price, 'Debate: Epistemological Restraint – Revisited,' *Journal of Political Philosophy* 8 (2000): 401–7.

47 To my knowledge, Charles Larmore is the only leading contemporary political liberal who explicitly distinguishes between epistemic and moral conceptions of reasonableness, so it is worth briefly identifying how his view is both similar to, and different from, the one defended here. On my reading, there are at least two key similarities, and two central differences. First, the similarities: (1) Larmore agrees that early modern theories of religious toleration, like Locke's, are a better model for liberal theory than what the late eighteenth or nineteenth centuries had to offer, because the classical arguments for liberalism – say, Voltaire's scepticism, Mill's experimentalism, and Kant's ideal of moral autonomy – will likely persuade only those antecedently convinced of the respective ethical or epistemological views at their core; and (2) since disagreement about controversial ethical ideals sets the political problem, the solution must lie in a procedural political form that abstracts from the very contested values under dispute. Larmore, then, is also suspicious of 'reasonable pluralism' (see chapter 8 below) as the basis for neutrality if, by that designation, one means that there are many viable conceptions of the good life that neither represent different versions of some single, homoge-

neous good, nor fall into any discernable hierarchy. Many (politically) reasonable people will reject this claim: 'Pluralism itself is one of the things about which reasonable people disagree.' Larmore, *The Morals of Modernity*, 12. While there are these motivational and structural similarities between our theories, there are also two central differences: (1) Larmore's norm of rational dialogue, which is implied by the requirement that governments treat those under their authority with equal respect, is (I think) cashed out in a way that cannot be detached from Kant's ideal of personal autonomy, so it falls prey to the same objection it was designed to evade, and (2) Larmore's search for 'a neutral justification of political neutrality' (Larmore, *Patterns of Moral Complexity*, 53) leads to an overly conservative ideal of public reason. On his view, people should respond to points of disagreement about constitutional essentials and matters of basic justice by retreating to neutral ground, by which he means to the beliefs *that they actually share*. They are to do this in order, either to 'a) resolve the disagreement and vindicate one of the disputed positions by means of arguments that proceed from this common ground, or b) bypass the disagreement and seek a solution of the problem on the basis simply of this common ground.' Larmore, 'Political Liberalism,' 135. A better starting point would appeal to moral norms that they *ought* to share, whether or not they, in fact, do so. This makes more sense in the context of an egalitarian political morality, and it actually better coheres with what Larmore says in his celebrated essay 'The Moral Basis of Political Liberalism': 'We would be wrong to suppose that the moral principle of respect for persons has the political significance it does because reasonable people share a commitment to it. On the contrary, the idea of respect is what directs us to seek the principles of our political life in the area of reasonable agreement. *Respect for persons lies at the heart of political liberalism, not because looking for common ground we find it there, but because it is what impels us to look for common ground at all*' (608; emphasis mine). I agree, but this leads away from the conservative norm of rational dialogue that Larmore specifies, and towards a more critical norm of public reasoning of the kind defended in this book.

48 See, for example, Joseph Raz's *The Morality of Freedom* for a liberal-perfectionist view that dispenses with equality as a foundational principle.

49 An anonymous *Political Studies* reader doubted that perfectionist critics of neutrality would be persuaded by my argument until the precise nature of this connection was set out at greater length. But why *shouldn't* a state committed to treating its members as equals devise different procedural mechanisms for resolving political disputes concerning, say, compulsory tax rates from those arising out of rival ethical claims over what is ultimately valuable in life, and how everyone should lead it? The first type of controversy is

rooted in conflicting perceptions of how a given community's resources should be distributed to satisfy a variety of *shared* social, economic, and political goals. But the second one prompts deeper identity-based questions about the background preconditions of political membership itself, namely *who* is to share, and what are the ethical *boundaries* of the relevant community?

7. Democratic Equality

1 Jonathan Quong thinks that dispensing with epistemology renders contractualism circular, and he cites my argument in the last chapter as a case in point. See his 'Disagreement, Asymmetry, and Liberal Legitimacy,' *Politics, Philosophy & Economics* 4, no. 3 (2005): 301–30. Chapters 7–9 of this book, though not directly addressed to Quong's diagnosis, explain why it is wrong.

2 Ronald Dworkin, 'The Original Position,' in *Reading Rawls*, ed. Norman Daniels (Oxford: Blackwell, 1975), 18.

3 John Rawls, *A Theory of Justice* (Cambridge, MA: Harvard University Press, 1971).

4 Thomas Scanlon, *What We Owe to Each Other* (Cambridge, MA: Harvard University Press, 1998).

5 Rawls, *A Theory of Justice.*

6 Martha Nussbaum, *Frontiers of Justice: Disability, Nationality, Species Membership* (Cambridge, MA: Harvard University Press, 2006).

7 Robert Nozick, *Anarchy, State and Utopia* (New York: Basic Books, 1974).

8 G.A. Cohen, 'On the Currency of Egalitarian Justice,' *Ethics* 99, no. 4 (1989): 906–44.

9 Richard Arneson, 'Equality and Equal Opportunity for Welfare,' *Philosophical Studies* 56 (1989): 77–93.

10 Ronald Dworkin, *Sovereign Virtue: The Theory and Practice of Equality* (Cambridge, MA: Harvard University Press, 2000).

11 Richard Arneson, 'What, If Anything, Renders All Humans Morally Equal,' in *Peter Singer and His Critics*, ed. Dale Jamieson (Oxford: Blackwell, 1999), 105–6.

12 Rawls, *A Theory of Justice*, 506.

13 Elizabeth Anderson, 'What Is the Point of Equality?' *Ethics* 99, no. 2 (1999): 287–337.

14 Samuel Scheffler, 'What Is Egalitarianism?' *Philosophy & Public Affairs* 31 (2003): 17–18.

15 Ibid., 31.

16 Rawls, *A Theory of Justice*, viii.

17 John Rawls, *Political Liberalism* (New York: Columbia University Press, 1993), 18.

18 For a very illuminating discussion of some of the ways that justice as fairness is appropriate for a constitutional democracy, see Joshua Cohen, 'For a Democratic Society,' in *The Cambridge Companion to Rawls,* ed. Samuel Freeman, 86–138 (Cambridge: Cambridge University Press, 2003).

19 Cohen thinks that Rawls may safely ignore this question without rendering the argument for liberal democracy unduly relativistic: 'In asking what the most reasonable conception of justice is for a democratic society, we answer a question of considerable importance: we address a disagreement among people who all accept an understanding of persons as equals but who dispute the implications of that understanding. In answering this question, we need not also decide whether the understanding of persons as equals is a compelling cultural assumption, or the most reasonable way to regard people, or a truth of religion or morality' (ibid., 88–9).

20 For contemporary liberal political philosophers such as Barry, Nagel, and Rawls, the relevant fact is one of '*reasonable*' pluralism, and not pluralism per se, but this is a mistake.

21 As Rawls says, we enter political society 'only by birth and exit only by death.' *Political Liberalism,* 68.

22 My argument *does not* commit me to the view that pluralism and coercion are exhaustive as defining features of politics. I have not addressed or, for that matter, tried to address the question 'what is politics?' I have argued only that, whatever else politics is, it is at least these two things, and that these things lead to the idea of democratic equality.

23 'Since the seventeenth century, finding a solution to this problem has been a major preoccupation of political philosophers. Bearing in mind that conflicting conceptions of the good are what create the problem, we may pose it by asking what might provide a form of argument capable of moving people to forgo or at any rate limit their pursuit of the good as they conceive it. The answers that I shall examine ... can all be (though they do not have to be) cast in the form of social contract theory. This is natural because the essence of a contract is that each of the contracting parties voluntarily accepts constraints on the pursuit of his own ends. And that is precisely what we are looking for: a mutually acceptable basis for restraint in the pursuit of one's conception of the good.' Brian Barry, *Justice as Impartiality* (Oxford: Oxford University Press, 1995), 31.

'Granted that politics is as often the scene of conflict as of cooperation, we are looking for principles to deal with conflict that can at some level be endorsed by everyone – principles that will both motivate and command respect and that will therefore give authority to results which are reached in accordance with them, even if those results do not in themselves command unanimous support. This sort of legitimacy is the ambition of thinkers as widely separated in their assumptions about human nature as Hobbes and Rousseau.' Thomas Nagel, *Equality and Partiality* (Oxford: Oxford University Press, 1991), 24.

'While political power is always coercive – backed by the government's monopoly of legitimate force – in a democratic regime it is also the power of the public, that is, the power of free and equal citizens as a corporate body. But if each citizen has an equal share in political power, then, so far as possible, political power should be exercised, at least when constitutional essentials and questions of basic justice are at stake, in ways that all citizens can publicly endorse in the light of their own reason. This is the principle of political legitimacy that justice as fairness is to satisfy.' John Rawls, *Justice as Fairness: A Restatement* (Cambridge, MA: Harvard University Press, 2000), 91.

'A social and political order is illegitimate unless it is rooted in the consent of all those who have to live under it; the consent or agreement of these people is a condition of its being morally permissible to enforce that order against them. (I shall state that here as a *necessary* condition, leaving open the possibility liberals may want to allow other things to vitiate political legitimacy besides lack of consent). Understood in this way, the liberal position provides a basis for arguing against some arrangement or institution inasmuch as one can show that it has not secured, or perhaps could not secure, the consent of the people. And it provides a basis for arguing in favor of an arrangement or institution if one can show that no social order which lacked this feature could possibly secure popular consent.' Jeremy Waldron, 'Locke, Toleration, and the Rationality of Persecution,' in *Liberal Rights: Collected Papers 1981–1991* (Cambridge: Cambridge University Press, 1993), 50.

24 Jürgen Habermas, 'Reconciliation through the Public Use of Reason: Remarks on John Rawls's *Political Liberalism*,' *Journal of Philosophy* 92 (1995): 128.

25 Glen Newey, *After Politics* (Basingstoke: Palgrave, 2001).

26 Ibid., 160.

27 Newey's argument that contemporary political liberalism, and normative theory generally, are anti-political relies on his own account of politics, which has three key features: (1) politics is marked by pervasive disagreement about what politics actually is, (2) even where/when agreement obtains about what politics actually is, endemic disagreement persists about how the mutually identified terrain should be interpreted, and, finally, (3) politics is about the use of power. Newey takes this account of politics to be both relatively uncontentious and problematic for liberal political thought, mostly because the latter's preoccupation with normative questions allegedly divorces it from how

and why power is actually exercised and distributed in the real world. While the world of politics is a Machiavellian one in which contingency reigns, liberalism retreats from that world in a Kantian effort to transcend contingency. As Paul Kelly points out, however, there are several problems with Newey's indictment: 'The first feature of politics, namely endemic conflict about what counts as politics, would seem to weaken Newey's argument immediately. The very concept of politics allows endemic disagreement about whether it is or is not a distinct and autonomous mode of experience or sphere of practice. If politics is what it is and not another thing, and people have construed it in as many and as conflicting ways as they have (even looking at only the western tradition of political thinking), then it is hard to see how we can support a non-arbitrary conception of the autonomy of the political. Why does Machiavelli represent the experience of politics any more than Kant, or, more importantly, Locke, Madison and Montesquieu, all of whom were aware of the darker side of politics, the realm of passion, unreason, force and power, as well as the brighter side of reason, agreement and the good of life?' *Liberalism* (Cambridge: Polity, 2005), 106. Newey is also wrong to think that endemic disagreement about the nature of politics precludes the normative vision of political liberalism. Even if we concede that Newey's own account of the political is accurate, his indictment does not flow from it – at best, all it precludes is elevating the normative vision of political liberalism into an *exclusive account* of the political. Political liberals can continue to defend the priority of their normative theories as important correctives to the contingencies of political power and inequality, provided that they are also willing to supplement those theories with other resources for institutional and constitutional design, *if* the normative theories do not already possess those resources. See Kelly, *Liberalism*, for a fuller rebuttal of Newey's case.

28 Newey develops this idea more forcefully than anyone else does, but several other critics join him in condemning political liberalism's *apolitical* tendencies. See John Gray, *Enlightenment's Wake* (London: Routledge, 1995); Gray, *Two Faces of Liberalism* (Cambridge: Polity, 2000); Bonnie Honig, *Political Theory and the Displacement of Politics* (Ithaca: Cornell University Press, 1993); and Chantal Mouffe, *The Return of the Political* (London: Verso, 1993).

29 Charles Larmore illustrates this point well in connection with ethically neutral principles of justice: 'Neutrality understood procedurally leaves open to a large extent the *goals* that the liberal state ought to pursue. Of course, some ends (e.g., the establishment of a state religion) are impermissible, because there can be no neutrally justifiable decision to pursue them. But any goals for whose pursuit there exists a neutral justification are ones that a liberal state may pursue. I do not think that the protection of life and property are the only

310 Notes to pages 196–7

goals that will satisfy this condition. The ideal of neutrality would not prevent a state from undertaking to ensure a particular pattern of wealth distribution, so long as the desirability of this pattern does not presuppose the superiority of some views of human flourishing over others held in society.' *Patterns of Moral Complexity* (Cambridge: Cambridge University Press, 1987), 44.

30 Scanlon, *What We Owe to Each Other,* 198–9.

31 I borrow this formulation from Brian Barry in *Justice as Impartiality,* 143.

32 This is exactly how Ronald Dworkin interprets Rawls: 'We must therefore treat the argument from the original position as ... a device for calling attention to some independent argument for the fairness of the two principles – an argument that does not rest on the false premise that a hypothetical contract has some pale binding force.' 'The Original Position,' 19.

33 See John Rawls, 'The Idea of Public Reason,' in *Deliberative Democracy: Essays on Reason and Politics,* ed. James Bohman and William Rehg, 93–130 (Cambridge, MA: MIT Press, 1997); and Rawls, 'The Idea of Public Reason Revisited,' in *Collected Papers,* ed. Samuel Freeman, 573–615 (Cambridge, MA: Harvard University Press, 1999).

34 See Amy Gutmann and Dennis Thompson, *Democracy and Disagreement* (Cambridge, MA: Harvard University Press, 1996).

35 Locke responds to this problem with a conception of political authority as 'umpire' that seems to weaken much of the force of Newey's critique of liberalism. See Gerald F. Gaus's discussion of the 'Lockean Solution' in his 'Reason, Justification and Consensus: Why Democracy Can't Have It All,' in *Deliberative Democracy,* ed. Bohman and Rehg, 205–42.

36 There are three general ways of relating deliberative procedures to political justification and legitimation. Some theorists, such as David Estlund, defend deliberative procedures in terms of their epistemic value. The idea is that under the right deliberative conditions, majority rule is the most reliable way of reaching collective decisions that track outcomes that are justified by process-independent standards. Other theorists, such as Joshua Cohen, defend the weaker epistemic claim that democratic procedures embody norms of reasonableness. Finally, there are defenders of fair proceduralism such as Gerald Gaus and Thomas Christiano. For them, public deliberation has instrumental value; it is an instrument for making informed and reasoned collective decisions. This yields a disjunctive procedural norm, which Christiano states as follows: 'Although public deliberation itself is not a requirement of justice on this account, when there is public deliberation, justice requires that each be able to participate as equals.' 'The Significance of Public Deliberation,' in *Deliberative Democracy,* ed. Bohman and Rehg, 258. I endorse a variant of fair proceduralism.

37 For a critique, see Jon Elster, 'The Market and the Forum: Three Varieties of Political Theory,' in *Deliberative Democracy*, ed. Bohman and Rehg, 205–42.

38 Joshua Cohen, 'Deliberation and Democratic Legitimacy,' in *Deliberative Democracy*, ed. Bohman and Rehg, 77. In chapter 10, we see this in connection with the distinction between the public and private spheres. While a liberal theory does draw a boundary between them, the boundary is not fixed pre-politically by a scheme of antecedently defined individual rights.

39 This fairness-based claim should not be confused with the civic republican or perfectionist one that human beings find their highest good fulfilled in and through politics.

40 I follow Charles Larmore, 'The Moral Basis of Political Liberalism,' *Journal of Philosophy* 96 (1999): 599–625.

41 Jürgen Habermas, 'Popular Sovereignty as Procedure,' in *Deliberative Democracy*, ed. Bohman and Rehg, 35–66.

42 As Larmore points out, there is a striking similarity between Habermas's conception of autonomy and Rawls's demand that political principles be free-standing. On the free-standingness of Rawlsian political principles, see chapter 8 below.

43 Larmore, 'The Moral Basis of Political Liberalism,' 614.

44 Ibid., 622.

8. Against the Epistemic Turn

1 To my knowledge, the most elaborate contemporary defence of the general relevance and centrality of cognitive psychology and epistemology to liberal theories of political justification has been made by Gerald F. Gaus: 'Given the actual disagreement in our Western societies over liberal ideals, it is manifest that justificatory liberalism cannot explicate "publicly acceptable" principles as those to which each and every member of our actual societies, in their actual positions, actually assent. If that is the test of public justification, justificatory liberalism is most unlikely to vindicate substantive liberal principles. Justificatory liberals require a *normative theory of justification* – a theory that allows them to claim that some set of principles is publicly justified, even given the fact that they are contested by some. And this, in turn, appears to call for a moral epistemology, in the sense of an account of the conditions for justified moral belief, or at lest justified adherence to social principles.' *Justificatory Liberalism: An Essay on Epistemology and Political Theory* (Oxford: Oxford University Press, 1996), 3. For defenders of what I am calling the reasonableness as fairness strategy of contractualism whose arguments have taken the epistemic turn in varying degrees, see Charles Larmore, 'Political Liberal-

ism,' in *The Morals of Modernity* (Cambridge: Cambridge University Press, 1996), 121–51; John Rawls, *Political Liberalism* (New York: Columbia University Press, 1993); and Rawls, *Justice as Fairness: A Restatement* (Cambridge, MA: Harvard University Press, 2001).

2   Rawls, *Political Liberalism*, 55–6.

3   Samuel Freeman, 'Introduction,' in *The Cambridge Companion to Rawls*, ed. Samuel Freeman, 1–61 (Cambridge: Cambridge University Press, 2003).

4   Rawls, *Political Liberalism*, 15.

5   'Considered judgments are simply those rendered under conditions favorable to the exercise of the sense of justice, and therefore in circumstances where the more common excuses and explanations for making a mistake do not obtain. The person making the judgment is presumed, then, to have the ability, the opportunity, and the desire to reach a correct decision (or at least, not the desire not to).' John Rawls, *A Theory of Justice* (Cambridge, MA: Harvard University Press, 1971), 48.

6   Ibid., viii.

7   See Rawls, *Political Liberalism*, 16–19.

8   Ibid., 16.

9   As we shall see, while the features themselves remain largely unchanged from *Theory* to *Political Liberalism*, both their underlying justification and presentation are altered. The Kantian (comprehensive) doctrine of moral persons in *Theory* is transformed into the (political) conception of democratic citizenship in *Political Liberalism*.

10 Rawls, *A Theory of Justice*, 505.

11 In this section, we outline Rawls's argument *for* the social contract by establishing the connection between it and the ideals of social cooperation and person that lead to it; in the next, we outline his argument *from* the original position to the two principles of justice. This analytical distinction is useful because, as Charles Larmore suggests, readers of *A Theory of Justice* 'ought to wonder more than they do about the contractarian form in which Rawls presents his theory of justice as fairness.' 'Public Reason,' in *The Cambridge Companion to Rawls*, ed. Samuel Freeman (Cambridge: Cambridge University Press, 2003), 369.

12 Rawls, *Justice as Fairness*, 16.

13 See section 40 of *A Theory of Justice* for Rawls's Kantian interpretation of the original position: 'To express one's nature as a being of a particular kind is to act on the principles that would be chosen if this nature were the decisive determining element' (253).

14 Rawls links publicity to a reciprocal ideal of community as early as 1958: 'A practice is just or fair, then, when it satisfies the principles which those who

participate in it could propose to one another for mutual acceptance ... Persons engaged in a just, or fair, practice can face one another openly and support their respective positions, should they appear questionable, by reference to principles which it is reasonable to expect each to accept ... Only if such acknowledgment is possible can there be true community between persons in their common practices; otherwise their relations will appear to them as founded to some extent on force.' 'Justice as Fairness,' in *Collected Papers*, ed. Samuel Freeman (Cambridge, MA: Harvard University Press, 1999), 59.

15 Rawls, *A Theory of Justice*, 16.

16 Ibid., 13.

17 Rawls, *Justice as Fairness*, 15.

18 'In searching for the most favored description of [the original position] we work from both ends. We begin by describing it so that it represents generally shared and preferably weak conditions. We then see if these conditions are strong enough to yield a significant set of principles. If not, we look for further premises equally reasonable. But if so, and these principles match our considered convictions of justice, then so far well and good. But presumably there will be discrepancies. In this case we have a choice. We can either modify the account of the initial situation or we can revise our existing judgments, for even the judgments we take provisionally as fixed points are liable to revision. By going back and forth, sometimes altering the conditions of the contractual circumstances, at others withdrawing our judgments and conforming them to principle, I assume that eventually we shall find a description of the initial situation that both expresses reasonable conditions and yields principles which match our considered judgments duly pruned and adjusted. This state of affairs I refer to as reflective equilibrium.' Rawls, *A Theory of Justice*, 20. For a recent survey of the influence that this idea has had on contemporary political philosophy in the English-speaking world, see Wayne Norman's excellent discussion of it in 'Inevitable and Unacceptable? Methodological Rawlsianism in Anglo-American Political Philosophy,' *Political Studies* 96 (1998): 276–94.

19 This latest formulation of the two principles in *Justice as Fairness* (42) corrects the initial presentation of them found in *Theory* in order to respond to a number of objections raised by H.L.A. Hart in his critical review essay 'Rawls on Liberty and Its Priority,' *University of Chicago Law Review* 40 (1973): 551–5.

20 Rawls, *A Theory of Justice*, 62.

21 Since the publication of *A Theory of Justice*, much of the criticism directed at justice as fairness has focused on the question of whether or not socio-economic inequalities deriving from differences in natural talents or luck – those allegedly arbitrary from a moral point of view – are, in fact, undeserved and

therefore illegitimate. For a recent interpretation of Rawls that locates the value of redressing undeserved inequalities entirely *within* a normative ideal of democratic citizenship, rather than inferring that value from the putative cosmic unfairness of such inequalities themselves, see Samuel Scheffler, 'What Is Egalitarianism?' *Philosophy & Public Affairs* 31, no. 1 (2002): 5–39.

22 Rawls, *A Theory of Justice*, 5.

23 Ibid., 176.

24 'The principles of justice apply to the basic structure of the social system and to the determination of life prospects. What the principle of utility asks is precisely a sacrifice of these prospects. We are to accept the greater advantages of others as a sufficient reason for lower expectations over the whole course of our life. This is surely an extreme demand. In fact, when society is conceived as a system of cooperation designed to advance the good of its members, it seems quite incredible that some citizens should be expected, on the basis of political principles, to accept lower prospects of life for the sake of others. It is evident why utilitarians should stress the role of sympathy in moral learning and the central place of benevolence among the moral virtues. Their conception of justice is threatened with instability unless sympathy and benevolence can be widely and intensely cultivated' (ibid., 178).

'While persons in the original position take no interest in one another's interests, they know that they have (or may have) certain moral and religious interests and other cultural ends which they cannot put in jeopardy ... They do not have an agreed criterion of perfection that can be used as a principle for choosing between institutions. To acknowledge any such standard would be, in effect, to accept a principle that might lead to a lesser religious or other liberty, if not to a loss of freedom altogether to advance many of one's spiritual ends.' Rawls, *A Theory of Justice*, 327.

25 Ibid., 454.

26 Ibid., 499.

27 Ibid., 574.

28 See Samuel Freeman, 'Congruence and the Good of Justice,' in *The Cambridge Companion to Rawls*, ed. Samuel Freeman, 277–315 (Cambridge: Cambridge University Press).

29 Rawls calls this 'the fact of oppression': 'If we think of political society as a community united in affirming one and the same comprehensive doctrine, then the oppressive use of state power is necessary for political community. In the society of the Middle Ages, more or less united in affirming the Catholic faith, the Inquisition was not an accident; its suppression of heresy was needed to preserve that shared religious belief. The same holds, I believe, for any reasonable comprehensive philosophical and moral doctrine, whether

religious or non-religious. A society united on a reasonable form of utilitarianism, or on the reasonable liberalisms of Kant or Mill, would likewise require the sanctions of state power to remain so. Call this "the fact of oppression."' *Political Liberalism*, 37. The same applies, with equal force, to justice-as-fairness as initially presented in *A Theory of Justice.*

30 Rawls, *Political Liberalism*, 10.

31 Ibid., 11.

32 Ibid., 13.

33 Rawls, *Justice as Fairness*, 61.

34 Thomas Nagel, 'Rawls and Liberalism,' in *The Cambridge Companion to Rawls*, ed. Samuel Freeman (Cambridge: Cambridge University Press, 2003), 84.

35 Rawls, *Justice as Fairness*, 89.

36 Rawls later adopts a broader conception of public reason in which citizens may argue about constitutional essentials and matters of basic justice by appealing to non-political (partial or fully comprehensive) values provided that, in due course, political arguments are subsequently introduced to support their claims. See the discussion of this proviso in Rawls, 'The Idea of Public Reason Revisited,' in *Collected Papers*, ed. Samuel Freeman (Cambridge, MA: Harvard University Press, 1999), 584.

37 Rawls, *Political Liberalism*, 115.

38 Ibid., 50.

39 Ibid., 57.

40 Ibid., 59.

41 Ibid., 61.

42 Ibid., 62.

43 Ibid., 57.

44 Ibid., 59.

45 Ibid., 6.

46 Careful readers will probably wonder why characteristic 3 does not appear under the second aspect, given that it refers to reasonable comprehensive *doctrines*, and this tends to suggest that the underlying notion is an epistemic one. However, the only distinguishing feature of such doctrines aside from the three formal ones sketched above is that they are compatible with a (moral) political conception of justice. The circularity of the overlapping consensus argument for stability escapes us unless we notice this.

47 Rawls, *Political Liberalism*, 64–5; emphasis mine.

48 The first aspect is modelled by the reasonable constraints placed upon deliberators in the original position, while the second aspect limits what can be justified through the use of public reason.

49 See Ajume H. Wingo, *Veil Politics in Liberal Democratic States* (Cambridge: Cam-

bridge University Press, 2003), for the motivational limitations of constitutional principles and for the essential role of non-rational, emotive, and aesthetic factors in sustaining liberal-democratic institutions.

50 Rawls, *Political Liberalism*, 50.

51 Thomas Scanlon, *What We Owe to Each Other* (Cambridge, MA: Harvard University Press, 1998), 153.

52 Ibid., 170.

53 Ibid., 168. Charles Larmore is one important contemporary political liberal who conceives of the motivation underpinning contractual justification in related terms. See his discussion of equal respect in 'The Moral Basis of Political Liberalism,' *Journal of Philosophy* 96 (1999): 599–625.

54 Scanlon, *What We Owe to Each Other*, 195.

55 Ibid.

56 Ibid., 204.

57 'Generic reasons are reasons that we can see that people have in virtue of their situation, characterized in general terms, and such things as their aims and capabilities and the conditions in which they are placed. Not everyone is affected by a given principle in the same way, and generic reasons are not limited to reasons that the majority of people have. If even a small number of people would be adversely affected by a general permission for agents to act a certain way, then this gives rise to a potential reason for rejecting that principle. (This is a generic reason since it is one that we can see people have in virtue of certain general characteristics; it is not attributed to specific individuals.)' (ibid., 204–5).

9. Beyond the Basic Structure

1 George Sher, *Beyond Neutrality: Perfectionism and Politics* (Cambridge: Cambridge University Press, 1997).

2 The last sentence of Thomas Hurka's 'Review of *Beyond Neutrality: Perfectionism and Politics*' reads, 'As one finishes [Sher's] book, it is hard not to believe that the period of neutralist liberalism is now over.' *Ethics* 109, no. 1 (1998): 190.

3 Richard Arneson, 'Liberal Neutrality on the Good: An Autopsy,' in *Perfectionism and Neutrality: Essays in Liberal Theory*, ed. George Klosko and Steven Wall, 191–208 (New York: Rowman and Littlefield, 2003).

4 See Jeremy Waldron, 'Autonomy and Perfectionism in Raz's *The Morality of Freedom*,' *Southern California Law Review* 62 (1989): 1097–1152.

5 Brian Barry, *Justice as Impartiality* (Oxford: Oxford University Press, 1995), 161.

6 See Arneson's critique of Barry: 'We can fix a school curriculum by appealing only to neutral conceptions of people's individual rights coupled with uncontroversial ideals of the good. If everyone agrees that basic literacy and mathematical competency is good, we can appeal to the idea that it is fair that every person have fair opportunity to attain some reasonable threshold level of literacy and mathematic competence, and run public schools on this basis.' 'Liberal Neutrality on the Good: An Autopsy,' 29–30. More controversial subjects might be dealt with in the manner described by Mill: 'All attempts by the State to bias the conclusions of its citizens on disputed subjects are evil; but it may very properly offer to ascertain and certify that a person possesses the knowledge requisite to make his conclusions, on any given subject, worth attending to. A student of philosophy would be the better for being able to stand an examination both in Locke and in Kant, whichever of the two he takes up with, or even if with neither: and there is no reasonable objection to examining an atheist in the evidences of Christianity, provided he is not required to profess a belief in them.' *On Liberty and Other Writings* (Oxford: Oxford University Press, 1981), 119.

7 This distinction between rules and ethos appears in G.A. Cohen, *If You're an Egalitarian, How Come You're So Rich?* (Cambridge, MA: Harvard University Press, 2000). Cohen thinks of ethos in terms of attitudes and values that inform individual choices, and not necessarily political ones, so his meaning of the term is something different from mine. I examine the plausibility of his suggestion that (Rawlsian) liberalism presupposes a personal ethos that is inconsistent with the public acceptance of its political principles, or rules, in chapter 10.

8 W.D. Ross, *The Right and the Good* (Oxford: Oxford University Press, 1930).

9 We identify conceptions of the good not by ascertaining whether or not our ends satisfy certain cognitive standards, but rather by the expressive, symbolic, and functional roles they invariably play in defining who we all are as individual persons. Dworkin makes the point as follows: 'Each person follows a more-or-less articulate conception of what gives value to life. The scholar who values a life of contemplation has such a conception; so does the television-watching, beer-drinking citizen who is fond of saying "This is the life," though he has thought less about the issue and is less able to describe or defend his conception.' *A Matter of Principle* (Cambridge, MA: Harvard University Press, 1985), 191.

10 'Whatever conception of human good is appealed to in defending liberal institutions, it is one that reflects values any reasonable person could accept as the basis of moral claims; and that implies only that, whatever the effects of these institutions, they can be justified in terms of these values.' Peter De

Marneffe, 'Liberalism, Liberty, and Neutrality,' *Philosophy & Public Affairs* 19, no. 3 (1990): 254.

11 Rawls's 'primary goods' are one particularly well-developed example of what such interests might consist of. See his *A Theory of Justice* (Cambridge, MA: Harvard University Press, 1971); and *Political Liberalism* (New York: Columbia University Press, 1993).

12 In the literature, these three formulations are widely referred to as *consequential*, *intentional*, and *justificatory* neutrality, respectively.

13 One important exception is found in Robert Goodin and Andrew Reeve, 'Liberalism and Neutrality,' in *Liberal Neutrality*, ed. Robert Goodin and Andrew Reeve, 1–8 (London: Routledge, 1989); and Goodin and Reeve, 'Do Neutral Institutions Add Up to a Neutral State?' in *Liberal Neutrality*, ed. Goodin and Reeve, 193–210.

14 See Will Kymlicka, 'Liberal Individualism and Liberal Neutrality,' *Ethics* 99 (1989): 883–905.

15 'If a constitutional regime takes certain steps to strengthen the virtues of toleration and mutual trust, say by discouraging various kinds of religious and racial discrimination (in ways consistent with liberty of conscience and freedom of speech), it does not thereby become a perfectionist state of the kind found in Plato or Aristotle, nor does it establish a particular religion as in the Catholic or Protestant states of the early modern period. Rather, it is taking reasonable measures to strengthen the forms of thought and feeling that sustain fair social cooperation between its citizens regarded as free and equal. This is very different from the state's advancing a particular comprehensive doctrine in its own name.' Rawls, *Political Liberalism*, 195.

16 One problem that N3 confronts is the question of how exactly we are supposed to identify *the* justification for any particular piece of legislation or public policy, given the fact that different members of the democratic majority that enacted it will clearly have different and potentially incompatible reasons for supporting it. There are a few potential solutions to the problem of extending a motive or intention-based account of justification that is naturally well-suited to individual moral agents to collectivities of such agents, or to the state as a whole. We could say, for instance, that a law or public policy is (neutrally) justified if it is, in principle, susceptible to some ethically neutral justification. This formulation is far too weak, however, because almost any law or policy can be presented so that its justification satisfies it, regardless of the actual reasons underlying its adoption. Because democratic citizens owe one another neutral justifications for policies that adversely affect the interests of any of their number, we must ultimately be concerned instead with the actual reasons underlying their political proposals. The difficulty we

noted above with identifying people's actual reasons (individually or collectively) implies that justificatory neutrality at level 2 (after constitutional essentials have been settled at level 2) will be a matter of democratic ethos, not law. In this view, a law or policy that fulfils N3 will be one initiated, framed, and enforced on the basis of sincerely held neutral justifications.

17 Goodin and Reeve express this point as follows: 'Our goal is badly described by saying that the state should assist all citizens neutrally; rather, our goal is that the state assist all its citizens, neutrally. The goal is assistance.' 'Do Neutral Institutions Add Up to a Neutral State?' 201. Indeed, if N3 were itself the goal, the liberal state might actually satisfy it through even-handed indifference.

10. How Political Is the Personal?

1 On the distinction between agent-neutral and agent-relative reasons, see Thomas Nagel, *The View from Nowhere* (Oxford: Oxford University Press, 1986); and *Equality and Partiality* (Oxford: Oxford University Press, 1991). See also Samuel Scheffler's discussion of 'agent-centered prerogatives' in *The Rejection of Consequentialism* (Oxford: Clarendon, 1994); and *Boundaries and Allegiances: Problems of Justice and Responsibility in Liberal Thought* (Oxford: Oxford University Press, 2001).

2 See, for example, Matthew Clayton, *Justice and Legitimacy in Upbringing* (Oxford: Oxford University Press, 2006).

3 Susan Okin attributes this view to Rawls, but it is unclear whether he endorses it, or else something closer to the view defended here. See her *Justice, Gender and the Family* (New York: Basic, 1989), and Rawls's remarks on the family in 'The Idea of Public Reason Revisited,' in *Collected Papers*, ed. Samuel Freeman, 573–615 (Cambridge, MA: Harvard University Press, 1999).

4 Thomas Scanlon discusses this at some length in *What We Owe to Each Other* (Cambridge, MA: Harvard University Press, 1998).

5 As I have argued throughout this book, this discontinuity is one of the central features of the contractual view of political legitimacy.

6 This formulation is found in Nagel's *Equality and Partiality*; Rawls calls the idea an 'institutional division of labor'; Dworkin defends a similar claim in 'The Foundations of Liberal Equality,' in *The Tanner Lectures on Human Values*, 1–119 (Salt Lake City: University of Utah Press, 1990); and *Sovereign Virtue: The Theory and Practice of Equality* (Cambridge, MA: Harvard University Press, 2000).

7 Rawls, *Political Liberalism*, 268–9.

8 Dworkin, 'Foundations of Liberal Equality,' 292.

9 Nagel, *Equality and Partiality*, 117.
10 I borrow this formulation from Michael Ignatieff's vivid portrayal of the moral relations between citizens living in welfare states: 'As we stand together in line at the post office, while [old-age pensioners] cash their pension cheques, some tiny portion of my income is transferred into their pockets through the numberless capillaries of the state. The mediated quality of our relationship seems necessary to both of us. They are dependent on the state, not upon me, and we are both glad of it. Yet I am also aware of how this mediation walls us off from each other. We are responsible for each other, but we are not responsible to each other.' *The Needs of Strangers* (London: Vintage, 1984), 9–10.
11 Nagel describes the problem as follows: 'What we need is an institutional structure which will evoke the requisite partition of motives, allowing everyone to be publicly egalitarian and privately partial. *The trouble is that this is a pipe dream.* If we try to imagine actual institutions that would realize it, we encounter overwhelming problems – problems concerning the legal and the economic character of the necessary arrangements, and the political and economic motives necessary to sustain them.' *Equality and Partiality*, 86; emphasis mine.
12 In considering G.A. Cohen's and Liam Murphy's critiques of Rawls, Thomas W. Pogge notices that 'following Parfit, Cohen and Murphy like to express moral views in terms of goals or aims rather than, say, constraints or duties.' Pogge does not 'find the choice of language innocent. It creates a drift toward consequentialist reasoning, to which both authors are already sympathetic.' 'On the Site of Distributive Justice: Reflections on Cohen and Murphy,' *Philosophy & Public Affairs* 29, no. 2 (2000): 138n2.
13 Peter Singer, for example, defends this 'simple' solution to world poverty: 'Whatever money you're spending on luxuries, not necessities, should be given away.' 'The Singer Solution to World Poverty,' in *Writings on an Ethical Life* (New York: Ecco, 2000), 123. This implies that the average American household should give away any annual income over $30,000 (1999 value).
14 Liam B. Murphy, 'Institutions and the Demands of Justice,' *Philosophy & Public Affairs* 27, no. 4 (1999): 251–91.
15 G.A. Cohen calls Rawls's limitation of the principles of justice to the basic structure of society 'arbitrary' and 'lame.' See 'Where the Action Is: On the Site of Distributive Justice,' *Philosophy & Public Affairs* 26, no. 1 (1997): 23–4. Murphy concurs: 'Where people live within the domain of justice they must concern themselves with the substantive political/moral aim expressed in the principles of justice, be that the aim of equality, the aim of increasing weighted well-being, or some other aim. It is not credible that what funda-

mentally matters is that the relevant institutions promote equality or well-being, rather than that equality or well-being be promoted.' 'Institutions and the Demands of Justice,' 283.

16 See Karl Marx, 'On the Jewish Question,' in *Karl Marx: Selected Writings*, ed. David McLellan (Oxford: Oxford University Press, 1977), 39–62.

17 See G.A. Cohen, 'Incentives, Inequality and Community,' in *The Tanner Lectures on Human Values*, ed. G.B. Petersen, 262–329 (Salt Lake City: University of Utah Press, 1992); 'The Pareto Argument for Inequality,' *Social Philosophy and Policy* 12 (1995): 160–85; 'Where the Action Is,' 3–30; and *If You're an Egalitarian, How Come You're So Rich?* (Cambridge, MA: Harvard University Press, 2000).

18 While Cohen's critique focuses specifically on Rawls, its implications are much broader because the difference principle is only one prominent version of the oldest and still most influential justification of economic inequality – incentives are required to stimulate greater effort, efficiency, and thus productivity; this requires inequality; the resulting increased productivity generated by inequality benefits (or at least can be made to benefit) even those on the losing end of it. Locke illustrates the claim like this: 'There cannot be a clearer demonstration of any thing, than several nations of the *Americans* are of this, who are rich in land, and poor in all the comforts of life; whom nature having furnished as liberally as any other people, with the materials of plenty, i.e., a fruitful soil, apt to produce in abundance, what might serve for food, raiment, and delight; yet *for want of improving it by labour,* have not one hundredth part of the conveniences we enjoy: *and a king of a large and fruitful territory there, feeds, lodges, and is clad worse than a day-labourer in England.*' *The Second Treatise of Government,* in *Political Writings*, ed. David Wootton (London: Penguin, 1993), 25–6; last emphasis mine.

19 Cohen, *If You're an Egalitarian*, 126–7.

20 Ibid., 3.

21 Catharine MacKinnon, *Women's Lives*Men's Laws* (Cambridge, MA: Harvard University Press, 2005), 34.

22 See Cohen, *If You're an Egalitarian*, 22.

23 Nagel, *Equality and Partiality*, 24–5.

24 Cohen, *If You're an Egalitarian*, 118.

25 Liam Murphy, himself a critic of the institutional approach, agrees: 'To say otherwise seems to deny the reality of the family as a special social form; it would be to make any identifiable pattern of behavior in society, such as a major tendency to self-seeking behavior, as much of an institution as the family is.' *Institutions and the Demands of Justice*, 269.

26 The relevant publications are Joshua Cohen, 'Taking People as They Are,'

Philosophy & Public Affairs 30, no. 4 (2001): 363–86; David Estlund, 'Liberalism, Equality and Fraternity in Cohen's Critique of Rawls,' *Journal of Political Philosophy* 6, no. 1 (1998): 99–112; Thomas W. Pogge, 'On the Site of Distributive Justice: Reflections on Cohen and Murphy,' *Philosophy & Public Affairs* 29, no. 2 (2000): 137–69; Kok-Chor Tan, 'Justice and Personal Pursuits,' *Journal of Philosophy* 101, no. 7 (2004): 331–62; and Andrew Williams, 'Incentives, Inequality, and Publicity,' *Philosophy & Public Affairs* 27, no. 3 (1998): 225–47.

27 Even G.A. Cohen agrees: 'Only an extreme moral rigorist would deny that *every person has a right to pursue self-interest to some reasonable extent* (even when that makes things worse than they need be for badly off people). I do not wish to reject the italicized principle, which affirms what Samuel Scheffler has called an "agent-centered prerogative."' 'Incentives, Inequality, and Community,' 370–1.

28 For an argument that state neutrality between conceptions of the good requires an unconditional basic income, see Philippe Van Parijs, 'Why Surfers Should be Fed: The Liberal Case for an Unconditional Basic Income,' *Philosophy and Public Affairs* 20, no. 2 (1991): 101–31; and Van Parijs, *Real Freedom for All: What (If Anything) Can Justify Capitalism?* (Oxford: Oxford University Press, 1995).

29 For recent exceptions, see David Archard and Colin M. MacLeod, eds., *The Moral and Political Status of Children* (Oxford: Oxford University Press, 2002), especially MacLeod, 'Liberal Equality and the Affective Family,' 212–31; and Matthew Clayton, *Justice and Legitimacy in Upbringing* (Oxford: Oxford University Press, 2006).

30 Nagel, *Equality and Partiality,* 120.

31 Rawls, *Political Liberalism,* 174.

32 John Stuart Mill, *The Subjection of Women,* ed. John Gray (Oxford: Oxford University Press, 1998), 558–9.

33 In *A Theory of Justice* (Cambridge, MA: Harvard University Press, 1971), Rawls emphasizes the importance of loving parenting for the development of a sense of justice.

34 The term *ethos* is becoming widely used, but the best description is Jonathan Wolff's in 'Fairness, Respect, and the Egalitarian Ethos,' *Philosophy & Public Affairs* 27, no. 2 (1998): 97–122, which I borrow.

35 The distinction is Thomas W. Pogge's. See 'On the Site of Distributive Justice,' 155–6.

36 G.A. Cohen, 'Incentives, Inequality, and Community,' 370–1. *How* this claim is consistent with the direct/lexical constraint modes of applying equality to personal choice (which appears to be Cohen's view) is very unclear.

37 Samuel Scheffler, 'The Conflict between Justice and Responsibility,' in

Boundaries and Allegiances: Problems of Justice and Responsibility in Liberal Thought (Oxford: Oxford University Press, 2001), 85–6. See, in particular, Scheffler's discussion of the 'distributive objection' to associative duties throughout this collection.

38 Or so G.A Cohen maintains. See *If You're an Egalitarian*, 144.

39 This would be equally devastating for Marxists.

40 I follow Kok-Chor Tan, who distinguishes between '*individual* choices in general and *personal* choices in particular.' 'Justice and Personal Pursuits,' 336.

41 See J. Cohen's 'Taking People as They Are' for this interpretation of Rawls's difference principle.

42 Tan, 'Justice and Personal Pursuits,' 373.

43 A point emphasized by Estlund, Tan, and Williams.

44 Rawls, 'The Idea of Public Reason Revisited,' 600.

45 This construction of the family and its sources of value follow Colin MacLeod in 'Liberal Equality and the Affective Family,' except for his stipulation that a family requires children, which needlessly excludes couples who choose not to or cannot procreate.

46 Ibid., 226.

47 Ibid.

48 As an aside, I find it bizarre that so many Canadians (in conversation) link citizenship and health care in order to condemn private medicine, while refusing to draw the parallel link between citizenship and private education. If the fact that 'we are all Canadians' somehow implies that we should all have access to the same health care, then why doesn't this civic consideration similarly undermine the case for private schools? We spend *more* time in schools, during the *most* formative periods of our lives, so they probably exert much more influence on both our personal and civic identities. If the Reciprocal Identity Formation Thesis is sound, I doubt that it applies any less to the educational system.

49 See Thomas Nagel, 'Concealment and Exposure,' *Philosophy & Public Affairs* 27, no. 1 (1998): 3–30; and Ferdinand Schoeman, 'The Rights of Children, Rights of Parents, and the Moral Basis of the Family,' *Ethics* 91 (1980): 6–19.

50 MacKinnon, *Women's Lives*Men's Laws*, 122.

51 John Tomasi has recently challenged this claim by noting that the 'interface' between the public and non-public domains in liberal societies undermines any attempt to restrict the boundaries of normative political theory to questions about justified state coercion. For him, political liberalism crucially depends upon the domains of ethical and political value working tightly in conjunction: 'An awareness of political rights cannot help but play a role in structuring the self-understandings of liberal citizens throughout their lives.

324 Notes to page 266

In this sense principles of justice *are* applied directly to the internal life of families and other nonpublic associations. Rights do not simply "impose essential constraints" on such groupings: rights provide the supports across which nonpublic groupings in liberal societies are built. Our point of view as citizens *cannot* be distinguished in any clean way from our point of view as members of families and other nonpublic groups. Rather, our nonpublic points of view always include our shared public point of view as an essential constituent part. And, crucially, a nonpublic domain or space is *not* simply the upshot of how principles of justice are applied through the various branches of law. In a liberal society, every nonpublic domain or space is the upshot of how the claims of right set out by various branches of law are *interpreted and applied* by individuals seeking meaning and value in their lives.' *Liberalism beyond Justice: Citizens, Society, and the Boundaries of Political Theory* (Princeton: Princeton University Press, 2001), 54.

In places, Tomasi describes this interface in ways quite similar to the reciprocal identityformation thesis. However, from his diagnostic claim about the interpenetration of the personal and the political, he infers a conception of liberal citizenship, and ultimately of politics, that should be rejected. There are multiple ways that political principles might apply to the personal point of view, so even if Tomasi's analysis is correct. this does not automatically generate support for direct application, which is undesirable for the reasons enumerated above. In my view, what the reciprocal identity formation thesis shows is that what counts as political and is accordingly subject to collectively enforceable norms must itself be expanded to include various things henceforth deemed private or personal and thus beyond the reach of the state. This preserves the traditional Lockean conception of liberalism as a doctrine about the justification of state power – as opposed to a view about ethical well-being – but it expands the scope of public reason. For Tomasi, on the other hand, the criteria of good citizen conduct and virtue are not strictly or exclusively derivable from liberal justice or the norms of public reason: 'To be a good citizen is to be a good *person*' (71). Tomasi's project of elaborating a non-public liberal reason is actually similar, at least in motivation, to Ronald Dworkin's thin or structural perfectionism, and I think that it also fails. See my discussion in chapter 5 above.

Conclusion

1 As we saw in chapter 5, Ronald Dworkin is one liberal who defends this holism, one that is supposed to appeal to 'people who want a more integrated moral experience, who want their politics to match their convictions about

what it is to live well, rather than requiring them to set these convictions aside, to check them at the voting-booth door.' 'The Foundations of Liberal Equality,' in *The Tanner Lectures on Human Values* (Salt Lake City: University of Utah Press, 1990), 20. I have argued that this is a mistake, philosophically, because the positions that Dworkin (and Raz) wants to defend cannot be logically derived from the challenge model, and politically, because, on his argument, anyone who rejects the challenge model will *pro tanto* also reject liberalism.

2 I say 'likely,' because this book has sought primarily to develop and refine the contractual argument for liberalism. The next step is to see, in concrete terms, what legal and policy reforms the view yields. I only hint at some of these here.

3 It should go without saying that one's offence at the sight or thought of those activities cannot, itself, be counted as a negative externality – no free society can recognize a right not to be offended.

4 Witness the deference often shown to parental autonomy when urgent medical treatment is required for children, but which also violates their parents' cultural or religious beliefs and practices.

5 Brian Barry's 'sceptical uncertainty' and Rawls's 'burdens of judgment' are two notorious examples.

6 Thomas Nagel, 'Concealment and Exposure,' *Philosophy & Public Affairs* 27, no. 1 (1998): 10.

Bibliography

Aarsleff, Hans. 'The State of Nature and the Nature of Man in Locke.' In *John Locke: Problems and Perspectives*, edited by John W. Yolton, 99–136. Cambridge: Cambridge University Press, 1969.

Alexander, Larry. 'Pursuing the Good – Indirectly.' *Ethics* 95 (1995): 315–32.

Anderson, Elizabeth. 'What Is the Point of Equality?' *Ethics* 99, no. 2 (1999): 287–337.

Archard, David, and Colin M. MacLeod, eds. *The Moral and Political Status of Children*. Oxford: Oxford University Press, 2002.

Arneson, Richard. 'Equality and Equal Opportunity for Welfare.' *Philosophical Studies* 56 (1989): 77–93.

– 'Liberalism, Distributive Subjectivism, and Equal Opportunity for Welfare.' *Philosophy & Public Affairs* 19 (1990): 138–94.

– 'What, If Anything, Renders All Humans Morally Equal.' In *Peter Singer and His Critics*, edited by Dale Jamieson, 103–28. Oxford: Blackwell, 1999.

– 'Welfare Should Be the Currency of Justice.' *Canadian Journal of Philosophy* 30, no. 4 (2000): 477–524.

– 'Perfectionism and Politics.' *Ethics* 111, no. 1 (2000): 37–63.

– 'Liberal Neutrality on the Good: An Autopsy.' In *Perfectionism and Neutrality: Essays in Liberal Theory*, edited by George Klosko and Steven Wall, 191–208. New York: Rowman and Littlefield, 2003.

– 'The Cracked Foundations of Liberal Equality.' In *Ronald Dworkin and His Critics*, edited by Justine Burley, 79–98. Oxford: Blackwell, 2005.

Ashcraft, Richard. 'Locke's State of Nature: Historical Fact or Moral Fiction?' *American Political Science Review* 62 (1968): 898–915.

– 'John Locke's Library: Portrait of an Intellectual.' *Transactions of the Cambridge Bibliographical Society* 5 (1969): 47–60.

– *Revolutionary Politics and Locke's Two Treatises of Government*. Princeton: Princeton University Press, 1986.

Bain, Alexander. *John Stuart Mill: A Criticism.* London: Longmans, 1882.

Barry, Brian. *Justice as Impartiality.* Oxford: Oxford University Press, 1995.

Bellamy, Richard. 'T.H. Green, J.S. Mill, and Isaiah Berlin on the Nature of Liberty and Liberalism.' In *Jurisprudence: Cambridge Essays*, edited by H. Gross and R. Harrison, 257–85. Oxford: Clarendon, 1992.

Bentham, Jeremy. *An Introduction to the Principles of Morals and Legislation*, edited by J.H. Burns and H.L.A. Hart. London: Athlone, 1970.

Berger, Fred. *Happiness, Justice and Freedom: The Moral and Political Philosophy of John Stuart Mill.* Berkeley: University of California Press, 1984.

Berkowitz, Peter. 'Liberty, Virtue, and the Discipline of Individuality.' In *Mill and the Moral Character of Liberalism*, edited by E.J. Eisenach, 13–48. University Park: Penn State University Press, 1988.

Berlin, Isaiah. 'John Stuart Mill and the Ends of Life.' In *Four Essays on Liberty*, 173–206. Oxford: Oxford University Press, 1969.

Bohman, James, and William Rehg, eds. *Deliberative Democracy: Essays on Reason and Politics.* Cambridge, MA: MIT Press, 1997.

Bourne, H.R. Fox. *The Life of John Locke.* 2 vols. London: Knight, 1876.

Brandt, Richard B. *A Theory of the Good and of the Right.* Oxford: Clarendon, 1979.

– *Morality, Utilitarianism, and Rights.* Cambridge: Cambridge University Press, 1992.

Brink, David O. 'Mill's Deliberative Utilitarianism.' *Philosophy and Public Affairs* 21 (1992): 67–103.

Brown, D.G. 'Mill on Liberty and Morality.' *Philosophical Review* 81 (1972): 135–58.

Caney, Simon. 'Anti-perfectionism and Rawlsian Liberalism.' *Political Studies* 42 (1995): 5–42.

Capaldi, Nicholas. *John Stuart Mill: A Biography.* Cambridge: Cambridge University Press, 2004.

Chan, Joseph. 'Legitimacy, Unanimity and Perfectionism.' *Philosophy & Public Affairs* 29, no. 1 (2000): 5–42.

Christiano, Thomas. 'The Significance of Public Deliberation.' In *Deliberative Democracy: Essays on Reason and Politics*, edited by James Bohman and William Rehg, 243–78. Cambridge, MA: MIT Press, 1997.

Cicovacki, P. 'Locke on Mathematical Knowledge.' *Journal of the History of Philosophy* 28 (1990): 511–24.

Clarke, Simon. 'Contractarianism, Liberal Neutrality, and Epistemology.' *Political Studies*, 47, no. 1 (1999): 627–42.

Clayton, Matthew. 'Liberal Equality and Ethics.' *Ethics* 113, no. 1 (2002): 8–22.

– *Justice and Legitimacy in Upbringing.* Oxford: Oxford University Press, 2006.

Cohen, G.A. 'On the Currency of Egalitarian Justice.' *Ethics* 99, no. 4 (1989): 906–44.

– 'Incentives, Inequality and Community.' In *The Tanner Lectures on Human Values*, edited by G.B. Petersen, 262–329. Salt Lake City: University of Utah Press, 1992.

– 'The Pareto Argument for Inequality.' *Social Philosophy & Policy* 12 (1995): 160–85.

– 'Where the Action Is: On the Site of Distributive Justice.' *Philosophy & Public Affairs* 26, no. 1 (1997): 3–30.

– *If You're an Egalitarian, How Come You're So Rich?* Cambridge, MA: Harvard University Press, 2000.

Cohen, Joshua. 'Structure, Choice, and Legitimacy: Locke's Theory of the State.' *Philosophy and Public Affairs* 15 (1986): 301–24.

– 'Moral Pluralism and Political Consensus.' In *The Idea of Democracy*, edited by David Copp, Jean Hampton, and John Roemer, 270–91. Cambridge: Cambridge University Press, 1993.

– 'Deliberation and Democratic Legitimacy.' In *Deliberative Democracy: Essays on Reason and Politics*, edited by James Bohman and William Rehg, 67–92. Cambridge, MA: MIT Press, 1997.

– 'Taking People as They Are.' *Philosophy & Public Affairs* 30, no. 4 (2001): 363–86.

– 'For A Democratic Society.' In *The Cambridge Companion to Rawls*, edited by Samuel Freeman, 86–138. Cambridge: Cambridge University Press, 2003.

Colman, John. *John Locke's Moral Philosophy.* Edinburgh: Edinburgh University Press, 1983.

Committee on Homosexual Offences and Prostitution. *Report of the Committee on Homosexual Offences and Prostitution [Wolfenden Report].* London: Her Majesty's Stationery Office, 1957.

Cowling, Maurice. *Mill and Liberalism.* 2nd ed. Cambridge: Cambridge University Press, 1990.

Cranston, Maurice. *John Locke: A Biography.* London: Longmans Green, 1957.

De Marneffe, Peter. 'Liberalism, Liberty and Neutrality.' *Philosophy & Public Affairs* 19, no. 3 (1990): 253–74.

Devlin, Patrick. *The Enforcement of Morals.* Oxford: Oxford University Press, 1965.

Dunn, John. 'Consent in the Political Theory of John Locke.' *Historical Journal* 10 (1967): 153–82.

– 'Justice and the Interpretation of Locke's Political Theory.' *Political Studies* 16 (1968): 68–87.

– *The Political Thought of John Locke: A Historical Account of the Argument of the Two Treatises of Government.* Cambridge: Cambridge University Press, 1969.

– 'What Is Living and What Is Dead in the Political Theory of John Locke?' In *Interpreting Political Responsibility*, 9–25. Princeton: Princeton University Press, 1990.

Dworkin, Gerald. 'Non-Neutral Principles.' *Journal of Philosophy* 80, no. 14 (1974): 491–506.

– ed. *Morality, Harm, and the Law.* Boulder: Westview, 1994.

Dworkin, Ronald. 'The Original Position.' In *Reading Rawls*, edited by Norman Daniels, 16–52. Oxford: Blackwell, 1975.

– *Taking Rights Seriously.* Cambridge, MA: Harvard University Press, 1977.

– 'Liberalism.' In *Public and Private Morality*, edited by Stuart Hampshire, 113–43. Cambridge: Cambridge University Press, 1978.

– 'What Is Equality? Part 1: Equality of Welfare; Part 2: Equality of Resources.' *Philosophy & Public Affairs* 10, nos. 3 & 4 (1981): 185–246, 283–345.

– *A Matter of Principle.* Cambridge, MA: Harvard University Press, 1985.

– 'What Is Equality? Part 3: The Place of Liberty.' *Iowa Law Review* 73, no. 1 (1987): 1–54.

– 'What Is Equality? Part 4: Political Equality.' *University of San Francisco Law Review* 22, no. 1 (1988): 116–137.

– 'The Foundations of Liberal Equality.' In *The Tanner Lectures on Human Values*, edited by G.B. Peterson, 1–119. Salt Lake City: University of Utah Press, 1990.

– *Sovereign Virtue: The Theory and Practice of Equality.* Cambridge, MA: Harvard University Press, 2000.

– 'Equality, Luck and Hierarchy.' *Philosophy & Public Affairs* 31, no. 2 (2003): 190–8.

Elster, Jon. 'The Market and the Forum: Three Varieties of Political Theory.' In *Deliberative Democracy: Essays on Reason and Politics*, edited by James Bohman and William Rehg, 3–34. Cambridge, MA: MIT Press, 1997.

Estlund, David. 'Beyond Fairness and Deliberation: The Epistemic Dimension of Democratic Authority.' In *Deliberative Democracy: Essays on Reason and Politics*, edited by James Bohman and William Rehg, 173–204. Cambridge, MA: MIT Press, 1997.

– 'Liberalism, Equality and Fraternity in Cohen's Critique of Rawls.' *Journal of Political Philosophy* 6, no. 1 (1998): 99–112.

Feinberg, Joel. *The Moral Limits of the Criminal Law.* 4 vols. Oxford: Oxford University Press, 1984–8.

– *Harm to Self.* New York: Oxford University Press, 1986.

– *Harmless Wrongdoing.* New York: Oxford University Press, 1988.

Frankfurt, Harry. 'Freedom of the Will and the Concept of a Person.' *Journal of Philosophy* 68 (1971): 5–20.

Freeden, Michael. *Ideologies and Political Theory: A Conceptual Approach*. Oxford: Clarendon, 1996.

Freeman, Samuel. 'Congruence and the Good of Justice.' In *The Cambridge Companion to Rawls*, edited by Samuel Freeman, 277–315. Cambridge: Cambridge University Press, 2003.

– 'Introduction.' In *The Cambridge Companion to Rawls*, edited by Samuel Freeman, 1–61. Cambridge: Cambridge University Press, 2003.

Galston, William. *Liberal Purposes: Goods, Virtues, and Diversity in the Liberal State*. Cambridge: Cambridge University Press, 1991.

Gaus, Gerald F. *Justificatory Liberalism: An Essay in Epistemology and Political Theory*. Oxford: Oxford University Press, 1996.

– 'Reason, Justification and Consensus: Why Democracy Can't Have It All.' In *Deliberative Democracy: Essays on Reason and Politics*, edited by James Bohman and William Rehg, 205–42. Cambridge, MA: MIT Press, 1997.

Gauthier, David. *Morals by Agreement*. New York: Oxford University Press, 1986.

George, Robert P. *Making Men Moral: Civil Liberties and Public Morality*. Oxford: Oxford University Press, 1993.

Glover, Jonathan, ed. *Utilitarianism and Its Critics*. London: Macmillan, 1990.

Goodin, Robert, and Andrew Reeve. 'Do Neutral Institutions Add Up to a Neutral State?' In *Liberal Neutrality*, edited by Robert Goodin and Andrew Reeve, 193–210. London: Routledge, 1989.

– 'Liberalism and Neutrality.' In *Liberal Neutrality*, edited by Robert Goodin and Andrew Reeve, 1–8. London: Routledge, 1989.

Grant, Ruth. *John Locke's Liberalism*. Chicago: University of Chicago Press, 1983.

Gray, John. *Mill on Liberty: A Defence*. London: Routledge and Kegan Paul, 1983.

– *Enlightenment's Wake*. London: Routledge, 1995.

– *Two Faces of Liberalism*. Cambridge: Polity, 2000.

Griffin, James. *Well-Being: Its Meaning, Measurement, and Moral Importance*. Oxford: Oxford University Press, 1986.

– *Value Judgment: Improving Our Ethical Beliefs*. Oxford: Oxford University Press, 1996.

Gutmann, Amy, and Dennis Thompson. *Democracy and Disagreement*. Cambridge, MA: Harvard University Press, 1996.

Habermas, Jürgen. 'Reconciliation through the Public Use of Reason: Remarks on John Rawls's Political Liberalism.' *Journal of Philosophy* 92 (1995): 109–31.

– 'Popular Sovereignty as Procedure.' In *Deliberative Democracy: Essays on Reason and Politics*, edited by James Bohman and William Rehg, 35–66. Cambridge, MA: MIT Press, 1997.

Haksar, Vinit. *Equality, Liberty and Perfectionism*. Oxford: Oxford University Press, 1979.

Hampton, Jean. 'Contracts and Choices: Does Rawls Have a Social Contract Theory?' *Journal of Philosophy* 87 (1980): 315–38.

– 'The Moral Commitments of Liberalism.' In *The Idea of Democracy*, edited by David Copp, Jean Hampton, and John Roemer, 292–313. Cambridge: Cambridge University Press, 1993.

Hare, R.M. *Moral Thinking: Its Levels, Method and Point.* Oxford: Oxford University Press, 1981.

Harris, Ian. *The Mind of John Locke.* New York: Cambridge University Press, 1994.

Harrison, John, and Peter Laslett. *The Library of John Locke.* Oxford: Oxford University Press, 1965.

Hart, H.L.A. 'Are There Any Natural Rights?' *Philosophical Review* 64 (1955): 175–91.

– *Law, Liberty and Morality.* Oxford: Oxford University Press, 1963.

– 'Rawls on Liberty and Its Priority.' *University of Chicago Law Review* 40 (1973): 551–5.

– 'Between Utility and Rights.' In *The Idea of Freedom*, edited by Alan Ryan, 77–98. Chicago: University of Chicago Press, 1979.

– 'Natural Rights: Bentham and John Stuart Mill.' In *Essays on Bentham*, 79–104. Oxford: Clarendon, 1982.

Himmelfarb, Gertrude. *On Liberty and Liberalism: The Case of John Stuart Mill.* New York: Knopf, 1974.

Hoag, Robert W. 'Happiness and Freedom: Recent Work on John Stuart Mill.' *Philosophy and Public Affairs* 15, no. 2 (1986): 188–99.

Holmes, Stephen. 'Gag Rules or the Politics of Omission.' In *Passions and Constraint: On the Theory of Liberal Democracy*, 202–35. Chicago: University of Chicago Press, 1995.

– 'Pre-commitment and the Paradox of Democracy.' In *Passions and Constraint: On the Theory of Liberal Democracy*, 134–77. Chicago: University of Chicago Press, 1995.

– 'The Positive Constitutionalism of John Stuart Mill.' In *Passions and Constraint: On the Theory of Liberal Democracy*, 178–201 (Chicago: University of Chicago Press, 1995).

Honig, Bonnie. *Political Theory and the Displacement of Politics.* Ithaca: Cornell University Press, 1993.

Hurka, Thomas. *Perfectionism.* Oxford: Oxford University Press, 1993.

– 'Review of *Beyond Neutrality: Perfectionism and Politics.*' *Ethics* 109, no. 1 (1998): 187–90.

Ignatieff, Michael. *The Needs of Strangers.* London: Vintage, 1984.

Jones, Charles. *Global Justice: Defending Cosmopolitanism.* Oxford: Oxford University Press, 1999.

Jones, Peter. 'The Ideal of the Neutral State.' In *Liberal Neutrality*, edited by Robert Goodin and Andrew Reeve, 9–38. London: Routledge, 1989.

– 'Liberalism, Belief, and Doubt.' *Archiv für Rechts und Sozialphilosophie* 36 (1989): 51–69.

Kelly, Paul. *Utilitarianism and Distributive Justice: Jeremy Bentham and the Civil Law.* Oxford: Clarendon, 1990.

– 'Contractarian Ethics.' In *Encyclopedia of Applied Ethics*, 1:942. San Diego: Academic, 1997.

– *Liberalism.* Cambridge: Polity, 2005.

Kelly, Paul, and David Boucher. 'The Social Contract and Its Critics.' In *The Social Contract from Hobbes to Rawls*, edited by Paul Kelly and David Boucher, 1–34. London: Routledge, 1994.

Kelly, Erin, and Lionel McPherson. 'On Tolerating the Unreasonable.' *Journal of Political Philosophy* 9 (2001): 38–55.

King, Peter. *The Life of John Locke, with Extracts from His Correspondence, Journals, and Common-Place Books.* London: Colburn, 1829.

Kramer, Matthew. *John Locke and the Origins of Private Property: Philosophical Explorations of Individualism, Community, and Equality.* Cambridge: Cambridge University Press, 1997.

Kymlicka, Will. 'Liberal Individualism and Liberal Neutrality.' *Ethics* 99 (1989): 883–905.

– *Contemporary Political Philosophy: An Introduction.* Oxford: Oxford University Press, 2002.

Larmore, Charles. *Patterns of Moral Complexity.* Cambridge: Cambridge University Press, 1987.

– 'Political Liberalism.' In *The Morals of Modernity*, 121–51. Cambridge: Cambridge University Press, 1996.

– 'The Moral Basis of Political Liberalism.' *Journal of Philosophy* 96 (1999): 599–625.

– 'Public Reason.' In *The Cambridge Companion to Rawls*, edited by Samuel Freeman, 368–93. Cambridge: Cambridge University Press, 2003.

Lecce, Steven. 'The Clapham Omnibus Revisited: Liberalism against Democracy?' *Contemporary Political Theory* 2, no. 1 (2003): 89–108.

– 'Contractualism and Liberal Neutrality: A Defence.' *Political Studies* 51, no. 3 (2003): 524–41.

– 'Should Egalitarians Be Perfectionists?' *Politics* 25, no. 3 (2005): 127–34.

Lee, Simon. *Law and Morals: Warnock, Gillick and Beyond.* Oxford: Oxford University Press, 1986.

Locke, John. *A Second Letter concerning Toleration.* In *Works*, 6:60–137. London: Tegg, 1823.

– *A Third Letter concerning Toleration.* In *Works*, 6:139–546. London: Tegg, 1823.
– *Political Writings.* Edited by David Wootton. London: Penguin, 1993.
– *An Essay concerning Human Understanding.* Edited by John Yolton. London: Dent, 1996.

Long, Douglas G. *Bentham on Liberty: Jeremy Bentham's Idea of Liberty in Relation to His Utilitarianism.* Toronto: University of Toronto Press, 1977.

Lyons, David. 'Mill's Theory of Morality.' *Nous* 10 (1976): 101–20.

Macdonald, Margaret. 'Natural Rights.' In *Theories of Rights*, edited by Jeremy Waldron, 21–40. Oxford: Oxford University Press, 1984.

MacIntyre, Alasdair. *After Virtue: A Study in Moral Theory.* London: Duckworth, 1981.

MacKinnon, Catharine. *Women's Lives*Men's Laws.* Cambridge, MA: Harvard University Press, 2005.

MacLeod, Colin M. *Liberalism, Justice and Markets: A Critique of Liberal Equality.* Oxford: Clarendon, 1998.

– 'Liberal Equality and the Affective Family.' In *The Moral and Political Status of Children*, edited by David Archard and Colin M. MacLeod, 212–31. Oxford: Oxford University Press, 2002.

Marx, Karl. 'On the Jewish Question.' In *Karl Marx: Selected Writings*, edited by David McLellan, 39–62. Oxford: Oxford University Press, 1977.

McCabe, David. 'Joseph Raz and the Contextual Argument for Liberal Perfectionism.' *Ethics* 111 (2001): 493–522.

McClure, Kirstie M. *Judging Rights: Lockean Politics and the Limits of Consent.* Ithaca: Cornell University Press, 1996.

Mill, John Stuart. *Autobiography and Literary Essays.* Edited by John Robson and Jack Stillinger. Toronto: University of Toronto Press, 1981.

– *On Liberty and Other Writings.* Edited by John Gray. Oxford: Oxford University Press, 1993.

– *The Subjection of Women.* Edited by John Gray. Oxford: Oxford University Press, 1998.

Montefiore, Alan. *Neutrality and Impartiality.* Cambridge: Cambridge University Press, 1975.

Mouffe, Chantal. *The Return of the Political.* London: Verso, 1993.

Murphy, Liam B. 'Institutions and the Demands of Justice.' *Philosophy & Public Affairs* 27, no. 4 (1999): 251–91.

Nagel, Thomas. *The View from Nowhere.* Oxford: Oxford University Press, 1986.

– 'Moral Conflict and Political Legitimacy.' *Philosophy & Public Affairs* 16, no. 3 (1987): 215–40.

– *Equality and Partiality.* Oxford: Oxford University Press, 1991.

– 'Concealment and Exposure.' *Philosophy & Public Affairs* 27, no. 1 (1998): 3–30.

– 'Rawls and Liberalism.' In *The Cambridge Companion to Rawls*, edited by Samuel Freeman, 62–85. Cambridge: Cambridge University Press, 2003.

Newey, Glen. *After Politics*. Basingstoke: Palgrave, 2001.

Nidditch, Peter H. 'Introduction.' In *An Essay concerning Human Understanding*, edited by Peter H. Nidditch, vii–x. Oxford: Oxford University Press, 1979.

Norman, Wayne. 'Inevitable and Unacceptable? Methodological Rawlsianism in Anglo-American Political Philosophy.' *Political Studies* 46 (1998): 276–94.

Nozick, Robert. *Anarchy, State and Utopia*. New York: Basic Books, 1974.

Nussbaum, Martha. *Frontiers of Justice: Disability, Nationality, Species Membership*. Cambridge, MA: Harvard University Press, 2006.

Okin, Susan. *Justice, Gender and the Family*. New York: Basic Books, 1989.

Parfit, Derek. *Reasons and Persons*. Oxford: Oxford University Press, 1984.

Passmore, John. 'Locke and the Ethics of Belief.' *British Academy Proceedings* 64 (1980): 185–208.

Petitt, Philip. 'Consequentialism.' In *A Companion to Ethics*, edited by Peter Singer, 230–40. Oxford: Blackwell, 1991.

Pinker, Steven. *The Blank Slate: The Modern Denial of Human Nature*. New York: Penguin, 2002.

Pogge, Thomas W. 'On the Site of Distributive Justice: Reflections on Cohen and Murphy.' *Philosophy & Public Affairs* 29, no. 2 (2000): 137–69.

Pojman, Louis J., and Robert Westmoreland. *Equality: Selected Readings*. Oxford: Oxford University Press, 1997.

Price, T.L. 'Debate: Epistemological Restraint – Revisited.' *Journal of Political Philosophy* 8 (2000): 401–7.

Proast, Jonas. 1690. *The Argument of the Letter concerning Toleration Briefly Consider'd and Answered*. Reprinted as *Letters Concerning Toleration*, edited by P.A. Schouls. New York: Garland, 1984. Page references are to the 1984 edition.

Quong, Jonathan. 'Disagreement, Asymmetry, and Liberal Legitimacy.' *Politics, Philosophy & Economics* 4, no. 3 (2005): 301–30.

Rawls, John. *A Theory of Justice*. Cambridge, MA: Harvard University Press, 1971.

– *Political Liberalism*. New York: Columbia University Press, 1993.

– 'The Idea of Public Reason.' In *Deliberative Democracy: Essays on Reason and Politics*, edited by James Bohman and William Rehg, 93–130. Cambridge, MA: MIT Press, 1997.

– 'The Idea of Public Reason Revisited.' In *Collected Papers*, edited by Samuel Freeman, 573–615. Cambridge, MA: Harvard University Press, 1999.

– 'Justice as Fairness.' In *Collected Papers*, edited by Samuel Freeman, 47–72. Cambridge, MA: Harvard University Press, 1999.

– *Justice as Fairness: A Restatement*. Cambridge, MA: Harvard University Press, 2001.

Raz, Joseph. 'Professor Dworkin's Theory of Rights.' *Political Studies* 26 (1978): 123–37.

– *The Authority of Law.* Oxford: Oxford University Press, 1979.
– 'Liberalism, Autonomy, and the Politics of Neutral Concern.' *Midwest Studies in Philosophy* 7 (1982): 89–102.
– 'Right-Based Moralities.' In *Theories of Rights,* edited by Jeremy Waldron, 182–200. Oxford: Oxford University Press, 1984.
– 'Authority and Justification.' *Philosophy & Public Affairs* 14 (1985): 3–29.
– *The Morality of Freedom.* Oxford: Clarendon, 1986.
– 'Autonomy, Toleration, and the Harm Principle.' In *Issues in Contemporary Legal Philosophy,* edited by R. Gavison, 313–33. Oxford: Oxford University Press, 1987.
– 'Facing Up: A Reply.' *Southern California Law Review* 62 (1989): 1153–1235.
– 'Liberating Duties.' *Law & Philosophy* 8 (1989): 3–21.
– 'Liberalism, Skepticism and Democracy.' *Iowa Law Review* 74 (1989): 761–86.
– 'Facing Diversity: The Case of Epistemic Abstinence.' *Philosophy & Public Affairs* 19 (1990): 3–46.
– *Ethics in the Public Domain: Essays in the Morality of Law and Politics.* Oxford: Oxford University Press, 1994.
– 'Liberty and Trust.' In *Natural Law, Liberalism and Morality,* edited by Robert P. George, 113–29. Oxford: Oxford University Press, 1996.
– *Engaging Reason: On the Theory of Value and Action.* Oxford: Oxford University Press, 2000.
Rees, J.C. *John Stuart Mill's* On Liberty. Oxford: Oxford University Press, 1985.
Regan, Donald. 'Autonomy and Value: Reflections on Raz's *The Morality of Freedom.*' *Southern California Law Review* 62 (1989): 995–1095.
Riley, Jonathan. *Liberal Utilitarianism: Social Choice Theory and J.S. Mill's Philosophy.* Cambridge: Cambridge University Press, 1988.
Riley, Patrick. 'On Finding an Equilibrium between Consent and Natural Law in Locke's Political Philosophy.' *Political Studies* 22 (1974): 432–52.
– 'Locke on "Voluntary Agreement" and Political Power.' *Western Political Quarterly* 29 (1976): 136–45.
Ross, W.D. *The Right and the Good.* Oxford: Oxford University Press, 1930.
Rousseau, Jean-Jacques. 1762. *The Social Contract,* edited by G.D.H. Cole. London: Dent, 1973.
Russell, Paul. 'Locke on Express and Tacit Consent: Misinterpretations and Inconsistencies.' *Political Theory* 14 (1986): 291–306.
Ryan, Alan. 'Locke and the Dictatorship of the Bourgeoisie.' *Political Studies* 13 (1965): 219–30.
– *Property and Political Theory.* Oxford: Blackwell, 1984.
– *The Philosophy of John Stuart Mill.* London: Macmillan, 1990.
Sadurski, Wojciech. 'Joseph Raz on Liberal Neutrality and the Harm Principle.' *Oxford Journal of Legal Studies* 10 (1990): 122–33.

Sandel, Michael. *Liberalism and the Limits of Justice.* Cambridge: Cambridge University Press, 1982.

Scanlon, Thomas. 'Contractualism and Utilitarianism.' In *Utilitarianism and Beyond,* edited by Amartya Sen and Bernard Williams, 103–28. Cambridge: Cambridge University Press, 1982.

– *What We Owe to Each Other.* Cambridge, MA: Harvard University Press, 1998.

– *The Difficulty of Tolerance: Essays in Political Philosophy.* Cambridge: Cambridge University Press, 2003.

Scheffler, Samuel, ed. *Consequentialism and Its Critics.* Oxford: Oxford University Press, 1988.

– *The Rejection of Consequentialism.* Rev. ed. Oxford: Clarendon, 1994.

– *Boundaries and Allegiances: Problems of Justice and Responsibility in Liberal Thought.* Oxford: Oxford University Press, 2001.

– 'What Is Egalitarianism?' *Philosophy & Public Affairs* 31 (2003): 5–39.

Schoeman, Ferdinand. 'The Rights of Children, Rights of Parents, and the Moral Basis of the Family.' *Ethics* 91 (1980): 6–19.

Sen, Amartya, and Bernard Williams, eds. *Utilitarianism and Beyond.* Cambridge: Cambridge University Press, 1982.

Sher, George. *Beyond Neutrality: Perfectionism and Politics.* Cambridge: Cambridge University Press, 1997.

Sidgwick, Henry. *The Methods of Ethics.* London: Macmillan, 1907.

Simmons, A.J. 'Tacit Consent and Political Obligation.' *Philosophy and Public Affairs* 5 (1976): 274–91.

– 'Inalienable Rights and Locke's *Treatises.' Philosophy and Public Affairs* 12 (1983): 175–204.

– 'Locke's State of Nature.' *Political Theory* 17 (1989): 449–70.

– *The Lockean Theory of Rights.* Princeton: Princeton University Press, 1992.

Singer, Peter. 'The Singer Solution to World Poverty.' In *Writings on an Ethical Life,* 118–24. New York: Ecco, 2000.

Skinner, Quentin. *The Foundations of Modern Political Thought.* 2 vols. Cambridge: Cambridge University Press, 1978.

– 'Meaning and Understanding in the History of Ideas.' In *Meaning and Context: Quentin Skinner and His Critics,* edited by James Tully, 29–67. Princeton: Princeton University Press, 1988.

Stephen, James Fitzjames. *Liberty, Equality, Fraternity.* Chicago: University of Chicago Press, 1991.

Stocker, M. 'Mill on Desire and Desirability.' *Journal of the History of Philosophy* 7 (1969): 199–201.

Sunstein, Cass. 'Should Sex Equality Law Apply to Religious Institutions?' In *Is Multiculturalism Bad for Women?* edited by Susan Moller Okin, 85–94. Princeton: Princeton University Press, 1999.

Tan, Kok-Chor. 'Justice and Personal Pursuits.' *Journal of Philosophy* 101, no. 7 (2004): 331–62.

Taylor, Charles. *Philosophical Papers.* Vol. 2, *Philosophy and the Human Science.* Cambridge: Cambridge University Press, 1985.

– *Sources of the Self: The Making of the Modern Identity.* Cambridge, MA: Harvard University Press, 1989.

Ten, C.L. *Mill on Liberty.* Oxford: Oxford University Press, 1980.

Thompson, Martyn P. 'The Reception of Locke's *Two Treatises of Government.*' *Political Studies* 24 (1976): 184–91.

Tomasi, John. *Liberalism beyond Justice: Citizens, Society, and the Boundaries of Political Theory.* Princeton: Princeton University Press, 2001.

Tuck, Richard. *Natural Rights Theories: Their Origin and Development.* Cambridge: Cambridge University Press, 1979.

Tully, James. *A Discourse on Property: John Locke and His Adversaries.* Cambridge: Cambridge University Press, 1980.

– *An Approach to Political Philosophy: Locke in Context.* Cambridge: Cambridge University Press, 1993.

Van Parijs, Philippe. 'Why Surfers Should Be Fed: The Liberal Case for an Unconditional Basic Income.' *Philosophy & Public Affairs* 20, no. 2 (1991): 101–31.

– *Real Freedom for All: What, If Anything, Can Justify Capitalism?* Oxford: Oxford University Press, 1995.

Vernon, Richard. *The Career of Toleration: Locke, Proast and After.* Montreal and Kingston: McGill-Queens University Press, 1997.

– 'Liberals, Democrats and the Agenda of Politics.' *Political Studies* 46 (1998): 295–308.

– *Political Morality: A Theory of Liberal Democracy.* London: Continuum, 2001.

Waldron, Jeremy. 'Enough and as Good Left for Others.' *Philosophical Quarterly* 29 (1979): 319–28.

– 'Mill and the Value of Moral Distress.' *Political Studies* 35 (1987): 410–23.

– *The Right to Private Property.* Oxford: Clarendon, 1988.

– 'Autonomy and Perfectionism in Raz's *The Morality of Freedom.*' *Southern California Law Review* 62 (1989): 1097–152.

– 'John Locke: Social Contract versus Political Anthropology.' *Review of Politics* 51 (1989): 3–28.

– 'Locke, Toleration, and the Rationality of Persecution.' In *Liberal Rights: Collected Papers, 1981–1991,* 88–114. Cambridge: Cambridge University Press, 1993.

– 'Minority Cultures and the Cosmopolitan Alternative.' In *The Rights of Minority Cultures,* edited by Will Kymlicka, 93–119. Oxford: Oxford University Press, 1995.

– *God, Locke and Equality: Christian Foundations in Locke's Political Thought*. Cambridge: Cambridge University Press, 2002.

Wall, Steven. *Liberalism, Perfectionism and Restraint*. Cambridge: Cambridge University Press, 1998.

Walzer, Michael. *Spheres of Justice: A Defence of Pluralism and Equality*. Oxford: Blackwell, 1983.

Wilkinson, Martin. 'Dworkin on Paternalism and Well-Being.' *Oxford Journal of Legal Studies* 16, no. 3 (1996): 433–44.

Williams, Andrew. 'Incentives, Inequality, and Publicity.' *Philosophy & Public Affairs* 27, no. 3 (1998): 225–47.

Williams, Bernard. 'A Critique of Utilitarianism.' In *Utilitarianism: For and Against*, edited by B. Williams and J.J.C. Smart, 77–150. Cambridge: Cambridge University Press, 1973.

Wingo, Ajume H. *Veil Politics in Liberal Democratic States*. Cambridge: Cambridge University Press, 2003.

Wolff, Jonathan. 'Fairness, Respect, and the Egalitarian Ethos.' *Philosophy & Public Affairs* 27, no. 2 (1998): 97–122.

Wollheim, R. 'John Stuart Mill and Isaiah Berlin: The Ends of Life and the Preliminaries of Morality.' In *The Idea of Freedom*, edited by Alan Ryan, 253–69. Oxford: Oxford University Press, 1979.

– 'The Sheep and the Ceremony.' Leslie Stephen Lecture, University of Cambridge, 1979.

Wolterstorff, Nicholas. *John Locke and the Ethics of Belief*. Cambridge: Cambridge University Press, 1996.

Wootton, David. 'Introduction.' In *John Locke: Political Writings*, edited by David Wootton, 7–119. New York: Penguin, 1993.

Yolton, John W. 'Locke on the Law of Nature.' *Philosophical Review* 67 (1958): 477–98.

– *Locke and the Compass of Human Understanding: A Selective Commentary on the Essay*. Cambridge: Cambridge University Press, 1970.

Index

political morality, 46; and reasonable agreement, 43

political philosophy vs practical reason, 45

political problem: Locke on, 31

politics: artificiality of, 136; basic facts of, 191; scope of, 271

polygamy, 80, 266

pornography, 78

Price, T.L., 292n69, 304n46

primary goods, 212

priority of right over the good, 234

privacy, 262

Proast, Jonas, 4, 7–9, 19, 20, 29–37, 40–5, 64, 88, 89, 190, 192, 229, 276n11, 278n37, 278–9n40, 280n66, 281n79, 281n81, 282n83, 288n80

progress, 54

publicity, 39

public deliberation, 197

public justification, 186

public reason, 25, 42

Quong, Jonathan, 306n1

radical democracy, 199

Rakowski, Eric, 188

Rawls, John, 12, 14–16, 20, 45, 77, 103, 120, 157, 163, 165–6, 168, 170, 175, 177, 183, 187, 190–2, 194–7, 202–22, 224, 226–8, 230, 232, 234, 244–5, 249, 251, 257–8, 273n1, 273n2, 274n3, 274n6, 274n10, 281n78, 282–3n102, 283n104, 288n89, 289n3, 290n13, 291n52, 295n27, 298n88, 298n90, 302nn1–2, 303n8, 303n25, 303n30, 303–4n32, 304n38, 306n3, 306n5, 306n12, 306nn16–17, 307nn18–21, 307–

8n23, 310nn32–3, 311n42, 311–12n1, 312n2, 312nn4–5, 312n7, 312nn10–14, 313nn15–20, 313–14n21, 314n22, 314n24, 314n29, 315n30, 315n33, 315nn3–7, 315n47, 316n50, 317n7, 318n11, 318n15, 319n3, 319nn6–7, 320n12, 320n15, 321n18, 321–2n26, 322n31, 322n33, 323n41, 323n44, 325n5; on political liberalism, 45, 211

Raz, Joseph, 5, 9–12, 20, 75, 97–135, 138, 179, 274n8, 290n33, 292n69, 293nn1–7, 293–4n8, 294nn9–18, 295nn19–26, 295nn30–8, 296nn40–3, 296n46, 296nn48–55, 296n58, 296n60, 297nn61–80, 298nn81–7, 298n91, 298n93, 298n98, 298n104, 302n3, 304n44, 305n48, 324–5n1; on authority, 110; on consent, 120; on harm principle, 114

reason: and goals, 99–100; practical, 109; theoretical, 109

reasonable: agreement and political legitimacy, 45; comprehensive doctrines, 211–12; disagreement, 92; persons, 215–18; pluralism and stability, 210; pluralism as unnecessarily restrictive, 173; regret, 142, 148; rejection, 223; vs rational in Rawls, 214–15

reasonableness: as fairness, 174, 202, 270; as valid argument, 172, 202, 270; two concepts of, 169–77

Rees, J.C., 284n3, 284n13

Reeve, Andrew, 318n13, 319n17

reflexivity thesis, 162–9, 270; and epistemology, 176; failure of, 183

Regan, Donald, 130, 296n56, 298n102